RUNNING
Microsoft® Outlook™ 98

Alan Neibauer

PUBLISHED BY
Microsoft Press
A Division of Microsoft Corporation
One Microsoft Way
Redmond, Washington 98052-6399

Copyright © 1998 by Alan R. Neibauer

Library of Congress Cataloging-in-Publication Data
Neibauer, Alan R.
    Running Microsoft Outlook 98 / Alan R. Neibauer.
        p.   cm.
    Includes index.
    ISBN 1-57231-840-6
    1. Microsoft Outlook.   2. Time management--Computer programs.
    3. Personal information management--Computer programs.   I. Title.
    HD69.T54N44   1998
    005.369--dc21   98-4617
                                                               CIP

Printed and bound in the United States of America.

  2 3 4 5 6 7 8 9   QMQM   3 2 1 0 9 8

Distributed to the book trade in Canada by Macmillan of Canada, a division of Canada Publishing Corporation.

A CIP catalogue record for this book is available from the British Library.

Microsoft Press books are available through booksellers and distributors worldwide. For further information about international editions, contact your local Microsoft Corporation office. Or contact Microsoft Press International directly at fax (425) 936-7329. Visit our Web site at mspress.microsoft.com.

Microsoft, PowerPoint, and Windows are registered trademarks and Expedia, MSN, NetMeeting, and Outlook are trademarks of Microsoft Corporation.

Other product and company names mentioned herein may be the trademarks of their respective owners.

Acquisitions Editor: Kim Fryer
Project Editor: Saul Candib and Barbara Moreland
Manuscript and Technical Editing: Labrecque Publications

Chapters at a Glance

Table of Contents

Acknowledgments

There are many people who deserve my thanks and appreciation for making this book a reality. My thanks to Barbara Moreland and Saul Candib, who both served as project editor, coordinating everyone's efforts and keeping the entire process on track, and to Lisa Labrecque who served admirably as project manager.

I wish to thank Curtis Philips, technical editor, for his attention to details. It wasn't easy keeping track of the various changes as Outlook 98 went through its growing pains. Yet, Curtis was somehow able to keep on top of everything.

I thank Lisa Auer, who acted as copy editor. The copy editor is often the last defense against typos, confusing grammar, and other glitches that squeak past everyone else in the process, and Lisa didn't miss a thing. My appreciation to Lisa Bravo, compositor, for her work in creating the attractive pages that you will soon be reading, and Erin Milnes, the proofreader, for her keen eye and attention to detail. I also want to thank William Teel for processing the screen art for the Companion CD, and for standing in for other duties when it was needed.

My thanks to Kim Fryer, acquisitions editor, who brought me on board, to Claire Horne, my agent, for knocking on the right doors and calling the right numbers, and to Lucinda Rowley, managing editor.

Last, but never least, my undying love and appreciation to the remarkable woman I am blessed to call my wife, Barbara. We met 35 years ago, married three years later, and yet she still amazes and surprises me, proving that while our bodies may grow old, true love never ages.

Introduction

Microsoft Outlook 98 seems to have been created with one overriding goal—to make your life easier. The program combines powerful communications tools for both the Internet and your network with the organizational tools you need to manage the details of your professional and personal life.

In this book, you'll learn how to use this multifaceted program. If you are new to Outlook, you'll find easy-to-follow instructions for every phase of the program. Before you know it, you'll be mastering Outlook's communications and record-keeping tools. If you have used earlier versions of Outlook, you'll appreciate the powerful new features in Outlook 98.

Parts I and II of the book walk you through the basic features of the Outlook environment and explore how to manage communications by using the e-mail, fax, and address book features as well as remote work options. You'll also learn how to use Outlook Express as an alternate e-mail system and how to share ideas and information using newsgroups.

Parts III and IV look in depth at how to schedule people, appointments, tasks, events, and so on, and show you how to create your contact list and keep it up-to-date. You'll learn to take full advantage of the Journal folder and the Notes folder. And you'll learn how to conduct and participate in online NetMeetings using the latest voice and video technology, including how to work collaboratively online using a Whiteboard and how to share your applications. Part V provides all the details about folders and folder items—how to work with them and manage their contents efficiently.

Although this book is organized as a progression through Outlook's capabilities, you don't necessarily have to read the chapters in order. I suggest starting with Part I, however, to learn the basics of Outlook, how to set up profiles, and how to customize it to your tastes. You can then go directly to chapters that have the information you need for a particular job. If you need to record an appointment, for example, you can go directly to Part III. You can then go back to Part II when you're ready to use Outlook's communications features.

Folders and Folder Items

In Outlook, folders (which are similar to the folders you find in the My Computer and Microsoft Windows Explorer windows) contain all the various bits of information you create and work with on a day-to-day basis. Each Outlook folder contains its own particular type of folder item, as does any folder you add. You'll learn to create, store, view, and revise the following types of information in Outlook's built-in folders:

- Electronic mail (e-mail) messages

- Appointments and meetings

- Contacts (names, addresses, phone and fax numbers, and other personal information)

- Task lists (to-do lists)

- Journal entries (records of your activities in Outlook and in Microsoft Office applications as you perform them)

- Notes

- Disk folders on a disk connected to your computer (a shortcut for the My Computer window)

- Discussions (postings and replies in public folders)

You'll also learn how to add new folders for items that don't quite fit into Outlook's standard folders and how to set folder properties. To help you find and view items in folders, Outlook provides view options. You can modify these views and create your own.

Outlook and Servers

You can use Outlook as a stand-alone program or as a "client" for an e-mail server, which means that you use Outlook to manage your own schedule and to communicate over the Internet through an e-mail provider. You can also use Outlook to work with information and communications systems that are stored and passed through a server set up as a post office.

It's likely that a majority of people who use Outlook will be connected to a server running Microsoft Exchange Server. Because of the intimate connection Outlook has with Microsoft Exchange Server, in this book you'll see several illustrations of dialog boxes that show "Exchange" in their title bars. If you're on an e-mail system that doesn't use Microsoft Exchange Server, you'll see "Windows Messaging Service" in the title bars instead of "Exchange."

If you are not connected to a server, don't get confused between Microsoft Exchange Server and the Microsoft Exchange program that you may see on your Windows menu when you click the Start button on the taskbar and point to Programs. Although the two programs offer communications capabilities, they are quite different. The Microsoft Exchange program, a precursor to Windows Messaging, is a communications tool for non-networked systems to communicate via a modem and fax. Microsoft Exchange Server, by contrast, is a network communications program designed to run on Windows NT. If you are not connected to a network, features designed for the Exchange Server will not be available to you.

Outlook Installation Options

Outlook 98 offers you three installation options: Corporate or Workgroup, Internet Only, and No E-Mail. The Outlook features described in this book are those provided by the Corporate or Workgroup installation, which includes using Outlook as an e-mail client over Microsoft Exchange Server. The fax capabilities described use Microsoft Fax on a client computer running Windows 95.

The Internet Only installation provides for communications only through a dial-up internet service provider. This installation provides its own fax capabilities. If you are using this installation, some of the dialog boxes and menus you see will be different than those shown in this book.

The No E-Mail installation option provides Outlook's record-keeping and time-management tools but no communications capabilities.

Using the Companion CD

This book comes with a CD loaded with the following software and book information:

- A powerful, searchable HTML version of the book that enables you to quickly locate specific information, such as a procedure or a definition, with only a click of the mouse

- Outlook 98

- One free month of Internet access to MSN, the Microsoft Network

- Microsoft Internet Explorer 4.01

Installing Outlook 98

A complete copy of Outlook 98 is included on the companion CD. To install Outlook 98, go to the Start menu on your Windows 95 task bar, click Run, and then browse to the Outlook folder on the companion CD. Select the setup.exe file in the folder, and choose OK to run the installation program.

Installing Microsoft Internet Explorer 4.01

While you can use most Web browsers to view the online version of this book, the text is best viewed in Microsoft Internet Explorer 4.01. For this reason, a copy of Internet Explorer 4.01 is included on the CD. (If you install Outlook 98 from the companion CD as described above, Internet Explorer 4.01 will automatically be installed as well.)

To install Internet Explorer 4.01 from the CD, choose Run from the Start menu, and then type d:\IE40\ie4setup.exe in the Run dialog box (where d is the drive letter of your CD-ROM drive). Then follow the instructions for installation as they appear.

When you run Internet Explorer after installing it, you will see the Internet Connection Wizard. This wizard helps you set up an account with an Internet service provider or establish a connection to your current service provider. (You do not have to be connected to a service provider to use the files on the CD.)

Installing Microsoft Network (MSN)

The companion CD also includes the client software for Microsoft Network, along with one-month of free access to MSN and the Internet. To take advantage of this offer, choose Run from the Start menu, type d:\MSN\setup.exe, and then click OK (d: should be replaced with the letter of your CD-ROM drive, such as f: for a CD-ROM installed as drive F). Follow the installation instructions that appear on screen, and when you're asked for a registration number, type in *1A6H-RS-KW12*.

About the Electronic Book

The CD-ROM includes an electronic version of *Running Microsoft Outlook 98*. This is a powerful version of the book offering full-text search that enables you to locate specific information, such as a procedure or a definition, with only a click of the mouse.

Internet Explorer 4.0 or better is required to view the electronic books. As part of the installation process, the setup program will automatically install Microsoft Internet Explorer version 4.01 if it is not already installed on your system. Microsoft Internet Explorer 4.01 runs on Microsoft Windows 95 or on Microsoft Windows NT with Service Pack 3 installed. If you're running Windows NT, you must install Service Pack 3 (not included) before attempting to install the electronic books. For information about downloading the Microsoft Windows NT Service Pack 3, connect to http://backoffice.microsoft.com/downtrial/moreinfo/nt4sp3.asp.

To install the electronic version of the book, do the following:

1. Insert the CD-ROM into your CD-ROM drive.

2. On the Windows taskbar, click **Start**.

3. Choose **Run** from the **Start** menu.

4. Type **d:\ebook\setup** (where d is your CD-ROM drive letter).

5. Click **OK**.

6. Follow the setup instructions that appear.

7. The Setup program for the electronic book installs a desktop icon and a Start menu item identified with the title. If it does not already exist, the Setup program creates a Microsoft Press group for the item. To view the electronic book, you can either select from the Start menu or double-click the desktop icon.

Additional Information

Every effort has been made to ensure the accuracy of the book and the contents of this companion disc. Microsoft Press provides corrections for books through the World Wide Web at

http://mspress.microsoft.com/mspress/support/

If you have comments, questions, or ideas regarding the book or this companion disc, please send them to Microsoft Press via e-mail at:

MSPINPUT@MICROSOFT.COM

or via postal mail to:

Microsoft Press
Attn: Running Series Editor
One Microsoft Way
Redmond, WA 98052-6399

Please note that product support is not offered through the above addresses.

Microsoft Outlook 98 Support

For support information regarding Microsoft Outlook 98, you can connect to Microsoft Technical Support on the Web at:

http://www.microsoft.com/support/

In the United States, you can also call Microsoft Outlook 98 technical support at (425) 635-7031; in Canada, (905) 568-2294, weekdays between 6 a.m. and 6 p.m. Pacific time.

For late-breaking information, look for the readme file on the companion CD.

PART I

Getting Started

CHAPTER 1

Starting Out

Let's begin with the basics: starting and exiting Microsoft Outlook 98, logging on, and logging off. This chapter also takes a look at your personal profile, which sets up the options you'll use in each Outlook session. The Inbox Setup Wizard makes it easy to create, use, change, and remove profiles.

Starting Microsoft Outlook

Microsoft
Outlook

Starting Outlook is as easy as double-clicking an icon. A couple of other methods are available, too. To start Outlook, take one of the following actions:

- Double-click the Outlook icon on the desktop.

- Click the Start button on the Microsoft Windows taskbar, point to Programs, and then click Microsoft Outlook.

Outlook

- Click the Outlook button on the Microsoft Office shortcut bar.

Logging On

If you are logged on to your organization's computer network, Outlook knows who you are and doesn't ask for your logon name and password. Outlook will start connecting you to your e-mail server, usually. (See the sidebar "The Lines Are Down! What Now?" on page 6, for a different situation.) Your e-mail server is the computer that stores the messages you send and receive.

 TIP

> If you want to have Outlook request a logon every time you start the program, do the following: start Outlook, and choose the Services command from the Tools menu. In the Services dialog box, select Microsoft Exchange Server and click the Properties button. In the Microsoft Exchange Server dialog box, click the Advanced tab, drop down the Logon Network Security list and choose None. If you want to log on automatically again, choose NT Password Authentication from the list.

If your computer is part of a network but you're not logged on, you'll see the following dialog box. (You won't see the Domain field in the dialog box if you are working on a non-network computer, or if your workstation has been disconnected from the network.) Follow these steps to log on.

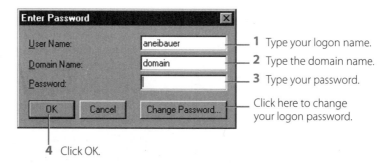

1 Type your logon name.

2 Type the domain name.

3 Type your password.

Click here to change
your logon password.

4 Click OK.

When Outlook connects you to your e-mail server, it refers to your user
profile to determine which options you'll be using (see "Developing
Your Profile," on page 7). The first time you start Outlook you will
probably have only one profile set up—a profile that was established
when you (or someone else) installed Outlook. If that's the case, Outlook simply begins using the profile when you log on, without asking
you any questions. But if you happen to have more than one profile
set up, and if you have turned on the option that prompts you to
choose a profile, Outlook displays the Choose Profile dialog box,
shown here:

1 Select the profile you want to use.

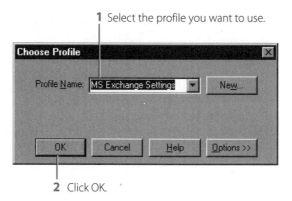

2 Click OK.

If the profile you're using is set up for use away from your network
connection, Outlook then displays a dialog box that asks whether you
want to connect to the network or work offline.

Connect. Click this button if the network is available via a direct connection or a continuous dial-up connection, and you want to connect
to your e-mail server to send and receive messages.

> **The Lines Are Down! What Now?**
>
> Networks and servers are wonderfully bizarre at times. They love to go down (that is, stop working) just to give some beleaguered system administrator something to do—namely, restart the network or server.
>
> If you try to connect to your server when the server or the network isn't working, you'll see a dialog box informing you that the server is unavailable. Click the Retry button to attempt a connection with the server again, or click Work Offline to load Outlook and work with the data on your personal machine, until the server becomes available again.

Work Offline. If you want to work offline (because the network is down, because you don't have a direct connection to it, or because you want to compose messages or perform other tasks before you connect), click the Work Offline button. When you work offline, you can compose messages for sending later, and you can review any messages that you have stored on your computer (rather than on your e-mail server). Later you can connect to the network or online service to send your messages and to receive any messages that are waiting for you.

When Outlook is running, you see the Outlook window. Chapter 2, "Looking Out into Outlook," explains what this window contains and how to use it.

Getting Off and Out—Exiting Outlook

You can exit Outlook and log off any services you were connected to, or you can just exit Outlook. To exit Outlook and log off at the same time, you must choose the Exit And Log Off command from the File menu. You can exit Outlook without logging off in all the usual Windows ways. Here's the list.

- Choose the Exit command from the File menu.

- Choose the Close command from the Control menu (or press Alt+F4).

- Click the Close button on the title bar.

- Double-click the Control-menu icon.

Developing Your Profile

Outlook keeps track of who you are and what you like. Whenever you log on, Outlook sets itself up to accommodate you—the way you work and the way you want Outlook to work. Each Outlook session is governed by a personal profile—the profile that was created when you (or some techno-guru) installed Outlook on your computer, a profile you created and told Outlook to use each time you run Outlook, or the profile that you select when you start the program.

If you always use Outlook in one place and in one way—say, on your desktop at work—a single profile is all you need. But if you use Outlook in different locations or to perform more complicated tasks, you might want several profiles. For example, you can set up one profile to use with Outlook when you're at your office, connected to a network. You can create other profiles for when you take your portable computer home with you or when you take it on your travels, business or otherwise. Or you might want a separate profile for those times when you send faxes from your computer over a telephone line that you also use for connecting to your mail server.

Creating a Profile

Suppose that Outlook is set up for your office, where you connect to your server through your organization's network. Now you go on the road with your laptop, and you want to connect to your server to read mail messages, to consult public folders, and to schedule appointments and tasks. Your original profile can be set up for both home and away, but you'll face a slower startup for Outlook because you'll see several dialog boxes on the way in.

For a more convenient and well-tailored startup, you can define a new profile for the on-the-road situation. To do this, you start the Inbox Setup Wizard as described next and create a new profile, which you'll use when you're away from your office. You can later select the original profile when you're back in the office.

If you have set up Outlook to prompt you to select a profile each time you start the program, you can click the New button in the Choose Profile dialog box to start the Setup Wizard. See "Using a Different Profile," on page 16.

You set up, change, and remove a profile using the Windows Control Panel. You can also change a profile, adding or removing services, from within Outlook itself. To create a new profile, follow these steps:

1 Open the Windows Control Panel, and double-click the Mail icon in the Control Panel window. Depending on your setup, the icon may be labeled Mail And Fax.

2 In the Properties dialog box, you'll see a list of the information services set up for the current profile.

3 Click the Show Profiles button.

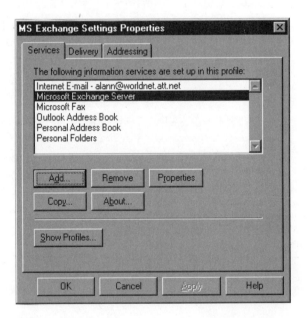

4 Click the Add button in the Mail dialog box to start creating a new profile.

5 The first panel of the Inbox Setup Wizard lets you select the services you want to include in the new profile. To include all possible services, leave all the check boxes turned on. To omit a service, click its check box to turn it off. (If you really know what you're doing, you can select the Manually Configure Information Services option and then select individual services and set them up the way you want. This book won't tell you all the things you need to know to take this path. You're better off letting the wizard supply the list and then selecting and omitting the services you want for each profile.)

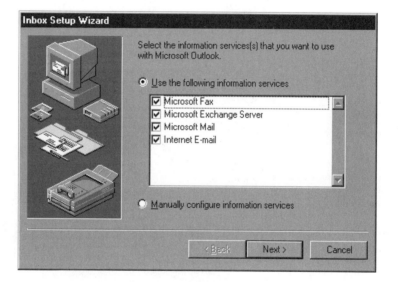

6 Click Next.

7 Type a descriptive name for the new profile in the Profile Name box.

8 Click Next.

9 From this point on, the wizard displays only those panels that apply to the services you selected in step 5. Fill in the information on each panel, and click the Next button until you get to the last panel. If you don't know the information you need, check with your service administrator.

10 Click Finish on the last panel to close the wizard.

11 In the Mail dialog box, you can choose a default profile in the box labeled When Starting Microsoft Outlook, Use This Profile.

12 Click the Close button.

You can use the Inbox Setup Wizard to create profiles specific to each location from which you use Outlook: office, home, and on the road. Or you can set up profiles specific to the different services you use in Outlook, such as Internet E-mail, MSN, or CompuServe.

Updating a Profile

Suppose you signed up for a new online service and want to add it to one or more of your profiles. You also bailed out of an online service that wasn't giving you what you wanted. Your profile is now out of date, so you want to update the online service information.

Here's how you do it.

1 Double-click the Mail icon in the Control Panel window to open the Properties dialog box.

2 Click the Show Profiles button to display the Mail dialog box.

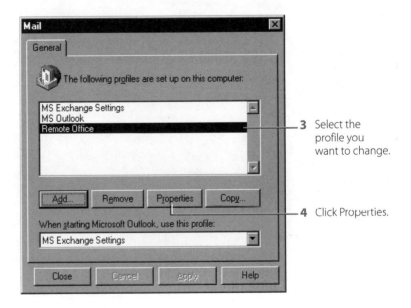

3 Select the profile you want to change.

4 Click Properties.

5 The following graphic shows the types of changes you might make to a profile:

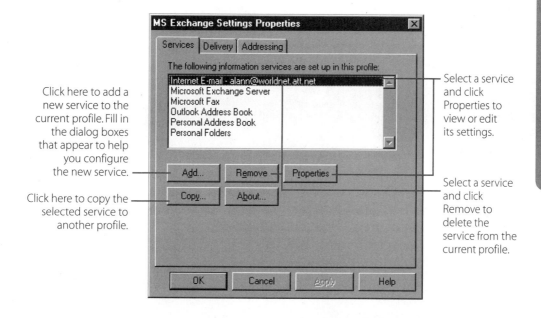

Click here to add a new service to the current profile. Fill in the dialog boxes that appear to help you configure the new service.

Click here to copy the selected service to another profile.

Select a service and click Properties to view or edit its settings.

Select a service and click Remove to delete the service from the current profile.

6 Click OK when you've finished modifying the profile.

7 If you want to make changes to another profile, repeat steps 3 through 6. Click the Close button in the Mail dialog box when you've finished.

Notice that the Properties dialog box also contains two other tabs: Delivery and Addressing. You can use these tabs to make additional changes to your profile.

On the Delivery tab, you can change the location to which your mail is delivered. If your profile includes two or more services that support mail with the same address type (for example, Microsoft Exchange and Internet Mail), you can specify the order in which those services should process outgoing mail.

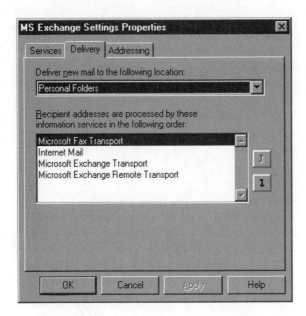

On the Addressing tab, you can specify which address list to display when you first open the address book, where to save new entries in your address book, and in which order to search address lists for recipient names.

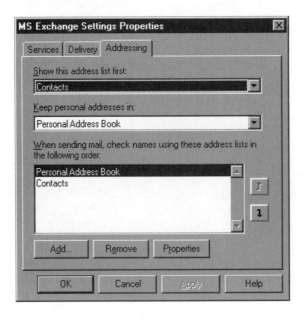

If you want to edit the profile you're currently using, you don't have to use the Control Panel. Just use either of the following techniques, then skip to step 5 on page 11:

- While working in Outlook, choose the Services command from the Tools menu.

- From the Windows desktop, right-click the Outlook icon (but *not* on a shortcut icon) and select Properties from the menu.

Setting Up Internet E-Mail

If you are setting up an Internet e-mail service on your computer, you'll need to get some information from your Internet service provider. In addition to your own e-mail address and logon password, you'll need to know these items:

- Outgoing mail server name (sometimes referred to as SMTP, which stands for Simple Mail Transfer Protocol)

- Incoming mail server name (sometimes referred to as POP, or Post Office Protocol)

- Your mail server logon name

- Your mail server password

If you want to use the news reader feature of Outlook, you'll also need the news server name. You'll learn more about setting up a news server in Chapter 7, "Communicating with Newsgroups."

Adding Fax Service to a Profile

SEE ALSO

For detailed information about sending and receiving faxes with Outlook, see "Getting the Facts About Fax," on page 150.

Sending faxes is a popular form of communication. The trouble with a stand-alone fax machine is that you need to print your message before you can send it. If your computer has a fax modem installed, you can create your message on the computer and then use Outlook to send the fax to its destination.

If you installed Outlook after Microsoft Fax was set up on your computer, the fax service may already be included in the profile. If you see a fax machine icon on the Windows taskbar when you run Outlook, then fax service is already installed.

▶ **NOTE**

If you set up Outlook using the Corporate or Workgroup option, you have to provide fax service using the Microsoft Fax software supplied with Windows, as explained in this chapter. If you set up Outlook using the Internet Only option, you can use the fax software provided with Outlook.

Before you can add fax service to Outlook, you need to install your fax modem and accompanying software. Installing a fax modem can be a tricky process. You can use the Windows Install New Modem Wizard to help you. Also consult your operating system manuals for instructions on how to install your fax modem software. With Windows 95, you have to install Microsoft Fax from the Windows CD. Use the Add/Remove Programs option in the Windows Control Panel, select the Windows Setup tab on the Add/Remove Programs Properties dialog box, and select the Microsoft Fax component.

★ **TIP**

If you use a single telephone line to connect to your mail server and to send faxes from your computer, set up a separate profile containing only Microsoft Fax service.

After you set up the software, take these steps to add fax service to an Outlook profile:

1 If you want to change the profile you're currently using while working in Outlook, choose the Services command from the Tools menu.

To change a profile other than the one you're using, open the Control Panel window, double-click the Mail icon, and then click the Show Profiles button. Select the profile you want to change, and then click the Properties button. When the Properties dialog box appears, be sure that the Services tab is showing and that the name of the profile you want to change appears in the title bar.

To add a profile, follow the steps outlined in "Creating a Profile," on page 7.

2 Click the Add button on the Services tab.

3 In the Add Service To Profile dialog box, select Microsoft Fax, and then click OK.

4 A message box asks whether you want to set up your fax modem for Outlook. Click Yes.

5 When the Microsoft Fax Properties dialog box appears, fill in as much of the information as you can. You must provide your fax number on the User tab.

6 If more than one modem is available to you, click the Modem tab, select the modem you'll be using, and then click the Set As Active Fax Modem button.

7 Click the Dialing tab, and then click the Dialing Properties button.

8 If you send faxes from only one location, you can set up the Default Location with the information that's needed. If you'll be sending faxes from several locations, click the New button, type a location name, and then click OK. Set up the necessary information for this new location. Click OK in the Dialing Properties dialog box.

9 Some of the telephone numbers that you call within your area code may require you to dial the area code to connect. If you call such a number, click the Toll Prefixes button. In the Local Phone Numbers list, select an exchange in your area code that requires you to dial your area code before you dial the number, and then click the Add button to move it to the list on the right. Repeat this step for each long-distance prefix that you will be dialing within your own area code.

 TIP

If most of the prefixes in the list require you to dial your area code first, click the Add All button, and then remove the few prefixes that are local to your number. If you aren't sure about which prefixes require you to dial the area code, you can work around this when you set up a fax entry in your address book.

10 Click OK in the Toll Prefixes dialog box, and then click the Message tab.

11 In the Time To Send area, select the time you want your faxes to go out.

12   In the Message Format area, select a message format. Click the Paper button to select how you want your fax transmitted: the size of paper, the image quality, and the orientation of the fax image on the paper.

13   If you don't want a cover page, click the Send Cover Page check box to turn it off. If you do want a cover page, select the one you want to use.

      If you want to change the cover page or see what it looks like, click the Open button. Or, if you want to create a new cover page of your own, click the New button. In both cases, the Fax Cover Page Editor starts up so that you can modify the existing cover page or create a new one.

      If you have cover page files available, you can click the Browse button to open one of them for use.

SEE ALSO

For information about setting up fax addresses, see the sidebar "Fax Addresses," on page 161.

14   When you've finished setting the fax properties, click OK in each of the open dialog boxes. If Outlook is running, you'll see a message telling you that you can't use the service until you log off and restart Outlook. The next time you start Outlook, you will be able to send faxes.

Using a Different Profile

If you have more than one profile set up, you can select which profile to use when you start Outlook. You can tell Outlook to use a particular profile all the time, or you can choose a profile each time you start the program.

To use the same profile all the time, do this:

1   In Outlook, choose the Options command from the Tools menu, and then select the Mail Services tab if it isn't already displayed.

2   Select the Always Use This Profile option, and then select the profile from the drop-down list.

3   Click OK.

If you prefer, you can choose a profile at the start of each Outlook session. For this option, follow these steps:

1 In Outlook, choose the Options command from the Tools menu, and then select the Mail Services tab if it isn't already displayed.

2 Select the Prompt For A Profile To Be Used option.

3 Click OK.

Once the Prompt For A Profile To Be Used option is turned on, you'll need to select a profile in the Choose Profile dialog box each time you start Outlook. (See "Logging On," on page 4.)

Removing a Profile

Suppose that your situation changes and you no longer need all of the profiles that you created. For example, perhaps you no longer have access to the network and want to delete the profile that includes the Microsoft Exchange service. To simplify your Outlook life, you can remove the unwanted and unnecessary profiles.

To remove a profile from Outlook, follow these steps:

1 Double-click the Mail icon in the Control Panel window.

2 In the Properties dialog box, click the Show Profiles button.

3 Select the profile you want to remove.

4 Click the Remove button, and then click Yes when asked whether you want to remove this profile.

5 Click the Close button.

Having a correct profile is critical to using Outlook. If you encounter problems running Outlook or accessing your e-mail service, carefully check your profile for the correct settings. If that doesn't correct the problem, create a new profile and try again.

Getting Started

CHAPTER 2

Looking Out into Outlook

After Microsoft Outlook 98 starts up, you see the Outlook window with your Inbox folder open, as shown in Figure 2-1, on the next page. Using the various elements displayed in this window as a starting point, this chapter describes the group panels of the Outlook Bar, shows you how to customize the Outlook window (including the Outlook Bar and toolbars), and explains how to set up your Outlook Assistants.

FIGURE 2-1.
The Outlook window with the Inbox folder open.

Outlook Bar

Standard toolbar

Status bar Click here to scroll this group.

Folder items

Using the Outlook Bar

The Outlook Bar, on the left side of the Outlook window, displays one of three groups of folders. The names of the groups will depend on how you installed Outlook 98. The groups will be called Outlook Shortcuts, My Shortcuts, and Other Shortcuts, or just Outlook, Mail, and Other. Don't worry about the group names, they work the same way whatever they are called.

When you click a group's label, the label moves to the top of the Outlook Bar, and the folders in that group appear on the bar. The folders are convenient places to store messages and other types of Outlook information. A number in parentheses next to a folder name indicates the number of *unread* messages in the folder, not necessarily the number of items in the folder. To open a particular folder, all you need to do is click it.

If the group contains a lot of folders (as the Outlook group does), you'll see small up and down arrows on the Outlook Bar, which you can click to scroll through the complete folder display. You can easily add folders to any of the three groups; for details, see "Adding a Folder to the Outlook Bar," on page 31.

Outlook Shortcuts Group

On the Outlook Bar, the Outlook Shortcuts group is displayed by default. On the panel for this group, you'll find at least these standard Outlook folders: Outlook Today, Inbox, Calendar, Contacts, Tasks, Journal, Notes, and Deleted Items.

Outlook Today

The Outlook Today page displays frequently used items, as shown in Figure 2-2, on the following page. You'll see a summary of any calendar events scheduled for the day, the number of unread messages in your inbox, and any assigned tasks that have to be performed. Click either the Calendar, Mail, or Tasks icons to see more information.

If you need to look up information about someone in an address book, such as a telephone number, enter the person's name in the Find A Contact text box and then click Go.

Click the Options command to set up the Outlook Today page. These are the options you can set:

- **When Starting Go Directly To Outlook Today.** Choose this option to start in the Outlook Today window rather than the Inbox.

- **Show __ Days In My Calendar**. Select the number of calendar days that contain appointments to display on the Outlook Today window. The default is five.

■ **In My Task List Show Me.** Choose whether to display all of your active tasks (the default) or just the current day's tasks.

■ **Show Outlook Today In This Style.** Choose a style for the Outlook Today window.

■ **Back to Outlook Today.** Accept your options and return to the Outlook Today window.

FIGURE 2-2.
The Outlook Today page.

Inbox Folder

For details about working with messages, see Chapter 4, "Exchanging Messages and Faxes."

The Inbox folder contains new messages you haven't read, plus any messages you've read and haven't deleted or moved to another folder. Figure 2-1, on page 20, shows examples of Inbox items. You'll typically work in your Inbox folder to create new messages and to read, forward, or reply to messages you've received.

Calendar Folder

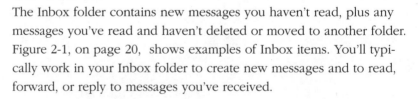

For more information about working with your calendar, see Part III, "Scheduling Your Time and Tasks."

The Calendar folder displays a calendar showing the appointments you have made and, depending on how you've arranged the window, a list of tasks you have recorded. Here's a view of a typical Calendar folder:

Date Navigator

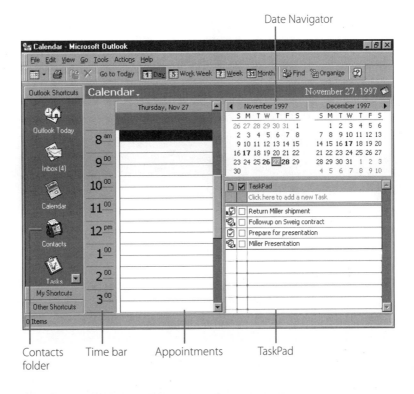

Contacts folder   Time bar   Appointments   TaskPad

Contacts Folder

? SEE ALSO

For more information about working with your list of contacts, see Chapter 13, "Managing Your Contacts."

You can use the Contacts folder to store names, street addresses, telephone numbers, e-mail addresses, and other information about people you deal with on a business or a personal basis. A typical Contacts folder looks like the illustration at the top of the following page.

Tasks Folder

? SEE ALSO

For more information about setting up and working with your list of tasks, see Chapter 12, "Controlling Your Tasks."

In the Tasks folder, you can compile a list of projects and the tasks that are involved in each project. You can describe and categorize each task, record its due date, and track its status. You can also sort the list in various ways—by category or by the name of the person assigned to the task, for instance. Your Tasks folder might look something like the illustration at the bottom of the next page.

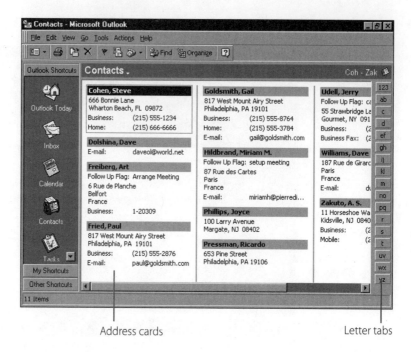

Address cards

Letter tabs

Click the plus sign to see entries in a group.

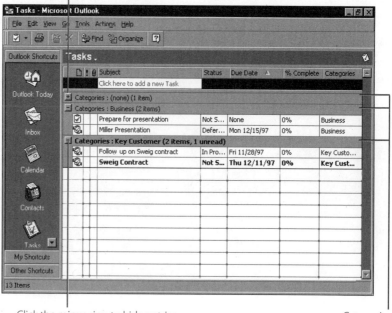

Click the minus sign to hide entries.

Categories

Journal Folder

 SEE ALSO

For more information about your journal, see Chapter 14, "Keeping a Journal."

The Journal folder contains a record of various actions you've taken, such as sending and receiving messages, assigning tasks (and the responses), creating documents in other Microsoft Office applications—even making phone calls. You can track the actions on a timeline, and you can sort the list of journal entries in different ways. The following illustration shows a typical Journal folder.

Click the minus sign to hide entries.   Timeline view

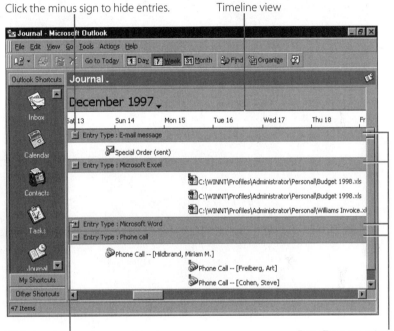

Click the plus sign to see entries in a group.   Entry Type groupings

Notes Folder

 SEE ALSO

For more information about the Notes folder, see Chapter 15, "Making Notes."

In the Notes folder, you can record notes about anything you like: meetings, personal reminders, comments, bits of useful information. A sample Notes folder is shown at the top of the next page.

Getting Started

Note label   Notes can appear in any of five colors.

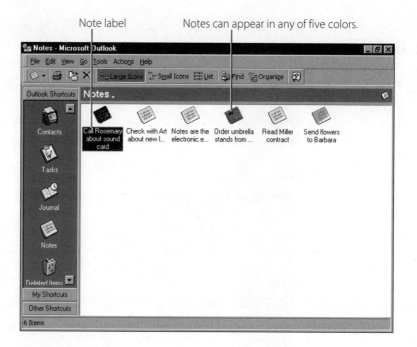

Deleted Items Folder

When you delete an item from any of your other folders, Outlook moves it to the Deleted Items folder. You can retrieve items from this folder as long as you haven't emptied it, but after you empty the folder, the folder items are gone forever. (You can empty the folder by right-clicking the Deleted Items icon and then choosing Empty "Deleted Items" Folder from the shortcut menu.) Until you empty the Deleted Items folder, it can contain any of the various kinds of folder items that you can set up or receive in Outlook—messages, appointments, task entries, contact entries, journal entries, notes, and documents. Each entry displays a distinctive icon to indicate what type of item it is. Here's an example of the Deleted Items folder:

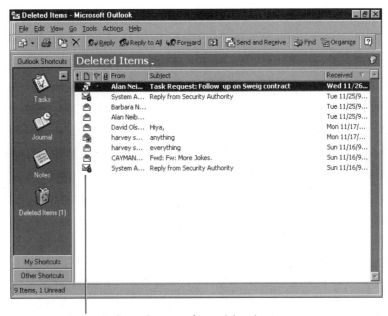

Icons indicate the type of item deleted.

Getting Started

> **⊕ TIP**
>
> You can set up Outlook to automatically remove the messages in the Deleted Items folder when you exit Outlook. Choose the Options command from the Tools menu, and then select the Other tab, if it isn't already displayed. Turn on the Empty The Deleted Items Folder Upon Exiting check box, and then click OK.

My Shortcuts Group

When you click the My Shortcuts group label on the Outlook Bar (it may be called Mail on your system), you see at least the three standard folders in the group: Drafts, Outbox, and Sent Items. (There may be additional folders depending on how you set up Outlook.)

Drafts Folder

The Drafts folder stores messages that you are not yet ready to send. They may be messages that you have not completed, or those that you are holding to send at a later time. You can open a message in the Drafts folder to complete and send it.

Outbox Folder

The Outbox folder temporarily holds messages you've sent that have not yet been pulled from your computer to your e-mail server for delivery. When you're connected to your server, messages stay in your Outbox folder for only a short time. If you're working offline, the Outbox folder holds your sent messages until you're connected again. When you're back online, Outlook sends your messages from the Outbox folder to your e-mail server. Internet e-mail messages sent while offline are stored in the Outbox until you go on-line. Then, depending on how Outlook is set up, outgoing mail might be sent automatically, or it may wait in the outbox until you use the Send And Receive command.

Sent Items Folder

The Sent Items folder contains copies of messages you've sent. You can use this folder as a record of the messages you've generated in case you need to refer to them again or in case you need to resend a message.

Other Shortcuts Group

The third label on the Outlook Bar refers to a miscellaneous group called Other Shortcuts. The folders you see when you click this label depend on your computer setup. Some typical folders in this group incude My Computer (the same as the My Computer icon on the Windows desktop), My Documents, Personal Folders (if these folders are set up in Outlook), Favorites, and Public Folders. You can add other disk folders, as well as Outlook folders, to the Other Shortcuts group; for details, see "Adding a Folder to the Outlook Bar," on page 31.

My Computer Folder

For more information about viewing disk contents in Outlook, see "Opening Documents or Starting Programs from Outlook," on page 484.

When you click the My Computer folder, the Outlook window displays icons for your computer's disk drives, the same icons you see when you double-click the My Computer icon on your desktop. You can then switch to any disk drive on your computer or to any network drive, just as you can in the My Computer window on your desktop. In this way, you can use Outlook as a substitute for My Computer and Windows Explorer to locate and open any folder, file, or document.

My Documents Folder

The My Documents folder on the Other Shortcuts group panel is a shortcut to the My Documents folder, if you have one, on your computer's hard disk. If, like me, you keep most of your documents in the My Documents folder or in a subfolder inside it, you can use the My Documents shortcut to find and open most any file or document that you want to work on.

When you open a file or document from the Outlook window, Windows starts the application that was used to create the document.

Personal Folders

? SEE ALSO

For information about setting up personal folders and using Outlook for remote mail, see Chapter 8, "Setting Up Outlook for Remote Work," and Chapter 9, "Running Outlook for Remote Work."

On the Other Shortcuts group panel, you might also see an icon labeled Personal Folders. This folder contains duplicates of your four Mail folders (Inbox, Deleted Items, Sent Items, and Outbox) and can include other folders as well. Personal folders are located on your computer's hard disk rather than on a server. These duplicate folders work in a manner similar to the Mail folders when you're working offline. In fact, you must install personal folders if you plan to use Outlook for remote mail. They also work as backup folders in which you can keep duplicates of the messages in your mail folders.

Favorites Folder

? SEE ALSO

For details about working with Favorites, see "Using Public Folder Favorites," on page 532.

Outlook's Favorites folder is a shortcut to the Favorites folder on your hard disk. This folder is inside the folder in which Windows is installed (usually called Windows). Icons or labels for the items in your Favorites folder also appear on the Favorites toolbar of your Office shortcut bar (if you have set it up) and on the list that appears when you click the Favorites button on the Microsoft Internet Explorer toolbar. You can set up and click the items in the Favorites folder to quickly jump to any disk folder, World Wide Web site (URL), application, or disk file.

Public Folders

? SEE ALSO

For more information about public folders, see Chapter 19, "Managing Folders."

If your e-mail server uses Microsoft Exchange Server, it provides some variety of public folders. These are folders that most people can use, containing messages that can be read by everyone who can open the folder. A public folder can also contain postings—notes that ask questions, provide answers, or state opinions and facts—as well as documents. Public folders are intended to present and record public discussion of a specific topic.

Some public folders might have limited access—that is, they might be available only to certain people. For example, only the members of a project team might have access to a project folder.

Getting Started

Depending on the generosity of your Exchange administrator and on the capacity of your Exchange server, you might have use of hundreds of public folders (especially if your Exchange administrator sets up public folders for Internet newsgroups) or possibly only a few.

Customizing the Outlook Bar

The Outlook Bar sits along the left edge of the Outlook window, as you saw in Figure 2-1, on page 20. Earlier, this chapter described the three groups that initially appear on this bar: Outlook Shortcuts, My Shortcuts, and Other Shortcuts. But you can do more with the Outlook Bar than switch groups and click a folder icon to open a folder. The following sections explain the various ways you can change the Outlook Bar.

Turning the Outlook Bar Off and On

SEE ALSO

For details about how to widen columns in the folder items list, see "Changing Column Width," on page 557.

When you are working with your e-mail messages or a list of tasks, at times you might want a better view of the columns of information displayed in the folder items list. If so, you'll want to use the entire width of the Outlook window for folder items so that you can widen the columns. To use the entire width of the Outlook window for the folder items list, you can turn off the Outlook Bar.

To turn off the Outlook Bar, do one of the following:

- Choose the Outlook Bar command from the View menu.

- Right-click an empty area of the Outlook Bar (don't click directly on a folder icon on the bar), and then choose Hide Outlook Bar from the shortcut menu.

To turn the Outlook Bar back on, choose the Outlook Bar command from the View menu again.

Changing the Size of Icons on the Outlook Bar

Initially, the folder icons on the Outlook Bar appear in large size, but you can make them smaller. When you change the size of the icons on the Outlook Bar, you change them only for the current group. When the folder icons are smaller, you can see more of them without scrolling the group, and you can also narrow the Outlook Bar to allow more space for the folder items list or to display the Folder List.

To display the Outlook Bar icons in small size, right-click an empty area of the Outlook Bar (don't click a folder icon), and choose Small Icons from the shortcut menu. To return the icons to large size, right-click the Outlook Bar again, and choose Large Icons from the shortcut menu.

Adding a Folder to the Outlook Bar

You can add any existing Outlook or disk folder to any group on the Outlook Bar. To add a folder to a group on the Outlook Bar, take these steps:

1   Switch to the group on the Outlook Bar to which you want to add the folder.

2   Right-click an empty area of the Outlook Bar (don't click a folder icon) and choose Outlook Bar Shortcut from the shortcut menu.

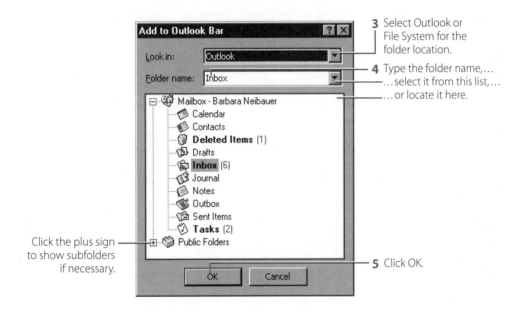

3 Select Outlook or File System for the folder location.

4 Type the folder name,...
...select it from this list,...
...or locate it here.

Click the plus sign to show subfolders if necessary.

5 Click OK.

Getting Started

If the Folder List is displayed, you can add a folder by dragging it from the Folder List to the Outlook Bar. Drag the folder until a horizontal line appears where you want to position the folder, and then release the mouse button.

Removing a Folder Icon from the Outlook Bar

To remove a folder icon from the Outlook Bar, follow these steps:

1 Switch to the group on the Outlook Bar from which you want to remove the folder icon.

2 Right-click the folder icon you want to remove from the Outlook Bar.

3 Choose Remove From Outlook Bar from the shortcut menu.

4 Click Yes in the message box that asks whether you're sure you want to remove the folder icon.

Removing a folder icon from the Outlook Bar doesn't remove the folder from Outlook. If you want to remove the folder, see "Removing a Folder," on page 529.

Renaming a Folder Icon on the Outlook Bar

The icons on the Outlook Bar are shortcuts to the actual folders. You can change the name of any icon that appears on the Outlook Bar.

Changing the name of a folder icon on the Outlook Bar does not change the name of the folder itself. For information on renaming folders, see "Renaming a Folder," on page 528.

Here's how to rename a folder icon on the Outlook Bar.

1 Right-click the folder icon you want to rename.

2 Choose Rename Shortcut from the shortcut menu. The icon's name becomes active (highlighted).

3 Type or edit the name of the folder icon, and then press the Enter key.

Adding a Group to the Outlook Bar

You might find that you'd like to add another group (or several more groups) to the Outlook Bar. You can easily add a group by following these steps:

1 Right-click an empty area of the Outlook Bar.

2 Choose Add New Group from the shortcut menu. Outlook adds a group label and activates it for naming.

3 Type a name for the new group, and then press the Enter key.

You can now add folder icons to your new group; see "Adding a Folder to the Outlook Bar," on page 31.

Renaming a Group on the Outlook Bar

If you want to change the name of a group on the Outlook Bar, take these steps:

1 Right-click the label of the group you want to rename.

2 Choose Rename Group from the shortcut menu. Outlook activates that group label for renaming.

3 Type a new name for the group, and then press the Enter key.

Removing a Group from the Outlook Bar

If one of the groups on the Outlook Bar is no longer useful to you, you can remove it from the bar. Simply right-click the label of the group you want to remove, choose Remove Group from the shortcut menu, and click Yes in the message box that asks whether you're sure you want to remove the group.

Customizing the Outlook Window

Outlook allows you to customize the appearance and functionality of the main Outlook window to fit the way you work and the tasks you perform most often. You can choose whether to hide or display such components as the Preview Pane, Folder List, the Outlook toolbars, and the status bar. You can also add, remove, rename, resize, or reposition various elements in the Outlook window.

Displaying the Preview Pane

To read the contents of messages directly from the Inbox, you can display the Preview Pane. The Preview Pane displays the contents of the message selected in the messages list, as shown in Figure 2-3. To display the Preview Pane choose Preview Pane from the View menu.

FIGURE 2-3.
The Preview Pane displays the contents of the highlighted message.

Preview Pane—

> ⭐ **TIP**
>
> Choose AutoPreview from the View menu to display the first three lines of every message directly under each item.

Displaying the Folder List

The first time you start Outlook, you see only a list of messages in your Inbox. If all you do with Outlook is read and send messages, this might suit you. But at some time or other, you'll more than likely want to open other folders and work with the items they contain. The easiest way to do this is to click the folder you want to open. If the folder you want isn't on the Outlook Bar, you can add it there (which can make the bar cluttered and slower to use), or you can display the Folder List.

Displaying the Folder List can be extremely useful if your work takes you frequently from folder to folder. Still, there might be times when you want to see more of the columns in the items list without having to scroll horizontally. In this case, you can either hide the Folder List or change its width. (For information about the latter choice, see "Changing List Widths," on the next page.) You can also display the Folder List temporarily, just long enough to select another folder.

To open the Folder List, choose Folder List from the View menu. To hide the list, repeat this command or click the Close button on the Folder List title bar.

Right-click here to display a drop-down menu of folder commands.

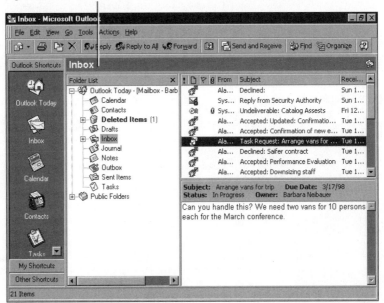

To display the Folder List temporarily, follow these steps:

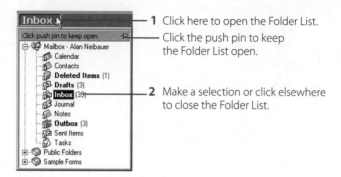

1 Click here to open the Folder List.
  Click the push pin to keep
  the Folder List open.

2 Make a selection or click elsewhere
  to close the Folder List.

Displaying the Status Bar

The status bar at the bottom of the Outlook window shows helpful information. In many windows, the status bar displays the number of items in the open folder and how many of the items are unread. In some form windows (if the form's designer set up the form this way), the status bar also provides messages that indicate what you should type or choose in a form field.

If none of this information is important to you—if you never or only rarely look at the status bar—you might want to hide the status bar to gain some extra space in the window. To hide or display the status bar, choose the Status Bar command from the View menu.

Changing List Widths

? SEE ALSO

The Calendar folder has additional sections that you can size. For details, see "Adjusting the Calendar Display," on page 312.

When you have the Outlook window set up to show the Outlook Bar, the Folder List, and the items list, you might want to change the width of one or more of these elements in order to see the full width of large-size Outlook Bar icons, to see all the folders you've expanded in the Folder List—particularly when the subfolders run several levels deep—or to see more columns of information in a list of messages or files.

Here's how to change the width of the Outlook Bar or the lists.

1 Position the mouse pointer on the vertical dividing line between the Outlook Bar and the lists or on the line between the lists. The

mouse pointer changes to a vertical line with two arrowheads pointing left and right.

2 Drag the vertical dividing line to the left or to the right to adjust the width of the Outlook Bar or the lists, and then release the mouse button.

Working with Toolbars

Like all good applications with a graphical user interface, Outlook provides toolbars in its windows. Clicking the toolbar buttons gives you a fast, easy way to take specific actions or perform common tasks. You can turn Outlook's toolbars on and off, you can reposition them, and you can change the size of the toolbar buttons.

Outlook contains two toolbars that you can use with any folder:

■ The Standard toolbar contains buttons appropriate to the actions you usually take for the type of item you've selected or opened. You'll see a version of the Standard toolbar in every folder you open in Outlook. The buttons on the Standard toolbar change for each type of folder or folder item.

■ The Advanced toolbar contains an additional set of useful buttons, which depend on the folder you have open. For example, there is a button for planning a meeting when you're using the Calendar folder, and for starting an online meeting when you're in the Contacts folder. The toolbar also contains some common buttons, such as ones to open the previous folder you were using, select a view for the current folder, group items, and undo your last action.

There are two other toolbars that you can access, depending on the task you are performing.

■ The Remote toolbar contains buttons for running a remote mail session. (See "Checking Out the Remote Toolbar," on page 294, for details.) You can see the Remote toolbar only in e-mail folders, which are designed primarily to hold messages.

- The Formatting Toolbar contains buttons for formatting text. You can only access this toolbar when working with any item (except notes) that contain text, such as an e-mail message, a meeting request, a task item, or a journal entry.

Displaying and Moving Toolbars

In most cases, Outlook will display the toolbar appropriate for the function you are performing. When you are composing a message, for example, Outlook opens the Formatting Toolbar so that you can format your text. You can easily display or hide toolbars and change their position on the screen to suit your tastes and working habits.

Turning Toolbars Off and On

Obviously, toolbars take up a certain amount of window space. If you'd prefer to use this space to see more folders or folder items, you can turn a toolbar off in either of these two ways:

- Point to Toolbars on the View menu, and then click the box beside the toolbar you want to turn off to clear its check mark. (A check mark in the box beside the toolbar means it is currently turned on.)

- Right-click any toolbar. On the shortcut menu, click the box beside the name of the toolbar you want to turn off to clear the check mark.

 NOTE

Only the names of toolbars that apply to the current folder or to the open folder item appear on the Toolbars submenu or on the Toolbars shortcut menu.

To turn a toolbar back on, you can use either of the two methods just described. Just choose the toolbar from the Toolbar submenu or open the shortcut menu to restore the check mark beside the name of the toolbar you want to turn on.

 TIP

If all the toolbars are turned off, you can right-click the menu bar to display the Toolbars shortcut menu, where you can turn on the toolbars you need.

Changing the Position of a Toolbar

You can reposition a toolbar on the screen by moving it to the top edge, bottom edge, right edge, or left edge of the Outlook window, or by floating the toolbar. (If the Outlook window is not maximized, you can even drag a toolbar outside the Outlook window.) To move a toolbar to a new position, drag the move handle at the left end of the toolbar to a different edge of the Outlook window or into the middle of the window.

You might want to float a toolbar that is too wide to display all of its buttons on the screen. (This sometimes occurs when you're using a 640 × 480 screen resolution.) You'll know the toolbar has more buttons than you can see if it shows a right-pointing chevron at the right end of the toolbar.

 TIP

To quickly float a toolbar, double-click its move handle. To quickly return a floating toolbar to the edge where you last docked it, double-click its title bar.

When a toolbar is floating, you can change its size in much the same way as you change the size of a window. To change the size and shape of a floating toolbar, simply drag a side of the toolbar frame.

Customizing Toolbars and Menus

The toolbars provided by Outlook are useful, but they may not offer all of the features you use often. For example, you may want to quickly set up an appointment from within any folder with a single click of the mouse, but the Appointment button is not on the Standard toolbar.

With Outlook 98, you can add and delete features from toolbars and menus, create your own custom toolbars, and change the icons on toolbar buttons. To start the process, use either of these methods:

- Point to Toolbars on the View menu, and then click Customize.

- Right-click a toolbar, and then choose Customize from the shortcut menu.

The Customize dialog box, shown in Figure 2-4, contains three tabs.

- Use the Toolbars tab to display or hide a toolbar; create, rename, or delete a custom toolbar; or reset the menu bar or an Outlook toolbar to its default layout.

- Use the Commands tab to add features to menus and toolbars.

- Use the Options tab to change the appearance of menus and toolbars.

FIGURE 2-4.
The Customize dialog box for creating and changing toolbars.

Adding Buttons to a Toolbar or Menu

You can easily add a feature to a menu or toolbar. You do this by choosing the category of the feature on the Commands tab of the Customize dialog box and then dragging the specific feature to where you want it to appear. Follow these steps:

1   Point to Toolbars on the View menu, and then choose Customize.

2   Click the Commands tab.

3   Click the category that contains the feature you want to add.

4   Click the feature you want to add.

5 Drag the feature to its new location on the toolbar or menu. As you drag over the toolbar or menu, an icon of a button with a plus sign moves with the mouse and an insert bar appears to guide you. If you drag to a menu, the menu will drop down so that you can position the new feature exactly where you want.

6 Release the mouse button to drop the feature into place.

Deleting and Changing Buttons and Menu Commands

You can also delete features from a menu or toolbar, change their position, and customize how they appear. First display any tab of the Customize dialog box, and then use one of these techniques:

- To remove a feature, drag it off of the menu or toolbar.

- To change the position of a feature, drag it to another location on the menu or toolbar, or to another menu or toolbar.

- To change the appearance of a button, right-click it and choose commands from the shortcut menu.

Be careful when customizing menus. When the Customize dialog box is displayed, if you drag one of the menu names, such as File or Edit, away from the menu, you will remove the entire new item and its commands. To remove a specific command from a menu, follow these steps after the Customize dialog box is displayed:

1 Click the menu name, and then release the mouse. The menu will open and display its commands.

2 Drag the specific menu command away from the menu.

To customize a toolbar button or menu command, right-click it to open the shortcut menu. The functions of the shortcut menu commands are shown in Table 2-1.

TABLE 2-1.   Customizing Buttons and Menu Commands

Command	What the Command Does
Reset	Restores the item to its default status
Delete	Removes the item from the menu or toolbar
Name	Determines the name displayed on the menu or ScreenTip: use the & symbol before the character you want underlined as a keyboard shortcut
Copy Button Image	Copies the icon to the Clipboard
Paste Button Image	Inserts the icon from the Clipboard onto the menu or toolbar
Reset Button Image	Restores the default icon image
Edit Button Image	Lets you customize the icon
Change Button Image	Displays a list of alternative icons
Default Style	Uses the default style of display for the item
Text Only (Always)	Displays only the name of the feature, no icon, in toolbars and menus
Text Only (in Menus)	Displays only the name of the feature on menus
Image and Text	Displays both the name and icon of the feature
Begin a Group	Inserts a vertical bar to separate toolbar buttons or a horizontal bar to separate menu commands

The Edit Button Image option on the shortcut menu opens the Button Editor so that you can design your own button icons, as shown in Figure 2-5.

FIGURE 2-5.
Editing a button image.

Click or drag with the mouse to draw with the selected color.

Select a drawing color.

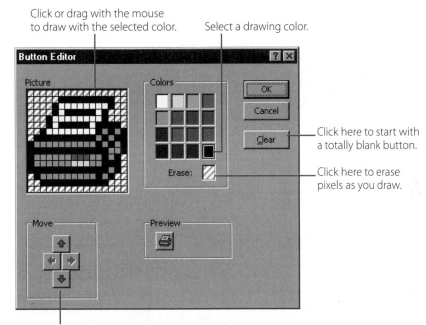

Click here to start with a totally blank button.

Click here to erase pixels as you draw.

Click to move the image around in its frame.

Changing the Appearance of Toolbars and Menus

Use the Options tab of the Customize dialog box to change the way toolbar buttons appear and the way menus are displayed.

You can choose to display toolbar icons in a large size (about twice the normal size), to display ScreenTips when you point to a menu or toolbar button, or to show keyboard shortcut key combinations along with the ScreenTips.

You can also choose the way drop-down menus appear. The default is no animation, in which the menu just appears when you click the menu bar. You can also choose to have menus open from the upper-left to the lower-right corner, slide down like a window shade, or open using the two styles randomly.

> **NOTE**

Large toolbar buttons are easier to see, but they also take up more space on your screen. With large toolbar buttons displayed, it's unlikely that the Standard toolbar can display all of its buttons within the width of the Outlook window, even on higher resolution screens.

Creating a New Toolbar

In addition to customizing Outlook's existing toolbars, you can create entirely new ones. You do this by creating a new blank toolbar and then dragging features to it as you just learned. To create a new toolbar, follow these steps.

1 Point to Toolbars on the View menu, and then choose Customize.

2 Click the Toolbars tab.

3 Click New.

4 In the box that appears, type a name for the toolbar (the default suggestion is Custom 1), and then click OK to display a small blank toolbar.

5 Click the Commands tab.

6 Drag the features you want to the new toolbar.

7 Click Close.

The toolbar will now be listed on the Toolbars submenu or shortcut menu. To delete a custom toolbar, point to Toolbars on the View menu, click Customize, click the toolbar in the Toolbars tab, and then click Delete.

Getting Help from Outlook Assistants

Outlook provides two assistants to help you work with messages that come to your Inbox: the Rules Wizard (formerly the Inbox Assistant) and the Out Of Office Assistant. The Rules Wizard can be set up to automatically sort messages or to forward messages that you always treat the same way. For those times when you're out of the office, you can set up the Out Of Office Assistant to tell people who send you messages that you are away, when you'll be back, and whom to contact or what to do during your absence. The Out Of Office Assistant can also automatically sort, move, forward, and delete messages while you are away.

> **NOTE**

You can use the Out Of Office Assistant only if you are using Outlook with Micro-soft Exchange Server. In addition, you must have the Exchange Extensions add-in installed in Outlook. For information about installing add-ins, see "Add-In Manager," on page 94.

Rules Wizard

For a variety of reasons over which you might have little control, your Inbox can become flooded with messages and items that you want to act on in very specific ways. You can, of course, take these actions yourself, attending to each message manually. But if you find a category of messages that you act on in a specific way every time, you can set up the Rules Wizard to take care of these actions for you. The Rules Wizard can automatically delete, forward, reply, move, and perform several other actions on items delivered to your Inbox.

? **SEE ALSO**

To quickly create a rule using the information in a specific message, see the sidebar "Creating a Rule," on page 139.

To set up the Rules Wizard, first choose the Rules Wizard command from the Tools menu to display the following dialog box:

In the Rules Wizard dialog box, click the New button to open the dialog box shown in Figure 2-6, on the facing page. In this dialog box, you select the general type of rule you want to create, as explained in Table 2-2. For example, if you want to place e-mail from a particular recipient in a folder other than the Inbox, select the Move New Messages From Someone option.

TABLE 2-2. General Types of Rules to Apply

Setting	What the Rules Wizard Acts On
Check messages when they arrive	Performs some action when a message is received
Check messages after sending	Performs some action after you send a message
Move new messages from someone	Automatically places new messages from a sender into a specified folder
Notify me when important messages arrive	Displays a specified notice on screen when a message with a specified priority is received
Move messages based on content	Places a message containing specified text into a selected folder
Delete a conversation	Deletes a message containing specified text
Flag messages from someone	Applies a selected flag for a set number of days when a message is received from a specified sender or group.
Assign categories to sent messages	Assigns a category to sent messages based on the recipient
Assign categories based on content	Assign a category to sent messages based on the contents
Move messages I send to someone	Moves sent messages into specific folders based on the recipient
Stop processing all following rules	Stops applying selected rules to messages

The Rule Description box displays the logic or action of the rule. The description will change and enlarge as you select specific actions from other Rules Wizard dialog boxes.

FIGURE 2-6.

Creating a new rule.

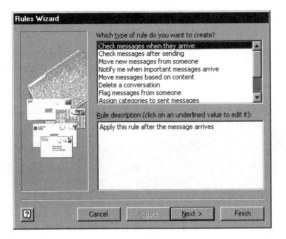

In some cases, the description will contain links, which appear as underlined text. This means that you must click the link to further refine the rule. If you select the Move Messages Based On Content rule, for example, you'll see the description shown here.

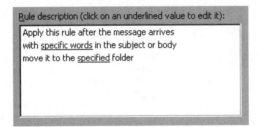

This means you have to click the specific words link to enter the text you want the rule to check for, and then click the specified link to choose the folder to place the message. If you see a link labeled people or distribution list in the description, it means you must click it to select a specific sender or group of senders to use for the rule.

After you choose the type of rule, click Next to select the conditions to apply to the rule. Most rules can be applied only when certain conditions are met, such as when a message is addressed to you or when certain words appear in the subject. The options offered by the Rules Wizard depend on the type of rule you are creating. In most cases, you can select more than one option to create rather sophisticated rules.

For example, you could create a rule that checks messages to determine if they are from the sender named Dave Olshina, have to do with budgets, and contain attachments. The list of possibilities is rather long, so a sampling is described in Table 2-3.

TABLE 2-3. Rules Wizard Dialog Box Options for Selecting Conditions

Setting	What the Rules Wizard Acts On
From people or distribution list	Items from a particular sender or group of senders
Sent to people or distribution list	Items sent to a particular recipient
Sent directly to me	Items with your name in the To box
Where my name is in the Cc box	Items with your name in the Cc box
With specific words in the subject	Items that include the specified text in the Subject box
With specific words in the body	Items that contain the specified text somewhere in the message body
Which has an attachment	Items that have attachments

? SEE ALSO
To learn how to create an Outlook template, see "Out of Office Automatic Replies," on page 55.

After you select conditions and click Next, the Rules Wizard asks What Do You Want To Do With The Message? and lists actions that can be taken. For example, if you want to send an automatic reply to a message, choose the action Reply Using A Specific Template. A few of the other actions you may choose include deleting the message, forwarding it to a preset list of recipients, playing a sound, or moving it to a folder you specify.

After you've chosen an action to be applied to messages matching a rule's conditions, the wizard asks if you'd like to make any exceptions to the rule. For example, after specifying that all messages from a certain sender be deleted, you could add an exception such as "except if it has an attachment."

When you've specified any possible exceptions to the rule, the Rules Wizard asks you to enter a name for the rule and turn it either off or on. If there are any links still shown in the description, you have to click them now and complete the definition.

When you click Finish in the last Rules Wizard dialog box, the new rule appears in the list of completed rules.

If you have more then one rule, they will be performed in the order in which they are listed in the box. To change the order of a rule, click it and then click either the Move Up or Move Down buttons depending on where you want to place the rule in the list.

You can also use the dialog box to copy, modify, rename, or delete rules. For additional control over how rules are applied, click the Options button to see these options:

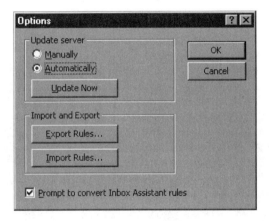

The Update Server section determines when the rules are applied. When set at Automatically, rules that you create or change are applied immediately. Choose Manually when you want to control when new or changed rules are put into effect. They are applied when you click Update Now.

Use the Import And Export section to save your rules to a file on your disk or to retrieve a set of rules that you already saved. If you import a set of rules saved with the Inbox Assistant from an earlier version of Outlook, you will be asked if you want to convert the rules to Outlook 98 format. Turn off the check box at the bottom of the Options dialog box if you do not want to be prompted.

Creating Rules with Organize

Outlook 98 includes Organize, a timesaving feature that lets you manage folders and folder items. Using Organize, you can quickly create a rule without going through all of the Rules Wizard dialog boxes. While you'll learn about Organize features throughout this book, here's how to use it to create a rule.

1 Click the Inbox folder if it is not already open. You can also create a rule from the Drafts, Sent Items, and Outbox folders in this same way.

2 Click Organize.

3 Click Using Folders. **4** Select From or Sent To.

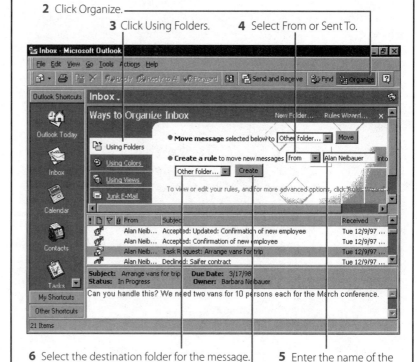

6 Select the destination folder for the message. **5** Enter the name of the sender or recipient.

7 Click here to create the rule.

The rule will be inserted at the top of the Rules Wizard list and will be turned on. Click Rules Wizard in the Organize pane if you wish to refine the rule as you just learned in "Rules Wizard," on page 45.

Out of Office Assistant

When you're away from your office—on vacation, for example—and you want to notify people that you're not available for a while, you can set up the Out Of Office Assistant to automatically send a reply each time you receive a message. Also, the Out Of Office Assistant can automatically perform specific actions on incoming items.

When you use the Out Of Office Assistant, you also create a set of rules for performing actions on messages. The basics of the rules are similar to those of the Rules Wizard, although the dialog boxes differ.

To set up the Out Of Office Assistant, take these steps:

1 Choose Out Of Office Assistant from the Tools menu.

2 Click to turn on the Out Of Office Assistant.

3 Type the message you want the assistant to send.

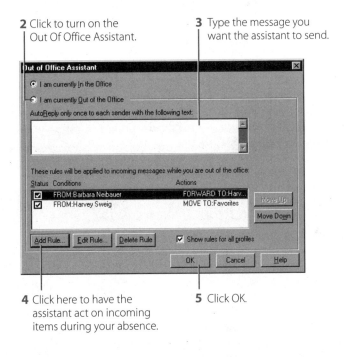

4 Click here to have the assistant act on incoming items during your absence.

5 Click OK.

When you click Add Rule, you'll see the Edit Rule dialog box, shown in Figure 2-7, on the next page. Use this dialog box to set up the rules for the types of items you want the Out Of Office Assistant to act on and the actions it should take for those items. The fewer settings you make in the upper area of the dialog box (When A Message Arrives…), the fewer items the Out Of Office Assistant is asked to deal with, and the faster your mail will be processed.

FIGURE 2-7.

The Edit Rule dialog box.

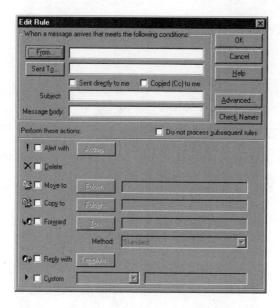

Click the Check Names button in the Edit Rule dialog box to check names in the From and Sent To boxes against the address lists in your address book. Here's how it works.

■ If Outlook finds a matching name, it underlines the name and turns it into a link to the address book entry.

■ If you type a partial name, such as just a first name, Outlook will complete the name with the full listing from the address book.

■ If Outlook locates multiple matches, such as several persons with the same first name, you'll be asked to select the correct name from a list.

■ If Outlook does not find a match, it asks if you want to create a new address listing.

If you need to identify the items further, you can fine-tune your description by clicking the Advanced button in the Edit Rule dialog box. Clicking this button opens the Advanced dialog box, shown in Figure 2-8, which provides additional settings. Consult Table 2-4 for a list of these settings and the items they describe. When you have set up the Advanced dialog box, click OK to close it and return to the Edit Rule dialog box.

FIGURE 2-8.
The Advanced
dialog box.

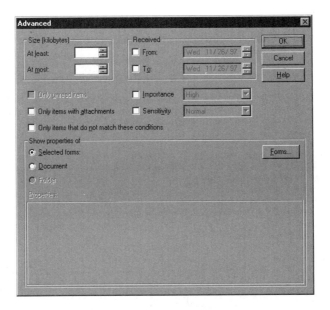

 TIP

> You can choose settings in the Advanced dialog box without making any settings in the Edit Rule dialog box.

TABLE 2-4.   Advanced Dialog Box Options for Identifying Items

Setting	What the Out Of Office Assistant Acts On
Size At least	Items that are larger than the size you set
Size At most	Items that are smaller than the size you set
Received From	Items received after the date you set (for items between two dates, also set a Received To date)
Received To	Items received before the date you set (for items between two dates, also set a Received From date)
Only unread items	Items you haven't read yet
Only items with attachments	Items that contain attachments (files or messages)

(continued)

TABLE 2-4. *continued*

Setting	What the Out Of Office Assistant Acts On
Importance	Items set to the specified level of importance—High, Normal, or Low
Sensitivity	Items with the specified level of sensitivity—Normal, Personal, Private, or Confidential
Only items that do not match these conditions	Uses the reverse of all the settings in both the Edit Rule and the Advanced dialog boxes
Show properties of Selected forms	Displays fields in the forms you select with the Forms button
Show properties of Document	Displays document properties
Show properties of Folder	Displays folder properties

After you return to the Edit Rule dialog box, having selected the kinds of items you want the Out Of Office Assistant to act on, you need to specify the actions you want the Out Of Office Assistant to take for these items. In the lower portion of the Edit Rule dialog box, choose the actions that should be taken for this set of items.

When the settings are complete, click OK in the Edit Rule dialog box to accept all the settings and return to the Out Of Office Assistant dialog box. If you want to specify different actions for other types of items, you can reopen the Edit Rule dialog box as described earlier, identify a new set of items, and select the appropriate actions. Repeat this procedure for each set of items that you want the Out Of Office Assistant to take care of—closing the Edit Rule dialog box and returning to the Out Of Office Assistant dialog box each time. Finally, when you've finished setting up the rules you want, click OK in the Out Of Office Assistant dialog box.

 TIP

You can set up the Out Of Office Assistant in advance and then turn it on and off as needed. You can leave rules you create intact so that you have to set them up only once. You can, of course, change the rules at any time to better suit your needs.

When the Out Of Office Assistant is turned on, the next time you start Outlook (if you connect to your e-mail server), you'll see a message telling you that the Out Of Office Assistant is on and asking whether you want to turn it off. Click Yes to turn off the Out Of Office Assistant; click No to leave it turned on.

The rules stay intact so that you can use them the next time you're out of the office without having to set them up again. Out Of Office Assistant rules are inactive as long as the assistant is turned off.

Out of Office Automatic Replies

To send an automatic reply using the Out Of Office Assistant, follow these steps:

1 In the Edit Rule dialog box, turn on Reply With, and then click the Template button.

2 To reply to others in addition to the sender, click the To button to select other names, or type them in the text box.

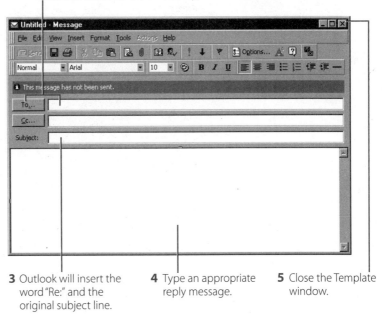

3 Outlook will insert the word "Re:" and the original subject line.

4 Type an appropriate reply message.

5 Close the Template window.

6 Click Yes in the message box to save your changes.

CHAPTER 3

Setting Outlook Options

You can start Outlook and begin using it exactly as it was installed on your computer. But just as you can customize the appearance of the Outlook window, as you learned in Chapter 2, "Looking Out into Outlook," you can also customize the way Outlook works. By setting options, you can fine-tune Outlook for the way you like to work, making it more efficient and comfortable.

Accessing Outlook Options

You use the Options command on the Tools menu to access all of the settings that you can customize. The Options dialog box contains as many as eight tabs. Several of the tabs also have buttons that display one or more pages of additional options. This indicates just how much you can customize Outlook—the way it works and the way it looks. The following sections describe the options on each tab.

Not all of the dialog box tabs and options described in this chapter will be available if you set up Outlook with the Internet E-mail Only option or if you are not connected to Exchange Server.

When you want to set options on more than one tab, you can click the Apply button instead of OK to apply your changes right away and keep the dialog box open. The Apply button is especially useful for options that change the appearance of the Outlook window. That way, you have a preview of the new look—and you can change it back before you close the dialog box if you don't like it.

Using the Preferences Tab

The Preferences tab of the Options dialog box, shown in Figure 3-1, lets you access a variety of options for controlling various Outlook features. There are a few options you set directly on the tab, but most you access using the provided buttons.

Setting E-Mail Options

Click the E-mail Options button on the Preferences tab to access a wide variety of options for controlling how e-mail is received, sent, and handled, as shown in the bottom figure on the next page.

FIGURE 3-1.

The Preferences tab of the Options dialog box.

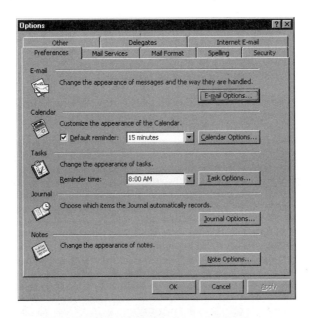

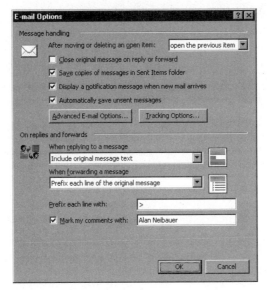

Message Handling

Your choices in this section of the E-mail Options dialog box determine what happens when you move, reply to, forward, or send a message.

After Moving Or Deleting An Open Item

As part of the process of deleting or moving a message that you've just read, Outlook must close the message window. What should Outlook do after closing the window? You can choose one of the following three options:

- Open The Previous Item is the standard setting. With this option selected, the previous message in the folder (the one listed just before the open one in the item list) is opened when you delete or move the current message.

- Open The Next Item opens the next item in the folder.

- Return To The Inbox is the setting to use if you don't want to open another message but just return to the Inbox folder.

Close Original Message On Reply Or Forward

After you send a reply or forward a message, Outlook leaves open the original item's window by default. This setting is handy if you like to read through all your messages and dispose of them as you go ("disposing" includes replying to and forwarding messages), continuing to move up or down the message list after you send a reply or forward a message. However, if you're working on a few scattered messages, you might want to turn on the Close Original Message On Reply Or Forward option.

Save Copies Of Messages In Sent Items Folder

For your own record keeping, you might want to have copies of the messages you send. Well, maybe you don't want a copy of every message, but it's safer to keep a copy of all the messages and then later cull out the ones you don't need to save.

By default, Outlook puts a copy of every message you send in your Sent Items folder. If you prefer to be more selective about which messages you keep, turn off this option. If you turn if off, remember to add yourself to the Cc box for any messages that you want to keep for your records.

Display A Notification Message When New Mail Arrives

Outlook will display a message on screen reporting that new mail has been received.

Automatically Save Unsent Messages

By default Outlook saves messages you're working on every three minutes. This option saves the messages in the Drafts folder.

On Replies And Forwards

The options in the On Replies And Forwards section determine how the contents of the original message appear when you reply to or forward it.

When Replying To A Message

Because replies to messages have a conversational context (the reply takes place as part of a conversation among correspondents), the standard Outlook setup is to include a copy of the original message in the reply. Also, to distinguish the original message from the reply, Outlook indents the original message. You have these additional choices for dealing with the original message in replies:

- The Do Not Include Original Message option omits the original message from your reply.

- The Attach Original Message option includes the original message as an attachment, which appears as a message icon. This choice saves space in the message window but requires you and the recipient to open the attachment to read it.

- The Include Original Message Text option includes the original message in the reply but does not indent it.

- The Prefix Each Line Of The Original Message option adds a prefix character before each line of the original message. Prefix Each Line With lets you choose the prefix character.

When Forwarding a Message

When you forward a message, you obviously want to include the original message text—that's the idea behind forwarding. Outlook is initially set up to simply include the original message text. You have these three other choices for how to do this:

- The Attach Original Message option includes the original message as an attachment, which appears as a message icon that you and the recipient must open to read.

- The Include And Indent Original Message Text option indents the original message text.

- The Prefix Each Line Of The Original Message option adds a prefix character before each line of the original message. Prefix Each Line With lets you choose the prefix character.

Mark My Comments With

When you're replying to or forwarding a message with the original message included, you might want to stick comments into the middle of the original message text. When you do, Outlook inserts a label that identifies you as the commentator. The label looks something like this:

[Alan Neibauer]

You can change the name that appears in the comment label by changing the name in the Mark My Comments With box. If you don't want your comments labeled, turn off this option.

Advanced E-Mail Options

Click the Advanced E-Mail Options button in the E-mail Options dialog box for even more settings that control what happens when you send and receive mail. The dialog box contains four categories of settings.

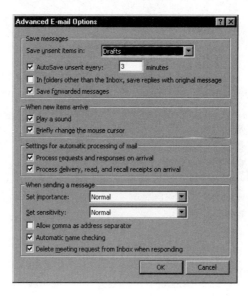

Save Messages

Set these items to control how your messages are saved. You can choose the folder in which to store unsent messages, specify how replies and forwarded messages are saved, and choose to have the messages you are working on saved automatically.

- The Save Unsent Messages In option lets you set the folder where unsent messages are stored. This is the folder used when you choose the Save command from the File menu when composing a message.

- Use the AutoSave Unsent Every setting to automatically save unsent messages at the number of minutes you specify. Turn off this option if you don't want to use the AutoSave feature.

- Use the In Folders Other Than The Inbox, Save Replies With Original Message option to save your replies with the original message in folders other than the inbox.

- Turn on the Save Forwarded Messages option to save messages that are forwarded. Turn off this option if you don't need to save copies of forwarded messages.

When New Items Arrive

You can choose how you want Outlook to notify you when a new message arrives in your Inbox.

- With the Play A Sound option turned on, you hear a beep when new messages arrive. (This option is turned on by default.) If you have a sound card installed in your computer, you can set the new-message sound to any .WAV file (using the Microsoft Office section from the Sound icon on the Control Panel). Turn off this option to squelch the beep or sound.

- With the Briefly Change The Mouse Cursor option turned on, you see the mouse pointer change briefly to an envelope when new messages arrive. (This option is turned on by default.)

? SEE ALSO

For other ways to
automatically handle
messages, see "Getting
Help from Outlook
Assistants," on
page 44.

Settings For Automatic Processing Of Mail

When you send meeting requests and task requests, you'll eventually
receive responses. You can specify the ways Outlook should process
these responses when they arrive.

- With the Process Requests And Responses On Arrival option
  turned on, Outlook places on your calendar any meeting requests
  you receive. When you receive responses to your meeting
  requests, Outlook records them on your meeting planner.

- The Process Delivery, Read, And Recall Receipts On Arrival
  option directs Outlook to record the response on the message
  containing your original request.

When Sending A Message

These settings let you control what happens when you send a message.
You can set the importance and sensitivity and choose other options for
sent messages and responses to meeting requests.

- Use the Set Importance option to set the priority for your messages. Most messages you send are of normal importance. That's
  why Outlook uses Normal as the standard importance setting. If
  all or most of your messages require top priority, select High from
  the drop-down list. Or, if all or most of your messages can be
  read at any time without compromising your work or the recipient's work, select Low.

  A message that you send with High importance displays a red
  exclamation mark to the left of its envelope in the message list; a
  message with Low importance displays a blue downward-pointing
  arrow. Your e-mail administrator might have set up your e-mail
  server to deliver messages sent with High importance faster than
  those sent with Normal or Low importance.

- Use the Set Sensitivity option to specify the nature of your messages. Most messages you send are not particularly sensitive.
  That's why Normal is the standard sensitivity setting in Outlook. If
  a message requires a different level of sensitivity, you have three
  other choices: Personal, Private, or Confidential.

  - The Personal setting displays the word *Personal* in the Sen-
    sitivity column of the message list.

Getting Started

- The Private setting displays the word *Private* in the Sensitivity column of the message list. This option prohibits recipients from changing your original message when they reply to it or forward it.

- The Confidential setting displays the word *Confidential* in the Sensitivity column of the message list. Confidential sensitivity notifies the recipient that the message should be treated according to the policies about confidentiality that your organization has set up.

 NOTE

> The Sensitivity column is not displayed by default. For information about changing the column display, see "Adding Columns from the Field Chooser," on page 554.

- With the Allow Comma As Address Separator option turned on (as it is initially), names in the To, Cc, and Bcc boxes of a message header are separated with a comma. You may prefer to separate names with a semicolon. If you regularly send messages to CompuServe accounts, which may have an internal comma in the address, you'll probably want to turn off this option.

- When the Automatic Name Checking option is turned on, Outlook checks the names in the To, Cc, and Bcc boxes of a message header against your address books. If a name doesn't appear in at least one of your address books, Outlook marks the name with a wavy red underline. You can ignore this underline as long as you're sure that the e-mail address is correct. You can also use the underline as a signal for you to add the name to your personal address book. If you find the underline annoying, you can turn off this option. You can then ask for name checking in a message window, either by clicking the Check Names button on the Standard toolbar or by pressing Alt+K.

- When the Delete Meeting Request From Inbox When Responding option is turned on, Outlook will delete a meeting request notification when you send a response to it.

Tracking Options

If it's important that most of your messages be received and read right away—or if you would at least like to have a record of when most of your messages were received and read—you can turn on either or both of the tracking options. If you need this information only for specific messages, you can adjust the tracking options in the Properties dialog box of the message or in the Message Options dialog box. To access these settings for all messages, click the Tracking Options button in the E-Mail Options dialog box.

NOTE

> Not all Internet Service Providers provide delivery and read receipts.

Tell Me When All Messages Have Been Delivered

If you like to know when messages have been delivered to the recipients, turn on this option. When your message arrives in the recipient's mailbox, Outlook delivers a message to your Inbox indicating when the message was received.

Tell Me When All Messages Have Been Read

If you want to know when recipients have opened your messages, turn on this option. When a recipient opens your message to read it, Outlook sends a notification to your Inbox.

Delete Receipt And Blank Responses After Processing

This option moves receipt notifications and responses that have no comments to the Deleted Items folder.

Setting Calendar Options

The Preference tab's Calendar options offer choices for setting up the calendar work week, your working hours, the standard reminder time for appointments, the font for dates, and the display of week numbers. You can also designate which calendar file to use, choose a time-zone setup, add holidays to your calendar, and adjust some advanced scheduling options.

When you've set up an appointment, Outlook can send you a reminder before the appointment's start time. By default, Outlook reminds you 15 minutes beforehand. You can change this lead time by selecting a different amount of time from the Reminder drop-down list. You have a wide range of choices, from a few minutes to several hours or even two days.

Click the Calendar Options button on the Preferences tab to display a separate box of Calendar options.

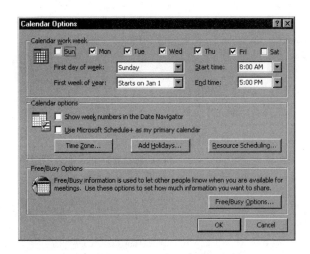

Calendar Work Week

You can specify your standard work week schedule for your Outlook calendar. You can indicate which days of the week you work, the first workday of the week, and the first workday of a new year.

Workdays

By default, Outlook's calendar sets up Monday through Friday as standard workdays. If your workdays are different, you can simply turn the appropriate days on and off to reflect your own work week.

First Day Of Week

Outlook also initially designates Sunday as the first day of a full week, although you can change this by selecting a day from this drop-down list. (In some European countries, for example, Monday is considered the first day of the week.)

First Week Of Year

This option allows you to specify exactly when your work calendar starts in a new year: January 1, the first four-day week in January, or the first full (five-day) week in January.

Start Time and End Time

A workday can start at various hours. Many people start at 8:00 AM, others at 9:00 AM. Flextime systems in modern companies can mean that individuals start work at various times during the day. You can set the start time and end time for your own workday so that your calendar can indicate to others the timeframe in which you might be available for meetings. The Start Time and End Time drop-down lists include both hours and half-hours for the entire day. If you need to set different times (for example, 8:45 AM or 9:15 PM), you can type in the time.

Calendar Options

The options and buttons in the Calendar Options section control a variety of settings for working with the Outlook Calendar.

Show Week Numbers In The Date Navigator Option

This option lets you number the weeks from 1 to 52 in the calendar.

Use Microsoft Schedule+ As My Primary Calendar

If you are switching to Outlook from Microsoft Schedule+ and you still need to use Schedule+ because some members of your organization haven't yet switched to Outlook, turn on this option. Outlook displays the appointments, tasks, and events that you set up in Schedule+, but it doesn't include your contacts. When this option is turned on, people who are still using Schedule+ can see your appointment schedule when they're trying to arrange a meeting.

If you turn on the Schedule+ option, you cannot use the Outlook Contacts folder as an address book. See the sidebar "Oh, No! The Show This Folder As An E-Mail Address Book Option Is Not Available!" on page 547.

Time Zone

People travel with their computers all the time. When you're on the road in another time zone, it's convenient to have that time zone's clock visible so that you can set appointments and task times to fit your location. Outlook gives you the means to set your current time zone and to show a second time zone. You can even swap the two zones when you travel from one to the other. Click the Time Zone button on the Calendar tab to open the Time Zone dialog box:

Setting Outlook Options **CHAPTER 3** **69**

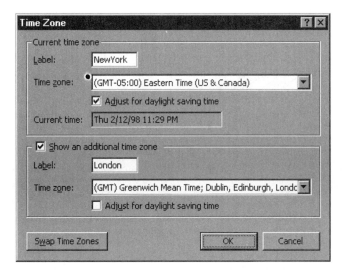

Getting Started

- In the Time Zone dialog box, select your current time zone from the drop-down list in the Time Zone box. In the Label box, type a label that represents the time zone; for example, you might use PT for Pacific Time. This label will appear above the time column on your calendar. If you want Windows to automatically adjust your computer clock and your calendar when daylight saving time begins and ends, leave the Adjust For Daylight Saving Time option turned on.

- When you travel to another time zone and plan to use your calendar there, you can set up a second time zone for the calendar. To set it up, turn on the Show An Additional Time Zone option and complete the Label and Time Zone boxes just as you did for your current time zone. These times will appear to the left of the times for the current time zone.

- If you travel into the second time zone and it becomes your current time zone, you can swap the zones. To do this, simply click the Swap Time Zones button. When you return home and want to switch back, click the Swap Time Zones button again. The current time zone displays closest to the appointment slots on your calendar.

Add Holidays

The Outlook calendar is initially set up to indicate the holidays observed in the country for which your computer is set up. If you also observe (or simply want to be informed about) holidays in other countries, click the Add Holidays button on the Calendar Options tab to add more holidays. In the Add Holidays To Calendar dialog box, turn on the check boxes for those countries whose holidays should appear on your calendar. Adding holidays for other countries makes particularly good sense if you do any business internationally—this way, you'll know when businesses in other nations are closed.

Resource Scheduling

Click the Resource Scheduling button to set up how Outlook should process meeting requests that are sent to you. You can choose to automatically accept meeting requests and process cancellations, automatically decline requests that conflict with your calendar, and automatically decline recurring meeting requests.

Free/Busy Options

The Free/Busy Options section of the Calendar Options dialog box lets you inform other people when you have time available for meetings. Click the Free/Busy Options button to determine just how much information about your schedule you want to provide.

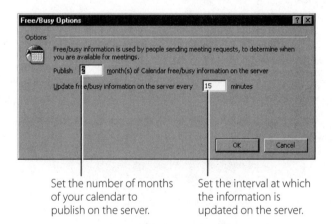

Set the number of months of your calendar to publish on the server.

Set the interval at which the information is updated on the server.

Setting Tasks Options

The Tasks section on the Preferences tab provides settings for task reminders. Set the time of day you want your task reminders to appear, and set the actions you want Outlook to take for tasks.

Click the Tasks Options button to choose display colors for overdue and completed tasks.

Setting Journal Options

Outlook is initially set up to record journal entries each time you create, open, close, or save any Microsoft Office file (a file created in Microsoft Access, Microsoft Excel, Microsoft Office Binder, Microsoft PowerPoint, or Microsoft Word). Click Journal Options on the Preferences tab to determine other activities that you want to record in your journal.

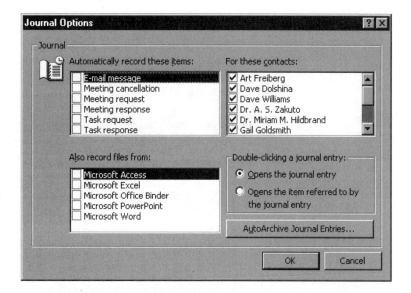

Automatically Record These Items

Turn on the appropriate options to have Outlook automatically record journal entries for e-mail messages, meeting cancellations, meeting requests, meeting responses, task requests, and task responses that are sent to or received from the contacts you select in the For These Contacts list.

For These Contacts

For each Outlook action, turn on the check boxes for the contacts that you want to record. This list includes only the names listed in your Contacts folder. If you have no contacts set up, this list is empty. If a name you want to select is not listed, close the Options dialog box, add the new contact, and then return to this tab.

Also Record Files From

Turn off the check box for any Office program whose actions you don't want to record. Other programs that are compatible with Office 97 might also appear in this list.

Double-Clicking A Journal Entry

Select what should happen when you double-click a journal entry. Outlook can either open the journal entry form itself or open the item associated with the entry (the e-mail message, the PowerPoint file, and so on). The setting you choose here for the double-click action also determines what is opened when you choose the Open command from the File menu in the Journal folder window, when you right-click a journal entry and choose Open from the shortcut menu, and when you press Ctrl+O.

AutoArchive Journal Entries

Click this button to change AutoArchive settings. For details, see Chapter 18, "Archiving Folder Items."

Setting Notes Options

Click the Note Options button on the Preferences tab to establish the format you prefer to use for new notes.

Color

Set the color of new notes in this box. Your choices are Blue, Green, Pink, Yellow (the standard color), and White.

Size

Select the standard size for notes (Small, Medium, or Large) in this box.

Font

To change the font for the text of notes, click this button to open the Font dialog box, where you can adjust the settings to your preference.

Using the Mail Services Tab

The options on the Mail Services tab of the Options dialog box, shown in Figure 3-2, let you fine-tune some choices from your established profiles. You can choose which profile to use by default and which services to check for e-mail.

FIGURE 3-2.
The Mail Services tab of the Options dialog box.

Selecting a Startup Profile

? SEE ALSO

For more details about profiles, see "Logging On," on page 4, and "Developing Your Profile," on page 7.

The options in the Startup Settings area of the Mail Services tab let you control which profile Outlook will use and which folder Outlook opens when it starts.

Prompt For A Profile To Be Used

If you switch between two or more profiles because you connect to several online services, or if you travel with your computer and you sometimes connect to your e-mail server, you might want to select the Prompt For A Profile To Be Used option. When this option is turned on, Outlook displays the Choose Profile dialog box when it starts up. This dialog box lists your profiles, allowing you to select the one you want to use for the current session.

Always Use This Profile

If you use only one profile, turn on the Always Use This Profile option, and then select the profile name from the list below the label. This option is most useful when your computer is always in one place and you use the same profile all the time.

Setting Mail Options

If you have more than one mail service set up, you can determine which to check for new mail by default. In the Mail Options section of the Services tab, turn on the box for each service that you want to check.

Synchronizing Folders

 SEE ALSO

For details about synchronizing folders, see "Synchronizing Folders," on page 274.

One variation of using Outlook remotely involves setting up offline folders. (See the sidebar "Offline Folders vs. Remote Mail," on page 262, for details.) When you use offline folders, you'll periodically connect to your e-mail server, either over a network or over a telephone line. You can then synchronize your folders, which means that Outlook adjusts the contents of your Exchange folders and the folders on your local machine so that they contain up-to-date data.

In the Mail Services tab, turn on the Enable Offline Access check box to activate the capability to synchronize folders. Leave this option turned off only if you prefer to manually synchronize your offline folders (with the Synchronize command on the Tools menu) while you're online. You can, of course, manually synchronize folders at any time you're online, even if this option is turned on.

With the When Online, Synchronize All Folders Upon Exiting option turned on, Outlook synchronizes all your offline folders with your online (server) folders when you exit Outlook. This way, your offline folders are consistent with your online folders when you start to work offline.

The remaining two options enable you to have Outlook synchronize your folders at intervals you choose. The online time interval is in effect while you're online, while the offline option will connect to the server at the interval you specify and synchronize your folders.

Using the Mail Format Tab

On the Mail Format tab of the Options dialog box, shown in Figure 3-3, you select the format for your messages. You can also set up Microsoft Word 97 as your e-mail editor.

FIGURE 3-3.
The Mail format tab of the Options dialog box.

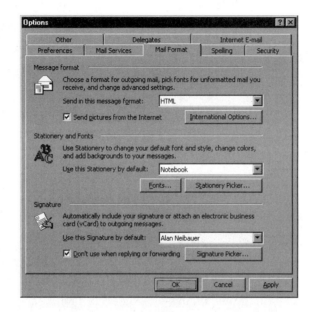

Selecting a Message Format

In the Message Format section of the Mail Format tab, choose the default format. You can select either HTML or Microsoft Exchange Rich Text to send formatted documents, Plain Text for messages without formats, or Microsoft Word to use Word as your e-mail editor. Select HTML to send messages to a wide variety of users, complete with fonts, colors, and other decorative features. Choose Plain Text if you know your recipient's e-mail system cannot accept formatted messages.

 NOTE

When sending replies, Outlook always uses the format of the original message to ensure that the reply can be read when received.

Instead of using Outlook message forms and the Outlook text editor for messages, you can choose to use Microsoft Word 97 as your e-mail editor. When you do this, you have at your disposal all of the word processing power of Word for creating a message. You can use tables, formulas, fields, and Word's wealth of formatting features. You can also attach to your message any object from any Microsoft Office 97 program. To use this option, you need to have Microsoft Word 97 installed and you must select Microsoft Word in the Send In This Message Format list.

> You can also choose to use Microsoft Word for individual messages, rather than as the default. You'll learn more about this in Chapter 4, "Exchanging Messages and Faxes."

Turn on the Send Pictures From The Internet option if you want to include graphics and background images.

The International Options button opens a dialog box with one check box labeled Use US English For Message Headers On Replies And Forwards. If you're using a version of Outlook for a language other than English, turning on this option directs Outlook to use English labels in the message header (To, Subject, From, and Sent). Turn off this option to keep message header labels in the language of the version of Outlook you're using.

Selecting Stationery and Fonts

The options in the Stationery And Fonts section of the Mail Format tab let you select the default font or page design for all new messages.

Stationery

A stationery is a preformatted design consisting of a background picture and perhaps a special design, font, and text. Outlook includes a number of attractive stationery designs, and you can also create your own.

To choose a stationery to use for all new messages, make your selection from the Use This Stationery By Default list. To use no stationery design and start with a blank message, select <None>. The Stationery

Picker button lets you create and edit stationery designs. You'll learn how to use it to create and modify stationery in Chapter 4, "Exchanging Messages and Faxes."

Fonts

To select a default font for all new messages, click the Fonts button. In the dialog box that appears, you can choose a font for new messages, for replying to and forwarding messages, and for reading and composing plain text messages. You can also choose to use your selected font rather than stationery fonts when using a stationery design. The International Fonts button on the Fonts dialog box lets you specify fonts for incoming messages that use international character sets.

Attaching a Signature

 SEE ALSO

For details about using the Signature Picker, see Chapter 4, "Exchanging Messages and Faxes."

A signature is a standard closing that you can attach to your messages. You can also attach a *vCard*, a special attachment that contains information from your address book listing. Once you create stationery files, you select the file to use for all messages from the Use This Signature By Default list.

Using the Internet E-Mail Tab

The Internet E-Mail tab, shown in Figure 3-4, on the next page, lets you control the format of mail sent over the Internet and the ways in which Outlook checks for new Internet mail.

Mail you send over the Internet must be encoded—converted to a format that the various computers that make up the Internet can handle. You can select from two formats: MIME (Multipurpose Internet Mail Extensions) and uuencode (UNIX to UNIX encoding).

If you choose MIME, you can select to actually use no encoding, Quoted Printable, or Base64. You can also choose to include certain special characters in headers without encoding.

When Sending Messages Wrap Text At

This option sets the length of lines. Some older e-mail systems cannot handle lines that are over 80 characters. Setting lines at between 72 and 76 characters allows room for indentations and prefix characters.

FIGURE 3-4.
The Internet E-Mail tab of the Options dialog box.

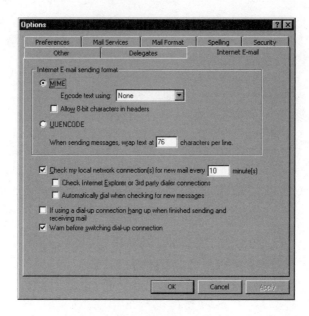

Check My Local Network Connection For New Mail

This option will check your mail server for new mail at regular intervals. If you connect to the Internet through a modem, you can choose to check mail using the connections already established with Internet Explorer or another browser and you can have Outlook dial the connection if you are not already online.

If Using A Dial-Up Connection Hang Up When Finished

You can turn on this option to have Outlook disconnect and hang up when it has finished sending and receiving mail.

Warn Before Switching Dial-Up Connection

This option, if turned on, will prompt you before disconnecting from one dial-up connection in order to start dialing another connection.

Using the Spelling Tab

When you check the spelling of messages, Outlook compares the words in your message text with a dictionary file. If the spelling checker can't find the word in its dictionary, it shows you the word in a dialog box and gives you a chance to correct the spelling, ignore the word (because it's a special word or a proper name), or add the word to the dictionary.

On the Spelling tab of the Options dialog box, shown in Figure 3-5, you'll find options for checking the spelling of messages. By default, Outlook suggests correct spellings for misspelled words. It also checks numbers, words that include numbers, and words that are written in all capital letters, as well as any original text in replies and forwarded messages. You can ask the spelling checker to ignore any or all of these types of information in message text.

FIGURE 3-5.

The Spelling tab of the Options dialog box.

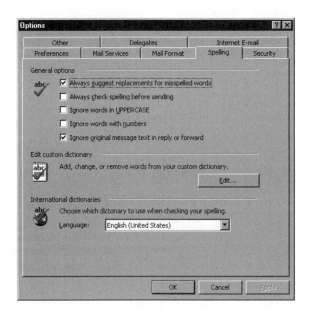

Always Suggest Replacements For Misspelled Words

If you don't want Outlook to automatically suggest correct spellings for words not included in the dictionary file it uses, turn off this option. When this option is turned off, you must click the Suggest button in the Spelling dialog box to get a suggestion from the spelling checker. If you prefer to always have a suggestion to work from, leave this option turned on.

Always Check Spelling Before Sending

If you're someone who always likes to check spelling before sending a message, the Always Check Spelling Before Sending option is for you. If you turn on this option, Outlook checks the spelling in your message text after you click the Send button but before the message is sent.

Ignore Words In UPPERCASE

To tell the spelling checker to ignore words that are written in all capital letters, turn on the Ignore Words In UPPERCASE option. The spelling checker then ignores words such as UNIX.

Ignore Words With Numbers

To tell the spelling checker to ignore numbers, turn on the Ignore Words With Numbers option. The spelling checker will then ignore words that contain a mix of numbers and letters (such as WSJ010846) and words that consist entirely of numbers (such as 123456789 or the 97 in Office 97).

Ignore Original Message Text In Reply Or Forward

The spelling checker is set up to ignore the original text included in replies and forwarded messages. If you want Outlook to check the spelling in the original text, turn off this option.

Using a Custom Dictionary

Proper names, jargon, and technical words may be properly spelled but not found in the dictionary file. Rather than have the spelling checker report these words as possible errors, you can add them to a custom dictionary when they are first encountered.

If you click the Edit button, a Windows Notepad window opens displaying the contents of the custom dictionary, one word per line. Edit the file to add or delete words, and then choose the Save command from the File menu in Notepad to save your changes.

You can obtain international dictionaries to use for checking spelling. If you have these dictionaries, choose the one you want to use by default in the International Dictionaries section of the Spelling tab.

Using the Delegates Tab

On the Delegates tab of the Options dialog box, shown in Figure 3-6, you can give others permission to perform Outlook tasks on your behalf. You may assign your assistant, for example, to act as a delegate on your behalf when you are out of the office or to handle certain types of requests and actions.

FIGURE 3-6.
The Delegates tab
of the Options
dialog box.

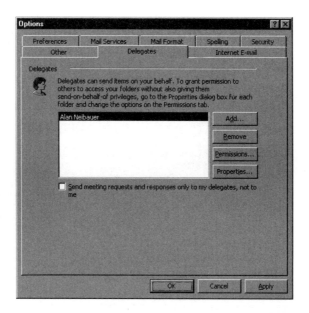

The Delegates box lists those people you have designated as your delegates. Use the buttons along the right side of the Delegates box to change the list or to change the types of permission you grant to a delegate.

Adding Delegates

To add a delegate to your list of delegates, follow these steps:

1   Click the Add button on the Delegates tab to open the Add Users dialog box, in which you can select persons to assign as delegates.

2   In the Type Name Or Select From List box, type the name of someone already listed, or select names from the list below the box. If necessary, you can look in another address book by selecting it from the Show Names From The list box.

3   Click the Add button, and then click OK to open the Delegate Permissions dialog box.

4 Select permissions for each Outlook folder.

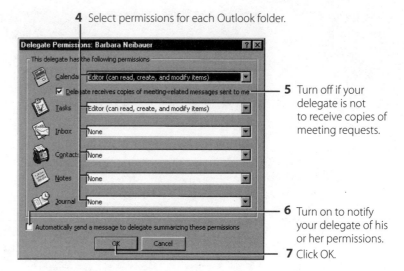

5 Turn off if your delegate is not to receive copies of meeting requests.

6 Turn on to notify your delegate of his or her permissions.

7 Click OK.

> If you type or select more than one name as a delegate, the Delegate Permissions dialog box shows the phrase <Multiple delegates> in its title bar. The permissions you set apply to all the delegates you selected. To set permissions for individuals, either add them one at a time or add them all at once and then change permissions for each one with the Permissions button. (See "Granting Permissions," below.)

Removing Delegates

To remove a delegate from your delegates list, simply select the name of the delegate in the Delegates box and click the Remove button. Outlook does not ask you to confirm deletion of a delegate.

Granting Permissions

When you want to change the level of permissions for a delegate, take these steps:

1 Select the name of the delegate in the Delegates box.

2 Click the Permissions button.

3 Change the permission settings in the Delegate Permissions dialog box.

4 Click OK in the Delegate Permissions dialog box.

Setting Delegate Properties

The Properties button displays the Properties dialog box for the name you select in the Delegates box. The Properties dialog box shows address book information, such as the delegate's e-mail name, title, and so on.

Sending Requests Only to Your Delegate

If you have arranged for a delegate to keep track of your calendar, you can take yourself off the meeting-request-and-response carousel. To set this up, take these steps:

1 In the Delegate Permissions dialog box, give the delegate you have chosen to take care of your calendar Editor permission for your Calendar folder.

2 Turn on the Delegate Receives Copies Of Meeting-Related Messages Sent To Me option.

3 Click OK in the Delegate Permissions dialog box.

4 On the Delegates tab, turn on the Send Meeting Requests And Responses Only To My Delegates, Not To Me option.

Using the Security Tab

SEE ALSO

For information about installing add-ins, see "Add-In Manager," on page 94.

On the Security tab, shown in Figure 3-7, on the following page, you'll find options for encrypting your messages, adding your digital signature to messages, setting your security file, changing your security password, setting up advanced security, logging off advanced security, and sending security keys. Security provides a layer of protection for your messages.

There are two levels of protection:

■ Encryption ensures that only someone who logs on to the e-mail server as a valid recipient can read your message. Without encryption, your messages are sent as readable text.

■ A digital signature assures the recipient that you are really the person who sent the message—in other words, that the message is not some bogus transmission sent by a pernicious computer hacker—and that the message has not been altered along the way.

FIGURE 3-7.
The Security tab of the Options dialog box.

In order to use these features, however, you must have a security certificate that verifies who you are to others. There are two types of certificates available in Outlook—an Exchange certificate to use over the network and a S/MIME certificate that you use over the Internet.

Getting a Digital Certificate

To get a digital certificate, follow these steps:

1   Choose the Options command from the Tools menu, and then click the Security tab.

2   Click the Get A Digital ID button.

   If you're not connected to a security-enabled Exchange Server network, you can only obtain a digital ID over the Internet. Clicking the Get A Digital ID button will launch your web browser and connect you to a site that provides information on security certificates. In this case, skip ahead to "S/MIME Internet Security," on page 86.

Getting Started

3 If the Get A Digitial ID dialog box appears, select Get A S/MIME Certificate if you want to get an S/MIME digital ID from an external certifying authority. Select Set Up Security For Me On The Exchange Server if you want an Exchange Key Management Server to assign you a digital ID.

4 Click OK.

5 If you chose the S/MIME option, skip ahead to "S/MIME Internet Security," on the next page. If you chose Exchange Server to get your digital ID, continue with the next section.

Exchange Server Security

To get an Exchange certificate, your network administrator must have security running on your Exchange server and must give you a special password, called a token. When you chose Exchange security in step 3 above, the Set Up Advanced Security dialog box should have appeared. Now follow these steps:

1 Type the token (or password) given to you by the network administrator into the Token box.

2 Accept your Keyset Name as it appears or correct it if necessary in the Keyset Name box.

3 Click OK to close the Setup Advanced Security dialog box and process your digital ID request.

4 When a message appears telling you that your request for security has been sent to your Exchange server, click OK.

5 Click OK again in the Security tab.

In a few moments (depending on how busy the server is), your Exchange server will send you e-mail verifying your token. When you open the message, a dialog box appears reporting that Outlook is writing the Exchange signing key to your system. Click OK to display a box reporting that Outlook is writing the encryption key to your system. Click OK again. Another message appears, reporting that you are now security enabled. This means that the certificate has been added to Outlook and that you now can send and receive encrypted and digitally signed messages.

> **NOTE**
>
> Once you enroll in Exchange security you do not have to do it again, unless you are notified by your system administrator to enroll with a new token.

S/MIME Internet Security

To use Internet security, known as S/MIME, you have to get a certificate from a third-party company by registering on their Web site. Most companies charge a small fee for their certificate services, although many offer a free trial period.

When you select Get A S/MIME Certificate From An External Authority in the Get A Digital ID dialog box, Outlook launches your Web browser and connects you to the appropriate site. Follow the instructions on the screen to apply for a digital certificate. In most cases, after you apply you'll be notified by e-mail that your certificate is ready and you'll have to connect to a Web site to accept it. When the site verifies your certificate, it will download it and install it on your system so you are ready to send and receive secure messages.

Changing Security Settings

If you are on a network and connected to the Internet, you can have both types of security certificates. On the Security tab of the Options dialog box, choose the setting to use as the default from the Default Security Setting list.

If you have problems using security procedures, something may not be set up properly. From the Security tab of the Options dialog box, click the Change Settings button to display the Change Security Settings dialog box. Generally, the settings in the Security Settings Name and Secure Message Format boxes should match. That is, if you are using the Exchange 4.0 Security setting you should also use the Exchange 4.0 secure message format, and if you're using the S/MIME setting you should also use the S/MIME format.

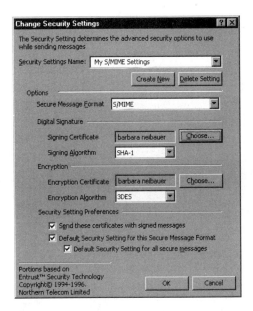

The following options at the bottom of the Change Security Settings dialog box determine when security is used.

Send These Certificates With Signed Messages

Choose this option to send a copy of your certificate with secure messages. The recipient will be able to use the certificate to send you encrypted messages. You cannot turn off this option when using Exchange Server security.

Default Security Setting For This Secure Message Format

Turn on this option to make the settings on this dialog box the default for the Secure Message Format you chose. If you chose the S/MIME format, for example, the settings will be used when you send a secure message using S/MIME. Turn on this option if you want to use different settings when sending S/MIME and Exchange Security secure messages.

Default Security Setting For All Secure Messages

Turn this option on to use these settings for all types of secure messages.

> **NOTE**

You can obtain more than one certificate. Click the Choose buttons in the Change Security Settings dialog box to select the certificate to use for your digital signature and for encrypted messages. You can also click the Choose buttons to display information about the certificate.

Securing Contents

E-mail messages using HTML formatting can also contain active content—elements that have the potential to run programs and perform operations on your computer. While it is unlikely that you will receive such a message, it pays to be careful. The Zone setting in the Secure Content area of the Security tab lets you control how active content is handled in both e-mail messages and attachments.

Selecting and Changing Zones

In the Zone list, you can select from two zones: Internet Zone and Restricted Sites Zone. The Internet Zone offers a medium level of security that will warn you before active content is accepted and run. The Restricted Sites Zone offers a high level of security that simply excludes any active content. To change the degree of security in a zone, click the Zone Settings button and then follow these steps:

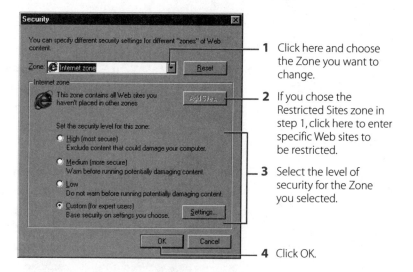

1 Click here and choose the Zone you want to change.

2 If you chose the Restricted Sites zone in step 1, click here to enter specific Web sites to be restricted.

3 Select the level of security for the Zone you selected.

4 Click OK.

If you choose the Custom level of security, you can then click Settings and choose to enable, disable, or warn for each of a list of specific types of content.

Securing Attachments

Active content can also be found in message attachments. Again, it is highly unlikely that you will receive an attachment with dangerous content, but by default, you will be warned of the potential problem when you save or open some attachments. If you do not want to receive this warning, click the Attachment Security button on the Security tab of the Options dialog box, choose None in the dialog box that appears, and then click OK.

Exporting and Importing Digital IDs

Security certificates are stored on your computer's hard disk. You can make a copy of the certificate on a floppy disk to transfer it to another computer, or as a backup in the event the security file becomes damaged. For example, suppose you use different computers at home and at the office. If you downloaded your S/MIME certificate at the office, you can make a copy of it to use at home.

To save your certificate, follow these steps:

1 Click Import/Export Digital ID on the Security tab of the Options dialog box.

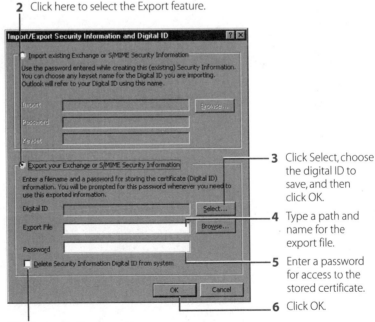

2 Click here to select the Export feature.

3 Click Select, choose the digital ID to save, and then click OK.

4 Type a path and name for the export file.

5 Enter a password for access to the stored certificate.

6 Click OK.

Click here only if you want to remove the certificate from your system after it is saved.

To get or restore the saved digital ID, turn on Import Existing Exchange Or S/MIME Security Information. Enter the path and name of the file to import, the password you saved it with, and the keyset if you are importing an Exchange certificate, and then click OK.

Using Security

Now that you've set up your digital ID, turn on the encryption and digital signature options at the top of the Security tab of the Options dialog box to use security with all messages:

- Turn on the Encrypt Contents And Attachments For Outgoing Messages option to encrypt your messages. Without encryption, your messages are sent as readable text.

- Turn on the Add Digital Signature To Outgoing Messages option to add a digital signature to each message you send.

- Turn on the Send Clear Text Signed Message option if you want recipients who cannot accept S/MIME to skip the verification of signatures.

(?) SEE ALSO

You'll learn more about sending and receiving secure messages in Chapter 4, "Exchanging Messages and Faxes."

You can, of course, turn off encryption and your digital signature on the Security tab, as explained earlier. If you do so, you can encrypt a single message or add your digital signature to a single message by clicking the Options button in the standard toolbar when composing a message, and then turning on the Encrypt Message Contents And Attachments check box, or the Add Digital Signature To Outgoing Messages check box. You can also use these check boxes to turn off security for an individual message.

When you are sending an encrypted message over the Internet, you must have the recipient's public key stored with his or her address in your address book. The public key (or coding scheme) the recipient sends you is stored with his or her address in your address book and is used to encrypt any messages you send the recipient. A complementary private key at the recipient's machine decodes the message. If you do not have this information, or if an Exchange recipient doesn't have security set up, you'll see a message box telling you this. You then have two choices for delivering the message:

- Click the Don't Encrypt Message button to send the message anyway. When encryption is turned on, this is the only way to send a message to a recipient who doesn't have advanced security.

- Click the Cancel Send button if you don't want to send an unsecured message.

Using the Other Tab

On the Other tab of the Options dialog box, shown in Figure 3-8, you'll find options that don't fit in any of the other tabs' categories.

FIGURE 3-8.

The Other tab of the Options dialog box.

Setting General Options

In the General area of the Other tab you can choose settings for managing deleted folder items, and for setting advanced options that control a variety of Outlook settings.

Turn on the Empty The Deleted Items Folder Upon Exiting check box if you want Outlook to empty your Deleted Items folder each time you exit Outlook. If you prefer to clear out your Deleted Items folder more selectively, be sure that this option is turned off.

Setting Advanced Options

Advanced options offer additional ways to set how Outlook acts. Click the Advanced Options button in the General area of the Other tab to determine how Outlook acts on startup, to specify how notes are displayed, and to access more advanced customization features.

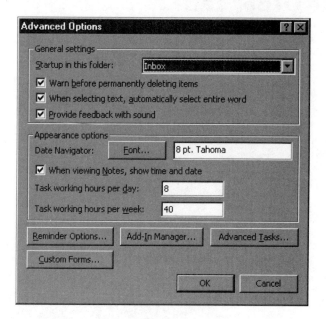

General Settings

Use this area to set some overall ways for Outlook to work. In addition to selecting which folder displays when you start Outlook, you can set the following options:

Warn Before Permanently Deleting Items

If this option is turned on, Outlook prompts you to confirm that you want to permanently delete items from the Deleted Items folder when you empty the folder or when you manually delete an item from it. (This option is turned on by default.) When you see the message, click Yes to delete the items. Click No to keep the messages in your Deleted Items folder. (You'll see a slightly different message if your Deleted Items folder contains subfolders or remote message headers.)

When Selecting Text, Automatically Select Entire Word

When you're editing a message and need to select text that includes a space, as soon as you select a single character beyond the space, Outlook selects the entire word. This setting can be handy if you usually select entire words. But if you need to select parts of two neighboring words, you will find this option frustrating and disruptive. If necessary, you can turn it off.

Provide Feedback With Sound

Turn on this option if you want Outlook to produce a sound for each action you take in the program—deleting a message, opening a file, and so on. If you don't have a sound card in your computer, the sound will be a simple beep. If you have a sound card, you can set the sound for each action by selecting the .WAV file you want Outlook to play when that action occurs. You set up these sounds through the Sound icon on the Windows Control Panel, using the options in the Microsoft Office category.

Appearance Options

Use these settings to control some aspects of the Outlook display.

Date Navigator

Click the Font button to choose the font to use with monthly calendars in the calendar folder.

When Viewing Notes, Show Time And Date

This option displays the time and date with notes in the Notes folder.

Task Working Hours Per Day

Set the number of working hours per day to use for tasks.

Task Working Hours Per Week

Set the number of working hours per week to use for tasks.

Reminder Options

Click the Reminder Options button on the Advanced Options dialog box of the Other tab to set how Outlook should notify you when a reminder you've set for a task or an appointment comes due.

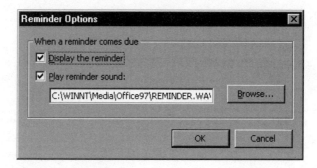

Display The Reminder

Turn on this option to have Outlook display a reminder message. In the message window, you can close the reminder if you don't need further reminding, you can reset the reminder to appear again after an interval you specify, or you can edit the task or appointment. For details, see "Setting a Reminder," on page 335, and "Setting a Task Reminder," on page 381.

Play Reminder Sound

Turn on this option to have Outlook play a sound to notify you that a task or an appointment is due. If you don't have a sound card, you'll hear a beep. If you do have a sound card, you can set the reminder sound to any .WAV file by typing its full pathname in this box or by clicking the Browse button to find the file.

Add-In Manager

Add-ins provide additional functionality to Outlook. Outlook comes with several add-ins, including ones for features such as NetMeeting and Internet Mail. Add-ins can also be third-party programs. Some add-ins are installed when you set up Outlook. To use certain Outlook add-ins (including Digital Security over your network), you must be running Outlook with Microsoft Exchange Server. If you need to install another of Outlook's add-ins or want to use a third-party add-in, you can install it by clicking the Add-In Manager button in the Advanced Options dialog box. To install or remove an add-in, take these steps:

1   Click the Add-In Manager button in the Advanced Options dialog box.

2 Turn off add-ins you don't want to use.

3 Click here to install additional add-ins.

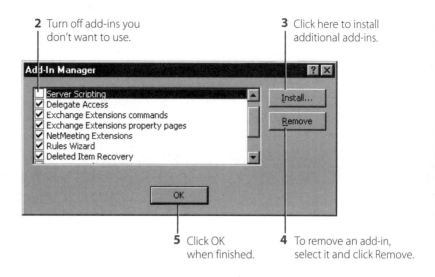

5 Click OK when finished.

4 To remove an add-in, select it and click Remove.

Getting Started

 NOTE

For information about the add-ins that come with Outlook, see Outlook online help.

Advanced Tasks

The Advanced Tasks button opens the Advanced Tasks dialog box, which contains the following options:

Set Reminders On Tasks With Due Dates

Leave this option turned on if you want Outlook to automatically set a reminder for a task that has a due date. The reminder appears on the due date at the time you set in the Reminder Time box. You can change the reminder date and time in the task item window.

Keep Updated Copies Of Assigned Tasks On My Task List

When you assign a task to someone else, you might want to receive updates on the task status as it changes. Leave this option turned on to keep a copy of the task in your task list so that Outlook can update the task status as it changes.

Send Status Reports When Assigned Tasks Are Completed

When this option is turned on, you will receive a status report when the person to whom you have assigned a task marks the assigned task as completed.

Custom Forms

Forms are an integral part of Outlook. You use forms to send and read messages, to set and request appointments, and to respond to meeting and task requests. Every folder item window in Outlook is a form. In addition, Outlook provides the tools for creating custom forms. In some cases, these forms are set up by an organizational forms designer. In other cases, you or a colleague might create a special form for your own purposes. To make forms work, you need to set aside some temporary storage space for them on your computer. Also, you can install forms that are included in form libraries to use in your work. For dealing with the necessary aspects of form life in Outlook, you click the Custom Forms button to open the Custom Forms tab. You can also use this command to change your Microsoft Windows NT network password and set several features of Outlook's Web services.

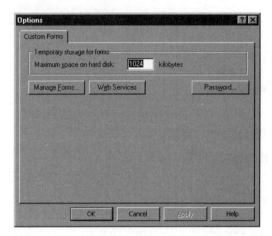

When you read a message or posting or when you create a message or posting with a form that isn't stored on your hard disk, Outlook downloads the form and stores it temporarily. This way, if you read or create an item that uses this form again in the next few days, it's ready at hand, and the process goes more quickly.

To prevent forms from taking up hard disk space that you need for other work, you can limit the amount of space Outlook can use for temporarily storing forms. In the Maximum Space On Hard Disk box, type a number (in kilobytes) for the amount of space you want to set aside for temporary form storage. If you use many different forms frequently and have plenty of free space on your hard disk, you might change this value to a higher number. Otherwise, the default setting (which depends on your system) is probably appropriate. When Outlook has filled the space you've set aside, it discards the oldest form stored in temporary storage to make room for the newest form you're using.

Manage Forms

Outlook downloads forms for reading messages when you need them. But when you want to use a form to send a message, you'll need to have the form installed. That's where the Manage Forms button comes into play. The Forms Manager dialog box helps you copy, update, and remove forms. To manage forms, do the following:

1 Click the Manage Forms button on the Custom Forms tab.

2 Click here to add more forms.

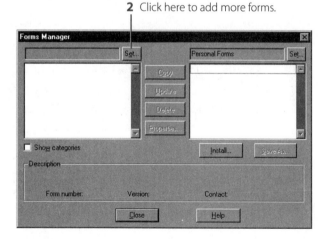

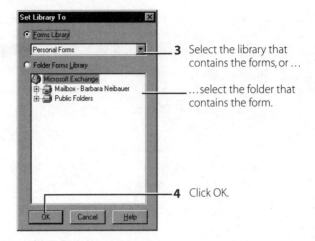

3 Select the library that contains the forms, or ...

... select the folder that contains the form.

4 Click OK.

5 When you've returned to the Forms Manager dialog box, select the forms that you want to add from the list at the left.

6 Click Copy. When Outlook has finished copying the forms, their names appear in the list at the right.

7 To copy forms from other folders, repeat steps 2 through 6.

8 Click the Close button in the Forms Manager dialog box.

Password

In some organizations, you might be required to change your password according to a certain schedule. Even if you aren't required to do this, it's a good idea to change your network password regularly, at least once every 60 days or so. Doing so helps maintain network security. The Password button on the Custom Forms tab opens the Change Windows NT Password dialog box.

Here's how to change your Windows NT password.

1 Click the Password button on the Custom Forms tab.

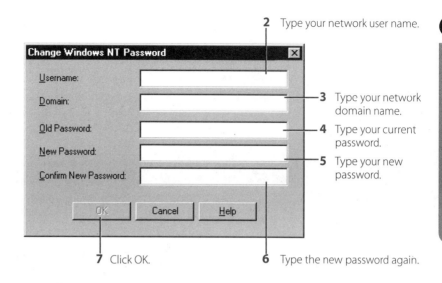

2 Type your network user name.

3 Type your network domain name.

4 Type your current password.

5 Type your new password.

7 Click OK.

6 Type the new password again.

Getting Started

Web Services

Communicating over the Web offers some unique challenges because of the variety of formats and the way information is transmitted.

Click the Web Services button on the Custom Forms tab, and then set these options in the Web Services dialog box:

Use Outlook Web Access To Open Messages Not Understood By Outlook Client.   If Outlook receives a form that it does not recognize and is not able to display, you can set Outlook to display the form in HTML format on your Web browser. When you turn on this option, you have to enter the path to your Web server and specify if you want to be notified before each such form is opened.

Activate Web Forms Link On Actions Menu.   You can add a command to the Actions menu that jumps to a library of HTML forms. When you choose to add this command to the menu, you must specify the path to the server where the forms are stored.

Setting AutoArchive Options

? SEE ALSO

You need to take additional steps to set up automatic archiving, especially for folders that don't contain e-mail messages. For details, see Chapter 18, "Archiving Folder Items."

E-mail and other items quickly accumulate in your folders, just as fast as they can accumulate on your desk. The AutoArchive feature on the Other tab of the Options dialog box will automatically move older items to special folders so they do not clutter up the inbox and other folders that you use often.

To control the AutoArchive feature, click the AutoArchive button on the Other tab of the Options dialog box. You can set the time span between archiving, ask for a prompt when archiving starts, direct Outlook to delete items after they're archived, and set the file that you want Outlook to use for archives.

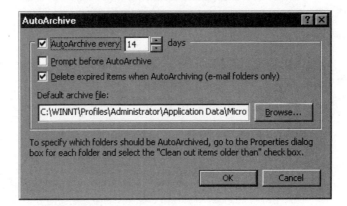

AutoArchive Every [ ] Days

To specify the time interval at which automatic archiving should take place, choose the number of days (1–60) in this box. Turn off this option to prevent all automatic archiving.

Prompt Before AutoArchive

Turn off this option if you don't want a prompt before the AutoArchive process begins.

Delete Expired Items When AutoArchiving (E-Mail Folders Only)

The AutoArchive process deletes expired items from e-mail folders by default. To prevent this, turn off this option.

Default Archive File

In this box, you can edit the filename or type a new filename. To locate or create another archive file in your file system, click the Browse button.

When the time period specified for AutoArchive is reached, you see a dialog box asking if you want to AutoArchive at that time. Select Yes to archive, No to skip archiving for the time being, and if you don't want to be prompted in the future, turn on the option labeled Don't Prompt Me About This Again.

Setting Preview Pane Options

The Preview Pane is a handy area to quickly review messages. Click the Preview Pane button on the Other tab of the Options dialog box to display the following options for setting the operation and appearance of the pane.

Mark Messages As Read In Preview Window

Turn on this option to mark a message as read after it appears in the Preview window for a set number of seconds.

Mark Item As Read When Selection Changes

Choose this option to mark the message as read when you move to another message.

Single Key Reading Using Space Bar

Enable this option to use the space bar to scroll through each message and then move on to the next message.

Preview Header

Click the Font button to choose the font of the text in the Preview Pane header.

PART II

Electronic Mail

Exchanging Messages and Faxes

You have something to say, and you wanna say it. Someone else has something to say, and you wanna hear it. You know something someone else needs to know; someone else knows something you need to know. You want to swap lies (as well as facts). Well, to swap tales with other people, you send them an e-mail message or a fax, or they send you one, through Microsoft Outlook 98.

Using electronic mail is a give-and-take process. You send a message to a hard disk somewhere (on a computer known as a server) so that the person you want to see the message (and only that person) can pull it down and read it. The messages you pull down from a server (receive), someone else sent up to the server.

Although sending a fax is usually more direct, it can be very similar: fax services can receive faxes for you and store them on a server from which you can retrieve them. In general, trading information has three important parts: composing the message you want to send, sending the message to the right place, and reading the messages others send to you.

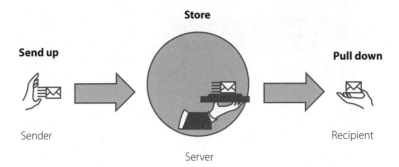

Store

Send up

Pull down

Sender

Server

Recipient

Your message, whether you send it by e-mail or fax, can include words and numbers (text), Web page addresses (URLs), pictures, charts and graphs, audio, and video; in fact, it can include any type of information that you can create in a Windows-based application. (See "Sending Files as Attachments," on page 132, and "Adding Links," on page 133.) You can also add special effects and decorations to the text—boldface, italic, underlining, color, bullets, and paragraph indention. (See "Formatting Text," on page 118, for information.)

After you compose and decorate (format) a message, you're ready to address the message so that you can send it to the right place for those people who should see it. The key to addressing a message is your address book. To find the right person, you need to use the right address book, and you need to make your address book as useful as possible. (See Chapter 5, "Mucking About in Address Books.") After you address the message, you push it along, by sending, forwarding, or replying.

And, of course, when someone else stuffs a message in your mailbox, you want to read it (maybe) and then deal with it in some way or other. Because a message can contain any object created by any Windows-based application, some parts of a message might appear as icons. You'll want to know how to make an icon open up and reveal its contents. You might also have more than one place to store mail messages—in various Outlook folders and in files outside Outlook. (See "Gathering Messages from the Beyond," on page 140, and "Moving a Folder Item," on page 463.)

Finally, for those days when nothing but a fax will do, you can find all the details about using Outlook to set up, send, and receive faxes at the end of this chapter—see "Getting the Facts About Fax," on page 150.

Using Message Windows

Messages appear in a message window. In Outlook, you can see messages in several types of windows. Two of the most common are the standard message window and a WordMail window. (You can also see messages in windows designed for meeting and task requests and responses, and in windows for messages based on special forms created by you or someone else.)

Standard Message Form

Unless you've turned on Microsoft Word as your e-mail editor, you'll see the standard message form, shown in Figure 4-1, when you open a message window.

We'll look at how to use this standard message form in the sections "Sending a Message," on the next page, "Replying to a Message," on page 141, and "Forwarding a Message," on page 143.

WordMail Messages

Outlook's standard message form is fine for many purposes, and it gives you some useful formatting options such as color, indention, paragraph alignment, and bullets. But, if you prefer, you can use Microsoft Word 97 to compose a new message or to read, reply to, or forward a message. By choosing Word as your electronic mail editor, you can incorporate tables, formulas, and fields in your message and use Word's entire array of formatting features when composing a message.

II

Electronic Mail

FIGURE 4-1.
Outlook's standard message form.

Standard toolbar   Message header boxes

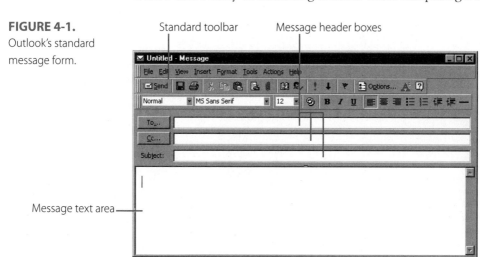

Message text area

To set up the WordMail tools, you must have Word 97 installed. Then follow these steps:

1 Choose the Options command from the Tools menu to open the Options dialog box.

2 Click the Mail Format tab.

3 Select Microsoft Word from the Send In This Message Format box.

4 Click OK.

After you turn on the Microsoft Word option, each time you compose a new message or read, reply to, or forward a message, you'll see a window that looks much like your Microsoft Word window.

You can also leave the default mail format set to HTML but use Word as your mail form for individual messages. To create a new message using Word, point to New Mail Message Using on the Actions menu and choose Microsoft Word.

Sending a Message

It's easy to create a new e-mail message—and Outlook gives you lots of options for protecting, formatting, delivering, and tracking your message, as well as for drawing attention to the message and adding attachments to it.

Creating a New Message

The fastest and easiest way to send a message is simply to type the text and click the Send button. In this basic case, your message looks tidy but unspectacular, and it also requires the least effort.

You can create a new message from any folder in Outlook. From the Inbox, Outbox, or Drafts folders, you click the New Mail Message button as described in the steps that follow. From another folder, open the list attached to the New button on the Standard toolbar and select Mail Message, or just press Ctrl+Shift+M. (The full name of the New button depends on the folder you have open.)

To send a simple message, do the following:

1 Click the New Mail Message button on the Standard toolbar, or open the list attached to the New button and choose Mail Message.

2 In the new message window, click the To button to display the Select Names dialog box.

3 Select the address book containing the recipient's name.

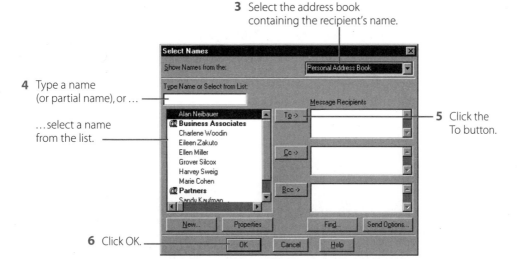

4 Type a name (or partial name), or ...

...select a name from the list.

5 Click the To button.

6 Click OK.

7 In the message window, click in the Subject box and type a brief description of the subject of your message.

8 Click in the message area, or press the Tab key to move to the message text area, and then type your message.

9 When your message is ready to send, click the Send button.

If you do not complete your message or are not ready to send it, choose the Save command from the File menu. Outlook stores the message in the Drafts folder. To complete the message, open the Drafts folder in the My Shortcuts (or Mail) group, and then double-click the message in the message list. Click Send when you are ready to send the message.

When you type the beginning of a name in the Select Names dialog box (step 4), Outlook jumps to the first name in the list that matches the letters you've typed. You can then scroll, if you need to, to find the name you want. You can also send a message to several recipients at one time. To do this, either select each name and then click the To button for each selection, or hold down the Ctrl key while you click all the names you want and then click the To button.

At the same time as you address your message to the main recipients, you can also designate who should receive courtesy copies (Cc) or "blind courtesy copies" (Bcc) of the message. To fill in the Cc and Bcc boxes of the message header at the same time as you fill in the To box, select the names of the recipients for the appropriate header box and click the related button (Cc or Bcc) in the Select Names dialog box.

NOTE

When you select a recipient from the address book, Outlook inserts the name in the message window with an underline. The underline indicates that the name is associated with an e-mail address.

Typing Recipient Names and Addresses

Instead of clicking the To button in the message window to address your message, you can simply type the names of the recipients. To send the message to more than one person, separate the names either with a semicolon or with a comma. (For commas to work as separators, the Allow Comma As Address Separator option must be turned on. You'll find it by choosing Options from the Tools menu, clicking the E-Mail Options button on the Preferences tab, and then clicking the Advanced E-mail Options button.)

TIP

For CompuServe e-mail addresses that contain a comman, substitute a period (to send mail to member 707,1765 use the address 707.1765@compuserve.com). With America Online addresses, remove spaces between words in screen names—send mail to Big Boss addressed to Bigboss@aol.com.)

When you send mail, Outlook checks all the recipients that you entered in the To and Cc headers to make sure that your mail can be delivered. To check the recipients before sending the message, click the Check Names button on the Standard toolbar or choose the Check Names command on the Tools menu.

Outlook will underline complete Internet e-mail addresses indicating that they use the correct syntax. The address must be in the format

name@service.something

Outlook will also underline names that have matching entries in the Contacts folder and use the actual e-mail address when transmitting the message. If Outlook cannot find a name or finds multiple matches or an incomplete Internet address, it displays the Check Names dialog box, shown in Figure 4-2.

FIGURE 4-2.
Outlook checks the name automatically.

Click here to create a new address listing.

Choose a name from the list found in the address book.

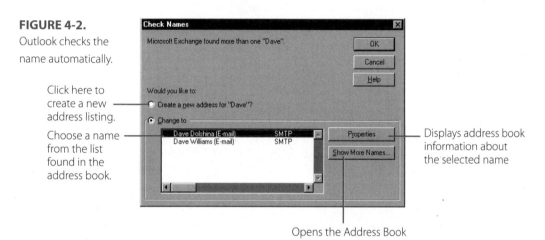

Displays address book information about the selected name

Opens the Address Book

Sending Your Messages

What happens when you click the Send button depends on how your system is set up and who the mail is addressed to. Mail sent to recipients on your Exchange Server is transmitted immediately. Mail to Internet recipients, however, is stored in the Outbox until you click the Send And Receive button on the Standard toolbar. Outlook will send any mail in the Outbox and check for new mail waiting for you. If you want to send mail without getting waiting mail, choose Send from the Tools menu. You can also set Outlook to automatically dial, send and receive, and disconnect at an interval you set in the Internet E-Mail tab of the Options dialog box.

If you have more than one mail service set up, the Send And Receive command will transmit all of your mail and check for mail on all of the services. If you want to send mail using a particular service point to Send And Receive on the Tools menu, and then choose the service you want to use.

SEE ALSO

To save a message in another format, such as an Outlook template, see "Saving Messages in Files," on page 144.

If the message service you select is one that you must sign on to, Outlook starts that service's logon routine. When you send a message, Outlook automatically saves a copy of it in the Sent Items folder. To check your sent messages, open the My Shortcuts (or Mail) group, and click the Sent Items folder.

Sending a Protected Message

When you want privacy for your messages, you can encrypt them. When you want to assure your recipients that *you* actually sent the messages they received in your name and that the messages weren't tampered with during transit, you can digitally sign them. You can both encrypt and digitally sign a message.

Stamping Your Signature

Have you ever received a message with a few standard closing lines at the end of it? Maybe the sender's name, an e-mail address, a postal address, and some pithy saying? Would you like to add such lines at the end of your messages? Outlook gives you the Signature command to do just that.

A Signature automatically adds whatever closing you want to your new messages. A Signature can also add a closing to replies and forwarded messages if you want.

You can create one or more standard closings, and then select the one to use by default for all messages or choose the appropriate one for each message. Here's how to choose a signature or set up your first signature when you are composing a message.

1 Click the message area of the message window.

2 Click the Signature button on the message window's Standard toolbar, or point to Signature on the Insert menu. If you have already created a signature file, select it from the list that appears. The signature will be inserted into the message.

3 To create a new signature file, click More.

4 If you have not yet created any signatures, a dialog box appears asking if you want to create one now. Click Yes.

Stamping Your Signature *continued*

5 Enter a name to use to select the signature.

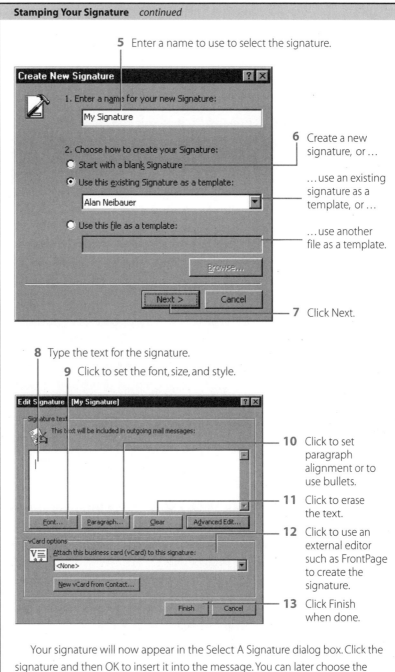

6 Create a new signature, or …

… use an existing signature as a template, or …

… use another file as a template.

7 Click Next.

8 Type the text for the signature.

9 Click to set the font, size, and style.

10 Click to set paragraph alignment or to use bullets.

11 Click to erase the text.

12 Click to use an external editor such as FrontPage to create the signature.

13 Click Finish when done.

Electronic Mail

Your signature will now appear in the Select A Signature dialog box. Click the signature and then OK to insert it into the message. You can later choose the same signature again from the menu that appears when you click the Signature button on the message window's Standard toolbar, or choose Signature from the Insert menu.

Swapping Security Keys

You can only send encrypted messages if both you and the recipient have security set up. To send an encrypted message over the Internet, you will first need the recipient's public key along with his or her certificate in your address book. The recipient's public key is like a personal "coding machine" that will encrypt the messages you send to him or her such that only the complementary private key kept by the recipient can decode them. To send protected messages within your organization, swapping security certificates isn't necessary—it's part of setting up Microsoft Exchange Server in your organization.

The people to whom you want to send encrypted messages must first send you a message that is digitally signed and includes their certificate. You'll have to give your public key to others to receive encrypted messages from them, so here are the steps.

1 Choose the Options command from the Tools menu, and then select the Security tab.

2 Click the Change Settings button.

3 Turn on the Send These Certificates With Signed Messages option.

4 Click OK in each dialog box.

Now send the recipient a message that is digitally signed, as you'll learn how to do next. When the message arrives, the recipient must drag it from the Inbox to the Contacts folder. This creates an address listing that contains the sender's public key.

Encrypting and Digitally Signing Messages

SEE ALSO

For information about reading an encrypted message or checking a digital signature, see "Reading a Protected Message," on page 138.

If you want to encrypt or digitally sign all messages that you send, choose Options from the Tools menu, select the Security tab, and turn on both the Encrypt Contents And Attachments For Outgoing Messages option and the Add Digital Signature To Outgoing Messages option.

If you don't want to turn on these options for all messages that you send, you can still encrypt or digitally sign a single message by following these steps:

1 Create the message.

2 Click the Options button on the message window's Standard toolbar to open the Message Options dialog box.

3 In the Security area of the Message Options dialog box, turn on Encrypt Contents And Attachments and Add Digital Signature To Outgoing Message.

4 Click Close.

5 Click Send.

If you are using Exchange Security, Outlook will display a dialog box reporting the level of security. Click the OK button in the dialog box.

 NOTE

If any of the intended recipients of your encrypted message do not have security set up or if you do not have their certificates, you'll see a message box telling you that the recipients cannot process encrypted messages. To send the message anyway, click the Don't Encrypt Message button. The message is then sent out without protection.

Using the Signature Picker

If you want to choose a signature to use for all messages, set it as the default on the Mail Format tab of the Options dialog box. You can also click the Signature Picker button on this tab to create, edit, or delete signatures.

To select a default signature, choose it from the Use This Signature By Default list. Once you select a signature, you can also choose to use it just for new messages, not for replies and forwarded messages. If you change your mind and decide not to use any signature by default, choose <None> in the list.

To create, edit, or delete signatures, click the Signature Picker button.

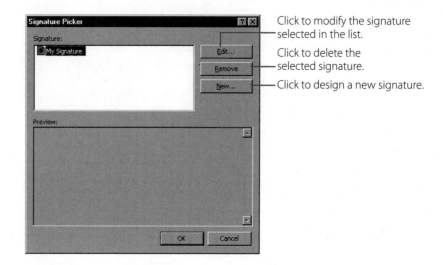

If you selected a default signature, the next time you send a message, Outlook will automatically add your signature at the end of the message. If you also chose to include the default signature on replies and forwards, Outlook will place it above the copy of the message you are responding to or forwarding.

Sending Business Cards

A vCard is a type of business card you attach to e-mail that includes information about a contact in your Address Book. When you include your personal vCard as a signature, recipients can read the information and add it to their address book with a simple click of the mouse—so it's better than sending recipients an actual printed business card.

To create this electronic business card, select an address in your Contacts list and save the listing to your disk as a vCard, with the .vcf extension. You can then select which vCard to use with a signature. To create and send a business card with your own information, first add yourself to the Contacts folder.

To create a vCard card from your listing in the Contacts folder, follow these steps:

1 Click the Contacts folder in the Outlook Bar.

2 Locate your own listing to make a vCard for yourself. If you want to make a vCard of another person, locate his or her listing.

3 Right-click the listing and choose Export To VCARD File from the shortcut menu.

In the VCARD File dialog box that appears, the person's name will be shown as the filename.

4 Click Save.

You select the card to use while creating or editing a signature. If you do not yet have any signatures, you can create one from a card. Otherwise, you can create or edit a signature using Signature Picker from the Mail Format tab of the Options dialog box. This is how to add a business card to a signature.

1 Choose the Options command from the Tools menu.

2 Click the Mail Format tab.

3 Click the Signature Picker button.

4 Select an existing signature and click Edit, or create a new signature by clicking New, typing a name for the signature, and then clicking Next.

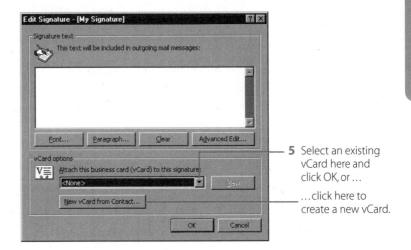

5 Select an existing vCard here and click OK, or …

…click here to create a new vCard.

If you chose to create a new vCard, continue at step 1, on the next page. If you're using an existing vCard, skip to step 7.

2 Select the listing to use for a card.

1 Choose the address book containing the address to use with the card.

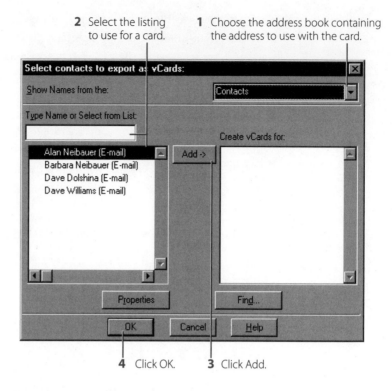

4 Click OK.

3 Click Add.

5 Make sure the new card is selected now in the vCard options list.

6 Click OK to close the Edit Signature dialog box.

7 Click OK to close the Signature Picker dialog box.

8 To use the vCard as the default signature, select it in the Use This Signature By Default list of the Mail Format tab.

9 Click OK to close the Options dialog box.

When you send your message, it will now include a paper clip icon indicating an attachment. The recipient can open and read the vCard just like any other attachment.

Formatting Text

A plain text message is quick and easy, but you might want to format the message's text a little, just to make e-mail life more lively. Outlook provides several ways to enhance the appearance of your mail messages.

You can use some basic text attributes to format a message, you can add background colors and pictures, and you can create electronic stationery for special events and effects.

Text formats are not available when you are using the Plain Text message format.

Applying Basic Text Formats

Basic text formats are easy to apply because they are available on the Formatting toolbar. To apply these formats to selected text in a message, use the buttons and boxes on the Formatting toolbar as shown below:

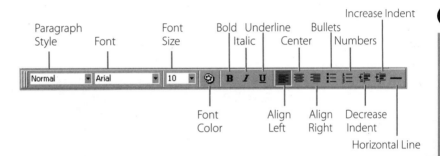

Besides using the toolbar, you can add and remove some text attributes using menu commands on the Format menu or common key combinations such as Ctrl+B for boldface.

You can also add text formats by selecting them from the Style list. Choose a style from the list on the far left of the Formatting toolbar, or point to Style on the Format menu and select the style you want. The list offers 15 options in addition to the normal text format. Most styles apply more than one type of formatting. The Heading 1 style, for example, formats text as Arial, 24-points, and bold.

Changing the Default Font

Outlook uses default fonts for new messages, text you type when replying to or forwarding messages, and plain text messages. Each of these message types can use different font settings. Set the default fonts by choosing the Fonts button on the Mail Format tab of the Options dialog box, as discussed in "Selecting Stationery and Fonts," on page 76.

Adding Pictures and Backgrounds

To create even more eye-appealing mail messages, add a graphic, add a color background, or fill the background with a repeating graphic. The graphic can even be an animated file that moves on the message, such as the animated GIF graphics common on the Internet.

To insert a graphic in a message, follow these steps:

1 Click in the message where you want the graphic to appear.

2 Choose Picture from the Insert menu.

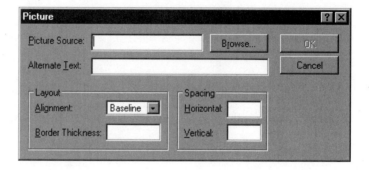

3 Type the path and filename for the graphic or use the Browse button to locate it.

4 Type the alternate text you want to appear as the image is loading onto the recipient's screen or when the image cannot be displayed on a reader's system.

5 Select an alignment for the graphic if you want it to appear somewhere other than at the location of the insertion point.

6 Enter the border thickness in pixels (use 0 for no border).

7 Enter the horizontal and vertical spacing between the picture and text, in pixels.

8 Click OK.

The picture will appear at the position you designated.

To change the size or position of the picture, click it. The graphic will be surrounded by a dotted border with eight small boxes, called handles. To move the graphic to another location in the text, point to it so that the mouse icon appears as a four-directional arrow and then drag. You can only drag the graphic within text, not to areas below the last text line.

To change the size of the graphic, point to one of the handles so that the mouse pointer appears as a two-directional arrow and drag as follows:

- Drag a center handle on the left or right border to change the width of the graphic.

- Drag a center handle on the top or bottom border to change the height of the graphic.

- Drag a corner handle to change the width and height.

You can also add a background to the entire message. To color the background, point to Background on the Format menu and select Color; then choose a color from the menu that appears. To fill the background with a picture, point to Background on the Format menu and select Picture.

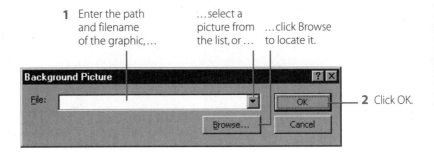

The picture will be tiled in the background—duplicated as many times as necessary to fill the message window.

Using Stationery

Stationery lets you design a message format and then use it as the default for every message or just for selected messages. Outlook includes a number of attractive stationery designs ready for you to use. You can edit these designs or create your own.

Selecting a Message Stationery

To format a specific message using one of Outlook's stationery designs, start a new message by pointing to New Message Using on the Actions menu. Until you use a stationery, the menu that appears offers two stationery options:

More Stationery.   Choose this command to select from existing stationery designs.

No Stationery.   Choose this command to use the standard Outlook text formats.

Once you select a stationery, it will be listed on this menu so you can later choose it again.

To select a stationery, click More Stationery, and then choose a stationery design to see it in the Preview window, as shown in Figure 4-3. If there is a scroll bar in the Preview window, scroll the window to see more of the design. If there is no scroll bar, the design will be repeated down the edge of the paper. Choose the design you want, and then click OK.

FIGURE 4-3.
Choose a stationery design to use for the message.

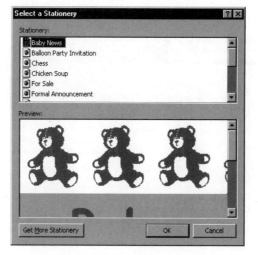

Click Get More Stationery to launch Internet Explorer, connect to the Web, and download additional stationary designs.

Some designs contain both background graphics and sample text. You can change the text as you would in any other message—just position the insertion point and add or insert text as desired.

Selecting a Default Stationery

You can also select a stationery design to use as the default for all new messages. It can be one of the designs provided with Outlook or one that you create yourself. To select a default stationery, follow these steps:

1 Choose Options from the Tools menu.

2 Click the Mail Format tab.

3 Select a design from the Use This Stationery By Default list.

4 Click OK.

Use the Stationery Picker button on the Mail Format tab to create, edit, and delete stationery forms. The Stationery Picker dialog box lists all of your stationery, including the ones provided by Outlook and those you create yourself.

Creating Stationery

If you have your own message design that you want to use frequently, save it as a stationery file. You can then use it as the default stationery or select it for individual messages by pointing to New Mail Message Using on the Actions menu.

You can create new stationery from scratch or use an existing stationery file or HTML file as a template. You can also edit a stationery file, changing the graphics, color, or font used for its default text. To create or edit a stationery file, follow these steps:

1 Choose Options from the Tools menu.

2 Click the Mail Format tab.

3 Click Stationery Picker.

4 Click New to create a new stationery file. (If you want to edit an existing design, select it from the list, click Edit, and then skip to step 8.)

II

Electronic Mail

5 Enter a name for the new stationery in the Create New Stationery dialog box.

6 You now have to choose from three options, just as you did when you created a new signature. Click Start With A Blank Stationery to start from scratch, click Use This Existing Stationery As A Template to choose a piece of stationery as a starting point, or click Use This File As A Template to pick an existing HTML file to start with, and then click Next.

7 If you chose to use an existing piece of stationery or an HTML file, a sample of it appears in the Preview Pane of the Edit Stationery dialog box, as shown in Figure 4-4. You can select either a picture or color for the background, but not both. If you select a picture, it will be tiled to fill the entire message background.

FIGURE 4-4.
Creating or editing stationery.

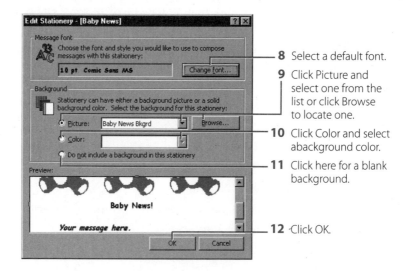

8 Select a default font.

9 Click Picture and select one from the list or click Browse to locate one.

10 Click Color and select abackground color.

11 Click here for a blank background.

12 Click OK.

The new stationery will now be listed with the others in the Stationery Picker dialog box. You can choose to use it as the default by selecting it on the Mail Format tab of the Options dialog box, or you can use it for individual messages by pointing to New Mail Message Using on the Actions menu and selecting it from the submenu.

Selecting Stationery Fonts

Most stationery designs include their own default font. You can choose to use the font associated with the stationery or to use the same default font for all messages. To do this, click the Fonts button in the Mail Format tab of the Options dialog box, and choose from these options:

Use The Font Specified In Stationery (If Specified).   Turn on this option to let the stationery font override the new message default font.

Use My Font When Replying And Forwarding Messages.   Turn on this option to use the stationery font for new messages but the default font with replies and forwarded messages.

Always Use My Fonts.   Turn on this option to make the default font always override the stationery font.

Saving Messages as Stationery

When you design a new piece of stationery using the Stationery Picker, you are not given the opportunity to enter and format text. If you want to include text in a piece of new stationery, take these additional steps:

1 Start a new message using the stationery design you want to add text to.

2 Enter and format the text as you want it to appear with each copy of the stationery.

3 Choose Save As from the File menu.

4 Make sure that HTML is chosen on the Save As Type list.

5 Enter a filename and then click Save.

6 Close the message.

7 Choose Options from the Tools menu.

8 Click the Mail Format tab.

9 Click Stationery Picker.

10 Click New to create a new stationery.

II

Electronic Mail

11 Enter a name for the stationery.

12 Click Use This File As A Template, click Browse, and then select the HTML file you saved in step 5.

13 Click Next to display the Edit Stationery dialog box.

14 Click OK.

You can now use the stationery as you would any other.

Setting Message Options

SEE ALSO

For information about setting up standard options on the tabs of the Options dialog box, see Chapter 3, "Setting Outlook Options."

Outlook sets up your new messages according to the options selected on the tabs of the Options dialog box. However, you might want to change the standard settings for a specific message. To do this, click the Options button on the message window Standard toolbar to display the options shown in Figure 4-5.

The settings you choose in the Message Options dialog box apply only to the message you're currently working on. Any changes you make here do not affect the standard settings on the tabs of the Options dialog box.

FIGURE 4-5.

Message options.

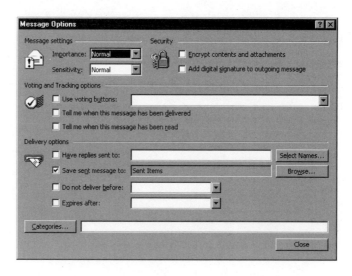

Message Settings

The first set of options in the Message Options dialog box lets you designate how important or sensitive a message is.

Importance

The default importance level for your messages is set in the Options dialog box (accessed by choosing Options from the Tools menu), but sometimes you might want to send a message with a different level of importance. Suppose, for instance, that you need to send an urgent message about a deadline change to members of your project team. It's important that they notice and read the message right away. You can click the Options button on the message window Standard toolbar and select High in the Importance box. When Outlook delivers that message, it adds a red exclamation mark to the left of the envelope in the recipient's message list, alerting the recipient that this is an important message. (Depending on how your e-mail server is set up, a High importance message might also be delivered faster than messages with Normal or Low importance levels.)

Likewise, if you've just heard a funny story that you'd like to pass along to a friend, but you know that the friend is busily working to complete a project, you can set a Low importance level for your message. When the message arrives, the recipient sees a blue downward-pointing arrow next to the envelope in the message list and knows that this message can wait until the project's work is done.

 TIP

> You can click either the Importance: High button (the red exclamation mark) or the Importance: Low button (the blue down arrow) on the Standard toolbar in the message window to quickly set the importance level for an individual message. If you change your mind and want to return the importance level of the message to Normal, click that toolbar button again.

Sensitivity

If a specific message requires a different level of sensitivity than you set as the default for all messages, you can designate this level in the Message Options dialog box. The four levels of sensitivity are Normal, Personal, Private, and Confidential.

Outlook shows the corresponding label—*Normal, Personal, Private,* or *Confidential*—in the Sensitivity column of the recipient's message list, provided that the Sensitivity column is displayed. If the Sensitivity column is not displayed, the recipient will see that the message has

II

Electronic Mail

SEE ALSO

For information about changing the column display, see "Setting Up Columns," on page 554.

been marked Personal, Private, or Confidential when she or he opens the message to read it.

The Personal designation is informational only. The Private designation prevents recipients from altering your original message if they reply to it or forward it. The Confidential sensitivity level notifies recipients to treat the message according to your organization's policies about confidentiality.

Security Options

The second set of options in the Message Options dialog box lets you encrypt the message and add your digital signature to it.

Voting and Tracking Options

The Voting and Tracking Options area of the Message Options dialog box helps you get responses to questions using voting buttons and asks for receipts when your mail has been delivered or read.

 NOTE

> Voting buttons can be used when sending mail through your network server. To use voting buttons with Internet e-mail, the recipient's e-mail address must be set to use Microsoft Exchange Rich Text format. See "Adding Someone," on page 171.

Did you ever send a message that asked people to respond to a proposal or an invitation? Outlook makes it possible to give your recipients an easy way to send a response to your proposal or invitation: voting buttons. When you turn on the Use Voting Buttons option in the Message Options dialog box, you'll see three choices in the drop-down list—Approve/Reject; Yes/No; and Yes/No/Maybe—which correspond to these three sets of voting buttons:

      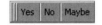

Select the set of buttons you want to include in your message, and send the message. (You will not see the buttons on your screen when you are composing the message, but they will appear with the message in the Sent Items folder.) When Outlook delivers the message, the recipients will see the buttons in the message window, along with the instruction *Please respond using the buttons above.*

SEE ALSO

To find out how to use a voting button in a message you receive, see "Replying Through Voting Buttons," on page 142.

You can even create your own set of voting buttons. Instead of selecting one of the choices in the list, replace the text that appears in the list box by typing in new text with the voting button names you want to use. Separate the names with semicolons, and don't include any spaces: for example, *Red;Green;Blue* or *Tuesday;Thursday*. When your message is delivered, it will display your custom buttons.

When recipients respond using the voting buttons, you'll receive an e-mail informing you of their selection. Read the e-mail to see the response and any additional comments. The message in your Sent Items folder will now be marked with a special icon indicating that responses have been received, and the message will contain a Tracking tab that records a list of all recipients and the status and date of their replies.

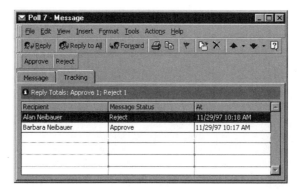

The default tracking options for your messages are set on the Preference tab of the Options dialog box, using the E-Mail Options button. (See "Tracking Options," on page 66.) But if you want to set a different tracking option for a specific message, you can do so in the Message Options dialog box.

To have Outlook notify you when your message arrives in the recipient's mailbox, turn on the Tell Me When This Message Has Been Delivered option. To have Outlook notify you when the recipient has opened your message, turn on the Tell Me When This Message Has Been Read option. You can choose either or both of these options. When your message arrives (or when the recipient opens it), Outlook delivers a message to your Inbox conveying this information.

> NOTE

Bear in mind that even though the label for the Tell Me When This Message Has Been Read option contains the word *Read,* Outlook can tell you only that the message was opened.

Delivery Options

The Delivery Options section of the Message Options dialog box contains four check box options:

Have Replies Sent To.   Set this option to send replies to your message to another address. For example, you might invite staff members to a staff party but want your assistant to receive the replies in order to set up a list of attendees or to supply a proper attendance figure to the caterer.

Save Sent Message To.   Use this option when you want to save an occasional message in a folder other than the Sent Items folder. At other times, you might not want to save a particular message at all. You can make both of these adjustments with the Save Sent Message To option.

Do Not Deliver Before.   To set up a delayed delivery, turn on the Do Not Deliver Before option and type or select the earliest date on which the message should be delivered.

Expires After.   To set an expiration date for a message, turn on this option and type or select an expiration date for the message.

> NOTE

You can use delayed delivery only if you are running Outlook with Microsoft Exchange Server.

Categories

? SEE ALSO

For more information about categories, see "Working with Categories," on page 560.

A handy way to organize messages is to group them into categories. By assigning a message to a category, you can match it up with other messages that belong to a specific project, an activity, a group, or any other designation. This lets you collect similar items for easy review and retrieval. To assign a message to a category by using the Message Options dialog box, follow these steps:

   1 Click the Categories button in the Message Options dialog box for the message.

To create a new category, type the name here,…

…and click here.

Click here to add new categories from the Master Category list.

3 Click OK.

2 Turn on the check boxes to assign the message to those categories.

Setting Message Properties

Another way to control various aspects of the message is through the Properties dialog box. From the message window, choose Properties from the File menu. In the General tab of the Properties dialog box, you can set the importance and sensitivity levels, and choose whether to AutoArchive the message and save a copy of the sent message, request a read receipt and a delivery receipt for the message, and set delayed delivery and expiration times for the messsage.

On the Security tab of the Properties dialog box, you can choose to encrypt the message and add a digital signature, and you can choose the default security setting.

Flagging a Message

> ⓘ Follow up by Friday, November 28, 1997 5:00 PM.

Even though you can make a Subject line informative and can include instructions within message text, you still might find it useful to add a

II

Electronic Mail

"flag" to a message. A message flag is a line that appears in the message header that has information about the nature of the message or that requests a response to the message. Follow these steps to flag a message:

1   Click the Flag button on the message window Standard toolbar (alternately, choose Flag For Follow Up from the Actions menu or press Ctrl+Shift+G) to display the Flag For Follow Up dialog box.

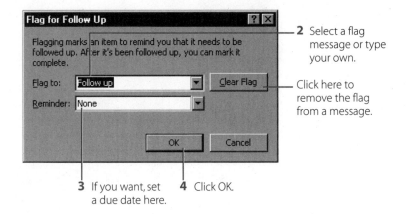

Flag for Follow Up

Flagging marks an item to remind you that it needs to be followed up. After it's been followed up, you can mark it complete.

Flag to: Follow up

Reminder: None

OK   Cancel

2 Select a flag message or type your own.

Click here to remove the flag from a message.

3 If you want, set a due date here.   **4** Click OK.

In the recipient's message list, a flagged message displays a flag beside its icon (assuming the Flag Status column is displayed). When the flag is red, the recipient hasn't yet responded. When the flag is white, a response has been made.

Message flag

To remove a message flag, click the Clear Flag button in the Flag For Follow Up dialog box.

Sending Files as Attachments

Have you ever mailed a cover letter accompanied by other documents? These other documents are called attachments because they are attached to a letter that introduces them. You can also send attachments with mail messages. An attachment is a file on your disk that you want to send to the recipient of the e-mail. The attachment can be any file that you'll find on your disk.

The contents of an attachment do not appear directly on screen with the message but are shown as an icon. The recipient can easily open the attachment to display its contents, play the sound or movie, or run the executable program. You can attach files to a new message, a forwarded message, or a reply.

To attach a file to a message, follow these steps:

Insert File

1   Click the Insert File button (the paper clip) on the message window Standard toolbar, or choose File from the Insert menu.

2   In the Look In box, select the disk and the folder that contains the file.

3   Select the file or files you want to attach.

4   Select Attachment in the Insert As box. This shows the file as an icon, which the recipient opens and reads in the program used to create the file.

5   Click OK.

In the Outbox folder next to the message, you'll see a paper clip icon in the Attachment column (the column is marked with a paper clip in the header). This lets you know that the message includes one or more attachments.

If you have a plain text file stored on disk (for example, a file saved in Windows Notepad), you can add it as an attachment or insert the text of the file directly into the message. To add the contents of the file to the message itself, in the Insert File dialog box, select the text file, click the Text Only option in the Insert As section, and then click OK.

Adding Links

Outlook provides a way to add two types of links to a message as described next. The first type of link is to a website, the second type is to an e-mail address.

II

Electronic Mail

Recalling, Replacing, or Resending a Message

Let's say you sent a message to your project team on the Microsoft Exchange Server but inadvertently included the incorrect date of the next team meeting. Rather than send an entirely new message, you can do any of the following:

- Recall the message you've already sent, removing it from the recipient's inbox.

- Resend the same message after correcting or updating it.

You can only recall or replace messages to recipients who are logged on and using Outlook and who have not read the message or moved the message out of their Inbox.

First find the message you've already sent by opening the My Shortcuts (or Mail) group on the Outlook Bar, opening the Sent Items folder, and double-clicking the sent message to open it.

To recall or replace the message, follow these steps:

1 Choose Recall This Message from the Tools menu.

2 In the Recall This Message dialog box, do one of the following:

- To recall the message, select the Delete Unread Copies Of This Message option, and then click OK.

- To replace the message with another, select the Delete Unread Copies And Replace With A New Message option, and then click OK. In the new message window that appears, type the new message, and then click the Send button.

3 To receive a notification about the success or failure of recalling or replacing the message for each recipient, turn on the Tell Me If Recall Succeeds Or Fails For Each Recipient option.

To simply resend the message (rather than recall or replace the message), follow these steps:

1 Choose Resend This Message from the Tools menu.

2 In the message window that appears, make any necessary changes, and then click the Send button.

Sending a URL in a Message

To find out how to use a URL in a message, see "Working with Links," on page 140.

So you've been surfing the World Wide Web, and you've found a Web site you want to share with someone. The easiest way to do this is to send the Web site address (URL) to your friend. So how do you get the URL into a message? You can either type it or copy and paste it.

In fact, if the URL begins with *www*, you can even leave off the *http://* designation. For example, if you type *www.microsoft.com* and then press the Spacebar or Enter key, Outlook automatically formats the URL as a link to the Web page, displaying it something like this:

www.microsoft.com

The URL is formatted with an underline and in blue.

If the URL does not start with *www*, type *http://* and the remainder of the address. When you're done, the text will be formatted as a link, underlined and in blue.

You can change the type of a link, from *http:* to *https://* or *gopher://*, for example, by changing its properties. Right-click the link and choose Properties from the shortcut menu to see this dialog box.

Although the Internet requires a complete URL to find a site, the format of the address may be confusing to mail recipients. Rather than have a URL in the message itself, you can use any text as a link for the reader to click to move to a location on the net. Here's how.

1 Select the text that you want to serve as a link. It can be text that you've already typed in the message or a separate note telling the recipient when to click. For example, if you want the user to jump to the Microsoft Press Web page, you could type *Click here to learn more about Microsoft Press* and then select the entire sentence.

2 Choose the Hyperlink command from the Insert menu.

3 Choose the type of link.

4 Enter the complete URL of the address.

5 Click OK.

The hyperlink will appear underlined and in blue.

Including an E-Mail Link

For an alternative way to have responses to a message sent to another e-mail address, see "Delivery Options," on page 130.

From time to time, you might want to send a message that offers your recipients an e-mail address to which they can send questions or comments rather than sending their replies to you. For example, let's say you want to encourage your friends to send a message to the President of the United States at *president@whitehouse.gov*.

To make it easy for your recipient to do this, simply type the e-mail address you want the recipient to contact, such as *president@white-house.gov*. When you press the Spacebar or Enter key after the address, Outlook formats the address as a link.

Outlook technically creates a Mailto link. If you right-click the link and choose properties, you'll see that the URL starts with *mailto:* as in

mailto:president@whitehouse.gov.

You do not have to type *mailto:* yourself, and it will not appear in the message. When the recipient clicks on the link, a new message window will open with the address already in the To: section.

Attaching Messages

Usually, to send a copy of a message to one or more people you just forward the message. That's fine if you want to send only *one* message. But suppose you want to forward several related messages all at one time? For that, you need to attach messages to your new message. You can attach other messages to any message you send, even if the message you're sending is itself a forwarded message or a reply.

To attach an existing message to the message you're working on, take these steps:

1 Choose Item from the Insert menu in the message window.

2 Select the folder containing the items you want to attach.

4 Select the form the items should take in your message.

5 Click OK.

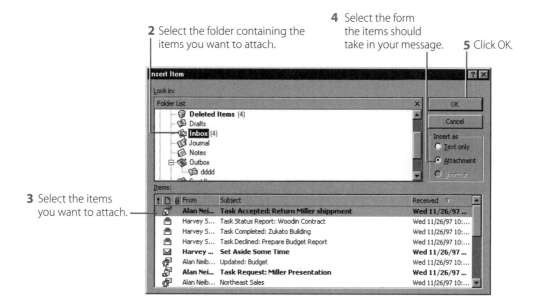

3 Select the items you want to attach.

Reading a Message

When a message arrives in your inbox, you can read and respond to it, forward it to others, view or open attachments, and respond using URL or e-mail links.

⭐ **TIP**

To learn how to automatically dispatch incoming messages that you don't want to read to the dustbin or to other places in Outlook or your file system, see "Rules Wizard," on page 45.

As you learned earlier in this chapter, a mail message can contain text that you read in the message window as well as attachments ("other stuff") that you have to open (as you would open an envelope that contains a paper letter). A message can also contain a link to a World Wide Web page (a URL), an e-mail response link, or voting buttons.

Electronic Mail

II

> **NOTE**
>
> Mail messages that you receive over the Microsoft Exchange server are automatically inserted into your Inbox. To receive messages from the Internet, you have to use the Send And Receive command, or you have to set up Outlook options to check for mail automatically at regular intervals.

You can read a mail message in the Preview Pane or in a separate window. If the Preview Pane is not displayed, choose the Preview Pane command from the View menu.

To quickly read mail message text when the Preview Pane is displayed, click the message in the Inbox message list. If part of a long message falls below the bottom of the Preview Pane window, scroll through the message window to read the rest of the message.

> **TIP**
>
> To see the first three lines of messages directly in the message list, choose Auto-Preview from the View menu.

To read the message in its own window, simply double-click the message line in your Inbox's message list.

> **TIP**
>
> Once you've opened a message in its own window, you can use the Next Item and Previous Item buttons on the message window Standard toolbar to move from message to message. Beside each of these buttons is a down arrow that you can click to see a list of commands that let you move more quickly to the messages you want to read. For example, you can move to the next or previous message from the same sender or to the next or previous unread message.

Reading a Protected Message

> **SEE ALSO**
>
> For information about sending an encrypted or digitally signed message, see "Sending a Protected Message," on page 112.

What if someone sends you a message that's encrypted or digitally signed? If the message came through your Microsoft Exchange server, you must be set up with a digital certificate, as explained in Chapter 2, "Looking Out into Outlook." To read a protected message, double-click the message line in your Inbox's message list. If the message is protected with Microsoft Exchange security, a message appears reporting the level of security. Click OK to read the message.

Creating a Rule

In Chapter 2, "Looking Out into Outlook," you learned how to create a rule to channel messages using the Rules Wizard (see "Rules Wizard," on page 45). Most of the time, you'll be creating a rule based on a specific sender or subject matter. If you already received a message that meets the conditions for the rule you want to set, you can save yourself time by creating the rule from the message itself.

1 Double-click the message to open it in its own window.

2 Choose Create Rule from the Actions menu. The Rules Wizard appears with the message's sender, recipient, and subject already listed as conditions.

3 Select the conditions that you want to apply.

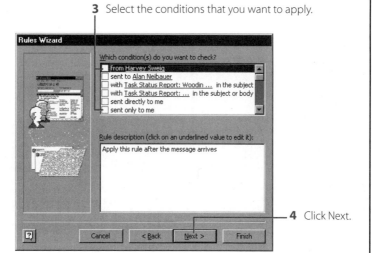

4 Click Next.

5 Select an action to apply to the rule, and then complete the rule as you learned how to do in Chapter 2.

You can create multiple rules from one message, and you can later delete or change them using the Rules Wizard command on the Tools menu.

You don't have to do anything special to read encrypted mail over the Internet. For someone to send you encrypted mail, the sender has to have a copy of the public key that comes with your certificate. This means you'll have to send the person your certificate ahead of time as explained in "Sending a Protected Message," on page 112. The message will be decrypted automatically when it arrives in your Inbox.

Electronic Mail

Checking a Digital Signature

A digital signature assures the recipient that the person named in the From line of a message actually sent the message. A digital signature also indicates that the message has not been altered or tampered with while being sent.

To check a digital signature, follow these steps:

1   Double-click the message line of the digitally signed message in your Inbox's message list. (The message might also be encrypted.)

2   If the Microsoft Exchange security dialog box appears, click OK.

   3   Click the Verify Digital Signature button on the Standard toolbar.

4   In the Verify Digital Signature dialog box, check the information Outlook provides, and then click OK.

Working with Links

Using a link in a message is easy—just click the link.

When you receive a message that contains a URL (a Web site address), you can simply click the URL in the message text to visit the Web site. Windows starts your default Web browser and connects to the Web site.

When you receive a message that contains an e-mail response link in the message text, you can send a response, a question, or a comment by clicking the link. Outlook opens a new message addressed to the e-mail address in the response link and with the Subject line set up for you to fill in. Simply add your message text, and then click the Send button.

Gathering Messages from the Beyond

If you are signed up for other electronic mail services, you can use Outlook to read the messages you receive through these services. For example, you could have accounts on the Microsoft Network, Compu-Serve, America Online, or AT&T WorldNet.

When you use the Send And Receive button, Outlook automatically checks for mail on all of your services. To check for messages on a specific service, point to Send And Receive on the Tools menu and choose the service from the submenu.

If the message service you select is one that you must sign on to, Outlook starts that service's logon routine. After you log on (if necessary), Outlook collects your messages, and they appear in your Inbox, ready to read, just like any other messages you receive through Outlook.

Replying to a Message

Oftentimes a message provokes you to respond. So what do you do? Send back a reply. You can direct your response only to the person who sent the message, or you can respond to the sender and everyone who received it.

To reply to a message, do the following:

1   Select the message line in the message list, or open the message.

2   To reply to the person who sent the message, click the Reply button on the Standard toolbar. To reply to the sender and to everyone who received the original message, click the Reply To All button (also on the Standard toolbar).

3   Type your response anywhere in the message area.

4   Delete any parts of the original message that you don't need to send back.

5   Click the Send button on the message window's Standard toolbar.

 TIP

> If you modify the original message, Outlook puts your name in square brackets at the leading edge of your changes. For ways to change this behavior, see "Mark My Comments With," on page 62.

You'll notice that if the message is not in Plain Text format, Outlook indents the original message when you either reply or reply to all. Also, Outlook includes the entire original message in the reply. If you'd like to change the way Outlook handles replies, choose the Options command from the Tools menu, click the Preferences tab, click the E-Mail Options button, and then adjust the settings in the E-Mail Options dialog box. You can set up Outlook so that original messages are not indented in your replies. You can also choose to exclude the original messages from your replies, or you can opt for including them as attachments rather than text. In addition, you can select different font effects for your replies. For details about these options, see "Using the Preferences Tab," on page 58.

 TIP

> Too often, people simply add their comments to a message they've received and then reply to all. After half a dozen replies to everyone, the message gets quite long. Most of this extra baggage isn't really necessary, so it's best to throw it away. Keep the message short and crisp for the sake of your hard disk, the e-mail system's performance, and your recipients.

Replying Through Voting Buttons

When you receive a network message that contains voting buttons, simply click the button that corresponds to your vote. Outlook displays a dialog box asking whether you want to send the response now or edit your response first.

If you select Send The Response Now, Outlook immediately sends the message without opening a reply form. The message arrives with your response inserted in front of the original Subject line, for example, *Approve: Special Offer.*

If you select Edit The Response Before Sending, Outlook opens a reply message addressed to the proper e-mail address and with the Subject line included. You can add additional comments if you like. Then click the Send button to send your reply. The message arrives with your response inserted in front of the original Subject line and your comments placed in the message area.

Replying to a Message Flag

When you receive a message with a flag and a due date, you can easily record your response to the flag when you've finished taking the action the flag requests:

1 Open the message.

2 Click the Flag button on the Standard toolbar.

3 Turn on the Completed option in the Flag For Follow-Up dialog box.

4 Click OK.

The flag area of the message displays the date on which you marked the action completed. You now have a record that you can store in an Outlook folder.

> ℹ Follow up by Wednesday, December 10, 1997 5:00 PM.
> Completed on Thursday, November 27, 1997 11:53 AM.

Forwarding a Message

❓ SEE ALSO

To set up Outlook to automatically forward messages of interest, see "Rules Wizard," on page 45.

Let's say someone has sent you a really important message. You think that other people might want or need the information in the message, even though they weren't originally recipients. In this case, you can forward the message to other interested parties.

To forward a message, follow these steps:

1 Select the message line in the message list, or open the message.

2 Click the Forward button on the message window Standard toolbar.

3 In the To box, add the names of those who should receive the message. Remember that you can use group names, too. (See "Using Personal Distribution Lists," on page 175, for information about personal groups.)

4 If you want to add your own remarks to the message, type them anywhere in the message area. You can use text formatting just as you can for a new message.

5 Delete any parts of the original message that you don't need to send on.

6 Click the Send button.

⭐ TIP

> If you modify an original message that is not in Plain Text format, Outlook puts your name in square brackets at the leading edge of your changes. For ways to change this, see "Mark My Comments With," on page 62.

II

Electronic Mail

Saving Messages in Files

Even though Outlook automatically saves a copy of your messages in the Sent Items folder, there may be a message that is so important or useful that you'll also want to save it in a file that you can open in another application.

To save a message in a file, do this:

1 Select the message from the message list, or open the message. You can save several messages in the same file by selecting all of them in the message list at the same time.

2 Choose Save As from the File menu to open the Save As dialog box.

3 If you select a single message, Outlook creates a name for the file by using the Subject line of the message. If you select more than one message, you need to enter a name for the file in the File Name box. You can select a different disk or select a different folder if you want by using the Save In box.

4 In the Save As Type box, select the format for the file you want to save.

5 Click the Save button.

 NOTE

If you are saving more than one message, Text Only will be the only format available. It will save the text of your messages but not the formatting.

Saving Message Attachments

When you receive a message with an attachment that is a file, you might decide that you want to save the attachment. If a message has more than one file attached, you can save one, some, or all of the files. You can open and save attachments from either the message list or from the open message window.

Saving Attachments from the Message List

In the message list, attachments are indicated by a paper clip icon next to the message name, and you'll see a paper clip above the Preview Pane, if you have it displayed. To see what files are attached, click the icon in the Preview Pane, which shows the names and sizes of the attached files.

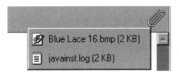

Click the filename that you want to open to see the Opening Mail Attachment dialog box. This dialog box will not appear, by the way, for some types of files, such as text and audio files—instead the file will be opened immediately.

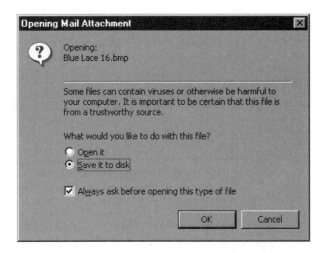

 NOTE

You may also see a paper clip icon next to the message name if the message contains a graphic or stationery background, even when it is not an attachment.

Click Save It To Disk to store the file in a location of your choice.

What happens when you click Open It depends on the type of file. Files such as Word documents and Excel worksheets are opened in their respective applications. Media files, such as audio and video files, are played.

You can also choose to save all or some of the files attached to a message using the File menu. With this technique, however, you won't see the Opening Mail Attachment dialog box. Here's how.

1 Select the message in the message list. A message with an attachment shows a paper clip icon on its message line.

2 Choose Save Attachments from the File menu.

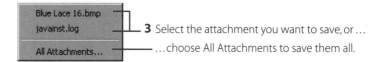

3 Select the attachment you want to save, or …

…choose All Attachments to save them all.

4 If you choose to save one attachment, you'll see the Save Attachment dialog box, where you can select the location and filename for the attachment.

5 To save additional individual attachments, repeat steps 1 through 4. If you choose to save all attachments, Outlook displays the Save All Attachments dialog box:

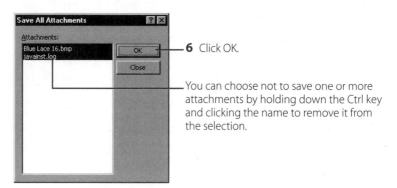

6 Click OK.

You can choose not to save one or more attachments by holding down the Ctrl key and clicking the name to remove it from the selection.

7 Select the folder where you want to store the attachment files.

8 Click OK.

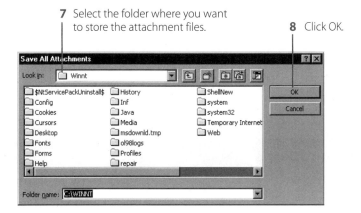

Saving Attachments from the Message Window

When you open a message by double-clicking it, attachments included with it are shown as icons below the message text.

Double-click an icon to display the Opening Mail Attachment dialog box, and then choose to open or save the attachment. If a message has multiple attachments, choose Save Attachments from the File menu to display the Save All Attachments dialog box. Hold down the Ctrl key and deselect any of the attachments that you do not want to save, and then click OK. Next choose the folder where you want to save the attachments, and then click OK.

Managing Junk Mail

As Internet e-mail becomes increasingly popular, you may receive a greater amount of junk e-mail, or *spam* as it is often called. Junk e-mail is any unsolicited messages about sales, offers, Web sites, or adult content. If left unmanaged, junk e-mail can quickly clog your Inbox.

Outlook lets you build a list of junk mail addresses—the e-mail addresses of persons or companies whose messages you identify as junk mail. You can automatically delete this e-mail, channel it into a special folder, or mark it with an identifying color on the message list.

II

Electronic Mail

For another way to
add a junk e-mailer's
address to the list, see
"Managing the Junk
and Adult Content
Senders Lists," on the
next page.

To place a sender's address on the junk mail list, follow these steps:

1 Right-click a message from the sender in the Inbox.

2 Point to Junk E-Mail on the shortcut menu and then choose either
Add To Junk Senders List or Add To Adult Content Senders List.

Channeling Junk and Adult Content Mail

One way to channel junk mail is by creating a rule in Rules Wizard.
The rule would instruct Outlook to look for incoming mail from persons on the junk mail list and perform some action on it, such as deleting the mail or moving it to a certain folder.

You can also channel junk mail using the Organize button by following
these steps.

1 Click the Inbox folder.

2 Click the Organize button on the Standard toolbar.

3 Click Junk E-Mail.

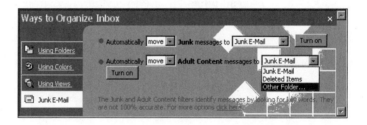

4 Select the types of mail you wish to move by choosing Move from
the first box on each line.

5 Open each folder list and select Junk E-Mail, Deleted Items, or
Other Folder.

6 You can refine the junk e-mail rules and download updated filters
by clicking the *click here* link.

7 Click Turn ON to activate the movement of the e-mail to the
selected folders. (The button changes to Turn OFF. Click on it if you
no longer want to channel junk e-mail to the designated folder.)

8 If you do not yet have a Junk E-Mail folder, Outlook will ask if
you want to create it. Select Yes to create the folder at that time.

The Junk E-Mail folder is not automatically added to the Outlook Bar, but it will be included in the Folder list.

9 Click the Close box on the Organize pane to remove it from the Inbox.

> If Outlook treats mail that you want to receive as junk mail, use the *click here* link to channel the mail to another location.

Color Coding Junk and Adult Content Mail

Rather than move or delete junk e-mail, you can choose to display it in a special color to set it apart from other mail.

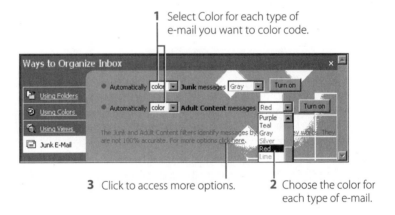

1 Select Color for each type of e-mail you want to color code.

3 Click to access more options.

2 Choose the color for each type of e-mail.

Managing the Junk and Adult Content Senders Lists

Rather than wait until you receive a message, you may want to add an address to the Junk Senders list or the Adult Content Senders list pre-emptively. You might also want to remove an address from one of the lists if you decide that the sender's messages might have some value after all.

To manage your junk e-mailers you have to display the Edit Junk Senders dialog box. Follow these steps:

1 Click the Inbox folder.

2 Click the Organize button on the Standard toolbar.

3   Click Junk E-Mail.

4   Click *click here*.

5   Click Edit Junk Senders and choose from these actions:

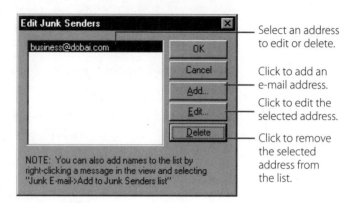

Select an address to edit or delete.

Click to add an e-mail address.

Click to edit the selected address.

Click to remove the selected address from the list.

6   Click OK to finish.

To manage the Adult Content Senders list, click Edit Adult Content Senders in step 5 above.

Getting the Facts About Fax

For details about setting up fax service as part of an existing profile or as a separate profile, see "Adding Fax Service to a Profile," on page 13.

One of the services you can add to your Outlook profiles is the ability to send and receive faxes. You can also set up a separate profile that you use only for faxes. The rest of this chapter describes the following procedures for using the Microsoft Fax service in Outlook:

■ Setting fax options

■ Adding fax addresses to your address book and Contacts folder

■ Sending a fax

■ Receiving a fax and retrieving a fax from a fax service

Remember, you'll know that Outlook is set up to send and receive faxes if the fax machine icon is in the system tray on the right side of the Windows taskbar.

Setting Fax Options

Most of the time, the faxes you send will be in a standard setup. (For exceptions, you can change the setup as you prepare a specific fax—see step 8 in "Sending a Fax," on page 163.) Although Outlook's default options for faxes might be just fine for your needs, you might want to review them. In particular, you'll want to check the setup of dialing and modem options.

> **NOTE**
>
> There are numerous programs available to provide fax capability to Windows and Windows programs. In this chapter, we discuss Microsoft Fax, which is supplied with Windows 95.

Here are the general steps for setting standard fax options:

1 Point to Microsoft Fax Tools on the Tools menu and choose Options from the submenu.

2 In the Microsoft Fax Properties dialog box, click the tab that contains the options you want to set—Message, Dialing, Modem, or User.

3 Set the options as appropriate on each tab—consult the specific instructions in the following sections.

4 When you've finished setting options, click OK.

Setting Message Options

On the Message tab of the Microsoft Fax Properties dialog box, shown in Figure 4-6, on the next page, you can select the time when you want Outlook to send your faxes, you can choose a standard message format, and you can set up a standard cover page. The following sections explain the various options on this tab.

Time To Send.   You can designate a time when Outlook should normally send your faxes.

- When you select the As Soon As Possible option, Outlook sends the fax right away if you're using a network-connected fax service and you're connected to the network. Outlook also sends the fax

II

Electronic Mail

FIGURE 4-6.

The Message tab of the Microsoft Fax Properties dialog box.

Select when to send faxes.

Turn off the cover page, select a different style, or click Browse to locate a different cover page style.

Select the message format.

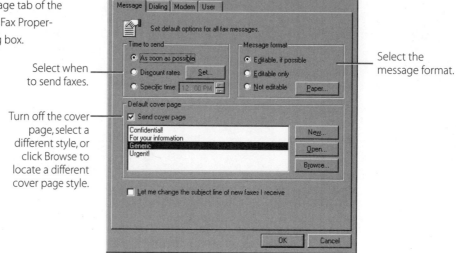

right away if you're working offline with a profile that has no online services but you have a fax modem in your computer. If you're working offline with a profile that includes an online service, Outlook sends the fax as soon as you connect to the online service that handles faxes.

■ When you select the Discount Rates option, Outlook sends faxes only during the hours when your telephone rates are discounted. To set the hours of discounted rates, click the Set button.

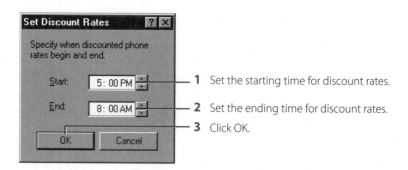

1 Set the starting time for discount rates.

2 Set the ending time for discount rates.

3 Click OK.

■ When you select the Specific Time option, Outlook holds faxes until the time you set in the box.

Message Format. You can decide whether you want recipients to be able to edit most of your faxes. To be editable, your fax must be sent to another computer. If most of your faxes are sent to paper fax machines, you'll want to choose the Not Editable option; choose the Editable Only option if you send most faxes to computers. The Editable, If Possible option sends the fax in editable format if it goes to a computer but otherwise sends it as not editable.

To set the paper setting for your faxes, follow these steps:

1 Click the Paper button.

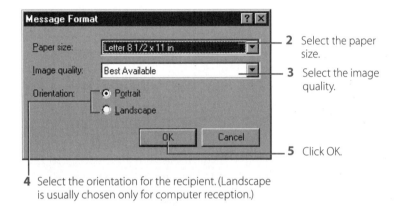

2 Select the paper size.

3 Select the image quality.

5 Click OK.

4 Select the orientation for the recipient. (Landscape is usually chosen only for computer reception.)

Default Cover Page. If you don't want to send cover pages with your faxes, turn off the Send Cover Page option. If you do want to send cover pages with your faxes, turn on the Send Cover Page option and select the style of cover page. The Confidential, For Your Information, and Urgent styles add these labels to the fax cover page.

You can create a new cover page (New button), change the design of the four listed cover pages (Open button), or choose a different cover page that's stored on a disk (Browse button):

- When you click the New button, Outlook starts the Fax Cover Page Editor with a blank sheet on which you can design your own cover page.

- When you click the Open button, Outlook starts the Fax Cover Page Editor and opens the cover page you selected in the list. You can then rearrange it to suit your needs and save it when you're done.

Electronic Mail

■ Click the Browse button to locate and open a cover page file not listed, such as one stored on a network server.

> If someone gives you a fax cover page file, copy it to the folder in which Windows is installed. That's where Outlook looks for cover page files when you open the Microsoft Fax Properties dialog box. If you want to remove a fax cover page from the list in this dialog box, move the file to a folder other than the Windows folder.

Let Me Change The Subject Line Of New Faxes I Receive. If you receive faxes on your computer, you might want to change the subject line of an incoming fax to make the subject line more descriptive of an action you must take or a point you want to note. The subject line appears in the folder items list of the folder where you keep the fax. If you want to be able to change the subject line of incoming faxes, turn on the option labeled Let Me Change The Subject Line Of New Faxes I Receive.

Setting Dialing Options

On the Dialing tab of the Microsoft Fax Properties dialog box, shown in Figure 4-7, you can set up the locations from which you send faxes, create a list of telephone numbers with toll prefixes, and specify how Outlook should handle retries when a fax doesn't go through on the first attempt.

FIGURE 4-7.
The Dialing tab of the Microsoft Fax Properties dialog box.

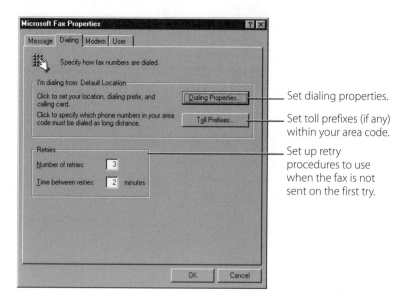

Set dialing properties.

Set toll prefixes (if any) within your area code.

Set up retry procedures to use when the fax is not sent on the first try.

Dialing Properties. When you need to set or change the standard dialing properties, click the Dialing Properties button to open the Dialing Properties dialog box:

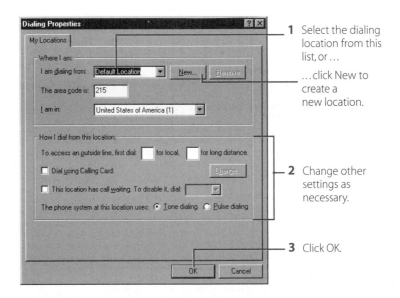

1 Select the dialing location from this list, or …

…click New to create a new location.

2 Change other settings as necessary.

3 Click OK.

SEE ALSO

For details about changing your calling card settings from the Dialing Properties dialog box, see "Setting Up Calling Card Dialing," on page 284.

If you dial a network or other e-mail or fax service from the same telephone all the time, you need to set up only one location. If you dial from several telephones, you need to set up a location for each telephone from which the dialing is different.

To create a new location for dialing, click the New button in the Dialing Properties dialog box. In the Create New Location dialog box, type the location name, and then click OK to return to the Dialing Properties dialog box, where you can set up the properties for the new location.

Toll Prefixes. Some telephone area codes cover a very compact geographical area in which all the prefixes can be called toll free. Other telephone area codes cover a wide geographical area in which only a few prefixes might be toll free. If the area code from which you send your faxes contains prefixes that aren't toll free from your location, you can provide a list of the prefixes that require dialing the area code first.

1 Click the Toll Prefixes button on the Dialing tab of the Microsoft Fax Properties dialog box.

II

Electronic Mail

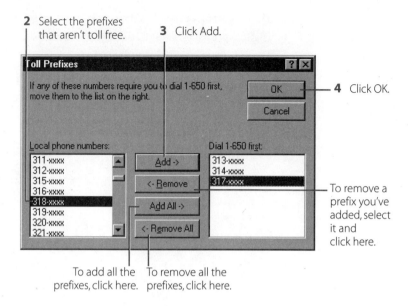

2 Select the prefixes that aren't toll free.

3 Click Add.

4 Click OK.

To remove a prefix you've added, select it and click here.

To add all the prefixes, click here.   To remove all the prefixes, click here.

 **TIP**

If you can call toll free to only a few prefixes in your area code, click Add All in the Toll Prefixes dialog box, and then remove the few prefixes that you *can* call toll free.

Retries.   A fax doesn't always reach its destination on the first attempt—possible problems include a busy line, a faulty connection, or a faulty or missing fax machine. You can decide how many times Outlook should try to get your fax through to the recipient—simply set the number in the Number Of Retries box on the Dialing tab. You can also decide how long you want Outlook to wait between retries. Because the most common problem with sending a fax is probably a busy line, you might want to wait the two minutes initially set up in Outlook.

Setting Modem Options

The Modem tab of the Microsoft Fax Properties dialog box, shown in Figure 4-8, lets you select the modem Outlook will use for faxes and set the options for that modem.

FIGURE 4-8.

The Modem tab of the Microsoft Fax Properties dialog box.

Select the modem to use for faxes.

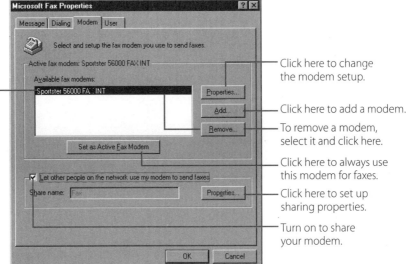

Click here to change the modem setup.

Click here to add a modem.

To remove a modem, select it and click here.

Click here to always use this modem for faxes.

Click here to set up sharing properties.

Turn on to share your modem.

II

Electronic Mail

Adjusting Modem Properties

You can set up your modem to answer incoming calls, and you can adjust the modem speaker volume and set your call preferences. To set modem properties, select the modem from the list on the Modem tab, and click the Properties button. You can then change the settings in the Fax Modem Properties dialog box, shown in Figure 4-9, on the next page.

In this dialog box, you can specify how your modem should answer incoming calls:

- If you use your telephone line primarily for fax reception and you want your computer fax modem to automatically answer every incoming call, select the Answer After option and set the number of rings the fax modem should allow before it answers. If you use the line only for faxes, you can set the number of rings to one. The standard setting of three rings gives you a chance to answer in case you occasionally receive voice calls on this line. This setting also ensures that you're not receiving a single-ring call made in error.

FIGURE 4-9.
The Fax Modem Prop-
erties dialog box.

Select the type of
answering you want.

Turn on to silence the modem after
connecting; turn off to listen during transmission.

Set the modem speaker volume.

Turn this option
off if you're using
a shared network
modem that
collects and
sends faxes.

Fax Modem Properties

Answer mode
○ Answer after [3] rings
○ Manual
◉ Don't answer

Speaker volume
Off   Loud
☑ Turn off after connected

OK
Cancel
Advanced...

Call preferences
☑ Wait for dial tone before dialing
☑ Hang up if busy tone
After dialing, wait [60] seconds for answer

Turn on to hang up
when the line is
busy; turn off to
stay connected.

Specify how long Outlook
should wait for the
recipient modem to answer.

Click here for
advanced options.

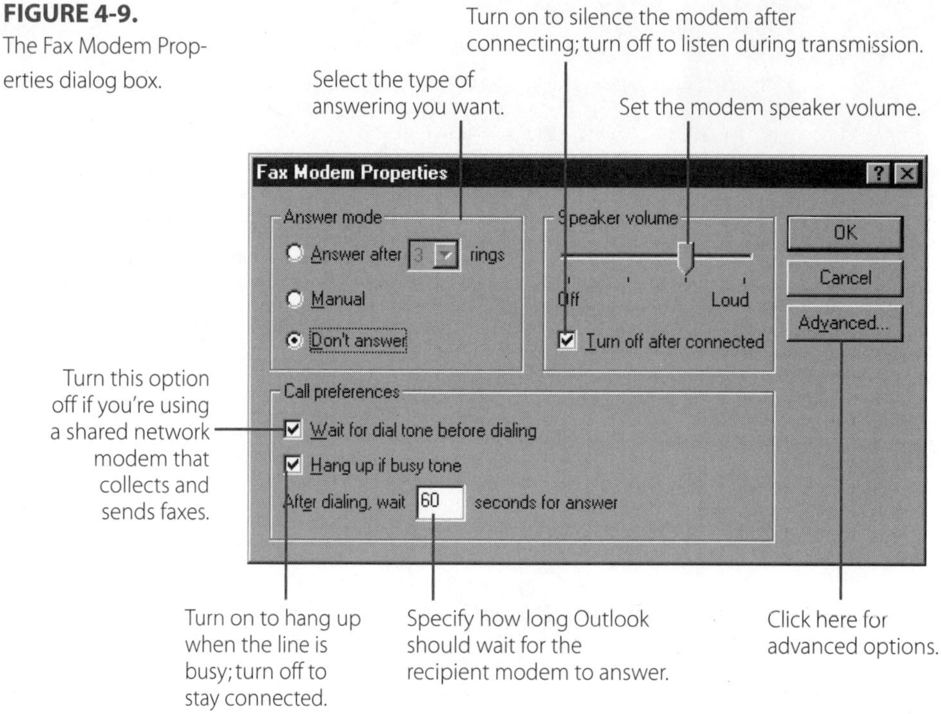

■ If you use your telephone line for both voice and fax and you
want to manually switch on fax reception, select the Manual
option. When a call comes in and you hear the fax warble, click
the Answer Now button in the Microsoft Fax Status window. (See
"Receiving a Fax," on page 165.)

■ If you don't want your computer to answer a telephone line at all,
select the Don't Answer option. You should select this option if
you receive your faxes from a fax service or a stand-alone fax
machine rather than directly through you computer.

Clicking the Advanced button in the Fax Modem Properties dialog box
displays a dialog box in which you can set more options for fax transmission and reception:

Turn on this option if you can't reliably send or receive faxes at speeds higher than 9600 bits per second (bps).

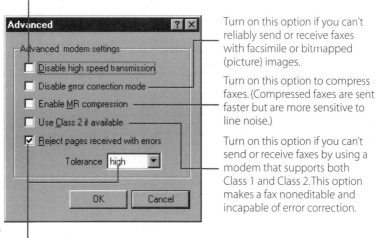

Turn on this option if you can't reliably send or receive faxes with facsimile or bitmapped (picture) images.

Turn on this option to compress faxes. (Compressed faxes are sent faster but are more sensitive to line noise.)

Turn on this option if you can't send or receive faxes by using a modem that supports both Class 1 and Class 2. This option makes a fax noneditable and incapable of error correction.

Turn off this option if you don't care about receiving errors. If you turn it on, set the degree of error tolerance—High permits more errors than Low.

Adding a new modem.   If the modem you want to use is not listed on the Modem tab of the Microsoft Fax Properties dialog box, you can add it. You can add either a local modem (a modem in your computer or attached to it) or a network modem.

To add a modem, take these steps:

1 Click the Add button on the Modem tab to open the Add A Fax Modem dialog box.

2 Select a local modem or a network fax server.

3 Click OK.

4 If you selected a local fax modem, work through the Install New Modem Wizard. If you selected a network fax server, type the share name of the modem and click OK.

Sharing properties.   If your organization has fewer modems than computers, you might need to share your modem with others. When your modem is shared, the people to whom you give the proper permissions can send their faxes through your modem.

To share your modem, follow these steps:

1 On the Modem tab of the Fax Properties dialog box, turn on the option labeled Let Other People On The Network Use My Modem To Send Faxes.

2 Click the Properties button to set up sharing. Outlook displays the NetFax dialog box. (The first time you share your modem, Outlook first displays the Select Drive dialog box. In this dialog box, select the drive on which you will share your modem, and then click OK.)

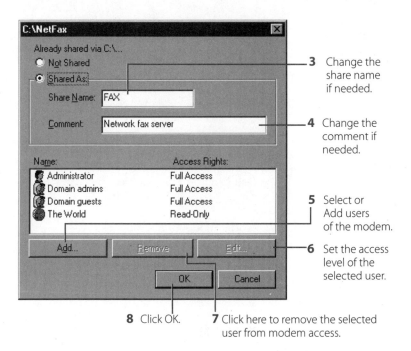

3 Change the share name if needed.

4 Change the comment if needed.

5 Select or Add users of the modem.

6 Set the access level of the selected user.

8 Click OK.

7 Click here to remove the selected user from modem access.

Setting User Options

On the User tab of the Microsoft Fax Properties dialog box, shown in Figure 4-10, on page 162, you set up your sender information. Note that the entries you supply can appear on your fax cover sheet and can be used by recipients as your return fax address.

Sending a Fax

When you've set up your fax service and modem, you're ready to send a fax. You have two ways to do this—by using Outlook's Compose

Fax Addresses

In Outlook you have three ways to set up a fax address, two of them in your address book and one on the spot. You can add a fax number to an e-mail address in your Personal Address Book or to a contact entry in your Contacts folder, which becomes an entry in the Outlook Address Book. For information about setting up entries in your address books, see "Adding Someone," on page 171, and "Setting Up Your Contact List," on page 408.

Follow these steps to set up a fax address in your Personal Address Book:

1 Choose Address Book from the Tools menu.

2 In the Address Book dialog box, select Personal Address Book from the Show Names From The box, and then click the New Entry button.

3 In the New Entry dialog box, select Other Address from the list and click OK.

4 Fill out the New Address tab, following the example of the one shown here:

5 Type the recipient's name.

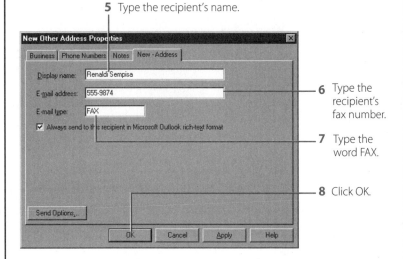

6 Type the recipient's fax number.

7 Type the word FAX.

8 Click OK.

Depending on how you set up Outlook, the New Entry dialog box may include the type FAX. If so, choose that type rather than Other Address, and then add the recipient's name and fax number in the New Address tab.

To address a fax on the spot, fill in the name and telephone number in the second Compose New Fax Wizard panel, as explained in "Sending a Fax," beginning on the previous page.

Electronic Mail

FIGURE 4-10.

The User tab of the Microsoft Fax Properties dialog box.

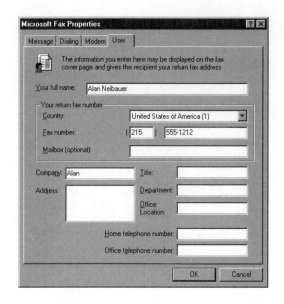

? SEE ALSO

For details about settings you might want to adjust through the Dialing Properties button and the Options button in the Compose New Fax Wizard, see "Setting Message Options," on page 126, and "Setting Dialing Options," on page 154.

New Fax Wizard or by addressing a message to a fax recipient from your address book and clicking Send.

The Compose New Fax Wizard lets you send a cover page with a note and attached files. Here are the steps for using the wizard:

1   Choose New Fax from the Actions menu. Outlook starts the Compose New Fax Wizard.

2   Click the Dialing Properties button if you need to change your dialing location or how your call is dialed.

3   Click Next.

4   On the second panel of the wizard, type the recipient's name in the To box, and select the appropriate country from the drop-down list. Type the recipient's fax number, and turn on the Dial Area Code option if needed. Then click the Add To List button. (Note that when you click the Add To List button, Outlook sets up a fax address in your Personal Address Book.) Repeat these steps for each recipient if the fax is being sent to several people. (Alternatively, you can click the Address Book button to select names of recipients.)

5   Click Next.

6 Choose whether to include a cover page.

7 Select a style for the cover page, if appropriate.

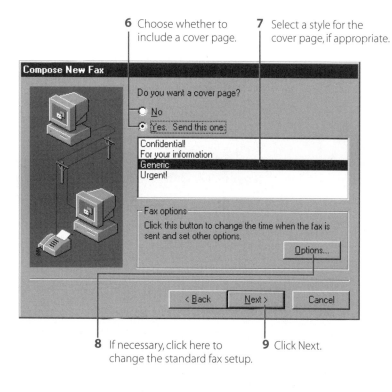

8 If necessary, click here to change the standard fax setup.

9 Click Next.

10 Type a subject line.

11 Type a note (optional). This could be the entire message.

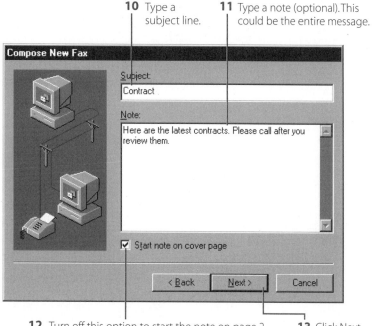

12 Turn off this option to start the note on page 2, turn on to start the note on the cover page.

13 Click Next.

14 On this panel of the wizard, you can add a file to the fax by clicking the Add File button. Select the file you want to include and click Open. Repeat this procedure for each file that you want to send in your fax. The files will appear as icons in your message.

15 Click Next.

16 On the Finish panel of the Compose New Fax Wizard, click the Finish button.

To send a fax using the message window, you must have the recipients set up with a fax address in your address book. (See the sidebar "Fax Addresses," on page 161, for information about how to do this.)

First open a new message, and then follow these steps:

1 Click the To button, select the address book you need from the Show Names From The box, and then select the fax recipient or recipients from the address book. Click OK in the Select Names dialog box.

2 In the message window, enter a subject and a message as you would for a regular e-mail message. You can format the message and add attachments as you can for other messages. When you've finished composing the fax message, click the Send button.

3 You'll see the Microsoft Fax Status dialog box, informing you of the status of the fax as Outlook prepares the fax message, initiates the fax modem, and then sends the fax.

> **NOTE**
>
> To quickly create a fax address from within the message window, choose the Fax Addressing Wizard from the Tools menu. Enter the recipient's name and fax number, click Add To List, and then click Finish.

Checking the Status of Outgoing Faxes

If you set up a number of faxes to send, you might want to know which fax is being sent and how many more are in the fax queue. To check the status of outgoing faxes, do the following:

1 Point to Microsoft Fax Tools on the Tools menu, and choose Show Outgoing Faxes to see a list of outgoing faxes.

2 To cancel an outgoing fax, select it from the list and then choose Cancel Fax on the File menu.

Receiving a Fax

You can set up Outlook to receive faxes in your Inbox. Before you can receive faxes, however, you must perform the following two actions:

- Set up your modem to answer incoming calls by selecting one of the Answer Mode options in the Fax Modem Properties dialog box. (See "Setting Modem Options," on page 156.)

- Decide whether you want to be able to change the subject line of the faxes you receive. On the Message tab of the Microsoft Fax Properties dialog box, turn on (or off) the option labeled Let Me Change The Subject Line Of New Faxes I Receive. (See "Setting Message Options," on 151.)

If you usually have Outlook set up to receive faxes and you want to discontinue doing so, select Don't Answer as your Answer Mode option.

After you complete these two actions, you're ready to receive a fax. How you do this depends on the Answer Mode option you've chosen:

- If you selected the Answer After option, simply let Outlook answer the call and receive the fax.

- If you selected the Manual option, when a call comes in and you hear the fax warble in the handset, click the Answer Now button in the Microsoft Fax Status window and hang up the handset.

TIP

If the Microsoft Fax Status window is not visible when the telephone rings, click the Fax icon at the right end of the Windows taskbar.

Received faxes appear in your Inbox, just as e-mail messages do. You can then treat the faxes just as you treat any folder item in Outlook.

Electronic Mail

Retrieving a Fax from a Service

If you have your faxes sent to a fax service instead of directly to your computer, you can request that the service send your faxes to you. To request faxes from your fax service, follow these steps:

1 Point to Microsoft Fax Tools on the Tools menu, and then choose Request A Fax from the submenu. You'll see the first panel of the Request A Fax Wizard.

2 Select this option to retrieve all available faxes, or ...

... select this option to request a specific fax, and then type the title and password (if applicable).

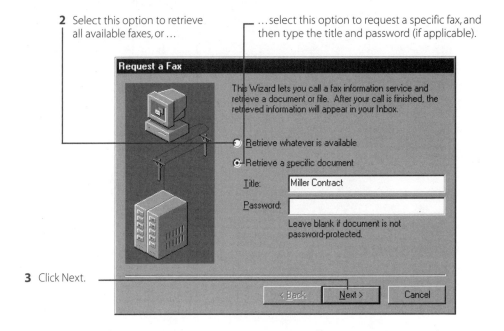

3 Click Next.

4 Type the name of the fax service in the To box, and select the appropriate country from the drop-down list. Type the fax service's fax number, and then click the Add button. (Alternatively, you can click the Address Book button to select names.)

5 Click Next.

6 Select the time you want Outlook to send the request.

7 Click Next.

8 Click the Finish button.

9 When the faxes arrive, receive the faxes as described in "Receiving a Fax," on the previous page.

CHAPTER 5

Mucking About in Address Books

I f you're like most users of Microsoft Outlook 98, you have more than one address book. First and foremost, you have organizational address books—one for the entire organization (called the Global Address List), one for your department (your network domain), possibly some for other departments (other network domains), and perhaps an Offline Address Book. Second, you have your Personal Address Book, in which you keep the names and addresses of the groups and people to whom you send e-mail most often. (If your Outlook setup does not include a Personal Address Book, you can add one—see the sidebar "Adding a Personal Address Book to Your Profile," on page 169).

You can also have the Outlook Address Book, which is created automatically from entries in your Contacts folder for which you've included an e-mail address or a fax number. And finally, you can also have a separate address book for each online service you use to send and receive e-mail. For example, if you use MSN (the Microsoft Network), you can have a separate address book for your MSN e-mail account.

 NOTE

What's a network domain? It's a collection of computers and users that share a common database and a common security policy.

Opening an Address Book

Who'd have ever thought that adults would need directions for opening an address book? How hard can it be? Actually, it's not hard at all, once you know where to go and what to do.

To open an address book, simply choose Address Book on the Tools menu, or click the Address Book button on the Standard toolbar when the Inbox, Outbox, Sent Items, or Drafts folder is open. Outlook displays the names that are in your default address book.

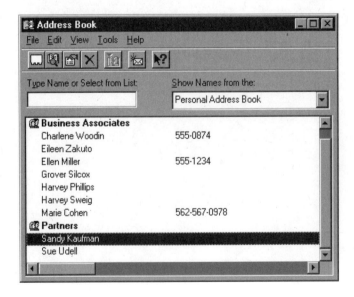

Adding a Personal Address Book to Your Profile

If you want to add a Personal Address Book to the profile you are using, follow these steps:

1 Choose Services on the Tools menu.

2 On the Services tab, click the Add button.

3 In the Add Service To Profile dialog box, select Personal Address Book, and then click OK.

4 In the Personal Address Book dialog box, enter a name for the Personal Address Book in the Name box.

5 In the Path box, enter the path of the Personal Address Book file, or click the Browse button to locate a Personal Address Book file that already exists.

6 Click OK in the Personal Address Book dialog box, and then click OK again in the message box that appears.

7 Click OK in the Services dialog box, and then exit and restart Outlook.

To add a Personal Address Book to a profile other than the one you are currently using, double-click the Mail icon on the Windows Control Panel. On the Services tab, click Show Profiles. On the General tab, click the profile you want in the Profile box, click Properties, and then follow steps 2 through 7 above.

II

Electronic Mail

Switching Address Books

When you have more than one address book, some names and addresses might not be included in all of them. You'll sometimes need to switch between address books to find the person you want to contact with e-mail or a fax.

To switch address books, do the following:

1 Choose Address Book on the Tools menu, or click the Address Book button on the Standard toolbar.

2 Click the Show Names From The box. From the drop-down list, select the address book you want to open.

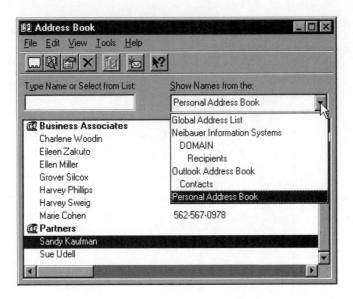

The names contained in the selected address book appear in the window.

Finding People

Even if you have only one or two address books, the number of names an address book can hold can make finding a certain person time-consuming and even tiresome. You need a way to locate a name quickly and efficiently so that you can get on with creating and sending a message and then move on to other tasks. Outlook provides a helpful tool for locating that certain someone easily and quickly.

To find a name in an address book, take these steps:

1 Choose Address Book from the Tools menu, or click the Address Book button on the Standard toolbar.

2 In the Show Names From The box, select the address book you want to look in.

3 Type the beginning of the name in the Type Name Or Select From List box. Outlook jumps to the spot in the list that matches the name you've started to type. You can, of course, simply scroll the list of names in the window to find the name you're looking for.

TIP

> To locate a person without first opening the address book, click Outlook Today in the Outlook Bar, type the name of the person in the Find A Contact text box, and then click Go to open the person's address book entry. If Outlook cannot locate a match, it displays the Check Names dialog box.

Adding Someone

When you first start using Outlook, your address books will contain a standard list of people within your organization or members of an online service. You can, of course, simply type an e-mail address in each message you send, but e-mail addresses are singularly weird. It's really hard to remember them. Consider, for example, a traditional CompuServe address: nine numbers with a comma in the middle. And you have no way of knowing who the heck resides behind some random number. On most other online services, people can select their own "handle"—or unique identification— which seldom looks anything like their legal name.

To avoid confusion, to reduce memorization, and to make sure you use the correct e-mail address every time, you should add names and addresses to your Personal Address Book or to your Outlook Contacts folder.

You can add new names, change names, and remove names as often as you want, and an electronic address book is much easier to keep straight than a paper address book. No ugly erasures, no running out of space. And your Personal Address Book—as well as all the other address books you use—can help you find names in many different ways.

NOTE

> You can add new names only to your Personal Address Book. Only e-mail administrators can add names to organizational address books. To add names to your Outlook Address Book, you must add names to your Contacts folder. For details, see "Setting Up Your Contact List," on page 408.

To add a name and address to your Personal Address Book, do the following:

1 Choose Address Book on the Tools menu, or click the Address Book button on the Standard toolbar.

Electronic Mail

New Entry

2 Click the New Entry button on the Address Book toolbar.

3 Select the type of address you want to add.

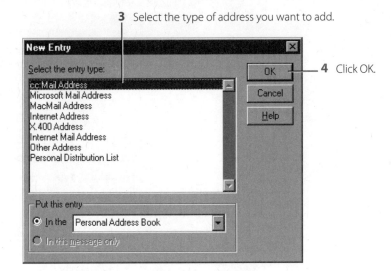

4 Click OK.

5 The next dialog box you see depends on the type of entry you selected in the New Entry dialog box. For most new entries, you'll enter information such as the name to display in the address book and the e-mail address. The following example is based on selecting Other Address.

6 Type the name to show in the address book (required).

7 Type the e-mail address (required); for example, alann@worldnet.-att.net.

8 Type the designation for the e-mail system. SMTP is a common format for Internet e-mail.

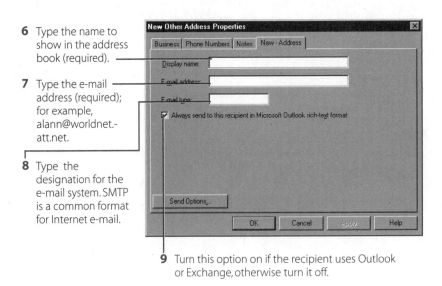

9 Turn this option on if the recipient uses Outlook or Exchange, otherwise turn it off.

10 Fill in the boxes on the other tabs with as much information as you want. For example, the Business tab provides boxes for addresses and a phone number. The Phone Numbers tab contains boxes for various phone numbers, including a box for the person's fax number. If you want to send a fax to this person, be sure to enter the fax number.

11 When you finish filling out the tabs, click OK.

Note that if you use the Other Address entry type to set up a fax number for an entry in your address book, you should type the fax number in the E-Mail Address box (step 7) and type *FAX* in the E-Mail Type box (step 8). If your system offers a Fax type, however, choose that when setting up a fax address.

When you add a name and address, Outlook requires only that you fill in the boxes on the initial tab. You can leave the other tabs blank and

---

Copying an Address to the Personal Address Book

You can easily add to the Personal Address Book an address already in another address book, such as Contacts or the Outlook Address Book. Just follow these steps:

1 Choose Address Book on the Tools menu, or click the Address Book button on the Standard toolbar.

2 Select the address book containing the name you want to add from the Show Names From The list.

3 Click the name in the list.

4 Click the Add to Personal Address Book button on the Address Book toolbar.

5 Close the Address Book dialog box. The listing is now duplicated in the Personal Address Book.

If you already have an address card open from the Contacts folder, there may be a button labeled Add To Personal Address Book on the General tab. Click that button to copy the listing to the Personal Address Book.

Properties

fill them in later by double-clicking on the name in the Address Book dialog box, or by using the Properties button on the Address Book toolbar. Clicking the Properties button displays the same dialog box that you saw after you clicked OK in the New Entry dialog box.

> You can send meeting requests to other users of Outlook and have them respond to accept or decline the invitation. To send such requests over the Internet, create an address book listing by selecting the Other Address type in step 3 above, and make sure the option labeled Always Send To This Recipient In Microsoft Outlook Rich-Text Format is turned on, as discussed in step 9 above.

Internet Encoding Methods

When you add an entry to your Personal Address Book, you will often be adding an address for someone with whom you exchange e-mail over the Internet. Depending on your Outlook setup, you can use the Send Options button in the New Address Properties dialog box to select options for how to send messages and attachments to your Internet correspondents.

Turn on to specify encoding.

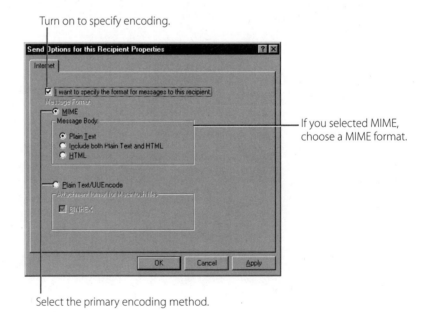

If you selected MIME, choose a MIME format.

Select the primary encoding method.

Different e-mail systems use different encoding methods for sending attachments and formatting across the Internet. These methods allow you to send whole documents, as well as files in other formats, through e-mail. The three most commonly used encoding methods are MIME (Multipurpose Internet Mail Extensions), which allows you to send highly formatted documents; uuencode, which converts binary files to text; and (for Macintosh files only) BINHEX (binary-hexadecimal). The standard encoding method for Outlook is MIME. If an e-mail address in your address book uses uuencode, select that option for the e-mail address.

For addresses that use MIME, you can select various formats for the body of your messages: Plain Text, HTML (Hypertext Markup Language—the encoding for World Wide Web pages), or both.

Using Personal Distribution Lists

Do you know a bunch of people to whom you want to send e-mail regularly? You can create personal groups—also called personal distribution lists. A personal group is a group of e-mail correspondents. You add their names to the personal group, and then when you want to send e-mail to all the members of the group, you simply select or type the group name. Outlook takes care of sending your message to all those lucky people.

Outlook provides the tools you need to create personal groups, to edit a personal group (to add and delete names), to delete personal groups, and to give a personal group a new name.

Creating a Personal Distribution List

Once you've decided to set up a personal group, the steps are pretty easy. You simply name the group, open the address book or books that contain the names you need, and select the names.

Here's how to create a new personal distribution list:

1 Choose Address Book on the Tools menu, or click the Address Book button on the Standard toolbar.

II

Electronic Mail

2 Click the New Entry button on the Address Book toolbar.

3 In the New Entry dialog box, select Personal Distribution List in the Select The Entry Type box, and then click OK.

4 Type a name for your personal group.

5 Click Add/Remove Members.

6 In the Edit Members Of dialog box, shown on the next page, use the Show Names From The box to select the address book containing the names you want to add to this personal group. You can switch to a different address book at any time if you want to add names from several address books. (Note that the title bar of the Edit Members Of dialog box displays the name of the personal distribution list. For example, if the group's name is Business Associates, the title bar shows Edit Members Of Business Associates.)

7 In the box on the left side of the Edit Members Of dialog box, select the names you want to add to the group. To add more than one name at a time, hold down the Ctrl key and click the names.

These names don't have to be listed consecutively. To add several consecutive names, select the first name, hold down the Shift key, and then click the last name. Outlook selects all the names from the first to the last that you clicked.

8 Click the Members button. The selected names now also appear in the Personal Distribution List box.

9 When you've finished adding members to your personal distribution list, click OK in the Edit Members Of dialog box.

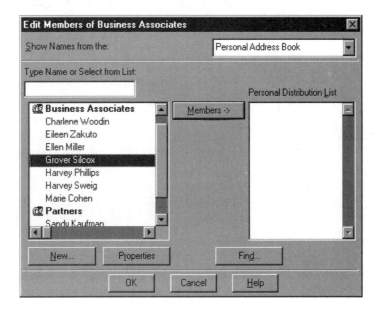

10 In the New Personal Distribution List Properties dialog box, you can click the Notes tab and enter any information that you want about this personal group. When the properties for this new personal distribution list are all set, click OK. The new personal distribution list now appears in your Personal Address Book with a "group" icon next to the name, as shown at the top of the next page.

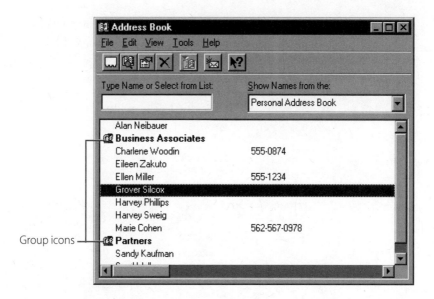

Group icons

★ **TIP**

You can add new names to your Personal Address Book as you're creating a personal distribution list. To do so, click the New button in the Edit Members Of dialog box and follow the steps for "Adding Someone," on page 171. You can also change the information for a person by selecting the name and clicking the Properties button in the Edit Members Of dialog box.

Editing a Personal Distribution List

People come and people go. From time to time, a personal distribution list changes. New people want to be in your club; others want out. (And there may be a few you just want to throw out!) For your personal distribution list to be fully useful all the time, you need to be able to add and remove names.

To add a name to an existing personal distribution list, follow these steps:

1 Choose Address Book on the Tools menu, or click the Address Book button on the Standard toolbar.

2 Select your Personal Address Book.

3 Select the personal distribution list you want to change.

4 Click the Properties button on the Address Book toolbar.

5 Click the Add/Remove Members button.

6 In the Show Names From The box, select the address book that contains the name you want to add, select the name from the Type Name Or Select From List box, and then click the Members button.

7 Click OK.

To remove a name from a personal distribution list, follow these steps:

1 Repeat steps 1 through 5 in the preceding procedure.

2 In the Edit Members Of dialog box, select the name or names you want to remove in the Personal Distribution List box.

3 Press the Delete key. Be sure to delete the extra semicolon and the space that separates the deleted name from the names surrounding it in the list.

4 When you've finished, click OK in the Edit Members Of dialog box, and then click OK in the Properties dialog box.

Deleting a Personal Distribution List

Sometimes groups disband—not even the Beatles lasted forever, though one fears that the Rolling Stones might. When you no longer want or need a personal distribution list, you can remove it from your Personal Address Book.

To delete a personal distribution list, take these steps:

1 Choose Address Book on the Tools menu, or click the Address Book button on the Standard toolbar.

2 Select your Personal Address Book.

3 Select the name of the personal distribution list you're removing, and then click the Delete button on the Address Book toolbar.

4 When Outlook asks whether you want to permanently remove the selected users from the address book, click Yes.

5 Close the address book.

Electronic Mail

> **NOTE**
>
> The individual names of the group members you added from other address books remain in your Personal Address Book after you delete a distribution list. If you want to remove individual names as well, select the names, and then click the Delete button on the Address Book toolbar.

Renaming a Personal Distribution List

Maybe a group changes its colors; maybe a group changes its mind; maybe you just want to use a different group name for whatever reason.

To rename a personal distribution list, do the following:

1 Choose Address Book on the Tools menu, or click the Address Book button on the Standard toolbar.

2 Select your Personal Address Book.

3 Select the group name you want to change.

4 Click the Properties button on the Address Book toolbar.

5 Type the new name of the personal distribution list in the Name box, and then click OK.

CHAPTER 6

Using Outlook Express

O utlook Express is an e-mail and newsreader program provided free with the latest version of Internet Explorer. You'll get Outlook Express with the Internet Explorer CD or when you download the standard or full version of Internet Explorer over the Internet. If you don't think you can get much of a program for free, think again. Outlook Express is a full-featured application that lets you send and receive e-mail over the Internet and subscribe to and trade messages with newsgroups. You can even use it with multiple e-mail accounts or to share a single account with several people. It is really quite a bonus.

You also get the newsreader portion of Outlook Express with Outlook, where it is called the Microsoft Outlook Newsreader. You'll learn how to use the newsreader in Chapter 7, "Communicating with Newsgroups."

Sending and receiving mail in Outlook Express is similar to sending and receiving mail in Outlook itself. So if you've read Chapter 4, "Exchanging Messages and Faxes," you're well on your way to using Outlook Express. Because Outlook Express is different from Outlook in many ways, however, don't skip this chapter even if you're an experienced Outlook user. You may still want to use Outlook Express for your Internet e-mail, and you'll need a basic understanding of how the program works to trade messages with newsgroups.

Setting Up Outlook Express

When you install Microsoft Internet Explorer 4.x on your system, you also get Outlook Express.

> If you already have Microsoft's Internet Mail and Internet News applications on your computer, Outlook Express automatically replaces them when it is installed, removing them from your system. All of your addresses and messages, however, are transferred to Outlook Express.

Outlook Express

To start Outlook Express, double-click its icon on your desktop, or click Start, point to Programs, point to Internet Explorer, and click Outlook Express.

The very first time you start Outlook Express you may have to tell it how to connect to the Internet to check your mail and newsgroups. If you already have a dial-up account established and you've been using it with another Web browser, for example, you can just select the same account. You can also create a new dial-up connection for an existing account, or you can start from scratch and select an Internet provider right online, from the comfort of your own home or office.

If you see the Internet Connection Wizard when you start Outlook Express, click Next in the Wizard box to display the options shown in Figure 6-1.

> Don't worry that you'll select the wrong option. You can access the Internet Connection Wizard again later from within Outlook Express itself.

Make your selection and then click Next. What happens now depends on your choice. For example, if you indicated that you already have an Internet service provider (ISP) and dial-up connection, just click Finish

FIGURE 6-1.

The Internet
Connection Wizard.

Click here if you do not yet have an
Internet account with an ISP.

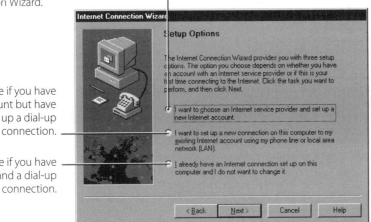

Click here if you have
an account but have
not set up a dial-up
connection.

Click here if you have
an ISP and a dial-up
connection.

in the next Wizard dialog box—you're ready to go. Outlook Express will use the dial-up connection that your system currently uses for Internet shortcuts.

If you indicated that you don't have an Internet account, you'll be taken through a series of steps to choose an online service and create a dial-up connection. While the Internet Connection Wizard lets you choose from a number of popular ISP's, it is better to shop around on your own ahead of time for the best prices and services. You can then install the software provided by the service you select and choose the service for Outlook Express later on. Refer to "Setting Up Accounts," on page 213.

The other option is for users who already have an account with an ISP but who have not yet set up their system to dial in and read e-mail and newsgroup messages. You'll be taken through a series of dialog boxes to select options.

If you choose to establish a dial-up connection, you'll need to know some information. So, check with your ISP and make sure you know the following:

- Your e-mail name, such as alann.

- Your account name, the name you use to log on to your ISP. It may be the same as your e-mail name or it might require an additional prefix, such as internet.usinet.alann.

- Your account password and your e-mail password, which are often the same but not always.

- The incoming (POP) mail server name, such as postoffice.worldnet.att.net or mail.earthlink.net.

- The outgoing (STMP) mail server name, such as mailhost.worldnet.att.net or smtp.best.com.

- The news service name, such as netnews.worldnet.att.net or nntp1.ba.best.com.

- The phone number to dial to reach your ISP. Try to find a local, toll-free number.

 NOTE

> You can change the information in your account and set up multiple accounts. See "Setting Up Accounts," on page 213.

Outlook and Outlook Express

You can have both Outlook and Outlook Express on your computer at the same time, and you can send and receive Internet e-mail with either one. However, because the two programs maintain their own separate set of address books and folders such as the Inbox and Outbox, they are not very good at sharing. While you can import Outlook Express addresses and mail into Outlook, they do not automatically share the information.

If you already have Outlook on your computer when you install Internet Explorer, Outlook—not Outlook Express—will become the default e-mail system used by the browser. This has the advantage of letting you use your current address book and folders whether you start your mail service from Outlook or from Internet Explorer. Each time you run Outlook Express and open the Inbox or Outbox, you'll be asked if you want to make Outlook Express the default mail reader. Click Yes to make it the default or No to continue using Outlook. You can also turn off the option labeled Always Perform This Check When Starting Outlook Express so that you are not asked this question each time you run the program.

You can choose to use Outlook Express as the default e-mail system. When you send mail, however, you won't be able to access your Exchange address book and network messages.

Running Outlook Express

Once you've completed the Internet Connection Wizard and each time you start Outlook Express, you may see the message shown here:

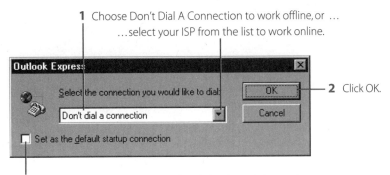

1 Choose Don't Dial A Connection to work offline, or …

…select your ISP from the list to work online.

2 Click OK.

Click here if you do not want to see this dialog box again. You can restore the dialog box using the Options menu.

If you choose to connect, Outlook Express dials up and logs onto to your ISP, but it does not automatically check for new mail or send mail from your Outbox.

Now let's take a look at the Outlook Express window, shown in Figure 6-2, on the following page.

Below the menu bar is the toolbar. You use the buttons on the toolbar to create, send, and receive messages, to work with your address book, and to connect to your ISP. The buttons on the toolbar depend on the folder being displayed, but you can create, get, and send mail from any folder in Outlook Express.

 NOTE

> If the Send And Receive button on the toolbar is unavailable, you do not have an Internet account set up.

Like Outlook itself, Outlook Express stores messages in folders, shown in the Folder List on the left side of the window. The folder you choose determines the contents of the larger pane to the right. Just click a folder name to open it.

Electronic Mail

FIGURE 6-2.

The Outlook Express window.

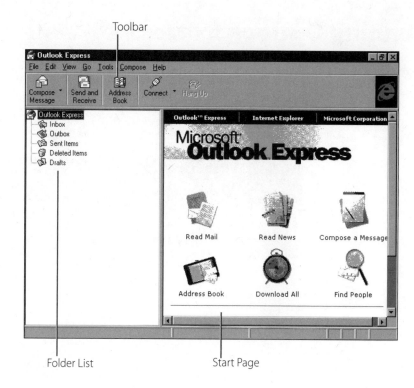

Toolbar

Folder List

Start Page

When you open Outlook Express you'll see the start page. (To return to the start page at any time, click Outlook Express at the top of the Folder List.) The options across the top of the start page let you connect to three sites at Microsoft Corporation to get information on Outlook Express, Internet Explorer, or the Microsoft Corporation itself. Click a button to launch Internet Explorer and move to the Web site.

The other icons on the start page perform these functions:

Read Mail.   Click this to open the Inbox folder so you can read mail that you've already received.

Read News.   Click this to read messages from newsgroups to which you've subscribed.

Compose A Message.   Click this to open a new message window to create e-mail.

Address Book.   Click this to open the Address Book window.

Download All.   Click this to connect to your ISP and download all new mail and news from your mail accounts and subscribed newsgroups.

Find People.   Click this to locate people by searching your address book or by searching popular online e-mail directory services.

If you want Outlook Express to automatically start in the Inbox rather than on this screen, turn on the check box labeled When Starting, Go Directly To My 'Inbox' Folder under the icons. Below that is a handy tip of the day.

Using the Outlook Express Address Book

The address book in Outlook Express is a simpler version of the one in Outlook, but it offers many of the same capabilities. You can, for example, organize addresses into groups and initiate online conferences if Microsoft NetMeeting is installed.

To access the address book, click the Address Book button on the toolbar, or choose Address Book on the Tools menu.

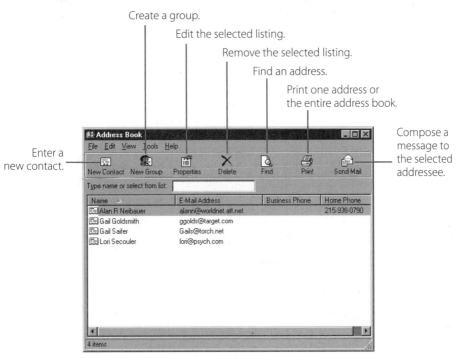

Create a group.

Edit the selected listing.

Remove the selected listing.

Find an address.

Print one address or the entire address book.

Enter a new contact.

Compose a message to the selected addressee.

Setting Up a vCard Reader

If you have Outlook installed as well as Outlook Express, Outlook may be set as the default vCard reader—the program used to display business cards on screen. This means that if you view a business card in Outlook Express, Outlook will actually open and display the card information in the Outlook address book format.

When you open the Outlook Express address book, you will be told if it is not the default card reader.

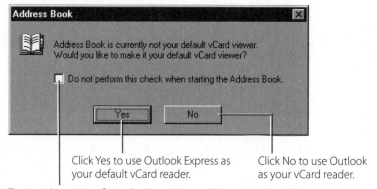

Click Yes to use Outlook Express as your default vCard reader.

Click No to use Outlook as your vCard reader.

Turn on this option if you don't want to see this message again.

Your choice for the default vCard reader will affect what happens when you open a business card and where information from business cards is stored. If you use Outlook as the default reader, the information will be stored in the Contacts folder of Outlook, not in the address book of Outlook Express. Use Outlook Express as the default vCard reader to save business card information in the Outlook Express address book.

? SEE ALSO

If you see a dialog box asking if you want to make Outlook Express the default vCard reader, refer to the sidebar "Setting Up a vCard Reader," above.

The Outlook Express address book only has one address type, and you cannot access addresses on your network server or in Outlook itself. To create a new listing, click the New Contact button on the Address Book toolbar. Figure 6-3 shows the address book form for creating a new address or editing an existing one.

FIGURE 6-3.
Entering or editing an
address listing.

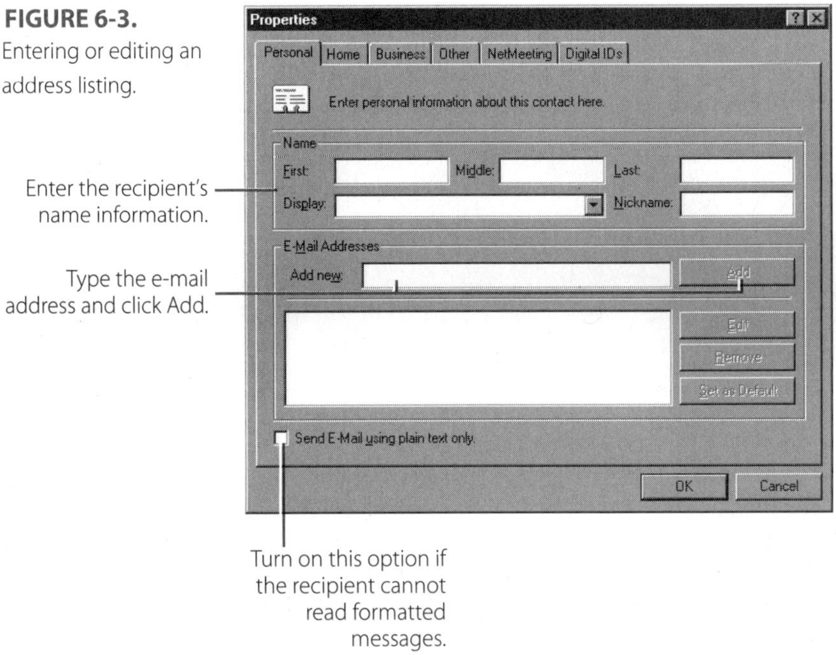

Enter the recipient's —
name information.

Type the e-mail
address and click Add.

Turn on this option if
the recipient cannot
read formatted
messages.

Use the other tabs of the dialog box to record home and business information, add notes and see group membership (on the Other tab), enter dial-up and server information for NetMeeting conferencing, and record Digital IDs to send encrypted mail.

Setting Up Groups

You often want to send the same e-mail to several individuals, such as members of a project team or a group of friends. You can create one or more groups in Outlook Express and then add members to it. To send an e-mail to the members of the group, you just select the group name in the address book rather than the names of each individual recipient.

To create a group, click the New Group button on the Address Book toolbar.

Click here to create and enter a new contact into the group.

Click here to add members from the Outlook Express address book.

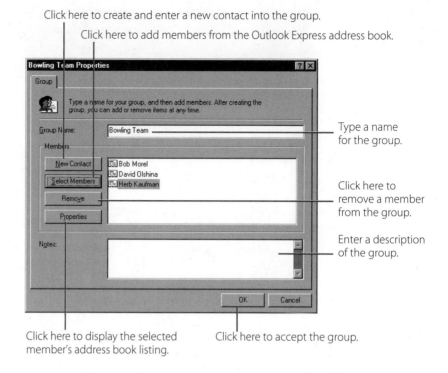

Type a name for the group.

Click here to remove a member from the group.

Enter a description of the group.

Click here to display the selected member's address book listing.

Click here to accept the group.

Sending Mail

Sending Internet mail in Outlook Express is just as easy as sending mail using Outlook, if not easier. If you are already using Outlook or another mail program as your default mail service, you'll see this dialog box when you compose your first message during each Outlook Express session:

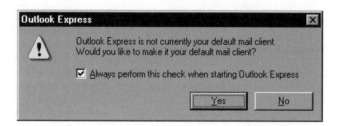

Click No if you do not want to make Outlook Express the default, such as when reading or sending mail from within Internet Explorer, or click

Yes to use it as the default mail program. Turn off the option labeled Always Perform This Check When Starting Outlook Express if you don't want to be bothered by this message again.

To send a simple message, do the following:

1 Click the Compose Message button on the toolbar, click Compose A Message On The Start Page, choose New Message on the Compose menu, or just press Ctrl+N.

2 To display the Select Recipients dialog box, click the card icon next to the To: text box or choose Select Recipients from the Tools menu.

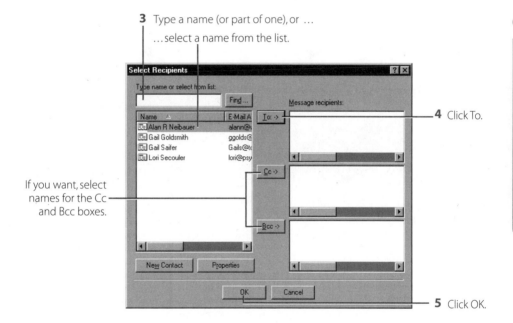

3 Type a name (or part of one), or …

…select a name from the list.

4 Click To.

If you want, select names for the Cc and Bcc boxes.

5 Click OK.

6 In the message window, click in the Subject box and type a brief description of the subject of your message.

7 Click in the message text area, or press the Tab key to move to the message text area, and then type your message.

8 When your message is ready to send, click the Send button.

Electronic Mail

TIP

> If you do not complete your message and are not ready to send it, choose Save from the File menu to store it in the Drafts folder, and then close the message without clicking Send.

Making Sure Your Messages Are Sent

Clicking on Send may or may not actually send your message. It all depends on how Outlook Express is set up.

If Outlook Express is set to send messages immediately, it will connect to your ISP if you are not already online and send your message. Otherwise, it merely adds the message to the Outbox and displays a dialog box reporting that you still have to send the mail.

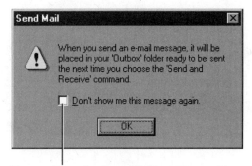

Turn on this option if you don't want to see this message again.

To remind you that you have mail to go out, the name of the Outbox folder will become bold and you'll see the number of unread Outbox messages. You'll also see a notice at the bottom of the start page reminding you that you have unsent mail.

• **You have 2 unsent message(s) in your** <u>**Outbox**</u>**.**

To send the mail in your Outbox, click the Send And Receive button on the toolbar. This sends any mail you have ready to go and checks for new mail at the same time. If you want to send mail without looking for new messages, choose Send from the Tools menu instead.

NOTE

> If Work Offline is selected in the File menu, you'll see a dialog box asking if you
> want to connect. Click Yes.

As Outlook sends your mail and checks for new messages waiting for
you, you'll see a dialog box reporting its progress. Click the Details
button in the box to expand it, as shown in Figure 6-4.

Outlook will first send any mail that you've composed and then download any mail that's waiting for you. If you have mail, you'll see an icon
on the right side of the Outlook Express status bar. In addition, the
word Inbox in the Folder List will become bold, and next to it will be
a number, which tells you how many messages there are that you
haven't read yet."

If you want Outlook to disconnect your phone line after it has received
messages, turn on the Hang Up When Finished option. Otherwise you
can hang up by choosing Hang-Up from the File menu, or by clicking
Hang-Up on the Start Page toolbar.

FIGURE 6-4.

Sending and receiving
messages.

II

Electronic Mail

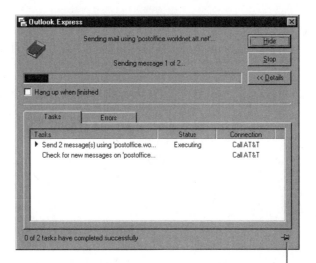

Click the push pin to keep the dialog box on screen after
messages are sent and received. Click it again to have the
box close after messages are processed.

Offline or Not Connected?

Technically, whenever you are not connected to the Internet you are working offline. However, Outlook Express and Internet Explorer have a special Work Offline mode that is different from simply not being connected. If you start Outlook Express and decide not to connect to the Internet at that time, you are still not in Offline mode. To use this mode you must choose Work Offline from the File menu.

When you are in Offline mode, you'll see a dialog box asking if you want to go online when you send and receive messages. In addition, when you launch Internet Explorer, it does not automatically dial-up your ISP and make the connection.

The setting that you make to the Work Offline command in one application also affects the other.

 TIP

Do not turn on the Hang Up When Finished option if you use Outlook Express as the default mail program with Internet Explorer. If Outlook Express sends and receives mail in the background while you are browsing, your dial-up connection will be terminated and so will your browsing.

Copies of all sent messages are stored in the Sent Items folder so you have a record of your communications.

Typing E-Mail Addresses

Instead of looking up a recipient in the address book, you can type the name or e-mail address of the recipient in the To section of the New Message window. To send the same message to more than one recipient, just separate the names with a semicolon.

 SEE ALSO

For more information about the Check Names dialog box, see "Typing Recipient Names and Addresses," on page 110.

As long as the recipient's name or e-mail address is in your address book, you only have to type the first few characters. As you type, Outlook Express scans the address book for an entry that starts with those characters and displays it highlighted on screen. If the name or e-mail address is correct, just move on and continue composing your message. If it is not, continue typing additional characters until Outlook Express finds the match you want.

Check Names

To confirm that all of your recipients have an e-mail address in the address book, click the Check Names button on the toolbar. Outlook Express will look up the names in the address book. If it cannot locate a name, you'll see the Check Names dialog box.

> You can also set up Outlook Express to search for recipients in online directories. See "Finding People," on page 227.

Adding a Signature

Although your e-mail address automatically appears on all of your messages, you may want to further identify yourself by including a standard signature closing. In Chapter 4, "Exchanging Messages and Faxes," you learned how to use a signature in Outlook. Signatures work the same way in Outlook Express, except you set them up differently.

To set up a signature in Outlook Express, follow these steps:

1 Choose Stationery from the Tools menu.

2 Click the Signature button on the Mail tab.

3 Click here to add your closing signature to all messages.

4 Type the text of your standard closing, or …
…select a file to be used as the signature.

Turn off this option to include the signature in replies and forwarded messages.

5 Click OK.

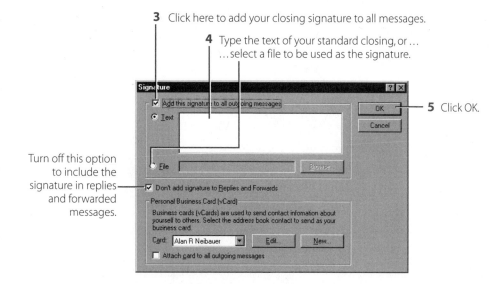

6 Click OK again to close the Stationery dialog box.

Electronic Mail

The next time you compose a new message, Outlook Express inserts the signature text into the message area. For replies and forwards, Outlook Express adds the signature above the copy of the message you are responding to or forwarding. Just type your message above the signature text.

Insert
Signature

You can also choose to manually insert your signature in selected messages. Follow all of the steps above to create the signature, but do not turn on the option labeled Add This Signature To All Outgoing Messages in step 3 above. When you want to add your signature to an e-mail, click the Insert Signature button on the New Message window's Standard toolbar or choose Signature from the Insert menu.

Creating a Business Card

As you learned in Chapter 4, "Exchanging Messages and Faxes," a business card is an attachment that includes information from your listing in the Address Book. When you include it as a signature, recipients can read the information and add it to their address books with a simple click of the mouse—so it's better than sending recipients an actual printed card.

The quickest way to add your business card to a message is to simply select your listing from the address book.

1 Choose Stationery from the Tools menu.

2 Click the Signature button.

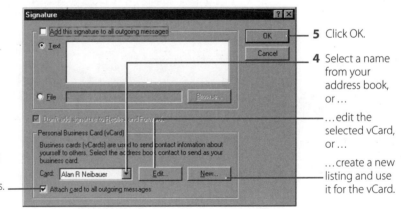

3 Click here to add a business card to your messages.

5 Click OK.

4 Select a name from your address book, or ...

...edit the selected vCard, or ...

...create a new listing and use it for the vCard.

Attached
Business Card

To learn how to read a
business card that you
receive with a mes-
sage, see "Reading
Business Cards," on
page 206.

The next time you send a message, Outlook Express will add your
business card as an attachment. When you compose a message, you'll
see an icon indicating that the card is attached. If you do not want to
include the card with a specific message, click the icon and choose
Delete from the menu that appears. Select Open from the same menu if
you want to edit the address book listing.

You can also add a business card as an attachment to a message without including it as a default signature. When composing a message,
choose Business Card from the Insert menu. Outlook Express inserts
the business card for the listing you chose in the Signature dialog box.

As an alternative, you can create and store business cards as individual files on your
disk, and then insert the card as an attachment. In the address book, select the listing that you want, and then point to Export on the File menu and choose the Business Card (vCard) command. The Save dialog box appears with the name of the
person you selected in the address book as the filename. Click Save.

Formatting Messages

Outlook Express lets you format messages in much the same way as
Outlook, but with some differences. You can use the Formatting toolbar and the Format menu to add pizzazz to your text, and you can also
add stationery and graphics files. To insert graphics use the Picture
command on the Insert menu or the Insert Picture button on the far
right of the Outlook Express Formatting toolbar. To add a background
picture or color, choose Background from the Format menu. You can
also change the default font used for new messages and use or create
stationery designs.

NOTE

Formatting is only available if you use HTML format rather than plain text for the
message. Select Rich Text (HTML) from the Format menu of the New Message
window to use this format for a specific message. To make this the default format, choose Options from the Tools menu of Outlook Express and select HTML
from the Send tab of the Options dialog box.

Electronic Mail

Changing the Default Font

Do you find yourself changing the font of every message because you just don't like the default font selected by Microsoft? Save yourself some time and choose another font, font size, or style as the new default. Follow these steps to change the default font:

1 Choose Stationery from the Tools menu to display the Stationery dialog box.

3 Click Font Settings to display the Font dialog box.

4 Choose a font, font style, size, effects, and color.

2 Make sure this option is selected.

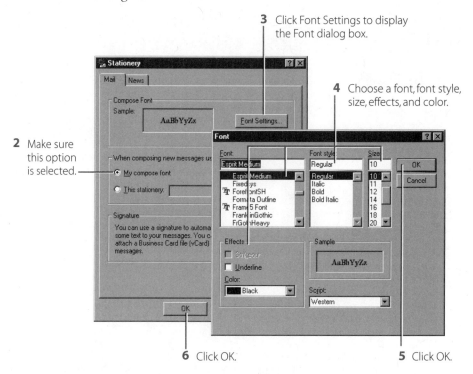

6 Click OK.

5 Click OK.

The selected font will now be used with all new messages. You can, of course, use the Formatting toolbar or Font command on the Format menu to choose a different font for individual messages, and you can select a new default font whenever you want.

Using Stationery

Although Outlook Express and Outlook do not share address books and folders, they do share stationery. In fact, new stationery that you create with one program will be available to the other. But while they share stationery files, the techniques for using stationery differ.

Composing a Message with Stationery

You may want to send most messages without a stationery design. Stationery does add to the time it takes to send and receive a message, and not all recipients are able to see background designs and graphics.

When you want to send a message using a stationery design, you can select it before composing the message. Don't click the Compose Message button on the toolbar, but follow these steps instead:

1 Click the small arrow on the Compose Message button on the toolbar, or point to New Message Using on the Compose menu.

2 Select one of the listed stationery designs and start your message, or click More Stationery to see additional designs and continue with step 3.

3 Select a design.

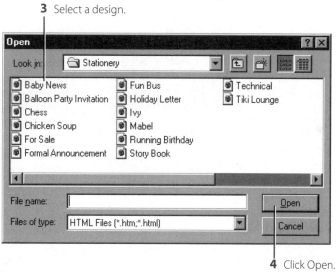

4 Click Open.

Remember, some stationery designs, such as Baby News, contain formatted text as well as a background pattern and pictures. You can edit or delete the formatted text if you do not want it in your message.

Choosing a Default Stationery

Now for an alternative. Suppose you have a great stationery design that you want to use for all your messages. Rather than choose it each time you send a message, set it as the default. Here's how.

II

Electronic Mail

1 Choose the Stationery command from the Tools menu to display the Stationery dialog box.

2 Click the This Stationery button.

3 Click Select.

5 Click OK.

CAUTION

The Edit option in the Select Stationery dialog box displays the selected stationery in HTML. Use this option only if you are familiar with editing HTML files.

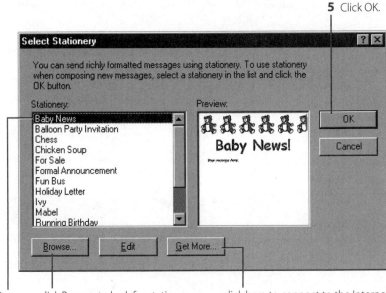

4 Select a design to use, or …

…click Browse to look for stationery files in other locations, or …

…click here to connect to the Internet and download additional stationery.

Choosing Something Other Than the Default

Just because you select a default stationery doesn't mean you *have* to use it for every new message. You may want to send a formal message to a business associate, a letter of complaint, or some other message that you just don't want formatted with the default stationery design. You may want to select a different design or just send a message with a plain background. It's your choice.

■ To send a message with a plain background, click the small arrow on the Compose Message button and choose No Stationery from the list.

■ To send a message with a different stationery, just select it using the techniques explained in "Composing a Message with Stationery," on the previous page.

Creating Your Own Stationery

Life is full of choices and so is Outlook Express. By adding background colors and pictures to a message you are actually creating your own stationery. If you want to use the same combination of colors and pictures again, you can save it as a stationery design, and then either use it as the new default or pick it for individual messages.

 NOTE

Unlike with Outlook, custom stationery you create with Outlook Express only includes a background color or picture, not text or a custom font unless you know how to edit HTML tags.

To create a custom stationery design, follow these steps:

1 Design the message with background colors or pictures. Selecting a small picture that tiles nicely behind your message will reduce the size of the messages you send compared to using a single, large background picture. A color will add the least amount of size to your messages.

2 Click Send.

3 Click the message in the Outbox or Sent Items folder.

4 Choose Save As Stationery from the File menu.

5 Type a name for the stationery in the File Name box.

6 Click the Save button.

Adding "Other Stuff" to Messages

E-mail is e-mail, regardless of what program you use to create it. Outlook Express offers the same capabilities as Outlook to include "other stuff" in your messages. You can include text from a file that you previously created, URL and mail links, and attachments. Again, the concepts are the same as for Outlook—it's just the techniques that differ.

Adding Text from a File

If you have a plain text or HTML format file stored on disk (for example, a text file saved in Windows Notepad or a Word document saved as HTML), you can insert the text from the file as part of your message. (HTML files can't be inserted if you've chosen the Plain Text format for your message. See "Sending Attachments," on the next page, for an alternative.) You can use Notepad or another word processing program to write and edit the text of a message and then just insert it into the New Message window. If you use a program other than Notepad, however, you must save the file as plain text or HTML. HTML gives you the advantage of adding formatted text to your messages.

 TIP

> You can always copy and paste text from a word processing program or other application into the Outlook Express message window.

To insert a file into a message, follow these steps:

1 Place the insertion point in the message where you want the text from the file to appear.

2 Choose Text From File from the Insert menu.

3 In the Insert Text File dialog box, select the type of file (text or HTML) and the name of the file to insert.

4 Click Open.

Including Links in Messages

A link is a clickable object. If you want the recipient to see a particular Web site, add a URL link. To make it easy for the recipient to send an e-mail to someone, add an e-mail link.

As with Outlook, just type URL links starting with either *www* or *http://*, and type e-mail addresses in the proper format. When you press the Spacebar or Enter key, Outlook Express formats the address as a link, underlined and in blue.

If you need to change the type of link, from *http:* to *ftp:*, for example, right-click the link and choose Properties from the shortcut menu to change the type of link or address. You can also select text and choose the Hyperlink command on the Insert menu to convert it to a link.

Sending Attachments

There will be times when you want to send a recipient more than just a message. You may want to send someone a document that you've created with Word, a sound file that you've recorded, a picture, or perhaps another file that you've found on the Internet.

You send these types of files as attachments. To send an attachment, follow these steps:

Insert File

1 In the New Message window, click the Insert File button on the toolbar or choose the File Attachment command from the Insert menu.

2 Select the file you want to send.

3 Click the Attach button.

The attachment will appear in a pane following the message, with an icon representing the file type and the file size.

When you view the message in the Preview Pane, a paper clip icon will indicate that the message contains an attachment. Graphics in formats such as BMP, GIF, and JPG will be listed under the message and the graphic itself will be displayed. Animated GIF graphics will even appear animated on the screen. Other graphics types can still be attached as files.

You can also choose to have multiple graphics attachments appear as a slide show with buttons to move from one to the other, or not to show graphics at all. See "Read Options," on page 220.

Getting Mail

Sending mail is only half the fun—getting mail is the other. To get new mail, click the Send And Receive button or choose Send And Receive from the Tools menu. If you are working offline, click Yes in the dialog box that appears. Outlook Express will send any messages in your Outbox, and then download any messages waiting for you. A dialog box will display its progress.

If you have mail, you'll see an envelope icon on the right of the status bar, and the word Inbox in the Folder List will become bold, and will be followed by the number of unread messages. If you are on the start page, you'll also see a note reporting the number of unread messages.

Remember, if you want Outlook to disconnect you from the Internet after it has received messages, turn on the Hang Up When Finished option. Otherwise you'll have to hang up by selecting Hang-Up from the File menu or by clicking the Hang-Up button on the Start Page toolbar.

Reading Mail

The mail in your Inbox won't do you much good until you read it. To read your mail, click Read Mail on the start page or click Inbox in the Folder List.

> If this is the first time you've used the Inbox and you have other e-mail systems installed, you'll be given a chance to import messages and address book information.

The Outlook Express window now contains three panels, as shown in Figure 6-5. Click a message to display it in the Preview Pane, or double-click the message to read it in a separate window.

FIGURE 6-5.

Reading messages in the Inbox.

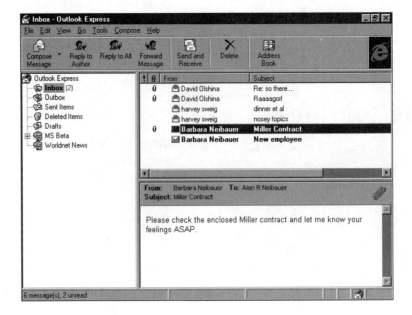

TIP

> To add the sender's address to your address book, double-click the message to display it in a separate window, and then right-click the sender's name and choose Add To Address Book from the shortcut menu that appears.

Saving Attachments

In the message list, attachments are indicated by a paper clip icon next to the message name, and you'll also see a paper clip in the Preview Pane header. Click the icon in the Preview Pane header to see the names and sizes of the attached files. Click the filename that you want to open to see the Open Attachment Warning dialog box. The box will not appear, by the way, for some types of files, such as text and audio files—these files will be opened immediately.

Click here to display the contents of the file in the associated application.

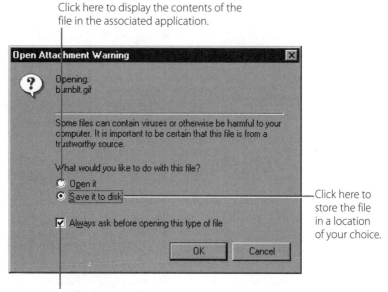

Click here to store the file in a location of your choice.

Turn off this option if you do not want to see this dialog box for this file type.

 NOTE

> You may also see a paper clip icon next to a message name if the message contains a graphic or stationery background, even when it does not have an attachment.

Electronic Mail

II

To save attachments using the File menu, see "Saving Message Attachments," on page 144.

If you double-click a message to open it in its own window, each attachment is listed along the bottom of the message window, showing an icon representing the type of file, the filename, and the file size. Double-click an icon to display the Open Attachment Warning dialog box, or right-click for a menu that lets you open, save, or print the file.

Reading Business Cards

If a message includes a business card, you'll see a paper clip icon next to the message header in the Inbox and a rotary file card icon in the Preview Pane header. If you double-click the message to open it in its own window, you'll see the icon in the header area.

Double-click to open
the attached vCard.

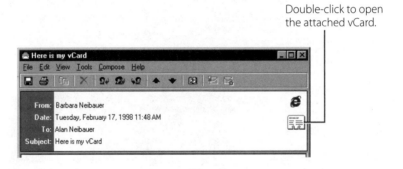

If you are using Outlook as the default vCard reader, click the card in the Preview Pane or double-click it in the message window to display the card in the Outlook address book format. If you are using Outlook Express as the vCard reader, clicking the card in the Preview Pane or double-clicking it in the message window gives you the option to open or save the card.

Once you open the card, you can just read the information or insert it into your address book. Using Outlook Express as the vCard reader, click the Add to Address Book button when the card is displayed to insert the contents of the card as a listing in your address book. If you are using Outlook as the vCard reader, click Save And Close to save the contents in Outlook's Contacts folder.

Replying to and Forwarding Messages

When you're ready to respond to a message you've received, use one of the buttons shown here. To respond to the sender, click the Reply To Author button on the Standard toolbar. To reply to the sender as well as any others who received the original message, click the Reply To All button (also on the Standard toolbar). To forward a message, click the Forward Message button.

With Outlook Express you can also forward the message as an attachment. When you add text to forwarded messages, they become difficult to read. Recipients have to distinguish between the new text and the original message. To send an e-mail message to another recipient while keeping it unchanged, forward the message as an attachment. This means that the entire forwarded message is attached to the new message. It appears as an envelope icon with the same name as the subject of the original message. When the user opens the attachment, it is displayed as an e-mail message just as you received it originally, including any attachments that were included with it.

To forward a message as an attachment, select the message in the Inbox or in another folder, and then choose Forward As Attachment from the Compose menu. The New Message window appears with the message attached. Compose your message as you would any other and then send it.

Setting Up Mail Security

The security measures available in Outlook Express are similar to those in Outlook but are designed for Internet mail, not Exchange mail. Although the security concepts are the same, there are some important differences, so we'll look at Outlook Express security in detail.

Security Zones

You set rules for the type of content that Outlook Express accepts with messages using security zones. You get two zones to select from—the Internet zone and the Restricted Site zone. You can control how each zone handles "active content," information that has the potential to change what's in your computer, such as ActiveX controls, scripts, and Java applets. You can also set the zone to a low, medium, high, or custom security level.

II

Electronic Mail

Low. This option does not warn you before accepting any active content.

Medium. This option warns you when the message contains active content, letting you decide whether or not to accept it.

High. This option excludes all active content without any prompts or messages.

By default, Outlook Express is set at the Internet zone, which uses medium security. You can change the setting of the Internet zone, or you can change to the Restricted Sites zone, which blocks active content from being received.

To change zone or zone settings, follow these steps:

1 Choose Options from the Tools menu.

2 Click the Security tab.

3 Click the Settings button in the Security Zones area.

4 Click OK in the dialog box that appears, warning you that you are about to change the zone settings.

The Security dialog box appears next.

5 Choose the zone you want to change.

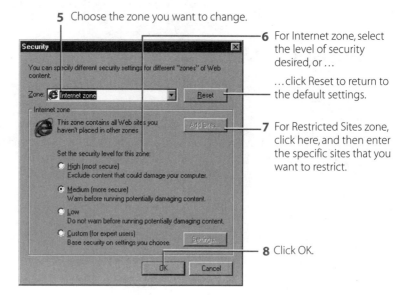

6 For Internet zone, select the level of security desired, or ...

... click Reset to return to the default settings.

7 For Restricted Sites zone, click here, and then enter the specific sites that you want to restrict.

8 Click OK.

9   Set the Zone box on the Security tab of the Options box to the zone you want to use, and then click OK.

Digital IDs

You can also secure your e-mail using a digital ID (also called a certificate). A digital ID lets you prove to recipients that the message actually came from you, and it allows others to send you encrypted mail. Before you can use a digital ID, however, you have to obtain one over the Internet from one of the organizations that provide them. These organizations also periodically verify that your digital ID is still valid.

 NOTE

Outlook Express shares S/MIME security certificates with Outlook.

Getting Your Own Digital ID

When you apply for a digital ID, you'll have to complete an online form, and then wait until you get a response from the security company. You will receive instructions for obtaining and downloading the security certificate.

You can get a digital ID by going to this site on the Internet:

http://www.microsoft.com/isapi/redir.dll?prd=OutlookExpress&pver=4.0&ar=cert

It is easier, however, to jump to the site directly from within Outlook Express by following these steps:

1   Choose Options from the Tools menu.

2   Click the Security tab.

3   Click Get Digital ID.

Outlook Express will launch Internet Explorer, connect to the appropriate site, and get you started with the enrollment process. Just follow the directions you see on the screen and those you receive with your confirmation by e-mail.

Associating the ID with Your Account

Once you get your ID, either through Outlook or Outlook Express, you have to associate it with your account. This lets Outlook Express know what ID to use with digitally signed messages.

1 Choose Accounts from the Tools menu.

2 Choose the account you want to associate with the ID, and then click Properties.

3 Click the Security tab.

4 Turn on this option to use the digital ID.

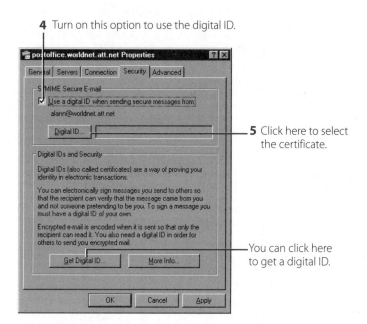

5 Click here to select the certificate.

You can click here to get a digital ID.

6 Choose the ID for the account.

7 Click OK.

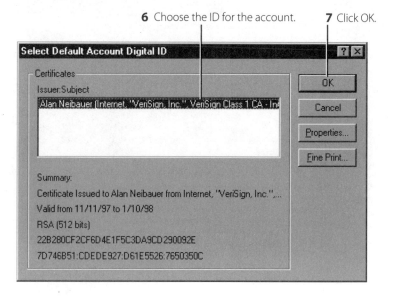

8 Click OK again to close the Properties dialog box.

A digital ID is made up of two codes, called keys. The public key is the code you send to people that you want to be able to send encrypted messages to you. The private key is stored on your computer, and it must be present in order for you to read encrypted messages. You should make a backup copy of your private key, because if the key is lost you will not be able to sign your mail with the ID or read encrypted mail. To make a backup copy, follow these steps:

1 Start Internet Explorer.

2 Choose Internet Options from the View menu.

3 Click the Content tab.

4 Click Personal to display the Client Authentication dialog box.

5 Click Export.

6 Enter a password.

7 Enter the name of the file, without an extension.

8 Click OK.

Use the Import button in the Client Authentication dialog box if you ever have to restore the digital ID or if you are installing it on another computer. Click Import, and then enter the password and the name and location of the digital ID file.

Sending a Digital Signature

Digitally Sign
Message

When you want the recipient to be sure that the message came from you, send the message with a digital signature. When you are composing a message, apply a digital signature by clicking the Digitally Sign Message button or by choosing Digitally Sign from the Tools menu. The Digitally Signed icon will appear in the message header.

If you receive a message with this icon, you know the message is digitally signed. You will also see a special screen before the message is displayed, informing you that the message is digitally signed. Click Continue to read the message. To avoid doing this for every digitally signed message you receive, turn on the option Don't Show Me This Help Screen Again before clicking Continue.

Swapping Keys

In order to send encrypted mail, you must know the public key of the recipient and it must be part of the entry for that person in your address book. In order for you to receive encrypted mail, the sender must have your public key.

To send your public key (so the recipient can send *you* encrypted mail), just send a digitally signed message. To get a key (so *you* can *send* encrypted mail), ask the sender to send you a digitally signed message.

When you receive the message, add the sender's key to your address book by following these steps:

1 Click the message in the Inbox.

2 Choose Properties from the File menu.

3 Click the Security tab.

4 Click the Add Digital ID To Address Book button to open the Properties dialog box for the message sender.

5 Click OK to add the digital ID and close the Properties box.

6 Click OK again to return to the Inbox.

You can visually verify whose public keys you have on file by opening the Address Book and looking for the digitally signed icon next to the entries' names. These are the people you can send encrypted mail.

 TIP

You can choose to digitally sign and encrypt all messages automatically from the Security tab of the Options dialog box.

Sending and Receiving Encrypted Mail

While it sounds like something out of a James Bond movie, there are good reasons to encrypt mail. In these days of computer networks, it is quite possible for your e-mail to be seen by someone other than the intended recipient. Encryption makes sure that your message is read only by the person to whom you sent it.

Encrypt
Message

To encrypt a message, click the Encrypt button or choose Encrypt from the Tools menu. Outlook adds the Encrypt icon (a blue padlock) to the message header to indicate an encrypted message.

When you receive an encrypted message, Outlook Express confirms that the key is indeed yours and then automatically decrypts the message.

Setting Up Accounts

When you first started Outlook Express, you had the opportunity to set up your connection and your mail and news accounts. You can also set up the accounts or change the specifics of the accounts later from within Outlook Express.

Outlook Express can manage multiple accounts. If you plan to use more than one e-mail account on your computer, for example, you can set up all of them. You can then send and receive mail through one or all accounts at the same time. Each account can have its own name and dial into its own ISP.

You can also set up Outlook Express to share one account with other members of your family and even have a separate Inbox folder for each person. In this case, you're only using one actual ISP, but you can send and receive messages under more than one name. That way, your spouse can send messages that don't have your name on it, and vice versa.

Changing Account Setup

There are a lot of reasons why your e-mail account can change. You may get fed up hearing busy signals from your ISP, so you switch to another provider and need to change your mail server and dial-up connection service. You may just want to change your e-mail password or the "friendly name" of your service that appears in the Internet Account dialog box and in the dialog box that opens when sending and receiving mail.

You are not tied to the original setup that you created when you first ran Outlook Express. To change account information, start Outlook Express and follow the next steps.

II

Electronic Mail

> **NOTE**
>
> If you change Internet service providers, you will probably have to make changes to your dial-up connection using the Dial-Up Networking resource in Windows. Make those changes first and then adjust your Outlook Express account as described below.

1 Choose Accounts on the Tools menu.

2 To see just mail or news accounts, click the appropriate tab.

3 Select the account you want to change.

4 Click Properties.

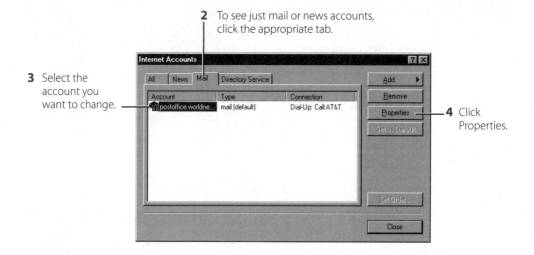

5 Change the desired settings in the Properties dialog box, using the appropriate tabs:

- Change your user information or e-mail address using the General tab.

- Change the name of incoming or outgoing mail servers and your mail logon name and password on the Servers tab.

- Change the dial-up connection on the Connection tab.

- Set security for the account on the Security tab.

- Set server port numbers, timeouts, and delivery rules (for advanced users only) on the Advanced tab.

6 Click OK.

Adding New Mail Accounts

When you first set up Outlook Express, you can establish only one account. You can later add other accounts to the setup for yourself or for other members of your family so that everyone can enjoy sending and receiving e-mail.

To share one account with other members of the family, create accounts for each person. Use the same e-mail address and server names, and just change the user-name and "friendly name" in the Internet Connection Wizard dialog boxes.

To add a mail account to Outlook Express, follow these steps:

1 Choose Accounts from the Tools menu.

2 Click Add.

3 Click Mail on the submenu to start the Internet Connection Wizard.

4 Complete the steps in the wizard and then click Finish in the final dialog box.

All your accounts will be listed in the Accounts dialog box.

Choose the account that you want to use as the default, and click Set As Default. —

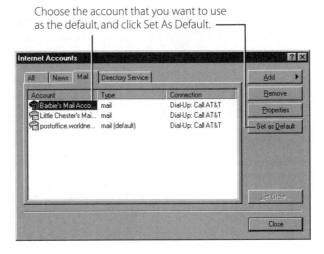

II

Electronic Mail

The default account will be used automatically for all mail that you send. You can tell which account is the default by looking for the word *(default)* in the list of accounts.

Sending Mail with Multiple Accounts

Although one account will be used as the default for all new messages, you can choose which account to use when you compose a message. The account determines the name in the From column on the recipient's screen and the e-mail account and server used.

Compose the message as you would normally, but in the New Message window, do not click Send. Instead, point to the Send Message Using or Send Later Using command on the File menu, depending on whether you want to send the message now or later, and then click the account name you want to use.

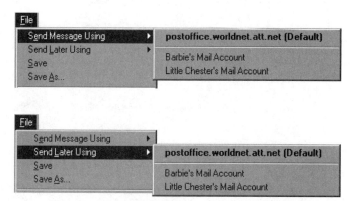

If you chose to send mail later, when you are ready to send the mail in your Outbox and receive mail, you can choose which account to use.

With the default properties for accounts, clicking the Send And Receive button sends all messages in the Outbox and receives mail for all accounts. If you would like the convenience of clicking one button to send and receive mail (the Send And Receive button on the toolbar) but would like to poll a subset of your accounts, you can exclude specific accounts from the global Send And Receive command. To exclude an account, choose Accounts from the Tools menu, select the account you want to exclude, and click the Properties button. On the General tab of the Properties dialog box, turn off the option labeled Include

This Account When Doing A Full Send And Receive. When you *do* want to send or receive via this account, point to Send And Receive on the Tools menu and choose the account.

 NOTE

> If you are sharing one e-mail account with more than one user, choosing to send and receive via a specific account sends just the current user's mail but downloads all mail waiting on the ISP's server.

Setting Message Options

Outlook Express is set to send and receive messages using popular default settings. You can change these settings if you don't like the way Outlook Express operates or if you want to customize it for your own personal tastes.

To change the default settings, choose Options from the Tools menu to see the Options dialog box.

General Options

The General tab of the Options dialog box, shown in Figure 6-6, on the following page, lets you designate some general ways in which Outlook Express works.

Check For New Messages Every [ ] Minutes.   If you want Outlook Express to automatically dial-up and check for messages at regular intervals, turn on this option and set the number of minutes between attempts.

Play Sound When New Messages Arrive.   When this option is turned on, a sound will play when new messages are downloaded. With this option turned off, you will still see an icon in the status bar reporting that you have new mail.

FIGURE 6-6.

The General tab of the Options dialog box.

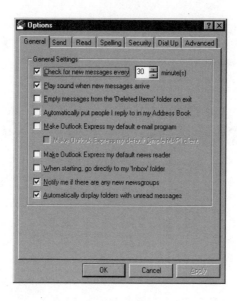

Empty Messages From The 'Deleted Items' Folder On Exit.   Turn on this option to automatically delete the messages you've moved to the Deleted Items folder when you exit Outlook Express.

Automatically Put People I Reply To In My Address Book.   Turn on this option if you want the address of the recipient to be inserted in your Address Book when you send a reply.

Make Outlook Express My Default E-Mail Program.   Turn on this option to use Outlook Express as the mail program when you send and receive from within your Web browser.

Make Outlook Express My Default Simple MAPI Client.   Turn on this option to use Outlook Express when you use the Send command from within another application, such as Microsoft Word.

Make Outlook Express My Default News Reader.   Turn on this option to have all requests for newsgroup messages access Outlook Express.

When Starting, Go Directly To My 'Inbox' Folder.   Turn on this option to have the Inbox folder open rather than the start page when you start Outlook Express.

Notify Me If There Are Any New Newsgroups.   Turn on this option to display a message reporting when there are new newsgroups when you access your newsgroup server.

Automatically Display Folders With Unread Messages. Turn on this option to expand and show in boldface folder names that contain unread messages.

Send Options

Use the Send tab of the Options dialog box, shown in Figure 6-7, to determine how and when your messages are sent.

Mail Sending Format. These options determine whether messages are sent in HTML or as plain text. Select Plain Text if you are sending mail to a recipient who has an older e-mail system that will not accept formatted mail. The default is HTML.

News Sending Format. These options determine whether news messages are sent as HTML or plain text. Plain Text is selected by default.

Save A Copy Of Sent Messages In The 'Sent Items' Folder. Turn off this option only if you are certain you will not need copies of your sent mail.

Include Message In Reply. Turn on this option to insert the text of the original message in your reply.

Send Messages Immediately. Turn on this option to send each message as soon as you click the Send button in the New Message window.

FIGURE 6-7.
The Send tab of the
Options dialog box.

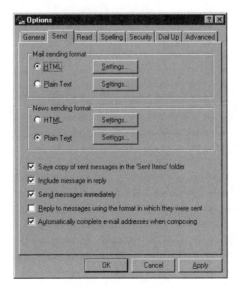

II

Electronic Mail

Reply To Messages Using The Format In Which They Were Sent.
Turn on this option to automatically reply in the same format (HTML or plain text) as the original message.

Automatically Complete E-Mail Addresses When Composing. Turn on this option if you want Outlook Express to try to complete the name or e-mail address that you start to type in the New Message window.

Read Options

The options on the Read tab of the Options dialog box, shown in Figure 6-8, determine how and when your incoming mail is read.

Message Is Read After Being Previewed For [ ] Seconds. Turn on this option to automatically mark a message as read after you've reviewed it in the Preview Pane for a specified number of seconds.

Download [ ] Headers At A Time. Turn on this option to limit the number of newsgroup headers to download at one time.

Automatically Expand Conversation Threads. Turn on this option to display all of the message headers in the message thread.

Automatically Show News Message In The Preview Pane. Turn on this option to have the Preview Pane display each news message as you select it, just like it displays mail messages you select.

FIGURE 6-8.
The Read tab of the Options dialog box.

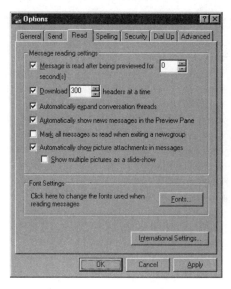

Mark All Messages As Read When Exiting A Newsgroup.   Turn on this option only if you want all your news messages marked as read when you leave the newsgroup, even messages you have not actually opened.

Automatically Show Picture Attachments In Messages.   Turn this option on to display graphics attachments in the Preview Pane rather than as icons that must be opened separately.

Show Multiple Pictures As A Slide-Show.   Turn on this option so that when more than one graphics file is attached to a message, you'll see one picture at a time, with buttons you'll click to move from picture to picture.

Font Settings.   Click Fonts to set the font that will be used to display plain text messages received in various languages.

Spelling Options

The Spelling tab of the Options dialog box, lets you control how the words in your message are checked. The options are the same as those for Outlook itself, discussed in Chapter 3, "Setting Outlook Options," with two additions. You can choose to not check the spelling of Internet addresses, and you can edit the custom dictionary by inserting names and other words that you know are correct but that are not contained in Outlook's dictionary.

Security Options

The Security tab of the Options dialog box, shown in Figure 6-9, on the following page, lets you control what active element contents are received with incoming messages by setting Security Zones. You can also choose to send your digital ID and encrypt all outgoing messages, and to connect to the Internet to receive a digital ID.

Use the Advanced Settings button on the Security Tab to choose an encryption method and whether you want to automatically send a decrypted copy of secure messages to yourself.

II

Electronic Mail

> **NOTE**

For details on using the Security tab, see "Setting Up Mail Security," on page 207.

FIGURE 6-9.

The Security tab of the Options dialog box.

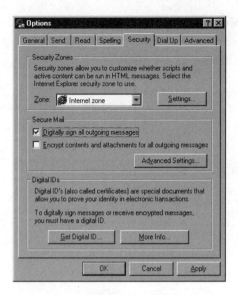

Dial-Up Options

Use the options on the Dial Up tab of the Options dialog box, shown in Figure 6-10, to determine how your connections are handled.

Do Not Dial A Connection.   Turn on this option to have Outlook Express start without asking for the type of connection and without dialing in.

Dial This Connection.   Turn on this option to automatically dial into the selected ISP when you start Outlook Express.

Ask Me If I Would Like To Dial A Connection.   Turn on this option to be asked if you want to dial in or not when you start Outlook Express.

Warn Me Before Switching Dial Up Connections.   If this option is turned on and you have more than one dial-up connection, Outlook Express will ask you if you want to try the second when the first is not working. Also, if you are connected with one dial-up account but have chosen an action (like downloading mail) linked to a different dial-up account, it will ask your permission before automatically disconnecting you from the first connection to dial the second.

FIGURE 6-10.

The Dial Up tab of the Options dialog box.

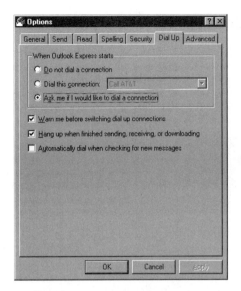

Hang Up When Finished Sending, Receiving, Or Downloading. If this option is turned on, Outlook Express automatically terminates the connection when all messages have been sent and received and all newsgroup messages have been downloaded.

Automatically Dial When Checking For New Messages. If this option is turned on, Outlook Express will connect without asking you when it checks for new mail.

Advanced Options

The options on the Advanced tab of the Options dialog box, shown in Figure 6-11, on the next page, are used less frequently than the others and should be changed with caution.

Delete Messages [ ] Days After Being Downloaded. Turn on this option to automatically delete newsgroup messages a specified number of days after their receipt.

Don't Keep Read Messages. Turn on this option to delete newsgroup messages after you read them.

FIGURE 6-11.

The Advanced tab of the Options dialog box.

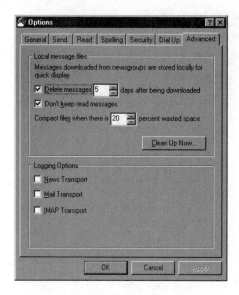

Compact Files When There Is [ ] Percent Wasted Space. Turn on this option to delete unused space from folders when the space reaches a set size.

Clean Up Now. Click this button to compact your folders and delete message bodies.

Logging Options. Turn on these options to make a log of commands sent to your news and mail services.

Using E-Mail Directories

You know that Outlook Express can complete a recipient's name that you start to type. It does so by checking the address book for names with matching characters. You can also set up Outlook Express to check online directories, such as BigFoot and Switchboard. If Outlook Express cannot find the e-mail address for a name in your address book, it will search one or more of the online directories before reporting that it cannot find a match.

To access a directory, you have to first set it up for your account. Follow these steps to set up one or more online directories:

1 Choose Accounts from the Tools menu.

2 Click the Directory Service tab.

3 Click a directory service that you want Outlook Express to use.

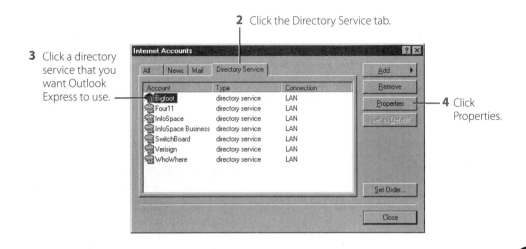

4 Click Properties.

5 Turn on this option to use the selected service when checking e-mail addresses.

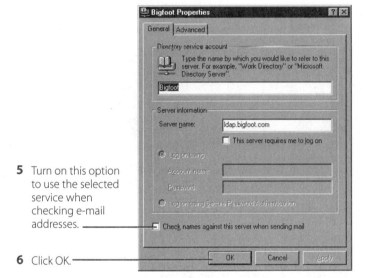

6 Click OK.

7 Repeat steps 3 through 7 for other directory services you want to check.

Unless you get specific instructions for setting up a directory service, leave the other options in the Properties dialog box set to their defaults. The Server Information section, for example, determines how the directory service is accessed. It includes the directory's Internet name and any login information that may be required. Some services, for example, require you to register to receive an account name and password.

If you set up more than one service, you can determine the order in which they are checked for e-mail addresses by following these steps:

1 In the Internet Accounts dialog box, click the Directory Service tab.

2 Click Set Order to display the Directory Services Order dialog box. The order of the services in the box determines the order in which they will be searched.

3 Click the service whose position you want to change.

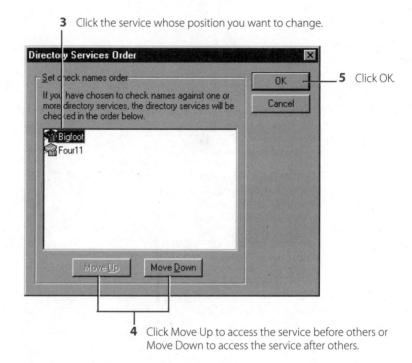

5 Click OK.

4 Click Move Up to access the service before others or Move Down to access the service after others.

As additional directory services become available, you can add them to the directory list. You'll need to get the directory's Internet server name (called the LDAP server) from your ISP. If the server requires you to log on, you'll also need an account name and password. When you have the information, open the Accounts dialog box, click Add and choose Directory Service to start the Internet Connection Wizard. Follow the steps in the wizard dialog boxes to complete the installation.

Finding People

In addition to using the directories to automatically locate e-mail addresses when composing messages, you can check them anytime you need to look up an e-mail address. You can use any of the following methods to search any directory service listed in Outlook Express, even if you haven't selected the service for e-mail address checking as described above.

- In the Address Book window, click the Find button on the toolbar.

- In the Select Recipients dialog box, click the Find button.

- From the Windows desktop, click the Start button, point to Find, and then click People.

   The Find People dialog box appears.

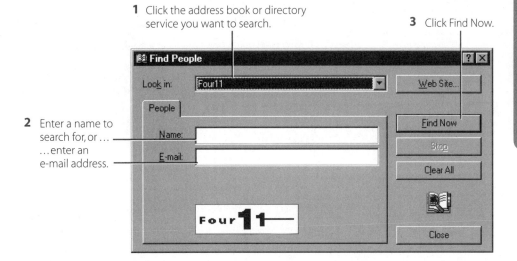

1 Click the address book or directory service you want to search.

3 Click Find Now.

2 Enter a name to search for, or ... ...enter an e-mail address.

NOTE

You must be online to search directory services.

If the directory locates any matches, the names and e-mail addresses will be listed.

■ Click Properties to read any other available information about the person, such as address and telephone number.

■ Click Add To Address Book to insert the name and e-mail address of the person in your Address Book.

■ Click Web Site to access the directory service's home page on the Internet, where additional options may be available.

When you search the Address Book rather than a directory service, the Find People dialog box also lets you search by address, phone number, or any text in the Address Book listing. When it locates a name, you can also select Delete to remove it from the Address Book.

Working with Folders

Outlook Express folders serve as storage containers for messages, much as the Windows folders store files. The initial folders provided by Outlook Express serve specific purposes:

Inbox. This folder stores messages that you receive.

Outbox. This folder stores messages ready to be sent.

Sent Items. This folder stores messages that have been sent.

Deleted Items. This folder stores messages you want to delete.

Drafts. This folder stores items that you are working on.

This arrangement of folders is convenient, but it may not serve all of your purposes. You may need additional folders to store messages for other accounts, for example, or you may want to subdivide a folder and create subfolders to organize messages further. Your Sent Items folder, for example, could contain a subfolder for each of your clients.

Working with folders is very easy. Your folders are organized in a hierarchy much like the directories on your hard disk. At the top of the hierarchy is the Outlook Express folder. All of the other folders are contained within it. Clicking the Outlook Express folder shows the start page.

To add a folder, follow these steps:

1 Right-click any folder in the list and choose New Folder from the shortcut menu that appears.

2 Type a name for the folder.

3 Click the folder that you want to contain the new one, if it isn't already selected.

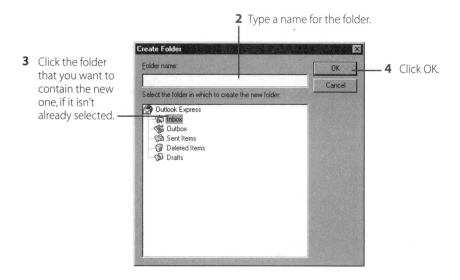

4 Click OK.

Folders that contain subfolders are marked with a plus sign. Click the plus sign to expand the listing; a minus sign is then displayed and the names of the subfolders are shown. Click the minus sign when you want to collapse the display so the names of the subfolders no longer appear.

To delete a folder, right-click its name—expanding the folder that contains it if necessary—and then click Delete on the shortcut menu. Click Yes in the message box that appears.

To rename a folder, right-click it and choose Rename from the shortcut menu. In the box that appears, enter the new name and then click OK.

You cannot rename or delete the default folders Inbox, Outbox, Sent Items, and Deleted Items.

Working with Messages in Folders

You do not have to leave messages in the folders where Outlook Express puts them. This is, after all, a free country.

To move a message to another folder, follow these steps:

1 Expand the folder list, if necessary, to see the folder where you want to place the message.

2 Open the folder containing the message.

3 Click the message you want to move.

4 Drag the message to the destination folder in the Folder List.

When you release the mouse, the message will be removed from its original folder and placed in the new folder.

 TIP

> You don't even have to open a subfolder before moving an item to one. Drag the item you want to move onto the visible "parent" folder, hold it there a moment, and the subfolders will open automatically. Continue to drag the item down to the destination folder, and then drop it in place.

To make a copy of a message in another folder, follow the same steps but hold down the Ctrl key when you release the mouse. You do not have to hold down the Ctrl key as you drag the message.

You cannot drag a message from the Deleted Items folder to the Outbox. If you accidentally delete a message from your Outbox that you want to send, double-click it in the Deleted Items folder and click Send on the message window standard toolbar.

As an alternative to dragging, you can also move or copy a message using a dialog box. Follow these steps:

1 Right-click the message and choose Move To or Copy To from the shortcut menu. You can also click the message and choose Move To Folder or Copy To Folder from the Edit menu. Outlook Express displays the Move or Copy dialog box.

2 Click the folder where you want to place the message.

3 Click OK.

Leaving Messages on the Mail Server

When you get a message from your mail server, it is downloaded to your computer and then deleted from the mail server. But, if you work in more than one location, you may want to leave a message on the mail server so you can pick it up later from another computer. For instance, you may want to read your mail on the road during a business trip but keep it on the server so it can be downloaded and filed on your main system when you return. In this scenario, you'd set your portable computer to leave messages on the server and your main system to remove them after they're received.

To set up Outlook Express so it leaves messages on the mail server, follow these steps:

1 Choose Accounts from the Tools menu.

2 Select your mail account from the Mail tab.

3 Click Properties.

4 Click the Advanced tab.

Electronic Mail

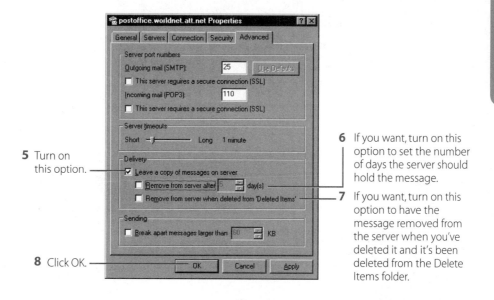

5 Turn on this option.

6 If you want, turn on this option to set the number of days the server should hold the message.

7 If you want, turn on this option to have the message removed from the server when you've deleted it and it's been deleted from the Delete Items folder.

8 Click OK.

If your mail server uses IMAP, as opposed to POP, the Advanced tab asks you for the root folder path, the location of your messages on the server. Enter the path, but do not end it with the / character.

Organizing Messages with the Inbox Assistant

In Chapter 2, "Looking Out into Outlook," you learned how to use the Rules Wizard and the Out Of Office Assistant to organize messages as they are received by Outlook. Outlook Express offers the Inbox Assistant, which operates similarly and includes additional options and features.

With the Outlook Express Inbox Assistant, you can set a rule to apply to all messages, or you can base the rule on the contents of the To, Cc, From, and Subject fields or on the account used and the message size. In addition to the Move To, Copy To, Forward To, and Reply With actions, you can also tell Outlook Express not to download the message from the server or to delete the message.

By using the Account criteria, for example, you can channel received messages to separate folders for each account recipient. So if you are sharing one account with several members of the family, each person can have a separate folder that automatically receives new messages. In another situation, you could presort the mail coming to you into various folders according to who sent it, text in the subject line, and so on.

Here's how to set it up:

1 Create a folder for each account or person in the household who will be receiving mail.

2 Choose Inbox Assistant from the Tools menu.

3 Click Add.

4 Turn on Account.　　　**5** Select the appropriate account from the list.

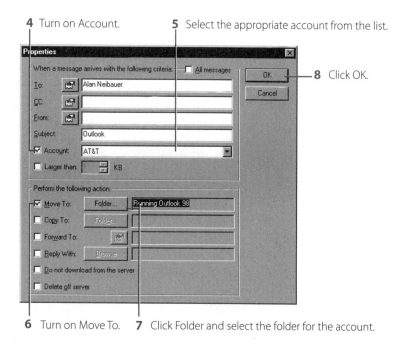

8 Click OK.

6 Turn on Move To.　　**7** Click Folder and select the folder for the account.

9 Repeat steps 3 through 8 for each account.

10 Click OK.

Now as new messages are received, they are inserted into the appropriate folder, rather than all placed in one Inbox.

Customizing the Outlook Express Window

Outlook Express lets you customize its appearance in a number of ways. You can change the size of the panes displayed on screen and choose whether to hide or display such components as the toolbar, status bar, Outlook Bar, and Folder Bar. The Folder Bar is an optional horizontal bar above the message list that shows the name of the currently open folder.

Viewing Read or Unread Messages

By default, Outlook Express displays all messages in a folder, showing the number of unread messages after the folder name. If your folders contain a large number of messages, you may find it tiresome to have to scroll to see those that are unread. To display just the unread messages, point to Current View on the View menu and choose the Unread Messages command. Outlook Express will hide read messages from the display. To redisplay all messages, point to Current View and choose the All Message command.

Working with Columns

You can add additional columns of information to those already shown in the message list pane, and you can remove those already there by default.

To insert and delete columns, follow these steps:

1 Click the folder that you want to change.

2 Choose Columns on the View menu to display the Columns dialog box.

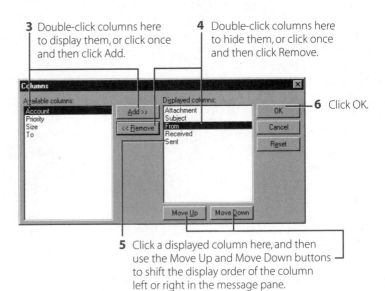

3 Double-click columns here to display them, or click once and then click Add.

4 Double-click columns here to hide them, or click once and then click Remove.

6 Click OK.

5 Click a displayed column here, and then use the Move Up and Move Down buttons to shift the display order of the column left or right in the message pane.

Rearranging Columns with the Mouse

When you want to quickly move a column to a new position in a folder window, just point to the column heading and drag it to the new location. As you move the column heading between existing columns, you'll see a shaded copy of the column heading indicating where the column will be inserted when you release the mouse button. When you release the button, the column moves to its new location and the columns to the right move over to make room.

Changing Column Width

To change column width using the mouse, first position the mouse pointer along the right edge of the column heading for the column that you want to widen or narrow. Then drag the right edge of the column heading to the right to widen the column. Drag the right edge of the heading to the left to narrow the column.

Getting the Longest Entry to Fit

Rather than trying to adjust the width of a column yourself, you can direct Outlook to set the width of the column so that the longest entry in it is fully displayed. To do this, double-click the right border of a column to set the column width to best fit.

Sorting and Grouping Messages

When messages are received, they are added to the list of messages already in the Inbox. You can sort the order of messages in the Inbox, or in any folder, by clicking the column headings.

Sorting with the mouse is quick and convenient, and you can sort items in either ascending or descending order. (Ascending order, depending on the column selected, means alphabetical, earlier time to later time, or lower number to higher number; descending order reverses the direction.)

You can tell how the messages are currently sorted by looking at the column heading. If you see an up-pointing triangle next to the column name, the messages are sorted in ascending order by that column. A down-pointing arrow means the messages are sorted in descending order.

II

Electronic Mail

If you want to sort the messages based on the information in a different column, click that column heading. Outlook Express uses that column for an ascending sort, displaying the up-pointing triangle. Then each time you click the column heading, Outlook Express reverses the sort direction.

You can also right-click a column heading and then choose either Ascending or Descending from the shortcut menu that appears.

As an alternative to using the mouse to sort columns, you can use the Sort By command on the View menu.

1 Select the folder that you want to sort.

2 Choose Sort By on the View menu.

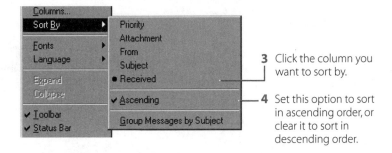

3 Click the column you want to sort by.

4 Set this option to sort in ascending order, or clear it to sort in descending order.

The Sort By submenu also offers the Group Messages By Subject command. When you choose this command, messages are arranged by subject and placed under the message that initiated each topic, indented and ordered according to who responded to whom, and in what order. Organizing messages in this fashion (also referred to as threading messages) allows you to follow the sequence of the conversation (or thread), reply to a specific previous reply, and have your message indented under the one you replied to. This is especially useful for newsgroups, where many people may contribute their thoughts on one subject, and where who is talking to whom about what aspect of the topic can quickly become confusing.

The first message on each subject is listed first and shown with a plus sign. The plus sign indicates that there are later messages on that same subject. Click the plus sign to expand the item, displaying the other messages. They will be indented to show their relationship to the first message. Click the minus sign to collapse the message group.

Changing Pane Size

The panes that make up the Outlook window are separated by gray bars. To change the size of a pane, just drag one of the bars. When you point to a bar, the mouse pointer will appear as a two-directional arrow.

For example, to enlarge the Preview Pane, drag the bar that is between it and the message list up toward the top of the screen. You cannot remove a pane by dragging a bar.

Working with the Toolbar

Chances are you'll be using the Outlook Express toolbar an awful lot. The toolbar buttons give you a fast, easy way to perform common tasks. You can turn the toolbar on and off, you can reposition it, and you can change the size of the toolbar buttons. You can also add new features to the toolbar for functions that you perform often.

Turning the Toolbar Off and On

Obviously, toolbars take up a certain amount of window space. If you'd prefer to use this space to see more folders or folder items, you can turn the toolbar off by clicking Toolbar on the View menu. Click it again to turn the toolbar back on.

Changing the Position of the Toolbar

You can reposition the toolbar on the screen by moving it to the top, bottom, right edge, or left edge of the Outlook Express window.

For another way to change its position, right-click any part of the toolbar and point to Align to see these options:

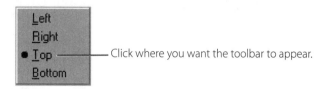

Click where you want the toolbar to appear.

Electronic Mail

Removing Text Labels

The default toolbar includes icons as well as text labels describing the button functions. This way you don't have to worry about memorizing what the icons represent. The text Send And Receive, for example, leaves nothing to the imagination, while the icon on that button may be obtuse for new users.

If you are familiar with the icons and want to make some extra room for messages, you can remove the text labels, cutting the size of the toolbar roughly in half. To remove, or later restore, the text labels, right-click the toolbar and then click Text Labels.

Customizing the Toolbar

Although the Outlook Express toolbar includes buttons for the most common functions, you can easily add additional features to the toolbar, such as a button to print a message or to move a message to another folder. You can also remove buttons that you do not use. If you find that you never use the Forward Message feature, for example, you can remove it to make room for another button.

To add or remove toolbar buttons, right-click the toolbar and choose Buttons to display the Customize Toolbar dialog box.

1 Click a button here and click Add to add it to the toolbar.

2 Click a button here and click Remove to remove it from the toolbar.

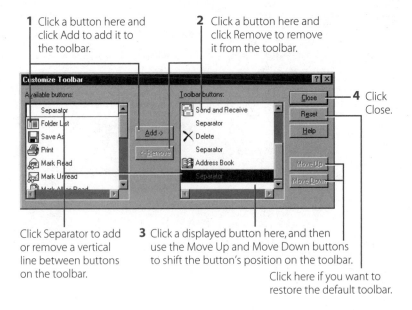

4 Click Close.

Click Separator to add or remove a vertical line between buttons on the toolbar.

3 Click a displayed button here, and then use the Move Up and Move Down buttons to shift the button's position on the toolbar.

Click here if you want to restore the default toolbar.

Changing the Window Layout

For additional ways to customize Outlook Express, use the Layout command on the View menu.

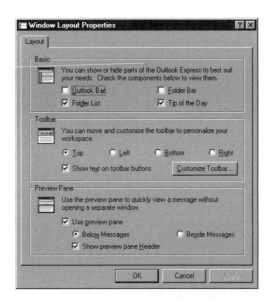

The Basic options in the Window Layout Properties dialog box let you add or delete screen elements. By default, you will see the Folder List along the left of the screen and the Tip of the Day at the bottom of the start page. You can also display the Outlook Bar and the Folder Bar, making Outlook Express look more like Outlook. The Outlook Bar displays folders as icons on the left side of the screen, and the Folder Bar shows the name of the currently open folder.

The options in the Toolbar section of the dialog box let you change the position of the toolbar, hide or display the text labels, and customize the toolbar by adding or deleting buttons. These are the same functions that you can perform using the menu that appears when you right-click the toolbar.

The Preview Pane options turn the pane off and on and control its position. When you choose to display the Preview Pane, you can also choose its position, either below or to the right of the message list, and you can display or hide the header, which shows the From, To, and Subject headings of the previewed message.

II

Electronic Mail

CHAPTER 7

Communicating with Newsgroups

A newsgroup is a group of individuals who share a common interest and who exchange messages with each other over the Internet. The collection of messages is also called a newsgroup. When a member *posts*, or sends, a message to the newsgroup, the message can be read and responded to by every other member of the group.

There are thousands of newsgroups, covering almost every imaginable topic—and some you probably couldn't even imagine! There are no membership fees or charges beyond what you pay your Internet service provider (ISP) for the Internet connection. You just sign up (*subscribe* in newsgroup parlance) and jump right in.

Setting Up for Newsgroups

In order for you to access newsgroups, your ISP must offer a news server, which is a computer that organizes newsgroups and handles the distribution of messages. Because of the popularity of newsgroups, it would be hard to find an ISP that doesn't offer such a server. Before accessing a newsgroup, you must be set up correctly to connect to the news server.

Outlook uses Outlook Express as its newsreader. A newsreader is a program that lets you access the news server, subscribe to newsgroups, and send and receive messages. If you did not install Outlook Express with Internet Explorer, Outlook will install a special version of it during its own installation process. When you start the newsreader from Outlook, you have access to the news features of Outlook Express but not to its Internet e-mail capabilities.

If you already set up Outlook Express as a separate program and configured it for at least one news server, it is ready and waiting. If you did not yet install any news servers, you'll have the chance to do so when you first access the newsreader.

Starting the Internet Connection Wizard

The easiest way to set up your news server is to use the Internet Connection Wizard. How you access the wizard depends on how you start the Outlook Express newsreader.

If you are running Outlook, choose News from the Go menu. Outlook Express opens and starts the Internet Connection Wizard if you don't already have a news server set up. If you have installed a different newsreader as your default newsreader, that one will open instead.

> If you installed Outlook Express as part of Internet Explorer, you can also start the Internet Connection Wizard by running Outlook Express and starting at step 2 on the next page.

You can also start the wizard from the Windows desktop by following these steps:

1 Point to Programs on the Start menu and choose Microsoft Outlook Newsreader.

2 When the newsreader starts, choose Accounts from the Tools menu.

3 Click Add, and then choose News from the menu that appears.

 NOTE

> Outlook Express users: When you start the newsreader from the Start menu, Outlook Express will not let you compose e-mail messages (other than to a newsgroup) or set up a mail account. In fact, the Mail tab will not be present in the Accounts dialog box. However, choosing News on the Go menu will open your *default* newsreader, which, if it's Outlook Express, *will* open with its mail features enabled.

Completing the Internet Connection Wizard

The Internet Connection Wizard is a series of dialog boxes in which you define your news server and prepare Outlook to communicate with it. You can set up the service to use a dial-up connection to your ISP, to connect through your network, or to let you manually connect using the dialer that comes with Internet Explorer or a third-party dialer.

To complete the Internet Connection Wizard, follow these steps:

1 Type your name and click Next.

2 Type your e-mail address and click Next.

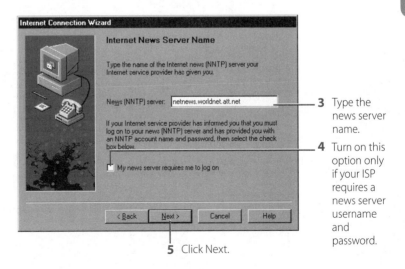

3 Type the news server name.

4 Turn on this option only if your ISP requires a news server username and password.

5 Click Next.

6 If you indicated that you need to enter a username and password, enter that information in the dialog box that appears and then click Next. You may need a username and password for some private newsgroups on company news servers but usually not for ISP news servers.

7 Enter a news server name that you would like to have displayed in the Folder List, and then click Next. By default, the Internet Connection Wizard uses the news server name, but you could use a less technical name, such as "AT&T Newsgroups."

8 Click here to use your phone line and a modem, or ...

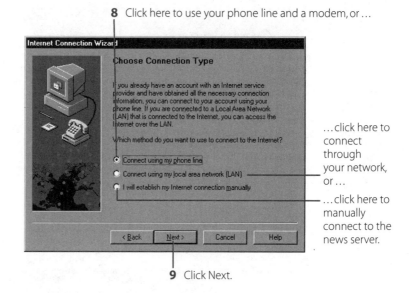

...click here to connect through your network, or ...

...click here to manually connect to the news server.

9 Click Next.

If you selected either a network or a manual connection, skip to step 13. If you selected a dial-up connection, continue with step 10.

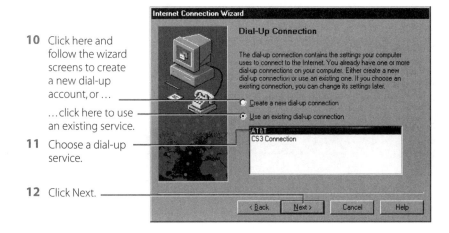

10 Click here and follow the wizard screens to create a new dial-up account, or …

…click here to use an existing service.

11 Choose a dial-up service.

12 Click Next.

13 Click Finish.

14 Click Close to close the Accounts dialog box. The name you chose for your news server will now appear at the bottom of the Folder List.

A message will appear asking if you want to download newsgroups from the server. See "Downloading Newsgroups," on the next page.

 NOTE

You can set up accounts for multiple newsgroup servers, and then switch between them in the Folder List.

To add an additional newsgroup account, you'll need to know the name of the newsgroup server. Then follow these steps:

1 Start Outlook Newsreader.

2 Choose Accounts from the Tools menu.

3 Click Add.

Electronic Mail

4 Click News to start the Internet Connection Wizard.

5 Complete the wizard as described above.

When you have more than one news account, you may wish to make one your default server. In the Internet Accounts dialog box, select one news account and click Set As Default.

If you need to update information for a news server account you've already created, follow these steps:

1 Choose Accounts from the Tools menu.

2 On the News tab of the dialog box, select the account you want to change.

3 Click Properties.

4 Change the desired settings.

5 Click OK, and then click Close on the Internet Accounts dialog box.

Downloading Newsgroups

You have to subscribe to a newsgroup before you can begin sending and receiving newsgroup messages. Subscribing to a newsgroup means marking it in Outlook so that it is displayed in the Folder List. However, before you can select groups to subscribe to, you'll have to download to your computer the entire list of newsgroups provided by your news server.

You'll be given an opportunity to download the list of newsgroups when you add or create a news server or the first time you click on a news server name in the Folder List.

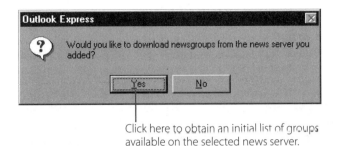

Click here to obtain an initial list of groups
available on the selected news server.

If you select a news server name in the Folder List and are not connected
to the Internet, you'll see another dialog box asking you if you'd like to
connect now. Click Yes to connect to your news server and download the
newsgroup names. Many news servers carry several tens of thousands of
newsgroups, so it may take several minutes to download the list. Once
downloaded, however, the names will be saved in the Newsgroups dialog
box, and you won't need to download the complete list again (see the
Newsgroups dialog box on the next page).

Subscribing to Newsgroups

Once you've downloaded the newsgroup list, you're ready to subscribe
to the newsgroups that interest you. If you do not subscribe to any
newsgroups, you'll see the following message each time you click on
the name of the news server in the Folder List:

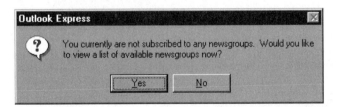

If you have already subscribed to at least one newsgroup and want
to open the Newsgroups dialog box, click the news server name
in the Folder List and then click the News Groups button on the
Standard toolbar.

Once the Newsgroups dialog box is displayed, subscribe to a news-group by following these steps:

1 Type a word or phrase to find a newsgroup of interest, or ... ... scroll the full list.

2 Click a newsgroup you want to subscribe to.   **3** Click Subscribe.

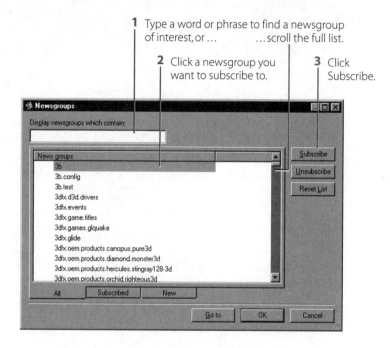

4 Repeat steps 1 through 3 for each group you wish to subscribe to.

Subscribed groups will have a newspaper icon next to their names. If you later want to unsubscribe to a newsgroup, click on it and click Unsubscribe.

 NOTE

> If you installed more than one news server, you'll see a News Servers bar on the left side of the dialog box. Click on the news server whose groups you want to list.

To view just the groups to which you are subscribed, click the Sub-scribed tab below the list.

From time to time, your news server may add more newsgroups to its list. When this occurs, you'll get a message whenever you log onto the news server asking if you want to download the new names. If you choose Yes, after Outlook Express downloads the new names, you can click the New tab of the Newsgroups dialog box to review the additional newsgroups and subscribe to any that interest you. To combine all the newsgroups into one list, click Reset List in the Newsgroups dialog box.

 **NOTE**

> To make sure that you are notified when new groups are added, choose the Options command from the Tools menu, click the General tab of the Options dialog box, and make sure the option Notify Me If There Are Any New News-groups is turned on.

Receiving Newsgroup Messages

Once you subscribe to newsgroups, when you click on the news server name in the Folder List, you'll see subscribed groups listed in the message list pane along with the total number of messages and the number of unread messages.

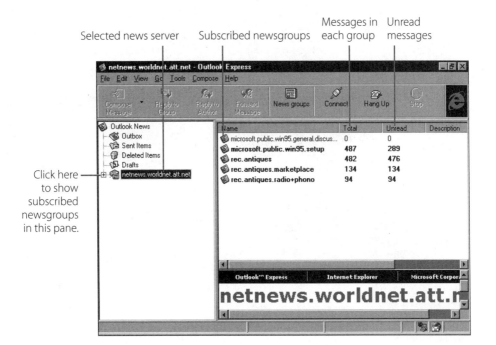

Selected news server Subscribed newsgroups Messages in each group Unread messages

Click here to show subscribed newsgroups in this pane.

To show the newsgroups in the Folder List, click the plus sign next to the news server name. The plus sign changes to a minus sign and your subscribed newsgroups appear indented beneath it, as is shown at the bottom of the next page.

Downloading Message Headers

To read newsgroup messages, you have to download them from the server. Because a newsgroup can have thousands of messages, many of which may not interest you, Outlook Express usually only downloads the message headers—the titles or subjects of the messages. You can then pick and choose which messages you want to read.

Click the newsgroup name that you want to read. Any messages that you already downloaded will be read from the cache and displayed in the message list. You'll see a message on the left of the status bar showing the total number of messages and the number that are still unread:

182 message(s), 182 unread

If you are online, Outlook will then automatically download up to 300 new message headers. (You can change this number on the Read tab of the Options dialog box.) A message on the left of the status bar will show the number of headers being received, and then they will appear in the message list. The list has four headings—Subject, From, Sent, and Size, although you may have to scroll the pane to see them all.

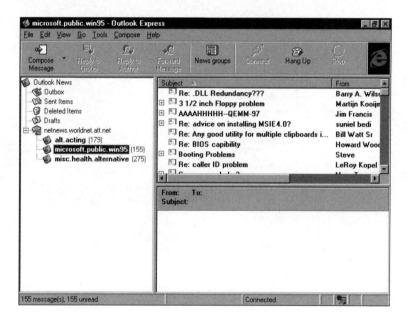

TIP

Choose Get Next 300 Headers from the Tools menu to download the next set of new headers.

If you are offline, you can connect to the news server and download new message headers by following these steps:

1   Select the newsgroup in the Folder List.

2   Choose Download This Newsgroup from the Tools menu.

3 Turn on this option.   **4** Select this option for the shortest download time.

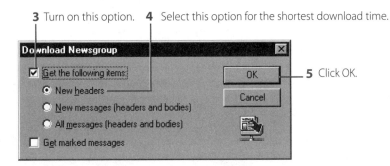

5 Click OK.

Outlook will connect to the news server, and then download new message headers (or whatever you requested in step 4 above) and display them in the message list.

Reading Messages

SEE ALSO

To change the number of messages read by default or other newsreader settings, see "Read Options," on page 220.

Now that you've downloaded the message headers, you can read messages that interest you. Messages that you have not read are shown in bold in the header list. Because only the header is actually downloaded by default, you can read the contents of messages as long as you are online but not if you disconnect.

To read a message, use either of these techniques:

■ Click the header to read the message in the Preview Pane.

■ Double-click the header to read the message in its own window.

If your newsreader window does not include a Preview Pane, follow these steps:

1   Choose Options from the Tools menu.

II

Electronic Mail

2 Click the Read tab.

3 Turn on the option labeled Automatically Show News Messages In The Preview Pane.

When you read a message, its contents will be temporarily stored in your computer's cache memory, so the message may be available even after you disconnect. Once the cache is cleared, however, the message contents will no longer be available offline unless you specifically download the message.

Working with Message Threads

A message thread is composed of an original message, all replies to it, replies to the replies, and so on. The thread usually relates to a single topic, though you shouldn't be surprised if messages get way off track as more replies are made.

Threads form a "conversation" about a subject that members are interested in. You can follow the thread to read the conversation in the order in which it actually took place.

Messages that contain threads are indicated with a plus sign in the header list. Threads tend to build up multiple levels with responses to responses and so on, as shown here:

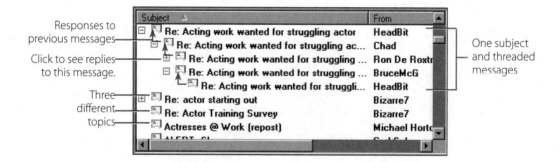

If your messages are not displayed in threads, point to Sort By on the View menu and choose Group Messages By Thread.

⭐ **TIP**

To display all message threads expanded, choose Options from the Tools menu and click the Read tab. Turn on the Automatically Expand Conversation Threads option.

When the thread is collapsed, the message header will be bold if at least one message in the thread is still unread (that is, unopened).

Downloading Messages

Reading messages while you are online can be time-consuming. You could easily run up huge phone bills and ISP charges if you are not on an unlimited plan. You can download the contents of all messages along with their headers, but that can also take a long time, and you may not even be interested in many of the messages. As an alternative, you can download selected messages and threads and then read them offline.

Reading Messages Offline

If you think you would be interested in every newsgroup message, you can set the newsreader to download both the headers of messages and their contents at the same time. You can then read the messages offline at your convenience. To set up a newsgroup for offline reading, follow these steps:

1   Right-click the newsgroup name in the Folder List or message pane window.

2   Point to Mark For Retrieval on the shortcut menu and choose one of the three download options, as shown below:

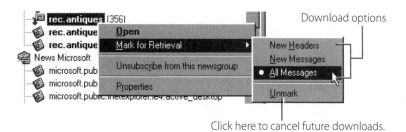

3   Repeat steps 1 and 2 for each newsgroup you want to set up.

When you want to download your messages, choose Download All from the Tools menu.

Use the Download This Newsgroup command from the Tools menu to download the messages from the selected newsgroup. Choose Download All from the Tools menu to download messages from all subscribed newsgroups on the server.

Downloading Selected Messages

You will probably find it more efficient to download only the messages that you are interested in reading. This way you don't take up a lot of disk space with uninteresting conversation, and you don't spend a lot of time waiting for the messages to be downloaded.

As you read through the message headers offline, mark those that you are interested in downloading. You can mark an individual message or an entire thread.

Here's how to mark and download individual messages.

1 Click a message header.

2 Point to Mark For Retrieval on the Tools menu and then choose the Mark Message command.

3 Repeat steps 1 and 2 for each message you want to download.

4 Choose Download This Newsgroup from the Tools menu.

5 Click OK.

Make sure this option is turned on. If it is not, go back and mark the messages again.

TIP

> To quickly mark a message for download, right-click it and choose Mark Message For Download from the shortcut menu (or just type the letter M). To mark multiple messages, select them by holding down the Ctrl key and clicking each message header. Then right-click any selected message header, and choose Mark Message For Download to mark all the messages.

To mark an entire thread, click the first message in the thread (the one with the plus sign). Point to Mark For Retrieval on the Tools menu and choose the Mark Thread command.

Displaying Messages

By default, Outlook displays all the message headers. With possibly thousands of messages in a newsgroup, it can take a long time to scan the list for ones you want to read.

Rather than display all the headers, you can choose to display certain ones. Point to Current View on the View menu, and then choose from these options:

All Messages.   This option displays all message headers.

Unread Messages.   This option displays only messages you have not yet read.

Downloaded Messages.   This option displays only messages that you downloaded.

Replies to My Posts.   This option displays replies to messages that you posted.

Just remember to change back to All Messages when you want to see all of the message headers!

Changing the Read Status of Messages

As you know, messages you haven't read are shown in bold in the message list. If you do not want to display only unread messages, you can use the bold indicator to scan the list for messages you still haven't read.

Once you're sure you are no longer interested in any unread messages in the list, you can mark them all as read. This way only new messages downloaded later will be shown in bold, and they'll be easy to identify.

To mark all of the messages in a selected newsgroup as read, follow these steps:

1 Point to Current View on the View menu, and then choose All Messages.

2 Choose Mark All As Read from the Edit menu.

The Edit menu also lets you mark individual messages or an entire thread as read, or you can mark a message as unread.

Finding Messages

When you're interested in messages about a specific topic, you'll find yourself scanning up and down the list looking for a key word or phrase in the headers. But because a newsgroup can contain hundreds, or even thousands of messages, you'll become bleary-eyed long before you reach the end of the list.

 TIP

> Remember, you can sort messages by clicking on the column heading in the message list. To sort by date, for example, click on the Sent header to toggle between an ascending and descending sort.

Rather than straining your eyes by scanning through the message list to find those you are interested in, have the newsreader find messages for you. The Find Messages command lets you locate messages by searching for a word or phrase in the header, by searching for a sender's name, or by searching for the date the message was posted. Here's how.

1 Select a newsgroup in the Folder List.

2 Choose Find Message on the Edit menu, and then enter as many specifications as needed in the Find Message dialog box.

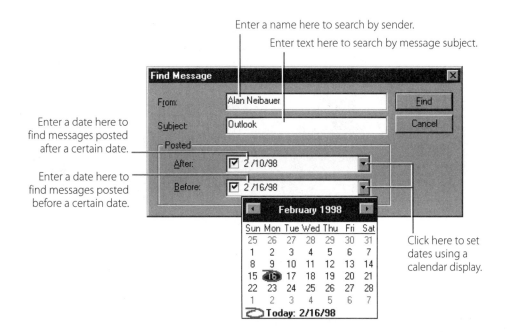

Enter a name here to search by sender.

Enter text here to search by message subject.

Enter a date here to
find messages posted
after a certain date.

Enter a date here to
find messages posted
before a certain date.

Click here to set
dates using a
calendar display.

Electronic Mail

3 Click Find.

Outlook will find and display the next message in the list that meets
the criteria. Press F3 to find the next and subsequent messages meeting
the same criteria.

Filtering Newsgroup Messages

The Find command displays messages that meet certain criteria. You
can use a filter to block messages that you are not interested in—for
example, from a certain sender, over a certain size that takes too long
to download, or on a specific subject.

A filter consists of one or more rules, much like the rules you create in
the Inbox Assistant. Messages that meet the conditions specified in the
rule will not be downloaded or displayed. You can turn the rules on
and off to control how and when the filter is applied. You can leave all
of the rules turned on, for example, to display just the messages you
are currently interested in, and then later turn off the rule to display all
the messages.

Follow these steps to create a filter:

1 Choose Newsgroup Filters from the Tools menu to display the Newsgroup Filters dialog box.

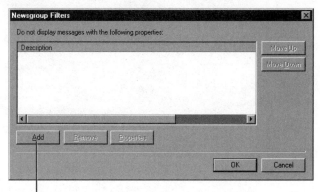

2 Click Add to display the Properties dialog box.

3 Select the server or newsgroups to apply the filter to, or select All Servers.

4 In any combination, enter or select from the Address Book a sender whose messages you want to exclude,…

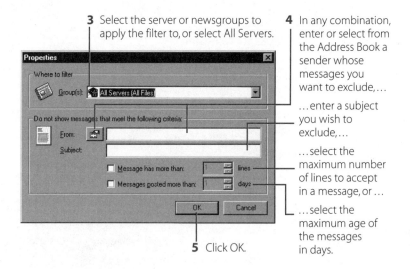

…enter a subject you wish to exclude,…

…select the maximum number of lines to accept in a message, or …

…select the maximum age of the messages in days.

5 Click OK.

6 Repeat steps 2 through 5 to create additional filter criteria.

The rules will appear in the Newsgroup Filters dialog box. If you no longer want to apply a certain filter, turn off all the rules or remove them from the Newsgroup Filters dialog box.

Turn off to ignore the rule.

Click to change the order in which the rules are applied.

Turn on to apply the rule.

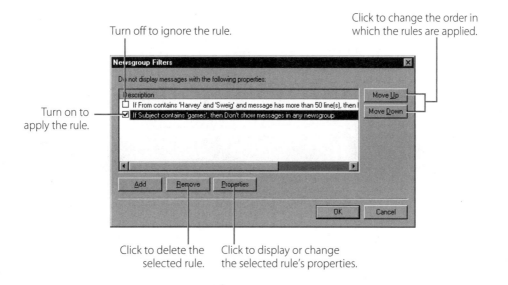

Click to delete the selected rule.

Click to display or change the selected rule's properties.

Electronic Mail

Checking Out a Newsgroup

You can also read newsgroup messages without subscribing to the newsgroup. This is useful if you're not sure that you want to subscribe to the group. Follow these steps:

1 Click the News Groups button on the Standard toolbar.

2 On the All tab, click on the newsgroup you may be interested in.

3 Click Go To.

Message headers will begin downloading to your computer. Because you are not subscribed to the group, the message headers will not be saved and the group will not be listed when you next start the Outlook Newsreader. To subscribe to the newsgroup you are viewing, choose Subscribe To This Group on the Tools menu.

Posting Newsgroup Messages

Sending mail to a newsgroup is very similar to sending regular e-mail. The main difference is that when you post a message, even a reply to someone else's message, you are sending it to the news server, where it can be viewed by every reader of the newsgroup.

As with e-mail, you can post a new message (start a new thread) or reply to a current message (add to an existing thread). With a newsgroup, you can also choose to reply personally to the sender or to forward the message to someone else via e-mail instead of through the group.

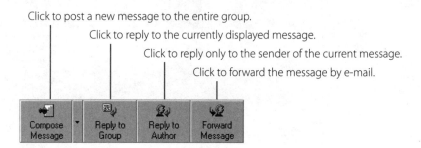

Click to post a new message to the entire group.

Click to reply to the currently displayed message.

Click to reply only to the sender of the current message.

Click to forward the message by e-mail.

When you post a new message or reply to the newsgroup, the To field of the New Message window will contain the name of the group. Do not edit the field. Complete the message, and then click Send in the message window to place it in the Outbox. Finally, click Send And Receive to post the message.

Setting Up Outlook for Remote Work

Many people never need to use Microsoft Outlook 98 beyond their workplace desktop. But you adventurous types who travel with your computers can set up Outlook to dial in to and connect to your e-mail server so that you can work with your e-mail and calendar.

When you're lodged in a hotel, you still might want to see the messages, postings, and meetings that are going on at headquarters. For times such as these, you can send and delete messages, set up appointments and tasks, request meetings, and respond to meeting and task requests. And, with some preliminary setup, you can also see the contents of public folders as well as your server folders.

This chapter introduces the various ways you can use Outlook to work from a remote computer. You'll find detailed instructions for setting up both online and offline work. This chapter focuses on the setup procedures involved in remote use. Chapter 9, "Running Outlook for Remote Work," focuses on how you use Outlook once your setup is complete—making connections, working with folders, sending messages, and so on.

Offline Folders vs. Remote Mail

When you use offline folders or Remote Mail, Outlook provides several ways for you to manage messages and other items from remote locations. If you run Outlook with Microsoft Exchange Server, it's probably better to use offline folders. With offline folders, you download a copy of your folders from Exchange Server onto your laptop, or whatever computer you are using to work offline. If you don't use Microsoft Exchange Server or if you simply need to download messages from your Inbox (and not use the calendar or other Outlook features), it's better to use Remote Mail. Remote Mail downloads new message headers when you connect, so you can choose which messages you want to read. Use the following descriptions to determine the method that is best for you.

You'll want to use the offline folders method in these cases:

- You use Outlook with Microsoft Exchange Server.

- You want to update the contents of any folder.

- You want to synchronize the folders between two computers—for instance, you want to have identical folder contents on the server and on your remote computer.

- You want to download your calendar or a task list to a remote computer.

- You don't need to worry about the cost of time on the telephone—for instance, you have an inexpensive local phone connection to your mail delivery service.

Use the Remote Mail method in these cases:

- You use Outlook with a server other than Microsoft Exchange Server.

- You want to retrieve messages for your Inbox only.

- You want to minimize time spent on the telephone—for instance, your computer at home has a slow modem, or you're connecting from a hotel or airport where the cost of telephone access is high.

You have three ways to work remotely with your e-mail:

- Work remotely online only (no offline work). See "Setting Up to Work Remotely—Online Only," opposite.

- Work online and offline, sometimes remotely, with offline folders. You can use this offline folders method only if you are running Outlook with Microsoft Exchange Server as your e-mail server. See "Setting Up to Work Remotely—Online and Offline," on page 266.

- Use Remote Mail to send and receive messages, but work offline most of the time. See "Setting Up Remote Mail and Offline Work," on page 276.

Before you decide between using offline folders or Remote Mail, consult the sidebar "Offline Folders vs. Remote Mail," on the facing page.

> **NOTE**

To work with Outlook remotely, your system administrator must set up your user account with dial-up access rights so that you can dial in to the network. Contact your system administrator for assistance.

II

Electronic Mail

Setting Up to Work Remotely—Online Only

You can dial in to your organization's network with the Dial-Up Networking feature in Microsoft Windows 95. After you connect to the network over the telephone line, you can then run Outlook just as if you were connected directly to the network. Using this method, you don't work with Outlook offline, so you don't need to make any changes to an Outlook profile, and you don't have to worry about offline folders. You do, however, need to set up Dial-Up Networking in Windows 95 so you can dial in to your network computer, as explained here:

1 Click the Start button on the Windows 95 taskbar, and then point to Programs. On the submenu that appears point to Accessories, and then click Dial-Up Networking.

If you have not created a dial-up networking connection before, you'll see the welcoming panel of the Make New Connection

Wizard. Otherwise, you'll see the Dial-Up Networking window shown here. (Your window may appear slightly different if you have selected a different view.)

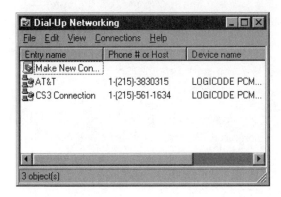

2 If the Dial-Up Networking window appeared, double-click Make New Connection.

SEE ALSO
See "Setting Up Calling Card Dialing," on page 284, for details about setting up Outlook to dial using your telephone calling card.

3 Type or accept the name for your connection.

4 Make sure your modem appears here.

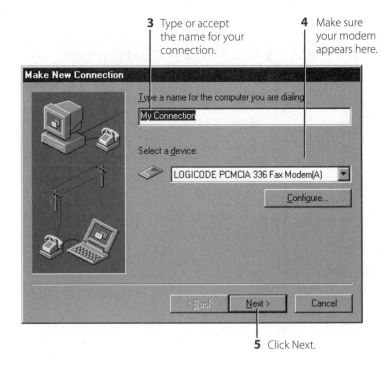

5 Click Next.

6 On the next screen, enter the area code and telephone number of your network computer.

7 Select the country location of the network server's phone number.

8 Click Next.

9 Click Finish on the final panel of the Make New Connection Wizard.

When you're ready to connect to the network computer, take the steps described in "Setting Up to Work Remotely—Online Only," on page 263. You can use a dial-up networking connection for all the tasks you would usually perform while directly connected to a network.

What About My Connections to Other Online Services?

If you have accounts on other online services, such as MSN (the Microsoft Network), CompuServe, America Online, or AT&T WorldNet, you can set up these services in a profile, and then use Outlook to send and receive mail through the service.

To set up an information service in a profile, first install any software that your service provided, or follow any directions they gave you to set up the dial-up service. This will create a dial-up networking account for the service. Then add an Internet e-mail service to your profile as explained in "Setting Up Internet E-Mail," on page 13. In the Connection tab of the Properties dialog box, turn on the Connect Using My Phone Line option, then select your ISP's connection in the Use the Following Dial-Up Network Connection list.

Note that typically you can add only one dial-in information service to a profile. Why? Because each dial-in information service requires a modem and a telephone line. When one service is using the modem and telephone line, a second service won't have access to the line. If, however, you have multiple modems connected to your computer and a telephone line for each modem, you can then set up one dial-in information service for each modem and telephone line.

II

Electronic Mail

Setting Up to Work Remotely— Online and Offline

Wouldn't it be a shame to have to give up the fancy tools you use with Outlook simply because you aren't connected to your Microsoft Exchange Server? You might not be connected either because you are away from your network connection or because the network or your Microsoft Exchange Server is currently not functioning. For these situations, you can use offline folders.

> **NOTE**
>
> You can use offline folders only if your e-mail server is Microsoft Exchange Server and you are using a profile for which you've indicated that you travel with your computer.

This method of working in Outlook parallels the method described in the preceding section, with one difference. For this method, you set up offline folders so that you can work on your messages, appointments, tasks, and other Outlook folder items without being connected to your e-mail server.

> **TIP**
>
> You can use a single Outlook profile for both online and offline work. If you do, you can have Outlook automatically detect your connection status when it starts, you can choose a default connection type, or you can ask to be prompted each time you start. To adjust these settings choose Services on the Tools menu, select Microsoft Exchange Server, select Properties, and then set your preferences on the General tab.

With offline folders, you can synchronize your Inbox folder, Calendar folder, Tasks folder, and any other folder from your remote location to make the contents identical to the contents of these folders on your e-mail server. You can download all the items in all offline folders in one step.

> If you use offline folders, you cannot use Remote Mail to download messages.

Here are the general steps involved in setting up Outlook for both online and offline work. You'll find the details for all five steps in the following six sections.

1 Set up an offline folder file.

2 Download the Offline Address Book.

3 Set up public folder favorites for public folders you want to open offline.

4 Designate other folders for offline use.

5 Filter the content of the offline folders.

6 Synchronize all offline folders.

Setting Up an Offline Folder File

To set up an offline folder file, take these steps:

1 Connect to your e-mail server for online work, either through a network connection or through Dial-Up Networking.

2 If necessary, switch to your Inbox.

3 Choose Services on the Tools menu.

> It really is much better to perform the steps for setting up an offline folder file while connected through a network connection than while connected through Dial-Up Networking. Why? Most dial-up networking connections run through modems that have much lower speeds than a network connection. Through a modem connection, the processes Outlook must perform before you can work offline can take a *very* long time. Over a direct network connection, the processes go relatively quickly.

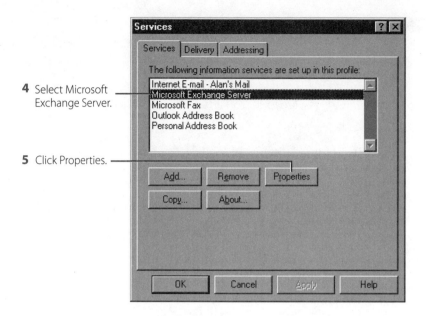

4 Select Microsoft Exchange Server.

5 Click Properties.

6 In the Microsoft Exchange Server dialog box, click the Advanced tab.

7 Click the Offline Folder File Settings button on the Advanced tab.

8 Accept the filename, type a new name, or ...

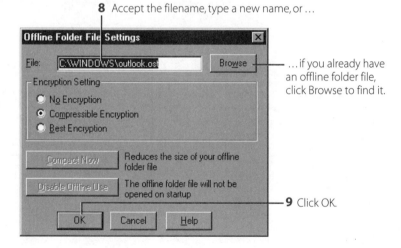

... if you already have an offline folder file, click Browse to find it.

9 Click OK.

10 When you are returned to the Advanced tab of the Microsoft Exchange Server dialog box, turn on the Enable Offline Use option.

11 Click OK, and then click OK in the Services dialog box. You're now ready for the next phase of setting up offline folders: downloading the Offline Address Book.

Turning Off Offline Folders

If you later want to discontinue using all offline folders, here's how to do it.

1 Connect to your e-mail server for online work, either through a network connection or through Dial-Up Networking.

2 If necessary, switch to your Inbox.

3 Choose Services on the Tools menu, select Microsoft Exchange Server, and then click the Properties button.

4 In the Microsoft Exchange Server dialog box, click the Advanced tab, and then turn off the Enable Offline Use option.

5 Click OK first in the Microsoft Exchange Server dialog box and then in the Services dialog box.

You can also turn off offline folders so they are disabled the next time you log on to Outlook. On the Advanced tab of the Microsoft Exchange Server dialog box, click the Offline Folder File Settings button and then click the Disable Offline Use button. Click Yes when Outlook asks whether you want to continue.

Downloading the Offline Address Book

When you're working offline, you'll probably want to compose new messages, reply to messages, and forward messages. Before you can specify the recipients of your message or place the message in your Outbox to be sent later, you need to have the Offline Address Book available. If you don't download the Offline Address Book, Outlook tells you that you can't compose or otherwise work with a message until you download the address book.

To download the Offline Address Book, do the following:

1 Connect to your network and start Outlook.

2 Choose the Synchronize command on the Tools menu.

3 Choose Download Address Book on the submenu.

4 In the Download Offline Address Book dialog box, select the level of detail you need in this address book. The first option downloads the address book with all its information. The second option omits details information. This second option is faster, but without details you cannot use encryption.

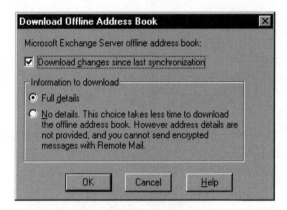

5 Click OK. You'll see a message that shows you how downloading is progressing. When downloading is complete, you're ready to work with messages offline.

Working Remotely with Public Folders

While you're working offline, you can't open the server's public folders, at least not directly. Outlook helps you get around this restriction through public folder favorites. If you've already set these up, you're in a good position to take advantage of them during offline work. If you haven't yet set up any public folder favorites, you must do so before you can work with the contents of a public folder offline.

Setting up public folder favorites is quite easy; simply follow these steps:

1 Find and open the public folder you want to add to your Public Folders Favorites folder. (You can do this by displaying the Other Shortcuts group on the Outlook Bar and clicking the Public Folders icon.)

2 Point to Folder on the File menu, and then choose Add To Public Folder Favorites from the submenu.

3 When the Add to Favorites dialog box appears, the folder you chose will already be highlighted in the Favorite Folder Name list. Click the Add button.

At this point, the folder you added displays the contents of its related public folder, and you can now set the folder in the Public Folders Favorites folder to be available offline. (See the next section, below.)

When you're working offline, the Public Folders Favorites folder contains the contents of the related public folder as they were the last time you synchronized the folders. You can read items in the folder, post new items, and reply to postings and messages. You can also delete items and add forms if you have permission to do so. Outlook copies the changes you make in the offline Public Folders Favorites folder to its related public folder the next time you connect to your Exchange server.

Designating Folders for Offline Work

Your Inbox, Outbox, Sent Items, and Deleted Items folders on your Exchange server are immediately available offline as well as online when you set up your offline folder file. (See "Setting Up an Offline Folder File," on page 267.) When you work offline, these folders contain all the items that were in the folders when you last exited Outlook. You can open and view these folders as you would while working online. You can compose messages, move messages, delete messages, and empty your Deleted Items folder—all while you're working offline. New messages won't be sent, however, and the other actions won't be posted to the server folders until you go online and synchronize the folders. Synchronizing means updating the contents of the offline folders on the remote computer so that they contain the same information that is in the server folders.

In addition to these folders, you can set up for offline use any other accessible folders on your Exchange server as well as any public folder favorites you have set up.

To designate a server folder or a favorite public folder for offline use, take these steps:

1 Right-click the folder you want to set up for offline use, and then choose Properties on the shortcut menu. As an alternative, you can click the folder, point to Folder on the File menu, and then choose Properties For on the submenu.

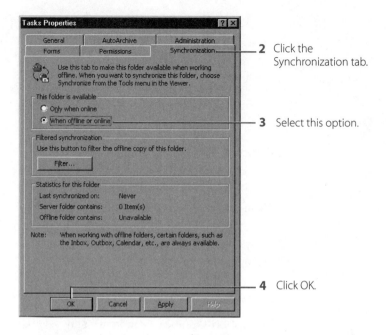

2 Click the
Synchronization tab.

3 Select this option.

4 Click OK.

This folder is now available for work offline as well as online. If you
no longer want a folder to be available for offline work, select the
Only When Online option on the Synchronization tab of the Properties
dialog box.

 NOTE

> You cannot set up your four main server folders—Inbox, Outbox, Sent Items, and
> Deleted Items—for exclusively online work unless you turn off offline folders. For
> instructions on how to do this, see "Turning Off Offline Folders," on page 269.

Filtering Folders for Offline Work

By default, your offline folders will be duplicates of your folders from
the Exchange server. Rather than duplicate all of the folder contents,
however, you can create a filter to determine what items are copied to
your offline folders when they are synchronized. Only items that match
the filter will be transferred into your offline folders. Create a filter from
the folder's Properties dialog box by following these steps:

1 Select the folder you want to filter.

2 Point to Folder on the File menu, and then choose Properties.

3 Select the Synchronization tab on the Properties dialog box.

4 Click Filter and then define any combination of the criteria shown.

Type words to be included in the filter. Choose the field.

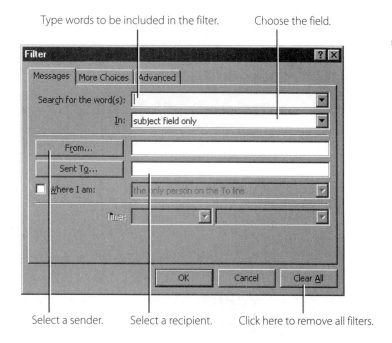

Select a sender. Select a recipient. Click here to remove all filters.

5 When finished with this tab, click the More Choices tab if you want to specify additional criteria.

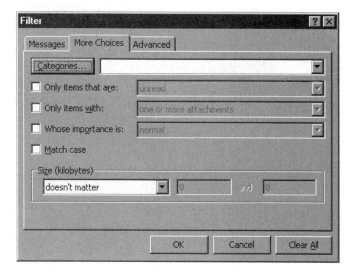

6 Specify any additional filter criteria, including categories and type of items. Then continue by clicking the Advanced tab if you want to specify additional criteria.

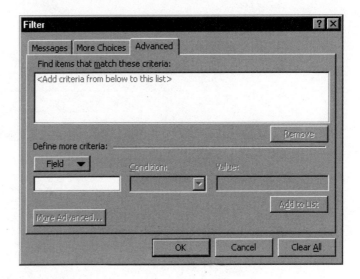

7 Define additional criteria based on the contents of fields.

8 Click OK.

Synchronizing Folders

After you set up folders for offline use, you need to periodically synchronize the offline folders with their related folders on the Exchange server. Outlook synchronizes your offline folders automatically whenever you connect to Microsoft Exchange Server. After a session of working online, you might want to synchronize your folders again. Before exiting Outlook, and while you're still connected to your Exchange server, you can synchronize any folders that you have set up to be available offline. To synchronize a single folder, do the following:

1 Select the folder that you want to synchronize.

2 Point to Synchronize on the Tools menu and choose This Folder from the submenu.

NOTE

Remember that publick folders reside on the server. If you want to use a public folder offline, you must add it to the Public Folder Favorites folder as explained in "Working Remotely with Public Folders," on page 270, and then choose to synchronize the copy of the folder in the Public Folder Favorites folder.

To synchronize all folders, point to Synchronize on the Tools menu, and then choose All Folders from the submenu. In either case—synchronizing a single folder or all folders—Outlook displays the progress of its synchronization in the Outlook status bar.

You can also set up Outlook to automatically connect remotely and synchronize folders. While working online in Outlook, choose Options on the Tools menu, and then click the Mail Services tab. Turn on the option labeled When Offline, Automatically Synchronize All Offline Folders, set the time interval, and then click OK.

NOTE

In the Mail Services tab of the Options dialog box, you can turn off the Enable Offline Access check box if you decide not to automatically synchronize folders.

Automatically Synchronizing All Offline Folders

When you use offline folders, you'll connect to your Exchange server at least occasionally, either over a network or with Dial-Up Networking. Outlook always synchronizes offline folders when you connect to your Exchange server. After that, you can synchronize any or all offline folders whenever you want while you're connected to the server. To further help you keep your offline folders synchronized, you can set an option to have Outlook automatically synchronize all offline folders with your online (server) folders when you exit an online Outlook session. To do so, follow these steps:

1   While working online in Outlook, choose Options on the Tools menu, and then click the Mail Services tab.

2   Turn on the option labeled When Online, Synchronize All Folders Upon Exiting, and then click OK.

II

Electronic Mail

With this option turned on, your offline folders are consistent with your online folders when you start to work offline. Leave this option turned off only if you prefer to manually synchronize your offline folders (by using the Synchronize command on the Tools menu) while you're working online. In the Mail Services tab, you can also select to automatically synchronize folders at periodic intervals, such as every 60 minutes, when you are online. You can manually synchronize folders at any time when you're online, even if you have also turned on one of the automatic synchronization options on the Mail Services tab. You can even set Outlook to synchronize while you're working offline, which means Outlook will automatically connect, synchorize, and disconnect at the time interval you specify.

Setting Up Remote Mail and Offline Work

If you need to work only with the messages in your Inbox, or if you want to spend as little time as possible on the telephone line, you can dial up your e-mail server with Remote Mail. By connecting to your e-mail server with Remote Mail, you get only a list of message headers. Remote Mail then disconnects from the server to save you from expensive phone charges. You mark the messages you want to read and the messages you want to delete and then you connect with Remote Mail again to download. When you reconnect to your e-mail server, Outlook downloads only those messages marked for download, deletes those messages marked for deletion, and disconnects again. You can then read the downloaded messages and perform all the actions—reply, delete, forward, move, and save—that you perform with messages when you're connected to your e-mail server through a network. You simply repeat the Remote Mail connection until you've finished receiving and sending messages.

 NOTE

If you use offline folders, you cannot use Remote Mail to download messages. If you have set up offline folders, either create a new profile without offline folders, or turn off these folders for the profile that you want to use for Remote Mail. See "Turning Off Offline Folders," on page 269.

Before you can connect through Remote Mail, you need to perform the following general steps:

1 Download the Offline Address Book while you're connected to your e-mail server. For details, see "Downloading the Offline Address Book," on page 269.

2 Set up personal folders, either in an existing profile or in a new profile. You can do this either online or offline.

3 Set up Remote Mail connections, providing Outlook with information such as your username and password.

4 Set up Remote Mail options, which you can do either online or offline.

Adding Personal Folders to a Profile

A personal folder file (which uses the .PST filename extension) is usually located on your computer's hard disk. Your personal folders mirror the set of folders used to store messages and other items on your e-mail server. Personal folders include the Inbox folder, the Calendar folder, and the other Outlook folders available on your server. You can work with items in personal folders even when the network or mail delivery service is unavailable. When you use Remote Mail in Outlook, a copy of your message is downloaded from your server to your Personal Folders Inbox.

? SEE ALSO

For information about setting up a profile, see "Creating a Profile," on page 7.

The easiest way to set up personal folders in Outlook is during the creation of a profile. When the Outlook Setup wizard asks whether you travel with this computer, choose Yes. The wizard then sets up personal folders for you.

To add personal folders to an existing profile, take these steps:

1 Select the Services tab of the Properties dialog box for the profile you want to change. If you're currently using the profile in Outlook, choose Services on the Tools menu and click the Services tab. If you want to change a profile that you aren't currently using, double-click the Mail icon on the Windows Control Panel. Click the Show Profiles button, select the profile you want to change, and then click the Properties button.

II

Electronic Mail

2 On the Services tab, click the Add button.

3 In the Add Service To Profile dialog box, select Personal Folders, and click OK.

4 In the Create/Open Personal Folders File dialog box, either type a name for a new personal folders file or select an existing personal folders file (one you use for another profile), and then click the Open button.

5 In the next dialog box that appears, type the name for your personal folders as you would like it to appear in Outlook's Folder List, or leave the default name, "Personal Folders."

6 If you're creating a new set of personal folders, enter a password for them and retype it for verification. It can be the same as your network logon password or your regular Outlook password. If you're using an existing set of personal folders, optionally click the Change Password button and type the old and then a new password.

7 To avoid typing the password each time you start Outlook, turn on the Save This Password In Your Password List option.

8 Click OK in each dialog box to complete the procedure.

Setting Up Remote Mail Connections

Before you can use Remote Mail, you must provide Outlook with information about your remote connection. To provide Outlook with this information, you need to set Dial-Up Networking options and Remote Mail options. Follow these steps:

1 Choose the Services command on the Tools menu, select Microsoft Exchange Server, and then click the Properties button.

2 Click the Dial-Up Networking tab.

3 Select the option for your Remote Mail connection. You have two choices:

- **Dial Using The Following Connection.** You'll want to select this option when you're working offline and you're going to use Remote Mail over a telephone line only. This option starts the dial-up process for you when you run Remote Mail. The connection names that are listed come from the Windows 95 Dial-Up Networking window.

- **Do Not Dial, Use Existing Connection.** You'll want to select this option when you're working offline and you're connected directly to your network or you've opened a dial-up connection through Windows 95 Dial-Up Networking. This option simply connects to your Exchange server through the existing connection rather than by dialing up.

4 If you select the Dial Using The Following Connection option, you can select an existing connection name from the drop-down list, or you can create a new connection by clicking the New button. If you need to modify a connection, click the Properties button. (For the additional steps involved in creating a new connection or modifying a connection, see "Setting Up to Work Remotely—Online Only," on page 263.) To change the location, click the Location button, and follow the instructions in "Setting Dialing Options," on page 154.

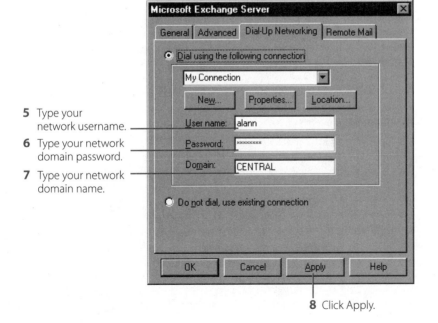

5 Type your network username.

6 Type your network domain password.

7 Type your network domain name.

8 Click Apply.

Electronic Mail

Setting Remote Mail Options

Remote Mail makes it possible for you to save time by screening message headers first, allowing you to mark messages for reading or deletion. You can then download in their entirety the messages that you have marked for reading.

We'll look at two options that can make Remote Mail work better for you:

■ Filtering Remote Mail so that you don't have to see messages you don't care about when you're away from your office

■ Scheduling automatic dial-in times so that you can keep your folders at home current

To set Remote Mail options, take the following steps. The specific options are detailed in the next two sections.

1 If the Dial-Up Networking tab of the Microsoft Exchange Server properties dialog box is still visible from the previous steps, click the Remote Mail tab. Otherwise, choose Services from the Tools menu, select Microsoft Exchange Server, click the Properties button, and then click the Remote Mail tab.

2 Choose to have Outlook process all marked items or …

…only items that match a filter.

3 Click here to set up a filter.

4 Turn this option off if you want to keep the Remote Mail connection open after processing.

5 Click here to schedule dial-up times.

6 Click OK.

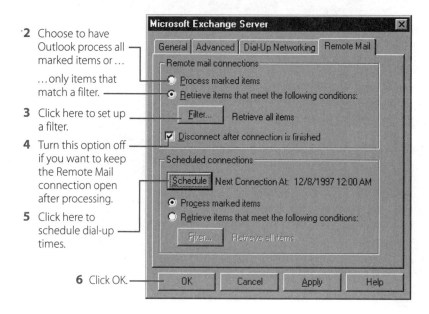

7 Click OK in the Services dialog box.

Filtering Remote Mail

A filter sets up conditions that tell the Remote Mail part of Outlook which message headers to download. A filter screens out messages you don't want to deal with and passes through only those message headers that you do want to see. This means shorter connection times while Remote Mail downloads the message headers and shorter work sessions for you because you aren't wading through extraneous messages.

Here's how to set up a Remote Mail filter.

1   Return to the Remote Mail tab of the Microsoft Exchange Server dialog box by choosing Services on the Tools menu, selecting Microsoft Exchange Server, and then clicking the Properties button.

2   In the Remote Mail Connections section of the dialog box, select the Retrieve Items That Meet The Following Conditions option, and then click the Filter button.

3   In the Filter dialog box, set up the criteria for the filter you want to use. You can fill in any or all of the four criteria, which can limit your remote mail transfers to messages from certain people, with a certain subject, and sent or copied directly to you.

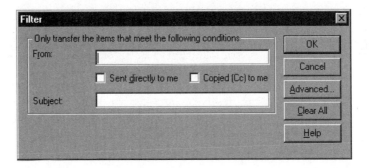

4   Click Advanced to see more criteria.

5   In the Advanced dialog box, set up any advanced criteria you need, such as accepting items of certain sizes, items within certain date ranges, items of specified importance and sensitivity levels, and items that are unread, contain attachments, or *don't* match the conditions you've set.

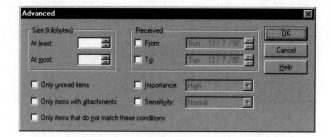

6 Click OK in all the open dialog boxes.

You can set up criteria in the Advanced dialog box either in addition to criteria you set up in the Filter dialog box or instead of setting criteria there. You don't have to fill out the Filter dialog box at all if you want to receive all your remote mail items.

Notice the option in the Advanced dialog box labeled Only Items That Do Not Match These Conditions. Selecting this option reverses all the other conditions you set up in the Filter and Advanced dialog boxes. For example, if you turn on this option and the Only Unread Items option, only items that you have already read will be delivered to you.

It's a simple matter to turn off a Remote Mail filter—click Process Marked Items on the Remote Mail tab.

This preserves your filter but deactivates it. It can be restored at any time by clicking Retrieve Items That Meet The Following Conditions again.

To remove the filter entirely, follow these steps instead:

1 Click the Filter button on the Remote Mail tab.

2 In the Filter dialog box, click the Clear All button, and then click OK.

Clicking the Clear All button clears both the Filter and the Advanced dialog box settings. The label beside the Filter button on the Remote Mail tab changes to Retrieve All Items. To make it clear that you aren't using any filter, you can select the Process Marked Items option, though with the filter turned off, either option will retrieve all your items.

Scheduling Remote Mail Connections

When you're away from your network connection, you might want to connect with Remote Mail at a specific time or at specific intervals or both. With Remote Mail scheduling, you can set the time and interval you want Outlook to use to dial in and connect.

To set up a dial-in schedule for Remote Mail, follow these steps:

1 Choose Services on the Tools menu, select Microsoft Exchange Server, click the Properties button, and then click the Remote Mail tab.

2 On the Remote Mail tab, click the Schedule button.

> **NOTE**
>
> You can set both a specific time and a time interval for the scheduled connections in the Schedule Remote Mail Connection dialog box. That's because the time interval you specify in the At box functions independently of the time you specify in the Every box. The At option establishes a single time connection; the Every option establishes a connection according to a time interval (such as one hour) from the *current system time*—not from the time you enter in the At box.

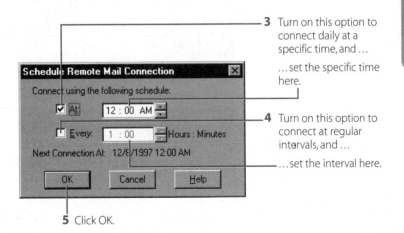

3 Turn on this option to connect daily at a specific time, and …

… set the specific time here.

4 Turn on this option to connect at regular intervals, and …

… set the interval here.

5 Click OK.

6 In the Scheduled Connections area, select the Process Marked Items option to have Outlook process all marked items, or select the Retrieve Items That Meet The Following Conditions option to

II

Electronic Mail

set up a filter. Click the Filter button in the Scheduled Connections area, then complete the filter as explained in "Filtering Remote Mail," on page 281.

7 Click OK in all the open dialog boxes.

Setting Up Calling Card Dialing

For various reasons, you might want to charge your dial-up calls to a telephone calling card. That's easy to set up. Here's what you do:

1 Use one of the following methods to open the Dialing Properties dialog box, which displays the My Locations tab:

- From within Outlook, choose Services on the Tools menu, select Microsoft Exchange Server, click Properties, click the Dial-Up Networking tab, and then click Location.

- In the Windows 95 Dial-Up Networking window, double-click a connection and then click Dial Properties.

2 Turn on this option to open the Change Calling Card dialog box, or ...

... if the option is already selected, click Change to change the calling card.

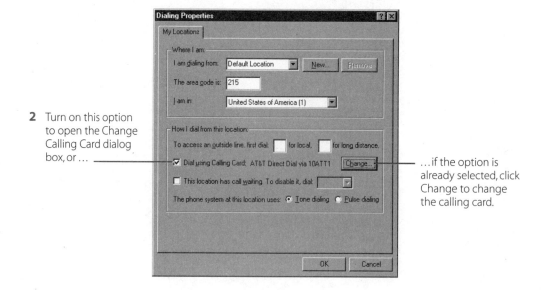

3 Select the specific type of calling card you want to use.

4 Type your calling card number.

5 To see the dialing rules for your calls, click the Advanced button in the Change Calling Card dialog box. Outlook opens the Dialing Rules dialog box. You can't change the dialing rules for the types of calling cards listed by Outlook. You can set up dialing rules for calling cards you add. For more information, see the next section.

Adding a New Calling Card

If the type of calling card you want to use isn't listed in the Change Calling Card dialog box, you can add it to the list. To add a new calling card, follow these steps:

1 In the Change Calling Card dialog box, click the New button.

2 Type the name of your calling card in the Create New Calling Card dialog box.

3 Click OK.

4 Enter your calling card number.

5 Click the Advanced button in the Change Calling Card dialog box to set up dialing rules for your calls. You may need to consult with your calling card provider to determine the appropriate rules.

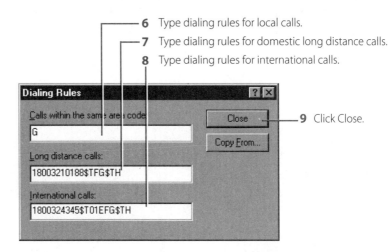

6 Type dialing rules for local calls.

7 Type dialing rules for domestic long distance calls.

8 Type dialing rules for international calls.

9 Click Close.

The dialing rules for calling cards are based on specific letters and symbols as well as numbers. To see an on-screen list of letters and symbols used in dialing rules, click the Help button in the upper-right corner of the Dialing Rules dialog box, and then click one of the rules boxes. The list will contain alphabetic characters and what dialing function each controls.

10 If the new calling card you're setting up can use dialing rules that have been set up for another card, click the Copy From button in the Dialing Rules dialog box. In the Copy Dialing Rules dialog box, select the calling card with the dialing rules you want to copy, and click OK.

You're now ready to access your mail remotely using a calling card.

Running Outlook for Remote Work

Now that you've set up Microsoft Outlook 98 for remote work (see Chapter 8, "Setting Up Outlook for Remote Work"), you're ready to work with Outlook remotely. In this chapter, you'll read about the ways you can run Outlook for remote work. The method you use will depend on your Outlook setup and the work you need to do.

You have three ways to run Outlook for remote work:

- Work remotely online only (no offline work). Use this method if you have a toll-free telephone connection to your e-mail server. If you still need to set up Outlook for this option, see "Setting Up to Work Remotely—Online Only," on page 263.

- Work online and offline, sometimes remotely; this method uses offline folders. You can use this offline folders method only if your e-mail server is Microsoft Exchange Server. Use this method when you prefer not to connect to your e-mail server full-time. If you still need to set up Outlook for this option, see "Setting Up to Work Remotely—Online and Offline," on page 266.

■ Use Remote Mail to send and receive messages but work offline most of the time. Use this method when you're away from a network connection and the telephone call to your e-mail server is a toll call. If you still need to set up Outlook for this option, see "Setting Up Remote Mail and Offline Work," on page 276.

Before you decide whether to use offline folders or Remote Mail, consult the sidebar "Offline Folders vs. Remote Mail," on page 262.

One of the beauties of working with Outlook remotely is that you can perform a lot of your work without being connected to your e-mail server. You can read new (and old) messages, create new messages, compose replies, and forward messages. You can also delete messages that you no longer need or want. Then, when you connect to your e-mail server, the messages you want to read are downloaded, the messages you want to send are sent to the server for routing, and the messages you want to delete disappear.

Running Outlook to Work Remotely—Online Only

When you're ready to connect to the network computer to work with Outlook remotely, take these steps:

1 Click the Start button on the Windows taskbar, and point to Programs on the Start menu. Point to Accessories, and then click Dial-Up Networking on the submenu.

2 In the Dial-Up Networking window, double-click the connection you set up to connect to your network dial-up computer.

3 Make sure your username is correctly entered here.

4 Type your password.

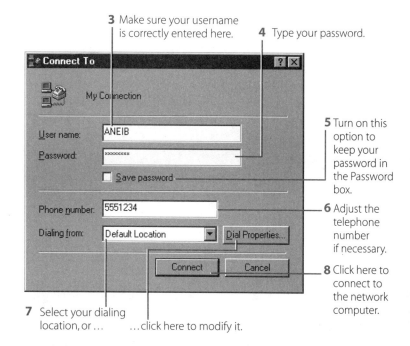

5 Turn on this option to keep your password in the Password box.

6 Adjust the telephone number if necessary.

8 Click here to connect to the network computer.

7 Select your dialing location, or …   …click here to modify it.

If you need to click the Dial Properties button to change or set a location (step 7), consult "Setting Up Calling Card Dialing," on page 284, for details.

9 When Dial-Up Networking has established the network connection, start Outlook as you do when you're connected directly to the network.

🌟 **TIP**

Turn on the Save Password option in the Connect To dialog box only if your computer is always secure. With this option turned on, anyone can use your dial-up networking connection to connect to the network. If you sometimes leave your computer where it's available to anyone, it's better to turn off the Save Password option. This means you'll have to type your password each time you want to establish a dial-up networking connection, but your computer will be much more secure.

II

Electronic Mail

Running Outlook to Work Remotely—Online and Offline

Working in Outlook both online and offline with offline folders is a simple matter of starting Outlook and connecting to your Microsoft Exchange server.

> You can use the offline folders method only if your e-mail server is Microsoft Exchange Server.

To work in Outlook when you have offline folders set up, do this:

1 Start Outlook.

2 In the dialog box that appears, click the button that fits the situation:

- Click the Connect button if your computer is connected to your Microsoft Exchange server through a network or if you have established a dial-up networking connection.

- Click the Work Offline button if your computer is not connected.

3 Perform your work in Outlook.

4 Choose Exit And Log Off from the File menu to exit Outlook.

Here are a few important points to keep in mind when you use Outlook for both online and offline remote work:

- If you choose Connect when you start Outlook, Outlook automatically synchronizes your folders in the background while it works on them. You can monitor the progress of the synchronization by checking the messages on the status bar.

- If you have turned on the When Online, Synchronize All Folders Upon Exiting option on the Mail Services tab of the Options dialog box (see "Using the Mail Services Tab," on page 73), Outlook also synchronizes your offline folders when you exit.

- You can direct Outlook to synchronize a single offline folder or all offline folders at any time. For directions, see "Synchronizing Folders," on page 274.

- If you choose Work Offline when you start Outlook, you must exit and log off Outlook and then restart Outlook to connect to your e-mail server.

Moving Items to Different Folders

(?) SEE ALSO

For information about how to move items to a different folder, see "Moving a Folder Item," on page 463.

While you're working offline, you might want to move an item to a different folder. This is a simple process: you move the item just as you would when you're connected to your Microsoft Exchange server. The next time you connect to your server, either remotely or through a network connection, the Microsoft Exchange server moves the items in the server folders to match the moves you made while you were working offline. This movement of items among folders is part of the synchronization process.

Running Remote Mail

To use Remote Mail, follow these steps:

1 Start Outlook.

2 In the dialog box that appears, click the Work Offline button.

3 Point to Remote Mail on the Tools menu, and then choose Connect from the submenu. Alternatively, you can click the Connect button on the Remote toolbar—see "Checking Out the Remote Toolbar," on page 294. Outlook starts the Remote Connection Wizard.

II

Electronic Mail

4 Turn on the service connection you want to make. If you want to check your dial-up settings before connecting, also turn on the Confirm Before Connecting option.

5 Click Next to proceed to the next panel of the Remote Connection Wizard.

6 To download and send all messages, choose Retrieve And Send All New Mail. To limit the remote connect options, select the Do Only The Following option, and then turn on the tasks you want to carry out. The specific actions you can choose from will vary.

7 Click the Next button as long as it's active. When it's no longer active, click the Finish button. For example, if you turned on the Confirm Before Connecting option on the first Remote Connection Wizard panel, click the Next button on the second panel. If you turned off the Confirm Before Connecting option, click the Finish button.

8 Outlook shows a message box telling you that your computer is dialing and then that your computer is connecting to your server. When the connection is established, you can work with messages using Remote Mail.

Breaking the Remote Mail Connection

Outlook doesn't keep a persistent Remote Mail connection. Remote Mail does its work and then disconnects to save you phone charges.

If you want to break the connection yourself before Remote Mail finishes, click the Disconnect button on the Remote toolbar or point to Remote Mail on the Tools menu, and then choose Disconnect from the submenu.

If you don't want Remote Mail to disconnect automatically, you can do the following:

1 Choose Services on the Tools menu, select Microsoft Exchange Server, and then click the Properties button.

2 Click the Remote Mail tab.

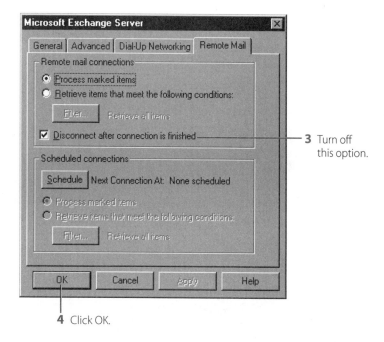

3 Turn off this option.

4 Click OK.

5 Click OK in the Services dialog box.

Working with Remote Mail

When the Remote Mail connection is made, Outlook performs the following actions in the order listed:

- Sends any messages you have set up to send—new messages, replies, forwards, and task and appointment responses

- Downloads the complete text of messages for the message headers you've marked for downloading

- Downloads message headers for messages that aren't already in the Inbox in your personal folders

- Deletes messages that you no longer want to keep on the Microsoft Exchange Server

- Disconnects the Remote Mail connection

II

Electronic Mail

You can now read and work with the new messages you received, mark new message headers for downloading, or delete messages or message headers.

Assigning a Delivery Point for Messages

If the Inbox folder in your personal folders hasn't been synchronized with your Inbox folder on your e-mail server, you'll see a message telling you that Outlook can't download your messages because there's no delivery point. In this case, you need to assign delivery to your personal folders Inbox. Of course, you must first set up personal folders. To do so, follow the steps described in "Adding Personal Folders to a Profile," on page 277.

Checking Out the Remote Toolbar

Outlook provides the Remote toolbar, which contains buttons for Remote Mail commands. Figure 9-1 shows the name of each button on the Remote toolbar.

To display the Remote toolbar, use one of the following methods:

- Point to Remote Mail on the Tools menu, and then choose Remote Tools from the submenu.

- Right-click a visible toolbar, and then click Remote on the shortcut menu.

- Point to Remote Mail on the Tools menu, and then drag the band at the top of the submenu into the Outlook window.

- Point to Toolbars on the Tools menu, and then choose Remote.

To hide the Remote toolbar, you can use any of these methods:

- Click the Close button on the Remote toolbar.

- Point to Remote Mail on the Tools menu, and then choose Remote Tools from the submenu.

- Right-click a visible toolbar, and then click Remote on the shortcut menu.

- If the Remote toolbar is floating in the Outlook window, click the Close box on the upper-right corner of the toolbar.

FIGURE 9-1.

The Remote toolbar.

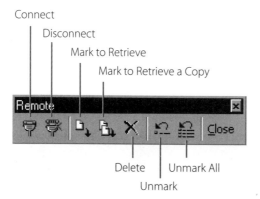

Connect

Disconnect

Mark to Retrieve

Mark to Retrieve a Copy

Delete

Unmark All

Unmark

Marking Messages for Downloading

Marking a message header for retrieval tells Remote Mail that you want to download the complete text of that message so that you can read and respond to it. Here's how to mark a message header for retrieval.

1 In the Inbox message list, select the messages you want to download. To select more than one message, hold down the Ctrl key as you click each message.

2 Click the Mark To Retrieve button on the Remote toolbar. Alternatively, you can point to Remote Mail on the Tools menu, and then choose Mark To Retrieve from the submenu.

The messages are now marked and ready to download the next time you connect to your Exchange server.

If you accidentally mark a message header for a message that you don't want to download, select it and click the Unmark button to unmark it. If you want to unmark all message headers, click the Unmark All button.

⭐ **TIP**

If you use separate profiles for Remote Mail and for connecting to your e-mail server over a network, use the Mark To Retrieve A Copy toolbar button or command rather than Mark To Retrieve. Mark To Retrieve A Copy puts a copy of the message in your personal folders Inbox and leaves the message in your e-mail server Inbox. If you use Mark To Retrieve, you'll end up with the same message in each of the two inboxes, which can be aggravating or confusing.

II

Electronic Mail

Deleting Messages When You Work Remotely

If you no longer want to keep a message, you can mark the message header for deletion. To delete a message header and the message from your e-mail server, simply select the message header, and then click the Delete button on the Remote toolbar. The message moves to your Deleted Items folder.

When you connect to your e-mail server, Outlook completes the deletion.

NOTE

> To delete the messages in their entirety after they've been downloaded, use the Delete button on the Standard toolbar. As with online messages, deleting offline messages sends them to the Deleted Items folder.

Sending Messages from a Remote Computer

SEE ALSO

For details about the standard procedures for sending e-mail messages, see "Sending a Message," on page 108.

When you're working offline and want to send a message, you simply compose the message as you would when you're connected to your e-mail server. You can also write replies and set up messages for forwarding. These processes aren't mysterious at all. You use the same commands and steps you use when you're connected. The only true difference is that the messages you set up to send don't go anywhere until you connect to your e-mail server. This connection can be through the network, through Dial-Up Networking, or through Remote Mail.

NOTE

> You must have a copy of the Offline Address Book in order to set up a message for sending. For more information, see "Downloading the Offline Address Book," on page 269.

After you create a new message, fashion your reply to a message, or set up a message for forwarding, the message lives in your Outbox until the next time you connect. Messages that you set up to send are displayed in your Outbox in italics.

PART III

Scheduling Your Time and Tasks

CHAPTER 10

Viewing the Calendar

Your Calendar folder in Microsoft Outlook 98 contains a calendar that shows the appointments you make, the meetings you're scheduled to attend, the events you want to be reminded of, and, usually, a list of the active tasks you have recorded. (In the next chapter, "Scheduling Appointments, Meetings, and Events," you'll learn how Outlook distinguishes among appointments, meetings, and events.)

You can view your calendar in a number of ways, and you can adjust the Calendar window (also called the Calendar folder) to suit your work and purposes (and aesthetics). First, however, let's briefly review the various parts of the Calendar window.

Using the Calendar Folder Window

Figure 10-1 shows a typical view of the Calendar folder window. In particular, notice the Appointments pane, the Date Navigator, and the TaskPad.

Time Display

 SEE ALSO

To set or change your work hours and other calendar options, see "Setting Calendar Options," on page 66.

The time display area of the Appointments pane shows the hours of the day, with each full hour numbered. Initially, Outlook is set up with half-hour time intervals; a line marks each half-hour increment.

The range of times that you can view at one glance varies from one hour to fifteen or more hours depending on the size of your Outlook window, the time intervals of your appointments, and the resolution of your monitor. If you need to see an appointment time that's out of view, use the scroll bar along the right side of the Appointments pane to scroll earlier or later times into view. When an appointment or meeting is out of view, you see a yellow rectangle that contains an arrowhead and an ellipsis.

FIGURE 10-1.
The Calendar folder window.

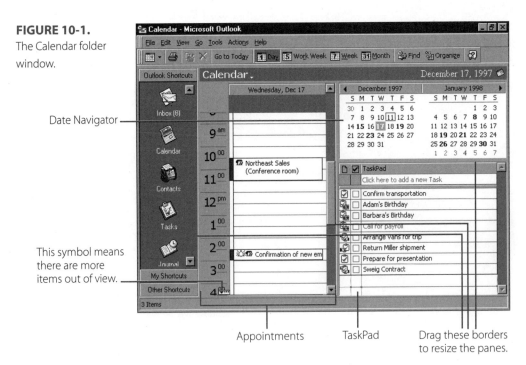

Date Navigator

This symbol means there are more items out of view.

Appointments   TaskPad   Drag these borders to resize the panes.

Changing the Time Intervals

You can change the time interval for your appointments to one that's convenient for your work at the moment. Outlook initially displays half-hour intervals, but you can adjust that from as short as five minutes to as long as sixty minutes. To change the time interval, take these steps:

1 Right-click anywhere in the time display area.

2 At the bottom of the shortcut menu, click the interval you want to use.

Showing Appointments in Two Time Zones

You can simultaneously display appointment times in two time zones. Typically, you'll use this second time zone when you conduct business across time zones. Outlook displays the second time zone to the left of the main time zone. If you travel to a location in the second time zone and want to use your calendar while you're there, you can swap time zones and display the second time zone next to your appointments (each time zone is labeled at the top of its column). To display a second time zone, see "Selecting and Changing Zones," on page 88.

Appointments

SEE ALSO

For information about scheduling appointments and meetings, see Chapter 11, "Scheduling Appointments, Meetings, and Events."

The Appointments pane of the Calendar lists your appointments by date and time. Each entry indicates whether the appointment is a group meeting or an online meeting, whether it is scheduled just once or on a recurring basis, whether it is private, and whether you've set a reminder for it. The entry also gives you information about the subject, location, and duration of the appointment.

Viewing Details of Appointments and Meetings

No matter what time span you choose to display for your appointments, you won't be able to see every detail in the Appointments pane. To see all the details of an appointment, locate it in the Appointments pane and then use one of the following methods:

- Double-click it.

- Right-click it and choose Open from the shortcut menu.

- Click it and choose Open from the File menu (or press Ctrl+O).

III

Scheduling Your Time and Tasks

TIP

In Day view (Calendar's default view, shown in Figure 10-1, on page 300), you can directly edit the subject and text of an appointment or meeting in the Appointments pane. To change other settings for the appointment, open the item using one of the three methods just described.

When you open an appointment, Outlook displays a window (with the same title as your appointment's subject) in which you can check or change any of the appointment's details. To close this window when you're finished, use one of the following methods:

- Click the Save And Close button. Be sure to use this method if you made any changes to the appointment.

- Click the Close box in the upper-right corner of the window. You can use this method if you made no changes to the appointment or if you don't want to keep any changes you made.

- Choose Close on the File menu (or press Alt+F4). Before you choose this command, however, you might want to choose Save on the File menu (or press Ctrl+S) to save any changes you made.

Date Navigator

 SEE ALSO

For information about how to work with the Date Navigator, see "Using the Date Navigator," on page 307.

Use the Date Navigator to see from one to several months at a glance. (See "Adjusting the Calendar Display," on page 312, for details about changing the range of dates visible in the Date Navigator.) Within the month or months shown in the Date Navigator, you can jump to a date simply by clicking it. You can also scroll the Date Navigator to jump months ahead or back. Outlook highlights the dates in the Date Navigator that are visible in the Calendar pane, as well as those that have appointments.

TaskPad

On the TaskPad, you see a summary of your tasks, as shown on the facing page.

Typically, the TaskPad shows your currently active tasks, including tasks that are overdue (shown in red instead of black) and tasks without a specific due date. When you click the Complete box (the check box in the second column), Outlook draws a line through the task.

Click column heads to sort tasks accordingly.

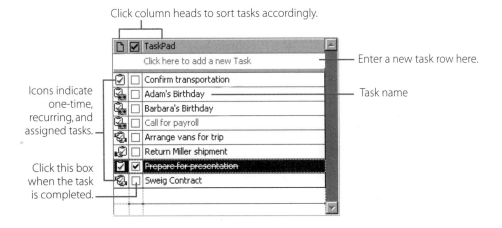

Enter a new task row here.

Task name

Icons indicate one-time, recurring, and assigned tasks.

Click this box when the task is completed.

SEE ALSO

For information about working with tasks, see Chapter 12, "Controlling Your Tasks."

When you've marked a task as completed and the due date passes, Outlook removes the completed task from the TaskPad.

Instead of switching to the Tasks folder to set up a new task, you can quickly add a new task to the TaskPad. To do so, follow these steps:

1 Click the text box labeled Click Here To Add A New Task on the TaskPad.

2 Type the subject of the task, and then press Enter.

SEE ALSO

For details about changing the setup of the TaskPad, see "Adjusting the TaskPad," on page 314.

The new task still has no due date. To set or change the properties of the task, you have to edit it. To edit a task on the TaskPad, double-click the task name, make your changes in the task item window, and then click the Save And Close button in the task item window. For more information about task properties, see "Setting Up a Task," on page 373.

Setting the Number of Days Displayed

SEE ALSO

To learn about other views available in the Calendar folder, see "Other Ways of Viewing the Calendar," on page 318.

The default Calendar view is the Day/Week/Month view. In this view, you can choose between four time spans: one day, one work week, one week, and one month. You set the time span by clicking one of these four buttons on the Standard toolbar:

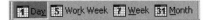

Scheduling Your Time and Tasks

TIP

> When you select dates in the Date Navigator, your selection affects how many days and which days appear in the Appointments pane. For details, see "Selecting Days," on page 311.

Day View

In Day view, you see the appointments for one day of your calendar, as shown in Figure 10-1, on page 300. To return to Day view after viewing your calendar in another time span, click the Day button on the Standard toolbar.

Work Week View

In Work Week view, you see the work days for the calendar week, as shown below.

The default work days are Monday through Friday, but you can change the days by clicking the Calendar Options button on the Preferences tab of the Options dialog box, as explained in "Setting Calendar Options," on page 66. If you set the work week from Monday through Saturday, for example, the Work Week view will display six days. (No matter how many days you assign to a work week, however, the Work Week button on the Standard toolbar will still display the number 5.)

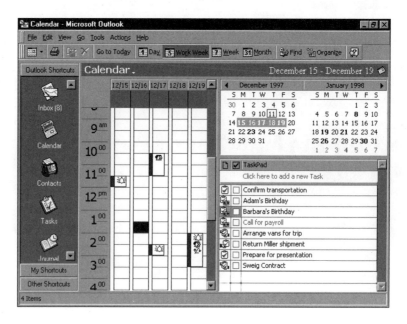

To display your calendar in Work Week view, click the Work Week button on the Standard toolbar. To display the appointments and meetings for one day of the week, click the date and then click the Day button on the Standard toolbar.

Week View

In Week view, you see one full week of your calendar, as shown below.

When you choose Week view, the time slots aren't included and the days appear in boxes. Depending on the resolution of your display and on how you've arranged the Calendar window, you may see the starting and ending times for appointments, as well as their characteristics (private, recurring), subjects, and place.

To display your calendar in Week view, click the Week button on the Standard toolbar. To display the appointments for any one day of the week, click the date and then click the Day button on the Standard toolbar.

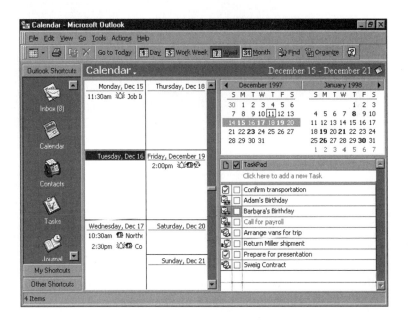

III

Scheduling Your
Time and Tasks

Showing Selected Calendar Days

In addition to the views available using the toolbar buttons, you can choose to show only selected days from the calendar.

From any view, just select the days in the Date Navigator. You can drag over any number of consecutive dates or hold down the Ctrl key and select any dates you want. Just the schedule for the selected dates will appear on the calendar.

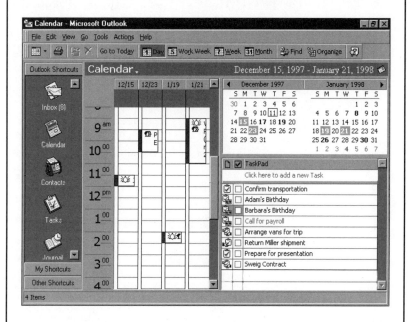

To change or reset the view, select other dates, or click one of the buttons on the toolbar.

Month View

In Month view, you see an entire month, as shown on the next page.

In Month view and in Week view, the days appear in boxes. Again, depending on your display resolution and window arrangement, entries for your appointments in Month view may show the starting time and as much of the subject as fits on one line of the date box.

To display your calendar in Month view, click the Month button on the Standard toolbar. To display the appointments for one day of the month shown, click the date box and then click the Day button on the Standard toolbar.

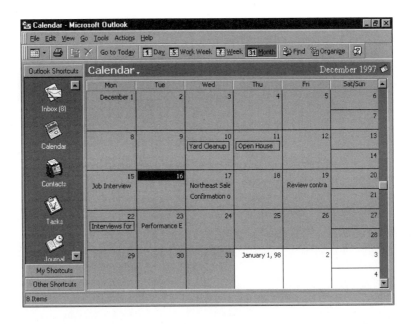

Getting a Date

SEE ALSO
You can use Outlook's Find Items command to find specific appointments, events, and meetings. For details, see "Searching Folder Contents," on page 475.

Much of your calendar work will usually focus on "today"—after all, today is the day you're living and working through. But setting appointments and scheduling meetings necessarily involves dates and times in the future. Also, when you want to review your schedule for the days, weeks, or months ahead, you need to jump to other dates. And if you want to review past appointments and meetings, you'll need to jump back in time. When you need to jump to another date, you can use the Date Navigator or the Go To Date command on the Go menu.

Using the Date Navigator

Depending on the size of the Outlook window, the resolution of your display, and the size of the Date Navigator pane, you can see a single month or several months at a time in the Date Navigator.

III

Scheduling Your
Time and Tasks

TIP

The Date Navigator is typically visible in Day view and Week view but absent from Month view. You can display the Date Navigator in Month view by placing the mouse pointer on the right window border, where it becomes a double vertical line with horizontal arrows, and dragging the border to the left toward the center of the calendar window.

To jump to another date, use one of the following methods:

■ If the date is visible in the Date Navigator, click the date.

■ If the date is not in view in the Date Navigator, click the left arrow in the top band of the Date Navigator to move back one month, or click the right arrow to move forward one month. Even if two or more months are visible in the Date Navigator, they scroll only one month at a time.

■ Click and hold the name of any month in the Date Navigator to open a list containing the three months before and the three months after the month you've clicked. Then drag the mouse pointer to the month you wish to view and release the mouse button:

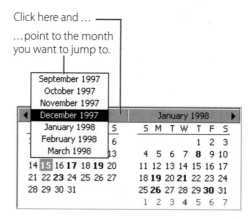

Click here and …

…point to the month you want to jump to.

After you've selected a new month and jumped to it, you can repeat this method to move three months before or after the newly displayed month.

When you click a month label and open the list of months, you can drag the mouse pointer to the top or bottom border of the list to scroll through an even larger list of months. You must hold the tip of the mouse pointer arrow exactly on the top or bottom border line to scroll.

Using the Go To Date Command

For dates that are further away than a few months, you'll probably want to use the Go To Date command, which can take you to any date within the Outlook date range.

To jump to any date, follow these steps:

1 From the Go menu, choose Go To Date.

2 Type the date you want to jump to, or …

…click here to display a calendar for the current month.

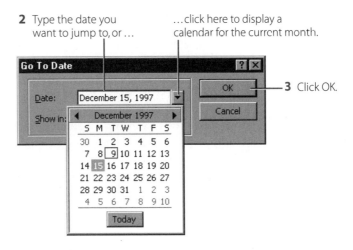

3 Click OK.

In the Date box of the Go To dialog box, you can type the date you want to see in any standard date format—for instance, to jump to October 13, 1999, you can type *10-13-99, 10/13/99, Oct-13-99,* or *October 13, 1999.* You should note the following points about typing dates:

- If you type a two-digit year number in the range 69–99, Outlook assumes that you mean 1969–1999. For the numbers 00–69, Outlook uses 2000–2069.

- If you want a year that's not within the century from 1970 to 2069, you must type the entire year number. The earliest date you can type in the Date box is April 1, 1601. The latest date you can type in the Date box is August 31, 4500. That range should just about cover it for your use of this version of Outlook.

- After you select or enter the date you want to see in the Go To Date dialog box, you can use the Show In list to choose to view the date in Day, Week, Work Week, or Month view.

TIP

After you type a date in the Date box of the Go To Date dialog box, click the down arrow beside the date to see the month calendar for the date you've typed. You can then refine your date jump if you need to.

Jumping Back to Today

When you've moved to a past or future date, you'll often want to jump back to today's date. You can do this in any of the following ways:

- If you're in the Day/Week/Month view of the calendar, click the Go To Today button on the Standard toolbar. This button is available whether you're viewing a day, work week, week, or month time span. Note, however, that on small and lower resolution displays, you might have to widen the Outlook window or even maximize it to see the Go To Today button. If the toolbar isn't large enough to display all the buttons, Outlook hides this button in preference to showing other ("more important") buttons.

- Click today's date in the Date Navigator (it is outlined to make it easy to find).

- Right-click any empty appointment slot or any date label in the Appointments pane, and then choose Go To Today from the shortcut menu.

- Choose Go To Today from the Go menu.

Selecting Days

As you use the TaskPad and Calendar, you might want to check the active or completed tasks for a selected number of days. You might also want to check on appointments for a set of selected days. You can select days either in the Appointments pane or in the Date Navigator pane. You can select a range of consecutive days in the Appointments pane, and you can select a range of consecutive days or scattered days in the Date Navigator.

Selecting Days in the Calendar

Here's how to select a range of consecutive days in the Appointments pane:

1   Display the calendar in Work Week view, Week view, or Month view.

2   Move to the week or month where you want to select days.

3   Use one of these methods to select the days you want:

   • Drag over the days you want to select.

   • Click the first date of the range, hold down the Shift key, and then click the last date of the range. You can select as many visible days as you like this way, including all the days that are visible in the Appointments pane.

> **NOTE**
>
> If you scroll the calendar after you select a range of days, Outlook automatically selects the similar range of dates. For example, if you select the first week of January when in Month view, then change to March in the Date Navigator, the first week of March will be selected.

Selecting Days in the Date Navigator

You can select consecutive days or scattered days in the Date Navigator. When you select days in the Date Navigator, Outlook changes the Appointments pane to display the days you selected. In this way, you can display ranges and numbers of days that differ from what the Day, Week, and Month views show.

To select a range of consecutive days in the Date Navigator, follow these steps:

1 Adjust the Date Navigator pane to show the months in which you want to select days.

2 Use one of these methods to select the days you want:

- Drag over the days you want to select. You can select as many as eight consecutive days or as many as six consecutive weeks this way. After you select the ninth day, the selection expands to selecting weeks at a time.

- Click at the left end of a week to select that week. (The mouse pointer must appear as a diagonal arrow pointing toward the upper right.) Drag down along the left end of weeks to select as many as six weeks.

- Click the first date of the range, hold down the Shift key, and then click the last date of the range. You can select as many as 14 days this way.

To select scattered days in the Date Navigator, follow these steps:

1 Adjust the Date Navigator pane to show the months in which you want to select days.

2 Click one of the days you want to select.

3 Hold down the Ctrl key while you click the other days you want to select. You can select as many as 14 days this way.

Adjusting the Calendar Display

Because the Calendar contains three panes, the amount of space for each pane is limited, especially if you work in an Outlook window that isn't maximized. Also, if you are using a lower-resolution display, you'll have less space available for the separate panes than if you are using a display with a higher resolution.

When you need to view or work in one of the panes and require a more expanded view of the pane's contents, you can adjust its borders to give it a larger portion of the Calendar window. (You can also hide the TaskPad and the Date Navigator, but you can't hide the Appointments pane.)

Between each of the panes in the Calendar window is a border that you can drag to adjust the size of the panes. (See Figure 10-1, on page 300.) When you position the mouse pointer on one of these borders, the pointer arrow changes to a double line with two arrows (pointing either up and down or left and right).

- Drag the vertical border separating the Appointments pane from the Date Navigator and the TaskPad to the left or right to change the width of the Appointments pane.

- Drag the horizontal border between the Date Navigator and the TaskPad up or down to change the height of these two panes.

- Drag the vertical border between the Appointments pane and the Outlook Bar to change the size of the Outlook Bar. This also changes the width of the other panes.

Hiding and Restoring the TaskPad

If you want to use the space the TaskPad occupies for either the Appointments pane or the Date Navigator, you can hide the TaskPad. To do so, perform one of the following actions:

- Drag the border along the right side of the Appointments pane to the right.

- Drag the bottom border of the Date Navigator down.

After you've hidden the TaskPad, you might want to see it again. Take the action that fits the circumstances in your Calendar window:

- If the Appointments pane extends to the right window border, place the mouse pointer on the right window border, and then drag the border to the left toward the center of the window.

- If the Date Navigator covers the TaskPad, place the mouse pointer on the bottom window border, just above the status bar, and then drag the border upward toward the middle of the Date Navigator.

III

Scheduling Your
Time and Tasks

Hiding and Restoring the Date Navigator

You can hide the Date Navigator to make extra room for either the Appointments pane or the TaskPad. To do so, use one of these methods:

- Drag the border along the right side of the Appointments pane to the right.

- Drag the top border of the TaskPad upward.

To restore the Date Navigator after you've hidden it, take one of the following actions:

- If the Appointments pane extends to the right window border, place the mouse pointer on the right window border, and then drag the border to the left toward the center of the window.

- If the TaskPad covers the Date Navigator, place the mouse pointer just above the TaskPad label, and then drag the border down to the middle of the TaskPad.

Adjusting the TaskPad

The TaskPad typically lists your active tasks. Overdue tasks appear in red. You can change the view of your tasks, and you can also change the formatting and arrangement of TaskPad columns.

Selecting a TaskPad View

② SEE ALSO

For more ways to view tasks, see "Viewing Your Tasks," on page 398.

When you point to the TaskPad View command on the View menu, you can select a view of the TaskPad from a submenu. Some of the views you can choose are similar to the views you have in the Tasks folder (discussed in Chapter 12, "Controlling Your Tasks"), but they have been modified to suit the TaskPad, where you have limited space and where you're more likely to be concerned about current tasks than tasks that are long past or far in the future.

All Tasks View

In All Tasks view, the TaskPad lists every task you have set up (for all days), including completed tasks, which have a line drawn through them. If you have many task items, you will have to spend a lot of time scrolling through the list to find what you need. If the TaskPad pane is small and you have many tasks, you may find this view quite useless.

To switch the TaskPad to All Tasks view, point to TaskPad View on the View menu and choose All Tasks on the submenu.

Today's Tasks View

Today's Tasks view is the default for the TaskPad. In this view, the TaskPad list contains only the tasks that are active for today (including overdue tasks). For the TaskPad and the Appointments pane, "today" means the date indicated by your computer clock.

To return to Today's Tasks view after selecting a different view, point to TaskPad View on the View menu and click Today's Tasks on the submenu.

Active Tasks For Selected Days View

You can select a range of days, either in the Appointments pane or in the Date Navigator, to have the TaskPad display tasks that are active during the selected days. You might want to use this view when you are thinking about a vacation, a business trip, or a professional activity (such as a conference, seminar, or trade show) that takes you away from work for several days or weeks. For vacation planning, you need to know which tasks must be completed before you leave and which can be rescheduled with new due dates after you return. For a business trip, the list of tasks might help you determine what preparations you need to make before you leave so that you have all the materials and information you need to take with you. For a professional activity that takes you away from the office, you might want to know all this—what to do before you leave, what to take with you, and what you can delay until after you return.

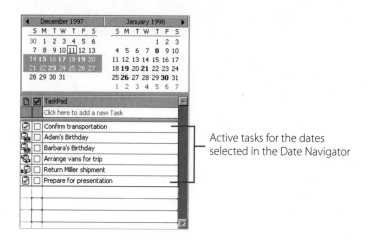

Active tasks for the dates selected in the Date Navigator

To switch the TaskPad to Active Tasks For Selected Days view, first select the dates you want to check. (See "Selecting Days," on page 311.) Then point to TaskPad View on the View menu and click Active Tasks For Selected Days on the submenu.

Tasks For Next Seven Days View

Sometimes you want to see all the tasks for the coming week (the next seven days). The Tasks For Next Seven Days view shows tasks with a due date that falls during the next seven days, including today. (If you have the Include Tasks With No Due Date option turned on, the list also includes tasks without a due date. To exclude these tasks so that the list contains only tasks with a due date during the next seven days, follow the steps in "Including Tasks with No Due Date," on the next page.) To switch to this view, point to TaskPad View on the View menu and click Tasks For Next Seven Days on the submenu.

Overdue Tasks View

When you're behind on some of your tasks and want to concentrate on cleaning up tasks that are past due, you can choose the Overdue Tasks view to display only overdue tasks in the TaskPad. (When you choose this view, you'll probably want to exclude tasks without a due date. For details, see "Including Tasks with No Due Date," on the following page.)

To switch the TaskPad to Overdue Tasks view, point to TaskPad View on the View menu and click Overdue Tasks on the submenu. Overdue tasks appear in red.

Tasks Completed On Selected Days View

From time to time, it's useful to review your accomplishments, especially during performance review time. You can select days, either in the Appointments pane or in the Date Navigator, to have the TaskPad display tasks that you completed on the selected days.

To switch the TaskPad to Tasks Completed On Selected Days view, first select the dates you want to check. (See "Selecting Days," on page 311.) Then point to TaskPad View on the View menu and click Tasks Completed On Selected Days on the submenu.

Including Tasks with No Due Date

In all the available TaskPad views, the list can either include tasks without a due date or exclude them. Initially, the TaskPad includes these tasks in its list of task items. To exclude tasks without a due date, simply point to TaskPad View on the View menu and click Include Tasks With No Due Date on the submenu to turn off this option. If you decide later that you would like to display tasks without a due date again, repeat this procedure to turn on the option.

Setting Up Parts of the TaskPad

You can set up your TaskPad to show additional or different columns or to group tasks. You can sort tasks, and you can format the view you use for the TaskPad. To change TaskPad settings, right-click a TaskPad column label to display this shortcut menu:

For information about all the commands on this shortcut menu see Chapter 20, "Organizing Folder Items." For information about the Format Columns command, see "Changing Column Format," on page 557. For information about the Customize Current View command, see "Modifying a View," on page 591.

Other Ways of Viewing the Calendar

? SEE ALSO

You can also set up views to look at your appointments and meetings in various ways. For information, see Chapter 21, "Setting Up Views." For information about grouping, sorting, filtering, and adding custom fields, see Chapter 20, "Organizing Folder Items."

Day/Week/Month view of the Calendar is the default view and is the view you'll probably use most often. In this view, you have the Date Navigator and the TaskPad available.

Day/Week/Month view is not, however, the only view that Outlook provides. The following sections describe five other views you can use for your Calendar folder. Each of the views is displayed by pointing to Current View on the View menu and then choosing the view you want from the submenu.

Day/Week/Month View With AutoPreview

To see additional details along with the subject and location, use the Day/Week/Month View With AutoPreview view. You'll be able to see up to the first 256 characters of the appointment details without having to open the item.

Active Appointments View

To see a list of all your active appointments and meetings—that is, future appointments and meetings—choose Active Appointments view. Active Appointments view displays appointments in a table arrangement, as shown at the top of the next page.

In this view, the appointments and meetings are grouped by recurrence status—nonrecurring, daily, weekly, monthly, yearly, and any other recurrence pattern an appointment might have.

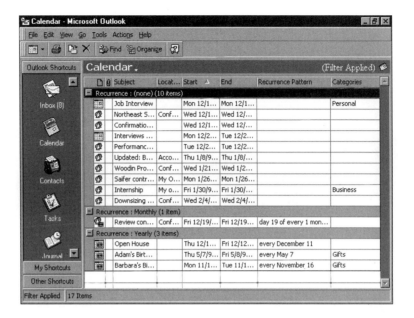

Events View

To see all events (including annual events) that you've added to your calendar, choose Events view, which displays events and annual events in a table, also grouped by their recurrence status.

In this view, events are separated by their recurrence: nonrecurring, daily, weekly, monthly, and yearly. Yearly recurrence means an annual event.

Annual Events View

If you want a list that contains only the annual events on your calendar, switch to Annual Events view, as shown on the next page.

Recurring Appointments View

For a list that contains only recurring appointments and meetings, switch to Recurring Appointments view.

III

Scheduling Your
Time and Tasks

In this view, appointments and meetings are grouped by recurrence status—daily, weekly, monthly, yearly, and so on. The difference between this view and Active Appointments view is that Recurring Appointments view does not show one-time appointments and meetings.

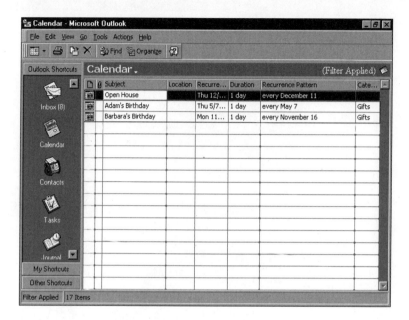

By Category View

If you assign categories to your appointments, you can see them listed by category. If you assign more than one category to an appointment, Outlook lists it in each category.

To see your appointments and meetings grouped by category, switch to By Category view.

In the next chapter, "Scheduling Appointments, Meetings, and Events," you'll learn how to set up and use appointments to keep track of where you need to be and when you need to be there.

Using Organize to Change Views

In addition to using the View menu to determine how the Calendar is displayed, you can use the Organize command. When the Calendar is displayed, click the Organize button on the toolbar or choose Organize from the Tools menu.

1 Click here.   **2** Select the view.   **3** Click this button to close the Organize pane.

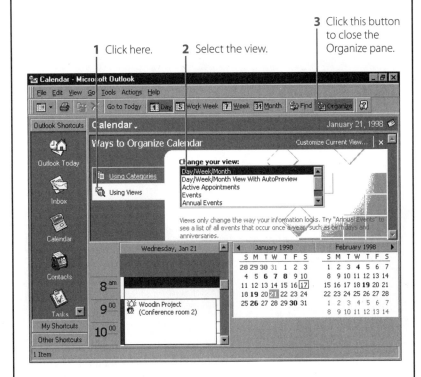

You can also point to Current View on the View menu and choose Customize Current View to modify the objects and appearance of the view. See Chapter 21, "Setting Up Views," for more information on customizing views.

Scheduling Appointments, Meetings, and Events

I n your Microsoft Outlook 98 Calendar folder, you can set up calendar items—appointments, meetings, and events. A meeting is an appointment to which you invite others using Outlook. Appointments and meetings have specific beginning and end times. In contrast, an event is an all-day affair to which you might or might not invite others. All three kinds of calendar items can be one-time occasions or affairs that recur at regular intervals (daily, weekly, monthly, or yearly).

In this chapter, you'll learn how to set up calendar items and how to change them—how to change the start and end times, how to set up recurring items, how to deal with reminders when they appear, how to adjust other properties, and how to copy items. You will also learn the fundamentals of planning and conducting an online meeting using Microsoft Net-Meeting. With NetMeeting, and the proper equipment on your computer, you can exchange written messages in real-time with others, speak with them, and even see them.

Setting Up a Calendar Item

 NOTE

Online meetings will be discussed separately later in this chapter.

To enter a calendar item, open the Calendar and move to the date of the affair. (See "Getting a Date," on page 307.) You can then use one of the following methods to create a new calendar item of the type you want:

New
Appointment

- An appointment

  - Click the New Appointment button on the Standard toolbar.

  - Choose New Appointment from the Actions menu.

  - Press Ctrl+N.

  - Right-click in the Calendar pane (the time area, an empty appointment line, or the date above the appointments area), and then choose New Appointment from the shortcut menu.

  - Point to New on the File menu, and then choose Appointment from the submenu.

- A recurring appointment

  - Choose New Recurring Appointment on the Actions menu.

  - Right-click in the Calendar pane, and then choose New Recurring Appointment from the shortcut menu.

  - Create a regular appointment, then click on the Recurrence button in the appointment window.

- A meeting

  - Choose New Meeting Request on the Actions menu (for an online meeting, choose New Online Meeting Request instead).

  - Press Ctrl+Shift+Q.

- Right-click in the Calendar pane, and then choose New Meeting Request (or New Online Meeting Request) from the shortcut menu.

- Point to New on the File menu, and then choose Meeting Request from the submenu.

- Choose Plan A Meeting from the Actions menu.

■ A recurring meeting

- Choose New Recurring Meeting on the Actions menu.

- Right-click in the Calendar pane, and then choose New Recurring Meeting from the shortcut menu.

- Create a regular meeting, then click on the Recurrence button in the meeting window.

■ An event

- Choose New All Day Event on the Actions menu.

- Right-click in the Calendar pane, and then choose New All Day Event from the shortcut menu.

■ A recurring event

- Right-click in the Calendar pane, and then choose New Recurring Event from the shortcut menu.

- Create an all day event, then click on the Recurrence button in the All Day Event window.

NOTE

If you invite others to an appointment, Outlook converts the calendar item to a meeting. When you invite others to an event, Outlook calls it an Invited Event.

When you create a calendar item, by whatever method, Outlook opens a calendar item window similar to the one shown in Figure 11-1, on the following page. The title bar indicates what type of item you're creating. Figure 11-1 points out various features of this window; you'll find information about these features throughout this chapter.

Scheduling Your
Time and Tasks

FIGURE 11-1.
A calendar item
window for an
appointment.

Type the subject.

Invite others to the meeting.

Set up an online meeting.

Type a location for the appointment or
click the down arrow to select a previous location.

Turn on this option for an online meeting.

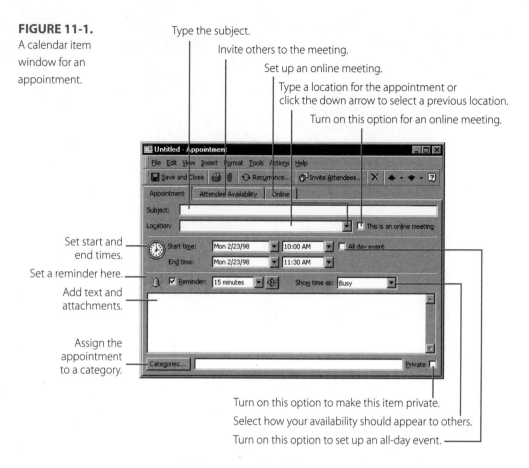

Set start and
end times.

Set a reminder here.

Add text and
attachments.

Assign the
appointment
to a category.

Turn on this option to make this item private.

Select how your availability should appear to others.

Turn on this option to set up an all-day event.

TIP

The calendar item window changes slightly for each type of item. For instance, if
you select New Meeting Request or create an Invited Event, the window will
have a To button and a box for the names of those you want to invite. Items with
invitations also have a colored band at the top of the Appointment tab that
shows the status of the invitations.

Quickly Setting Up a Calendar Item

To quickly set up a calendar item without worrying about the finer
points of settings such as location or invitations, take these steps:

1   Go to the date for the new entry. (See "Getting a Date," on
page 307.)

> **Creating a New Calendar Item from a Different Folder**
>
> If you're working in an Outlook folder other than the Calendar folder, you can set up a new meeting or appointment by using one of the following methods. Later you can change the item as necessary.
>
> - Click the down arrow at the right side of the New button on the Standard toolbar, and then choose Appointment or Meeting Request from the menu.
>
> - Point to New on the File menu, and then choose Appointment or Meeting Request from the submenu.
>
> - Press Ctrl+Shift+A for a new appointment; press Ctrl+Shift+Q for a meeting request.
>
> You can also drag other Outlook items to the Calendar folder icon on the Outlook Bar to create appointments. For example, if you are working in the Contacts folder, you can select a contact card and drag it to the Calendar folder icon. Outlook opens a meeting window addressed to the contact. Modify the meeting information—subject, location, start time, and end time—and then send the meeting request, as described next in "Planning a Meeting."

2 Click either the starting time or the text area pane to its right, and drag down to the ending time. (You can also click the ending time and drag up to the starting time.)

3 Type a name for the item. Outlook inserts the typed text in an appointment box in the Appointments pane.

4 Press Enter or click outside the appointment box. An appointment now appears on your calendar. It displays a reminder icon (set to the standard reminder time) but has no location, notes, or categories. To learn how to change the appointment setup, see "Changing a Calendar Item," on page 332.

Planning a Meeting

SEE ALSO

For more information about extending invitations, see "Changing Invitations," on page 340.

The main difference between scheduling a meeting and planning a meeting is the approach you take. Schedule a meeting when you know that the time you select is convenient for all those you are inviting to the meeting—you know they'll be there. Plan a meeting when you want to find a time that fits the schedules of those you are inviting.

III

Scheduling Your
Time and Tasks

You can start the process of scheduling a meeting and then use the Attendee Availability tab in the meeting window to check the schedules of the invitees. Planning a meeting merely reverses this course, tackling the issue of others' schedules before setting up the meeting details. In visual terms, when you schedule a meeting by creating a new meeting request you see the Appointment tab when the meeting window appears. When you plan a meeting, you see the Plan A Meeting dialog box first, and then you see the Appointment tab. The Plan A Meeting dialog box serves the same function as the Attendee Availability tab in the meeting window and is nearly identical to it.

To plan a meeting, take these steps:

1 Choose Plan A Meeting from the Actions menu.

2 In the Plan A Meeting dialog box, click the Invite Others button. You'll see the Select Attendees And Resources dialog box.

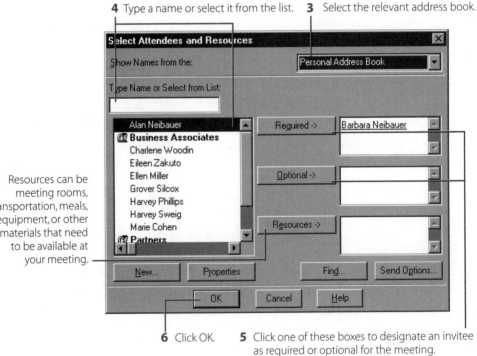

4 Type a name or select it from the list.   **3** Select the relevant address book.

Resources can be meeting rooms, transportation, meals, equipment, or other materials that need to be available at your meeting.

6 Click OK.   **5** Click one of these boxes to designate an invitee as required or optional for the meeting.

7 In the Plan A Meeting dialog box, you can now review the schedules for attendees, select the time for the meeting, and set other details for the meeting.

These bars show when
attendees are not available.

Drag these bars to set the meeting time.

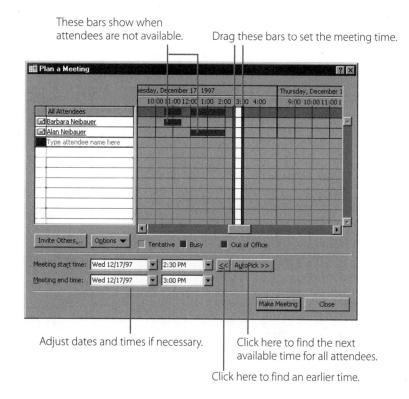

Adjust dates and times if necessary.

Click here to find the next
available time for all attendees.

Click here to find an earlier time.

8 Click Make Meeting when you've chosen a time.

9 Type a subject for the meeting.

10 Type a location for the meeting or select a previous location.

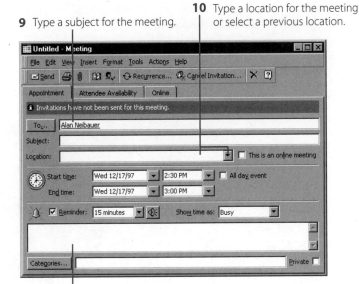

11 Type an agenda, notes, or comments; add attachments if necesary.

12 If you want to check meeting details again, click the Attendee Availability tab in the Meeting window. As mentioned earlier, this tab displays information you set up in the Plan A Meeting dialog box. On this tab, you can review and change the details of the meeting, review the schedules of the invited attendees, adjust the display of the schedule, and invite other attendees if necessary.

13 When you've finished reviewing the meeting details in the meeting window, click the Send button. Outlook then sends messages to the people you invited.

Inviting Resources to Your Meeting

Meeting resources include conference rooms, audio/visual equipment, and other equipment or material you need for a meeting. If your server administrator has set up rooms and equipment in the Global Address List, you can "invite" the resources to a meeting. When you invite a resource to a meeting, a message is delivered to the Inbox for the resource, which is (usually) handled by a staff person.

If you are the one in charge of monitoring the Inbox for a resource, you can set options for processing meeting requests automatically.

Handling a Meeting Request When You're Working Remotely

You can request meetings and respond to meeting requests you receive while you're working offsite—either working offline or working through a remote connection to your e-mail server. This is possible because meeting requests are sent as e-mail messages.

Before you can deal with meeting requests offline, you must take these steps:

1   Download the Offline Address Book. For information about how to do this, see "Downloading the Offline Address Book," on page 269.

2   Be sure that you're using Outlook for your scheduling. If you set up Outlook to use Microsoft Schedule+ 95 as your primary calendar, you won't be able to request or plan meetings. For more about this setup, see "Use Microsoft Schedule+ As My Primary Calendar," on page 68.

3   If you're working remotely in a time zone different from that of your office, you might want to display an additional time zone in the Appointments pane. For details, see "Showing Appointments in Two Time Zones," on page 301.

Choose Options from the Tools menu, click the Calendar Options button on the Preferences tab, and then click the Resource Scheduling button. You can set options so that Outlook will automatically accept meeting requests and process cancellations, automatically decline (or accept) conflicting meeting requests, and automatically decline (or accept) recurring meeting requests.

Updating Free/Busy Time

If you are using Outlook with Exchange Server, you can store your schedule information on the server. Individuals can use this information when planning meetings to ensure that all of the attendees are free at the scheduled date and time. (The Internet Only setup of Outlook lets you store and update free/busy time over the Internet, but you'll need a URL address where the information can be saved.) In fact, when you add a person to the list of invitees for a meeting or event, Outlook automatically retrieves their free/busy information from the server.

You control the publishing of your free/busy time on the server. To specify how often the information is uploaded to the server and how much information is sent, choose Options from the Tools menu, and

III

**Scheduling Your
Time and Tasks**

then click the Preferences tab. Click the Calendar Options button, and then click the Free/Busy Options button.

Enter the number of months of your schedule information to store on the server.

Enter the time interval for updating your schedule information on the server.

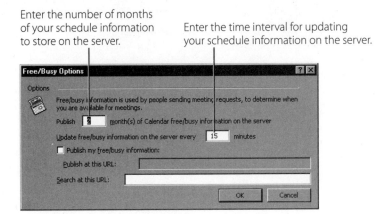

Changing a Calendar Item

Appointments, meetings, and events change. Sometimes the time changes, or perhaps the place. For some calendar items, you might want to add more notes and comments or insert files, messages, or other objects that pertain to the occasion you're scheduling. You might decide to alter the reminder setting, designate a calendar item as private, or adjust other properties. You might need to fine-tune appointments you set up quickly.

The general steps for changing a calendar item are as follows:

1 Open the calendar item in one of the following ways:

   - Double-click the calendar item.

   - Right-click the calendar item, and then choose Open from the shortcut menu.

   - Click the calendar item, and then choose Open from the File menu (or press Ctrl+O).

2 Change the calendar item as directed in the following sections. (You might want to refer to Figure 11-1, on page 326.)

3 Save and close the calendar item window in one of the following ways:

- Click the Save And Close button. Be sure to use this method if you made any changes to the calendar item details.

- Choose Close from the File menu (or press Alt+F4). If you made changes to the calendar item, Outlook will ask whether you want to save the changes. Click Yes to save the changes. Click No if you don't want to save the changes. You can also choose Save from the File menu (or press Ctrl+S).

 TIP

When your calendar is displayed in Day view, you can directly edit the subject and text of an appointment or a meeting in the Appointments pane. Just click the appointment to place the insertion point within it, then edit the text. Once the insertion point is in the text of an appointment or a meeting in the Appointments pane, however, you must double-click the border of the calendar item to open it for detailed editing, right-click the border and choose Open, or choose Open from the File menu.

Changing Times

After you set up a calendar item, you might need to change the beginning or end time of the item—perhaps a meeting must run longer because of added agenda items, or perhaps an appointment must be shortened or postponed because of your travel schedule. To change the times, first locate and open the calendar item. Then, in either the Start Time box or the End Time box (or both), select the new time. If the new time is other than on the hour or half-hour, select the nearest time and then edit the minutes. For example, if the new time is 11:45, select 11:30 and then change 30 to 45. (Notice that the list of times in the End Time box also shows the duration of the calendar item.) If you change the time for a meeting, click the Send Update button to send a message to attendees informing them of the new time.

 NOTE

If you change the specifics of a meeting and close it before clicking Send Update, Outlook displays a dialog box in which you can choose to send the updated notice to the invitees.

III

Scheduling Your
Time and Tasks

Dragging a Calendar Item to Change Its Time

Instead of opening a calendar item and setting the start time and end time, you can drag a calendar item to new times, as follows:

- To change the start time of a calendar item, drag the top border of the item up for an earlier time or down for a later time. The bottom border stays put, which means that you are also lengthening or shortening the calendar item time.

- To change the end time of a calendar item, drag the bottom border of the item up for an earlier time or down for a later time. The top border stays put, which means that you are also shortening or lengthening the calendar item time.

- To change the calendar item start time without changing the block of time for the item, point inside the item and drag, or drag the left or right border of the item. Drag up for an earlier time or down for a later time. Both the top and bottom borders move together.

- To move an item to another day, first make sure the new date is visible in the Date Navigator, and then drag the item from the Appointments pane and drop it on the new date in the Date Navigator. You can then go to that date and modify the time of the appointment or meeting as just described.

If you change the start or end time for a meeting by dragging the calendar item, Outlook displays a message asking whether you want to update the meeting attendees about the change in time. To send a message to attendees alerting them of the change, click Yes in the message box. Outlook opens the calendar item, which displays the new time. Click the Send Update button to send a message to the meeting attendees.

⭐ **TIP**

When you drag a calendar item, the box moves in increments reflecting the time span you have set for the Appointments pane. If you want to change these increments, see "Changing the Time Intervals," on page 301.

Dragging Invitation Times

In the Plan a Meeting window, and on the Attendee Availability tab in the meeting window, two vertical bars on the time grid show the start (the green bar) and end (the red bar) times of the meeting you are planning. (You can see the bars in the illustration on page 329; this view is displayed in the Attendee Availability tab when you select the Show Attendee Availability option.) You can drag these bars to change the start and end times. When you do, the start and end times also change in the time boxes at the bottom of the dialog box.

Setting a Reminder

? SEE ALSO

You can change the default reminder time for all of your calendar items; see "Reminder Options," on page 93.

Outlook is initially set up to remind you of a calendar item 15 minutes before the item's start time. In many cases, the 15-minute warning is sufficient. For some calendar items, however, you might want a reminder with a longer lead time; for other items, you might need less or none at all.

To change the reminder time for a specific calendar item, do this:

1 Locate and open the calendar item.

2 Click the Appointment tab, if it is not already displayed.

3 Click the down arrow at the right end of the Reminder box, and select the new reminder time from the drop-down list. You can also type the reminder time you want in the Reminder box.

4 Save and close the calendar item window.

If you don't want a reminder for a calendar item, turn off the Reminder option in the calendar item window. You can quickly turn off the reminder by right-clicking the calendar item in the Appointments pane, and then clicking Reminder from the shortcut menu.

Categorizing Your Calendar Items

? SEE ALSO

For information about working with categories in Outlook, see "Working with Categories," on page 560.

You can assign calendar items to categories so that organizing them is easier. By assigning a calendar item to one or more categories, you can then view your appointments, meetings, and events grouped by category. To assign a calendar item to a category, open the item and click the Categories button. (You can also type a category name in the text

III

Scheduling Your Time and Tasks

box to the right of the Categories button.) In the Categories dialog box, select the category or categories to which you want to assign the item and then click OK.

Describing Your Availability

When others are planning meetings, they can use the Attendee Availability tab to see when you have other engagements. The Attendee Availability tab usually shows that you are "busy" during the times of your appointments. Sometimes, however, even though you have an engagement, you might want your calendar to reflect that you are something other than "busy" during that time. That's where the Show Time As feature comes into play.

When you open a calendar item, the Show Time As box on the Appointment tab gives you four options to choose from:

Free. Even though you have an engagement scheduled, you might want to be available for an important meeting—your engagement can be moved or canceled.

Busy. This is the standard selection for new engagements.

Tentative. Sometimes you pencil in an engagement, either because you're not sure it will happen or because you want to be available for other engagements that might be more important.

Out of Office. If you're going to be away from the office for an engagement, you might want to make that clear to anyone planning a meeting to let them know that you can't be reached.

On the Attendee Availability tab, Outlook displays a legend of the color and pattern it uses to mark the status of your time.

Adding Attachments to an Item

In the box at the bottom of the calendar item window, you can type any text that you want to keep with the item. Because this box works the same as the message area in an e-mail message, you can attach

---

Categorizing Appointments with the Organize Button

The Organize button on the Standard toolbar provides some shortcuts for working with calendar items. In Chapter 10, for example, you learned how to use Organize to select the Calendar view.

You can also use Organize to create categories and to assign calendar items to a category. You'll learn how to create, delete, and manage categories in Chapter 20, "Organizing Folder Items." To quickly assign a calendar item to a category, however, follow these steps:

1   Open the Calendar folder.

2   Select one or more calendar items you want to assign to a category.

3   Click Organize on the Standard toolbar.

4   Click Using Categories.

5   You can either use the list next to the Add button to add the calendar items to an existing category or type a new category in the box below and click Create.

---

files, messages, and any other Microsoft Windows or Microsoft Office objects. For example, if you're sending a meeting request, you can type the agenda and include attachments for any background or preparatory material related to the meeting.

For information about attachments, "Sending Files as Attachments," on page 132, and "Attaching Messages," on page 136.

You can also include an attachment by embedding it as an object. This means that another Windows or Microsoft Office document is enclosed within the message itself. In order for the recipient to edit or change the contents of the embedded object, however, they must have the same program that you used to create it.

To embed an object, follow these steps:

1   Click in the message area, and then choose Object from the Insert menu.

III

**Scheduling Your
Time and Tasks**

2 Click Create New.   **3** Select the type of object.   **4** Click OK.

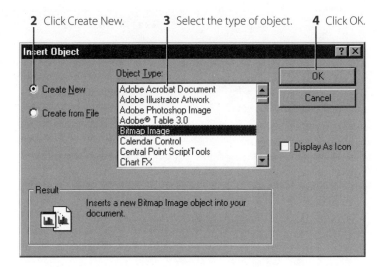

5 In the window that appears, create the object as you usually do in the application associated with the object. Here is an example of a bitmap image object window:

Use the bitmap toolbox to create an image in the bitmap object area.

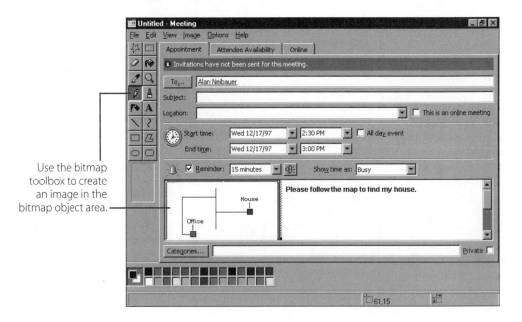

6 When you've finished creating the object, save and close it by clicking inside the message area, but outside the object area.

To insert an existing piece of "other stuff" from a file, follow these steps:

1 Click in the message area (this readies it to accept an insertion), and then choose Object from the Insert menu.

2 Click the Create From File option.

3 Click the Browse button to find the file, or type the path and file-name in the File box.

4 Turn on the Link option to create a link to the file.

5 If you want to display the file as an icon, turn on the Display As Icon option.

6 Click OK.

Linking Objects and Displaying Them as Icons

Anytime you include a very large file in a message, it's better to display it as an icon. An icon takes up less space in the message window, and usually it's easier for people reading the message to view a large file in the application used to create it.

Also, depending on the version of Microsoft Exchange Server and its configuration on your network, there may be a limit on message size. If you're sending a large file, it's better to link it, which reduces message size considerably. Remember that a linked file must reside on a disk and in a folder to which the recipient has read access. In addition, the recipient needs to have the same program you used to create the object to be able to read the contents.

Formatting a Message

If you enter text directly in the message area, you can format it using the buttons on the Formatting toolbar. (To turn on this toolbar, point to Toolbars on the View menu and choose Formatting from the sub-menu.) You can choose such attributes as font, font size, font style, color, alignment, indentation, and bullets or numbering.

Keeping Items Private

 SEE ALSO

For information about granting permissions and assigning delegates, see "Using the Delegates Tab," on page 80.

When you give others permission to view your Calendar folder, or when you assign a delegate who can perform actions such as responding to meeting requests on your behalf, these people can see the subject of a calendar item. If you have private calendar items that should not be seen by authorized users of your Calendar folder, open each item and turn on the Private option.

TIP

You can also turn the Private setting on or off by right-clicking the item in the Appointments pane and then choosing Private from the shortcut menu.

Changing Invitations

When you use the Plan a Meeting command on the Actions menu, you have the chance to select those whom you want to invite. You can later add and delete invitees, or even cancel all invitations, which converts a meeting to an appointment and an invited event to an event.

To select the additional attendees and resources you want to invite, open the calendar item and click the To button on the Appointment tab. You can also click the Attendee Availability tab and then click the Invite Others button. (If you want to change an appointment to a meeting, open the item and click the Invite Attendees button on the Standard toolbar to display the To button.) In either case, you see the Select Attendees And Resources dialog box, shown earlier on page 328. Select the people and resources you want to invite, and then click OK.

NOTE

To use Internet mail to invite others so they can schedule the meeting and respond, you must set their e-mail address to use Microsoft Exchange Rich Text Format. See "Adding Someone," on page 171, for more information.

Including but Not Inviting Others

For each attendee you invite, you can click the envelope icon to the left of the name to see a menu like the following.

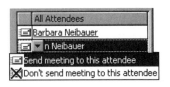

You'll probably use this menu most often with resources, which might not have e-mail addresses, even though you can type the resource's name in the Select Attendees And Resources dialog box. If you have a resource without an e-mail address, you can simply choose not to "send the meeting" to this "attendee." This prevents you from being notified that your message can't be delivered. You want others to know, however, that the people and resources you've invited will be available for the meeting.

If you want to remove a name from an invitation list, open the calendar item, select the name on the Attendee Availability tab, and then press the Delete key.

Canceling Invitations

A meeting reverts to an appointment and an invited event reverts to an event if you cancel all the invitations (after you've set them up but before you've actually sent them). To cancel the sending of invitations, click the Cancel Invitation button on the Standard toolbar, or choose Cancel Meeting from the Actions menu.

If you later change your mind and decide to issue the invitations after all, choose Invite Attendees from the Actions menu. Outlook uses the original invitation list on the Attendee Availability tab in the calendar item window.

Creating Recurring Items

When you create a recurring item, you have to designate when the appointment, meeting, or event occurs.

After filling out the information in the item's window, click the Recurrence button on the item's standard toolbar, choose Recurrence from the Actions menu, or press Ctrl+G to work with the recurrence pattern and series.

Outlook displays the Appointment Recurrence dialog box, shown in Figure 11-2. Adjust the recurrence schedule as shown in the figure. After you Click OK in this dialog box, any changes you have made—such as new meeting times or a new recurrence pattern—appear in the calendar item window, which you can now save and close.

> **NOTE**
>
> If you open an item already set up as recurring, you'll see the Open Recurring Item dialog box before the item itself opens. In this dialog box, choose whether you want to open this occurrence of the item or the full series of recurring items and then click OK. If you open a single occurrence of a recurring series of items, you can change the location, subject, or reminder time for that occurrence in the calendar item window. You can also change the start or end time for that occurrence (but not for the series). If you want to change the subject, location, or reminder for the entire series while working in the calendar item window for a particular occurrence, choose Edit Series from the Actions menu. Doing so opens a separate calendar item window that pertains to the entire series.

FIGURE 11-2.

The Appointment Recurrence dialog box.

If necessary, adjust the start, end, or duration.

Select a recurrence pattern and specify its details.

Set a start date for the series.

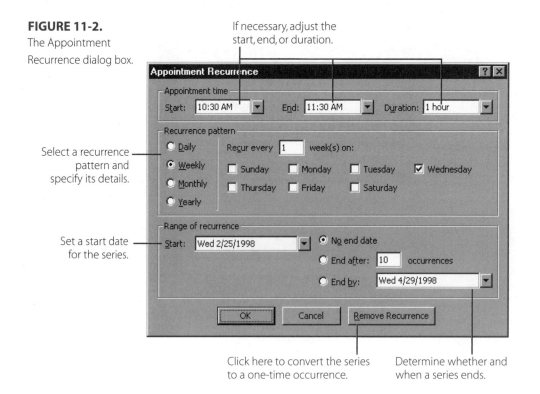

Click here to convert the series to a one-time occurrence.

Determine whether and when a series ends.

The following sections take a closer look at two parts of the Appointment Recurrence dialog box: the Recurrence Pattern area and the Range Of Recurrence area.

Recurrence Pattern

The recurrence pattern you select in the Appointment Recurrence dialog box tells Outlook how to set up your calendar for each engagement in the recurring series. Each recurrence pattern—Daily, Weekly, Monthly, and Yearly—has its own set of options, which appears to the right of the list of patterns. Select a recurrence pattern as follows:

Daily.   When an engagement recurs every day or recurs with a specific number of days between occurrences, you should select the Daily recurrence pattern. Select this recurrence pattern if you have an engagement that recurs every 30 days, for example. You can select a daily pattern that includes weekdays only (Monday through Friday), or you can specify a certain number of days between engagements by typing a number in the Every [ ] Day(s) box—from 1 (daily, including weekends) to 999 (about 2 years and 9 months).

Click here to set a day interval that includes weekend days.

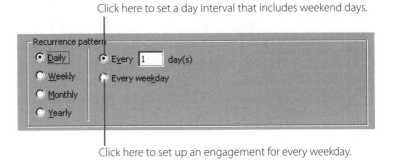

Click here to set up an engagement for every weekday.

Weekly.   You'll want to select the Weekly recurrence pattern when an engagement recurs on a specific day of the week or recurs with a specific number of weeks between occurrences. Type in a number to set the number of weeks between engagements—from 1 week to 99 weeks. You must also specify the day (or days) of the week.

III

Scheduling Your
Time and Tasks

Monthly. When an engagement recurs monthly on the same day or recurs with a specific number of months between occurrences, the Monthly recurrence pattern is your best choice.

When your engagement recurs on a specific date each month (or every so many months), select the first option on the right side of the Recurrence Pattern area. In the first box, type a number to set the specific date of the month. If the number you type for the date is greater than 28 (or 29 in leap years), Outlook notifies you that for months with fewer days than you specified, the engagement is set for the last day of the month. In the second box, type the number of months between engagements—from 1 month through 99 months.

When your engagement recurs in a specific pattern but not necessarily on the same date each time, select the second option on the right side of the Recurrence Pattern area, which specifies a relative day. For example, some organizations hold a meeting on the second Tuesday of each month. From month to month, the actual date changes—March 10 and April 14 are second Tuesdays in 1998, for instance. After you select this option, do the following:

1 Select the occurrence of the day during the month—first, second, third, fourth, or last.

2 Select the day pattern. In addition to the named days of the week, you can select Day, Weekday, or Weekend Day.

3 Set the number of months between engagements—from 1 month to 99 months (8 years and 3 months).

Yearly. Select the Yearly recurrence pattern when an engagement recurs annually on the same day every year.

Select the first option on the right side of the Recurrence Pattern area when your engagement recurs on the same date each year. Choose a month from the drop-down list, and type in a number to set the specific date. Outlook will not let you select a date that doesn't occur in a given month, for instance April 31 or February 29 in a non–leap year.

Select the second option on the Recurrence Pattern area, which specifies a relative day, when your engagement recurs in a specific pattern but not necessarily on the same date each time. If, for example, your club holds its annual party each year on the second Tuesday of December, the actual date was December 9 in 1997—but it will be December 8 in 1998. After you select this option, follow these steps:

1 Select the occurrence of the day during the month—first, second, third, fourth, or last.

2 Select the day pattern—Day, Weekday, Weekend Day, or the named days of the week.

3 Select the month.

Range of Recurrence

When you create a series of recurring engagements, Outlook doesn't set an ending date for the series. That's fine for recurring engagements that you expect to continue for many years or for those times when you don't know if a series is ever going to end. Sometimes you know when a series of engagements will end, for example, if you signed up for a workshop that lasts for six weeks. In such a case, you will want to set the end of the series.

In the Range Of Recurrence area of the Appointment Recurrence dialog box, you have three choices for ending a series: No End Date, End After, and End By. The No End Date option is self-explanatory. Use one of the other options under the following circumstances:

End After. If you know the number of engagements in the series, select the End After option and type the number in the box. (Setting the number of occurrences to 1 is the same as setting up a one-time engagement.) If your recurring engagements add up to more than 999, you will need to set an End By date instead.

> **Using The End After Option to Find the End By Date**
>
> If you set an End After number, Outlook sets the End By date to match the number of occurrences. You might not see this change until after you close the Appointment Recurrence dialog box and then reopen it. You can force Outlook to display the change, however, by setting the End After number and then clicking the End By option. You can then select either option to get the same result. Note, however, that this doesn't work in reverse—if you select a date in the End By box, Outlook does not change the number of occurrences. If you set a date past 999 occurrences, don't click the End After option. If you do, Outlook resets the End By date to the date of the last occurrence.

End By. If you know the date of the last engagement in the series, select the End By option. The End By box initially shows a date that matches 10 occurrences in the End After box (the default value). In the End By box, you can type a date, or you can click the down arrow to display a calendar from which you can select the end date.

Adjusting Calendar Item Properties

SEE ALSO

For information about the AutoArchive feature, see Chapter 18, "Archiving Folder Items."

Each calendar item has a Properties dialog box with options. To display the Properties dialog box for the calendar item, shown in Figure 11-3, open the calendar item, and then choose Properties from the File menu.

The contents of the Properties dialog box may vary depending on the type of calendar item, but the following options are typically included.

Importance. Select the level of importance: High, Normal, Low.

Sensitivity. Select the level of sensitivity: Normal, Personal, Private, or Confidential.

FIGURE 11-3.
A Properties dialog box
for an appointment.

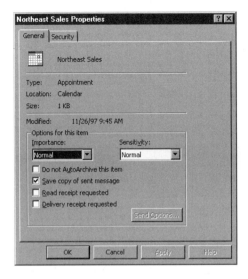

Do Not AutoArchive This Item.   Turn on this option to exclude this
calendar item when the folder is automatically archived.

Save Copy Of Sent Message.   Turn on this option to save a copy of
the message.

Read Receipt Requested.   Turn on this option to get a receipt when
your item is read (or at least opened) by the recipient.

Delivery Receipt Requested.   Turn on this option to get a receipt
when the message reaches its destination.

If you've enabled security features in Outlook, such as encryption or
digital signatures, you will also see a Security tab on the Properties
dialog box. Use this tab to control the security for individual messages.

Deleting a Calendar Item

When you need to delete a calendar item, first click the item to select
it. Then use one of the following methods to cancel (delete) the item:

■ Click the Delete button on the Standard toolbar.

■ Press Ctrl+D.

■ Choose Delete from the Edit menu.

III

Scheduling Your
Time and Tasks

- Right-click the calendar item, and then choose Delete from the shortcut menu.

- Open the calendar item, and then click the Delete button on the Standard toolbar in the calendar item window. For a meeting, you can also choose Cancel Meeting from the Actions menu.

Outlook moves deleted calendar items to the Deleted Items folder.

If you delete a calendar item that is part of a series, you see the following message:

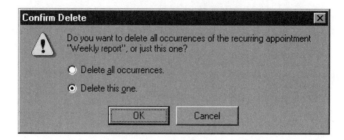

Choose whether you want to delete the entire series or just the selected occurrence, and then click OK.

If you open the series of a recurring item and delete the series, you won't see the Confirm Delete message.

No matter how you choose to delete a meeting or event to which others have already been invited, Outlook displays a dialog box in which you can choose to send a cancellation notice to the invitees or to delete the item without sending a notification.

Copying a Calendar Item

If you need to set up a calendar item that is similar to an existing one, you can copy the original item rather than starting over. You can either drag and drop the item to another date or use the Copy and Paste commands on the Edit menu.

Copying a calendar item using the mouse is similar to moving it, except that you hold down the Ctrl key when you drag the item from the Appointments pane to the new date on the Date Navigator. Remember to set the Date Navigator to show the new date before you start dragging the calendar item.

The steps for copying a calendar item using the Cut and Paste commands are as follows:

1 Locate the calendar item, and click its left border.

2 Choose Copy from the Edit menu (or press Ctrl+C).

3 Go to the date where you want to set up the new calendar item.

4 Click the appointment slot for the beginning time of the new calendar item.

5 Choose Paste from the Edit menu (or press Ctrl+V).

6 Fine-tune the copy of the calendar item as necessary to fit the new circumstances.

Dealing with a Reminder

As you've learned, Outlook helps you remember your scheduled engagements by displaying a reminder on the date and at the time you set for the reminder. Here's a picture of a reminder:

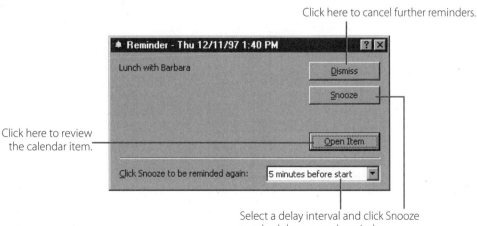

Click here to cancel further reminders.

Click here to review the calendar item.

Select a delay interval and click Snooze to schedule a second reminder.

If you want to be reminded again, select one of the predefined time intervals from the list. (You can't type a delay time.) Your choices range from five minutes to one week. If you postpone the reminder past the start time of the calendar item, the next reminder message displays the word *Overdue* in its title bar. If you need to reschedule the actual calendar item rather than the reminder, click the Open Item button to make the necessary changes.

You can only snooze in the Reminder message box, but you can change the initial reminder time in the calendar item window.

Receiving and Responding to a Meeting Request

When someone invites you to a meeting or an event, you receive an e-mail message that looks like the one shown here:

Click here to accept the invitation.

Click here if you might attend.

Click here if you can't attend.

Click here to see the item placed on your calendar.

Click here to forward the invitation to someone else.

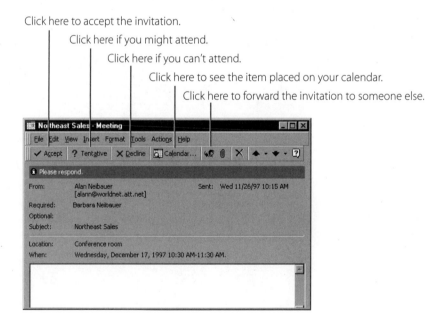

In order to process the meeting request, you must receive it using Outlook. The meeting request format is not compatible with Outlook Express.

If you click Accept, Tentative, or Decline, Outlook asks whether you want to send your response and whether you want to add comments to it:

Click here to add a comment to your response.

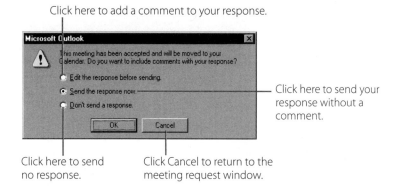

Click here to send your response without a comment.

Click here to send no response.

Click Cancel to return to the meeting request window.

Before responding to the invitation, however, you may want to check your schedule. If you click the Calendar button on the invitation's Standard toolbar, you will see the item placed on your calendar for the proposed date and time of the meeting. To see additional details of the meeting, open it as you would any other item in your Appointments pane, shown at the top of the next page.

Click the Attendee Availability tab to see a list of invitees and to check or update your free/busy time. After reviewing the details of the proposed meeting, you can use buttons on the Standard toolbar to accept, tentatively accept, decline, or forward the invitation.

If you want, Outlook can process meeting requests automatically. Choose Options from the Tools menu, click the Preferences tab, click the Calendar Options button, and then click the Resource Scheduling button. In the Resource Scheduling dialog box, you can select options for Outlook to automatically accept meeting requests, decline meeting requests that conflict with your existing schedule, and decline requests for recurring meetings. For more information, see "Resource Scheduling," on page 70.

III

Scheduling Your
Time and Tasks

Checking Attendees

When you receive a meeting request message, you can click the Attendee Availability tab to see a list of all the people and resources that are invited. Notice that the Attendee Availability tab for invitees does not include either the status of responses from others or an Invite Others button. You can turn on the Show Attendee Availability option to see the schedules for the other attendees.

When you open a calendar item for a meeting you requested, you see a slightly different version of the Attendee Availability tab. This version indicates the responses you've received so far to your meeting request and allows you to expand the list of invitees, by clicking the Invite Others button of the bottom of the screen.

Conducting Online Meetings

Ever get tired of going into the office or traveling out-of-town for a meeting? With Outlook and a program called NetMeeting that comes with it, you may not have to. You can participate in meetings from wherever your computer is located: at home, on the road at a convention or on vacation, or even in your car if you have the proper hardware. You can also use NetMeeting to chat online with friends, business associates, or even strangers!

For more information about NetMeeting, refer to the online help.	

With NetMeeting and the proper hardware, you can

- Talk and listen to others

- See other meeting participants who have video hardware

- Share programs

- Draw and annotate onscreen

If you do not have a sound-equipped computer, you can write and receive notes from others in the meeting.

You can use NetMeeting in conjunction with Outlook to plan and conduct meetings and to make Internet calls. An Internet call lets you connect to another person also running NetMeeting to hold a conversation. In addition, you can use NetMeeting as a separate program to make Internet calls and join online chats and conversations.

All of this is made possible by directory servers provided by Microsoft and other companies. The directory server is the link between you and others running NetMeeting, and it channels audio, video, typed chat, and shared programs between users.

Setting Up NetMeeting Conferences

A NetMeeting conference is simply a meeting conducted over the Internet through the directory server. To set up a NetMeeting conference, follow these steps:

1 Open the Calendar folder.

2 Choose New Online Meeting Request from the Actions menu.

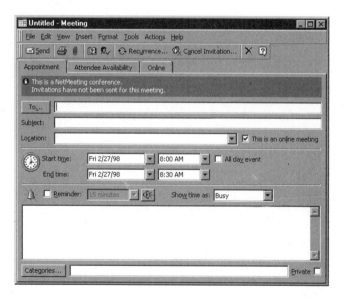

Notice that the This Is An Online Meeting option is already turned on.

3 Select or enter the invitees as you would for any other meeting.

> To invite a person to an online meeting, NetMeeting information must be in their Contacts folder listing. You'll learn how to enter NetMeeting information in Chapter 13, "Managing Your Contacts."

4 Enter the other specifics of the meeting.

5 Click the Online tab.

6 Select a directory server.

7 Enter your (or the meeting organizer's) e-mail address.

8 Turn on the Autostart option to start NetMeeting automatically 15 minutes before the meeting time, or click Start Meeting Now to start the meeting immediately.

> To convert an existing appointment or meeting to an online meeting, open the item and turn on the This Is An Online Meeting option.

Starting a Meeting

If you set the meeting to start automatically, Outlook will start NetMeeting 15 minutes before the meeting time and place the Internet calls to all the meeting invitees.

If you want to start the meeting manually, click the Start Meeting Now button when you're ready and Outlook will start NetMeeting and place Internet calls to the invitees.

Joining a Meeting in Progress

If you are not the meeting organizer or you miss the online meeting call, you can join the meeting in progress by following these steps:

1 Open the online meeting calendar item.

2 Click the Online tab.

3 Click Join Meeting Now.

Setting Up NetMeeting

The first time you run NetMeeting, you'll have to set it up on your system. Rather than wait until your first actual online meeting, you can set up NetMeeting beforehand using either of these techniques:

- Point to Internet Call on the Go menu, and then choose Internet Call from the submenu.

- Point to Internet Call on the Go menu, and choose From Address Book on the submenu. Choose the person you want to call, and then click OK.

- If you installed NetMeeting as a separate application, click Start on the taskbar, point to Programs, and then click Microsoft NetMeeting.

A series of dialog boxes begins in which you set up NetMeeting. The steps you see may vary slightly from the following description, depending on your system's configuration. Respond appropriately to each box described below and then click Next to move to the next one.

III

Scheduling Your Time and Tasks

1 The first dialog box simply explains some of the features available in NetMeeting. Click Next.

2 Leave this option turned on to log on to the server when you start NetMeeting. ——

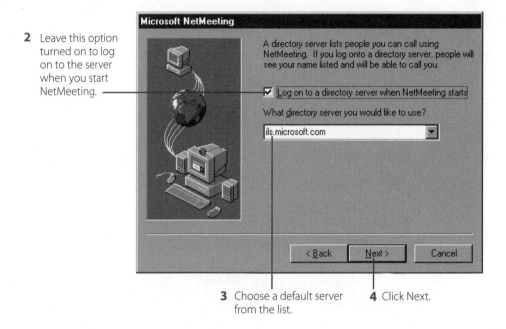

3 Choose a default server from the list. **4** Click Next.

5 On the next screen enter your name, e-mail address, and a brief comment about yourself that will appear onscreen to identify you to other NetMeeting users.

6 Click Next.

7 Specify the category of information that you plan to communicate over the Internet: personal, business, or adults-only.

8 Click Next.

9 Select the speed of your connection. The options are 14400 bps modem, 28800 bps or faster modem, ISDN, and Local Area Network.

10 Click Next.

11 If you have a video capture board or other video capability installed on your computer, you'll see a dialog box that asks you to confirm its use. Click Next to continue.

12 Next you may see a dialog box that asks you to select the devices that will record and play back sound on your system. Generally your sound card performs both functions. On some configurations this step may be skipped. After selecting the devices, click Next.

13 The next screen merely informs you that the Audio Tuning Wizard is about to help you tune your audio settings, and it instructs you to close all other programs that play or record sound. Click Next.

14 Click here to listen to sample audio.

15 Adjust the slider bar to a comfortable listening level.

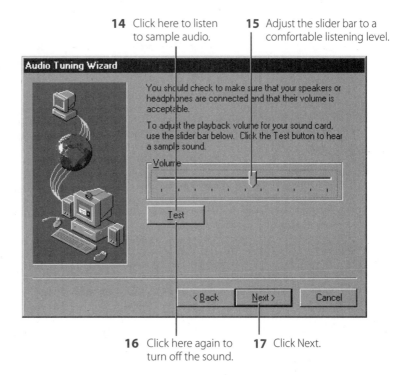

16 Click here again to turn off the sound.

17 Click Next.

Scheduling Your Time and Tasks

18 Read this sentence, speaking clearly and distinctly into your microphone.

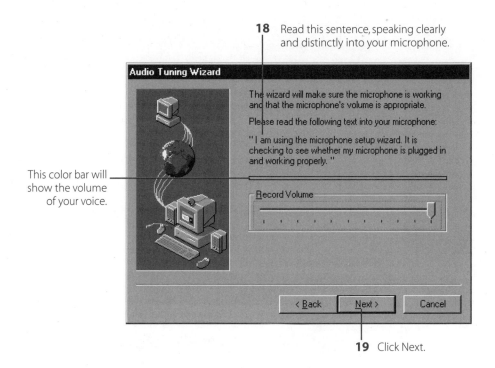

This color bar will show the volume of your voice.

19 Click Next.

20 Click Finish when the Audio Tuning Wizard reports that you have tuned your settings.

Once you start NetMeeting, you can change all of your setup options, and fine-tune Internet calling, audio, and video settings by choosing the Options command on the NetMeeting Tools menu.

When you click Finish, NetMeeting starts and connects to the directory server you chose earlier. Depending on your connection and configuration, you may need to click Connect if the Dial-up Connection box appears, or you may need to start your Dial-Up Connection manually and connect. The NetMeeting window appears as it attempts to connect to the server, as shown in Figure 11-4.

To manually log on to the directory server, choose Log On from the Call menu. Choose Log Off when you're ready to disconnect from the server and stop placing or accepting calls.

FIGURE 11-4.
The NetMeeting
window.

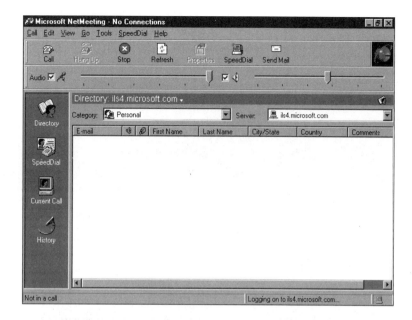

Using NetMeeting

When you place an online call, either for a meeting or just a one-on-one chat, NetMeeting connects to the directory server, checks that your invitee is also online, and then asks if the invitee wants to accept your call.

⭐ TIP

If you do not want to be bothered with calls, choose Do Not Disturb from the Call menu.

If the person selects to ignore the call, you'll be asked if you want to leave a message.

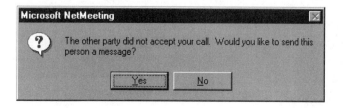

III

Scheduling Your
Time and Tasks

If you choose Yes, the familiar New Message window will be displayed, in which you can leave a message, attach a file, and so on.

If the person chooses to accept your call, the person's name is displayed in the Current Call folder of NetMeeting, as shown below, and you can start communicating.

You can only speak to and receive video from one person at a time. If there are more than two participants in the meeting, click the Switch button on the Current Call window toolbar and choose the person with whom you want to communicate.

To end the meeting, click the Hang Up button on the toolbar, or choose the Log Off command on the Call menu.

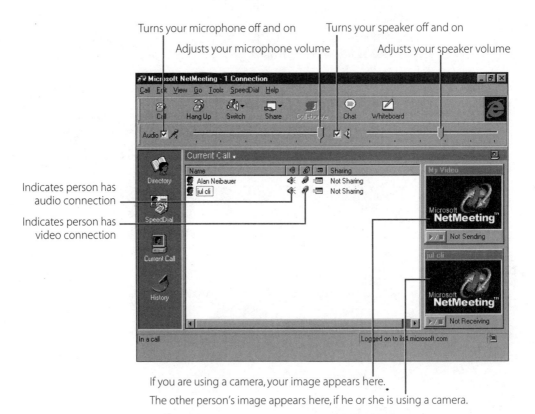

Turns your microphone off and on   Turns your speaker off and on

Adjusts your microphone volume   Adjusts your speaker volume

Indicates person has audio connection

Indicates person has video connection

If you are using a camera, your image appears here.
The other person's image appears here, if he or she is using a camera.

Chatting

Even with the proper equipment, the audio quality of a NetMeeting call may be poor, depending on the speed of your modem and the traffic on the directory server. You may wish to open a chat window and write messages to the other members of the meeting instead. Follow these steps:

1 Click Chat on the NetMeeting toolbar from the Current Call window, or choose Chat from the Tools menu to open the chat window.

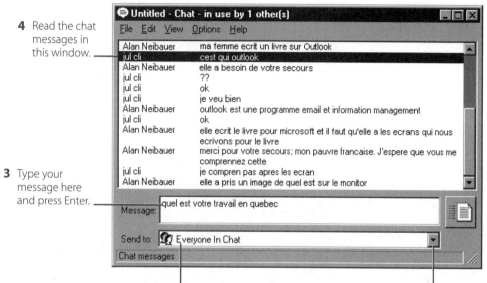

4 Read the chat messages in this window.

3 Type your message here and press Enter.

2 Send to everyone in the chat group or select a recipient from the list.

> **NOTE**

You can talk (speak) and chat (write) at the same time.

Using the Whiteboard

Sometimes you need to discuss something online that you can't easily express in words. Suppose, for example, that you want the participants in the meeting to review a drawing. You'd like to give each participant the opportunity to comment on the drawing or even make changes to it as the meeting progresses. Or suppose you're conducting an online training session and want to write out important points that you would use a flipchart for if this were an in-person meeting. In these instances you can use the Whiteboard.

III

Scheduling Your
Time and Tasks

The Whiteboard is a drawing window that you can display and share with all participants in the meeting. Whatever you draw on the Whiteboard appears simultaneously on the Whiteboards of all meeting participants. If you permit it, other meeting participants can add to your drawing using their Whiteboards.

To use the Whiteboard, follow these steps:

1 Click Whiteboard on the NetMeeting toolbar, choose Whiteboard from the Tools menu, or press Ctrl+W.

2 Draw on the Whiteboard.

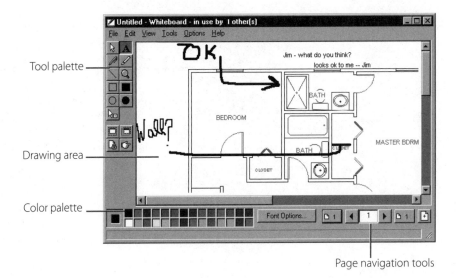

Use the tools on the Whiteboard tool palette, shown in Figure 11-5, to create drawings. The same features are also available on the Tools menu.

Selector. Use this tool to click or drag over objects you want to select. Drag the selected object to move it on the screen, or choose Delete, Copy, or Cut from the Edit menu.

Text. Use this tool to type in the Whiteboard. Choose a color from the color palette, or click the Font Options button that appears when you're using the tool to change the font, font size, and font style. You can also use the Colors and Font commands on the Options menu.

FIGURE 11-5.
Whiteboard tool palette.

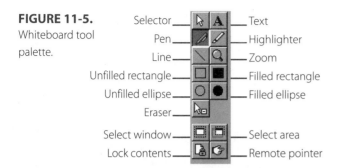

Selector
Pen
Line
Unfilled rectangle
Unfilled ellipse
Eraser
Select window
Lock contents

Text
Highlighter
Zoom
Filled rectangle
Filled ellipse

Select area
Remote pointer

Pen.   Use this tool to draw freehand on the screen by dragging the mouse.

Line.   Use this tool to draw straight lines by dragging the mouse from one point to the next. Select a line width from the window shown below, and choose a color from the palette. You can also use the Colors and Line Width commands on the Options menu.

Choose a width for a line or unfilled shape.
Choose a color for a line or shape.

Rectangle.   Use the rectangle tools to draw rectangles on the screen, choosing a line width and color from the palette. Choose Unfilled Rectangle to draw just a border; use Filled Rectangle to draw a solid rectangle of the selected color.

Ellipse.   Use the ellipse tools to draw filled and unfilled circles, choosing a line width and color from the palette.

TIP

> Use the Bring To Front and Send To Back commands on the Edit menu to layer overlapping objects in relation to each other.

Highlighter.   Choose a line width and a color, and then use this tool to drag over the area you wish to highlight.

III

**Scheduling Your
Time and Tasks**

Zoom.   Use this tool to toggle between normal and enlarged views. You can also use the Zoom command on the View menu.

Eraser.   Use this tool to erase objects by clicking them, or use it to drag a rectangle over an area, and all objects even partially within the area will be completely removed.

Select Window.   This tool works similarly to the Windows Clipboard. Click any window on your screen to copy the contents onto the Whiteboard; you can click even a partially obscured window. The Whiteboard will reopen with the window inserted as a graphic. You cannot open a file, other than a saved Whiteboard file, directly in the Whiteboard window.

Select Area.   Use this tool to drag a rectangle over the area of the screen you want to copy to the Whiteboard.

Lock Contents.   Turn on this tool to prevent others from changing the Whiteboard contents. Turn it off to allow others to change the Whiteboard.

Remote Pointer.   Turn on this tool to display a pointer and move it to the area of the Whiteboard you want others to look at. Click again to turn it off.

Use the Remote Pointer to show others where to look.

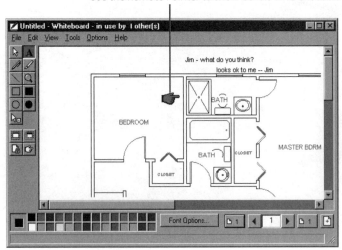

Working with Whiteboard Pages

If you were conducting an in-person meeting, you might use a flip chart to draw images and highlight important points. When one page gets full, you just fold it over and start with a fresh sheet. You can use the Whiteboard in the same way, changing pages as needed.

Use these buttons to add new pages or move from page to page:

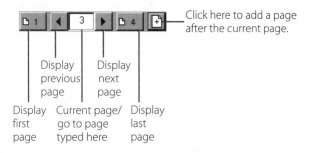

You can also add a new page before or after the current page using one of these menu commands:

- Choose Insert Page Before from the Edit menu to insert a page before the current page.

- Choose Insert Page After from the Edit menu to insert a page after the current page.

Choose Clear Page from the Edit menu to erase the current page, or choose Delete Page from the Edit menu to delete the page.

You can also work with pages using the Page Sorter command on the Edit menu to display a dialog box like the one at the top of the following page.

Normally, everyone in the meeting can see the same page that you have displayed on your screen. If you want to change pages without letting everyone see what you are doing, turn off Synchronize on the Tools menu.

III

Scheduling Your
Time and Tasks

Drag a page to a new position.

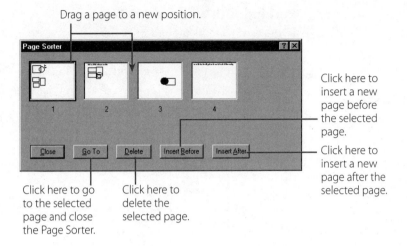

Click here to insert a new page before the selected page.

Click here to insert a new page after the selected page.

Click here to go to the selected page and close the Page Sorter.

Click here to delete the selected page.

Saving and Printing the Whiteboard

When your meeting is over, there is no need to lose the contents of your Whiteboard. While the Whiteboard is still displayed, each participant of the meeting can choose the Print command from the File menu to print a copy of the Whiteboard or the Save command from the File menu to save it. Whiteboards are saved in a special format, with the WHT extension, that can later be reopened in the Whiteboard using the Open command on the File menu.

If you close the Whiteboard without saving the contents, NetMeeting will ask if you want to save it at that time.

Sharing and Collaborating

In addition to sharing a drawing on the Whiteboard, you may want participants to share a program as well. This is especially true if your meeting is aimed at training or user support and you want to help participants use a program. You may also want users to interact with another program, even Outlook itself. That is the purpose of sharing and collaborating.

■ When you *share* a program with others, the meeting participants can see the program, but they cannot interact with it. The person sharing the program is called the *owner* and has control over who can work with it.

■ When you *collaborate* with others on a program, the meeting participants can also work with the program.

Sharing a Program

To share a program, follow these steps.

1 Start the program, and then switch back to NetMeeting.

2 Click Current Call to open the Current Call window.

3 Click this button on the NetMeeting toolbar.

4 Click the program to share.

You can also choose Share Application from the Tools menu. Other meeting participants will now be able to see exactly what you are doing with the shared program.

> If you share a window, such as My Computer, or a folder, every program in the folder will be shared during the meeting.

Collaborating

After you've shared a program, if you want meeting participants to be able to use it, click the Collaborate button on the Current Call toolbar or choose Start Collaborating from the Tools menu.

To work with the program, the meeting participant must click the Collaborate button on his or her own screen, and then click in the program window to begin using it. This transfers control of the program to the participant, and you are no longer allowed to use your cursor onscreen.

Press Esc to stop any participant who is currently working with the shared program and regain control over the program and your cursor. You can then click the Collaborate button to prevent others from using the program. Click the Share button to remove the program from others' screens.

Sending and Receiving Files

While you are in a meeting, you can send files to other participants and receive files from them.

Point to File Transfer on the Tools menu, and then choose one of these commands:

Send File.   This command lets you select the file to send.

Cancel Send.   This command stops the file transfer in progress.

Cancel Receive.   This command stops reception of the incoming file.

Open Received Files Folder.   This command opens a folder containing files received during meetings.

Using NetMeeting Directories

When you conduct an online meeting, you connect to persons who have NetMeeting information in their Contacts listing. You can also use NetMeeting as a separate application to contact other persons who are logged on to the same server.

1   Start NetMeeting and click the Directory button.

2 Choose a category of user.

3 Choose the server, if it's other than the one you are logged on to.

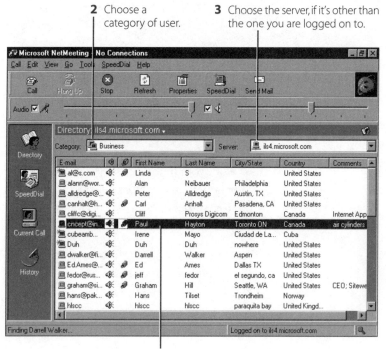

4 Right-click a person to contact, and click Call on the shortcut menu.

NetMeeting will place the call and ask the person to accept or decline your call. If the person accepts, the Current Call window appears and you can use all of the resources available to communicate.

To send e-mail to a person in the directory, select the name, and then choose the Call New Mail Message command.

Speed Dialing

When you place a call or when someone calls you, the other person's NetMeeting information is added to your SpeedDial list. The list is updated each time you start NetMeeting so you can quickly see who is currently available online. You can then call someone by following these steps:

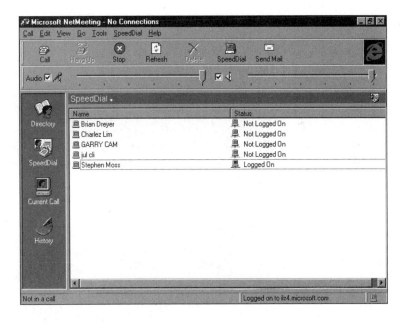

1 Click the SpeedDial button.

2 Double-click the person you want to call.

NetMeeting Etiquette

Treat the NetMeeting directory as you would a telephone book. Some people enjoy being called by strangers because they like experimenting with NetMeeting or just chatting with people from other parts of the world. Others do not appreciate calls from strangers.

Before placing a NetMeeting call, read the brief note in the Comments column of the directory window. It may indicate that the person wants to hear from anyone or only wants calls from friends, business associates, males, females, or whatever. For the full text of the comment, right-click the listing and choose Properties from the shortcut menu.

If you place a call and get a response that it was declined, don't try again. If you really have to reach the person, send an e-mail message. E-mail addresses are listed in the first column in the directory window or in the Properties dialog box.

To add a person to the SpeedDial list manually, choose Add SpeedDial from the SpeedDial menu.

1 Enter the person's address.

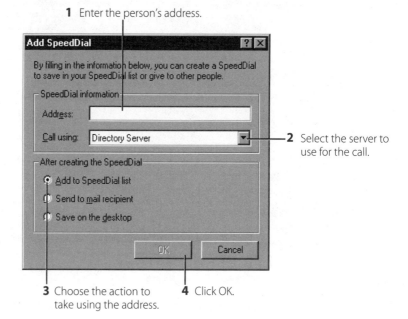

2 Select the server to use for the call.

3 Choose the action to take using the address.

4 Click OK.

Controlling Your Tasks

We all have tasks to perform, every day. For many daily tasks, we need a list to remind us. At home, you might have a "to do" note stuck on the refrigerator door; at work you may have a notepad that you check each morning to see the tasks for the day. A task list can help remind us what needs doing and when that doing must be done, especially for tasks with deadlines, for large tasks that continue for a long time, and for tasks that can be started at a future date but that we dare not forget to perform.

In your Microsoft Outlook 98 Tasks folder, you can set up tasks, describe them, specify start and end dates, set reminders, track the progress of your work on the task, estimate and track how much effort is expended, record costs, and note contacts and billing information. In Outlook you can assign a task to someone else (send him or her a task request), and someone else can assign a task to you (send you a task request). Outlook also provides tools that make it easy to report the status of an assigned task, while the task is under way and at its completion.

Other Ways of Looking at Tasks

You will probably work with tasks mostly from the Tasks folder. However, you can also perform some functions with tasks using the TaskPad and Outlook Today.

The TaskPad in the Calendar folder window is tied directly to entries you make in the Tasks folder. The TaskPad displays active tasks and tasks completed on the date showing on the calendar. You can open a task from the TaskPad and enter and change the details about a task, the same as you can by opening a task in the Tasks folder. You can also enter a new task in the TaskPad, and edit the information about a task that is displayed in the TaskPad. For more information about the TaskPad, see "Adjusting the TaskPad," on page 314.

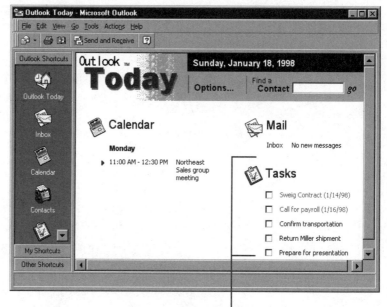

Accessing tasks from Outlook Today

You can also review active tasks from the Outlook Today window. The window displays all active tasks, each with a check box for you to mark when the task is completed.

Here's a typical Tasks folder, with the task list displayed in Simple List view:

One-time task —
Recurring task —

Assigned task —
Completed task —

Task assigned to you —

Setting Up a Task

Each task in Outlook is identified with a subject line and an optional description and is assigned settings for such items as the starting date, due date, priority, status, recurrence, and ownership. Recurrence determines whether the task is a one-time occurrence or one that recurs from time to time. Ownership designates the task as a job you do yourself or as a job you ask someone else to perform.

When you need to set up a new task, you can open the Tasks folder and use one of the following methods:

New Task

■ Click the New Task button at the left end of the Standard toolbar.

■ Choose the New Task command on the Actions menu.

III

Scheduling Your
Time and Tasks

- Point to New on the File menu, and then choose Task from the submenu.

- Press Ctrl+N.

- Double-click in the top row of the task list (which reads *Click here to add a new task*).

Outlook opens a task window, which initially displays the Task tab. On this tab, you can name the task, set due dates, assign a priority, and set up various other properties that will help you accomplish the task. Figure 12-1 shows an example of a task window and highlights some of the options you'll find on the Task tab. We'll discuss these options and settings throughout this chapter.

After you enter information for a task in the task window, click the Save And Close button to add the task to your task list. If you want to close the window without saving the information you've entered, click the Close button in the upper-right corner of the window (or choose Close on the File menu), and then click No when Outlook asks whether you want to save your changes.

FIGURE 12-1.

The Task tab of a task window.

Set due dates for the task.

Assign a priority to the task.

Set a reminder here.

Add notes and attachments here.

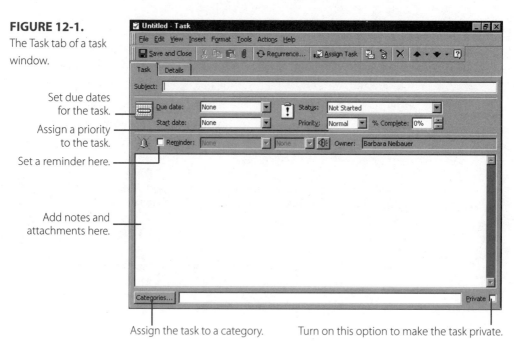

Assign the task to a category.   Turn on this option to make the task private.

Creating a New Task Anywhere in Outlook

If you're working in an Outlook folder other than the Tasks folder and need to set up a new task, use one of the following methods to create the task. Later you can fine-tune or change it as necessary.

- Click the small arrow on the Standard toolbar's New button (at the far left), and then choose Task or Task Request from the menu.

- Point to New on the File menu, and then choose Task or Task Request from the submenu.

- Press Ctrl+Shift+K for a new task or press Ctrl+Shift+U for a new task request.

Quickly Setting Up a Task

? SEE ALSO

In the Contacts folder, you can set up a new task that you will perform for a contact. For details, see "Assigning a Task to a Contact," on page 426.

When you need to set up a task quickly without worrying about the fine points of the settings, you can simply open the Tasks folder and do the following:

1 Click the top row of the task list (which reads *Click here to add a new task*).

2 Type the name of the task.

3 If applicable, click in the Due Date column and type a due date for the task, and then press Enter.

4 Continue adding tasks by repeating steps 2 and 3. When you are finished, press the Down arrow key or click the mouse in the list of tasks to deactivate the new task box.

The new tasks now appear in the task list. Later, if you want to add more information about a task or make any other changes, you can open the task item (by double-clicking it, for example, or by right-clicking the task item and choosing Open from the shortcut menu), make your changes in the task window, and then click the Save And Close button on the Standard toolbar.

III

Scheduling Your
Time and Tasks

To select a due date from a calendar rather than type the date, click the Due Date box and then click the down arrow that appears. Select a date from the calendar that Outlook displays. You can move around the calendar as you would the Date Navigator, described in "Using the Date Navigator," on page 307.

Setting Up a Recurring Task

If you have a task that must be repeated at a regular interval, you can set up a recurrence pattern for the task. This way, an occurrence of the task appears on your task list at the proper intervals so that you have an ongoing reminder of the work you need to do.

If you want to establish a recurrence pattern for a task that you assign to some-one else, you must set up the recurrence when you create the task. You can't add recurrence or change the recurrence pattern after you send a task request. For more details about task requests, see "Sending a Task Request," on page 385.

You can establish a recurrence pattern for a task when you first set up the task, or you can open one of your existing tasks and change it from one-time to recurring (or vice versa) or adjust its recurrence pattern. To do so, open the task item you want to work with and then take one of the following actions in the task window:

- Click the Recurrence button on the Standard toolbar.

- Choose Recurrence on the Actions menu.

- Press Ctrl+G.

In the Task Recurrence dialog box, shown in Figure 12-2, you can set the intervals at which the task should recur, and you can designate the start and end dates for the series of recurring tasks. You can also change a recurring task to a one-time task by clicking Remove Recurrence. Setting up a recurring task is very similar to setting up a recurring calendar item, as discussed in Chapter 11, "Scheduling Appointments, Meetings, and Events." In fact, the two areas of the Task Recurrence dialog box—Recurrence Pattern and Range Of Recurrence—also appear in the Appointment Recurrence dialog box, shown in Figure 11-2, on page 342.)

FIGURE 12-2.

The Task Recurrence dialog box.

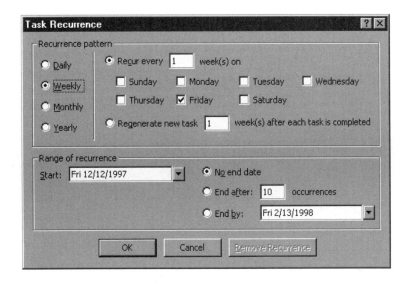

The recurrence pattern you set up in the Task Recurrence dialog box tells Outlook when each occurrence in the series of tasks is active and due. When you select one of the four recurrence patterns—Daily, Weekly, Monthly, or Yearly—a corresponding set of options appears on the right side of the Recurrence Pattern area. These options allow you to specify how Outlook should calculate the intervals between occurrences of a recurring task. When you complete an occurrence of the task, Outlook creates the next occurrence on the basis of the recurrence pattern you set and adds the next occurrence to your task list. The recurrence pattern options for tasks are nearly the same as those in the Appointment Recurrence dialog box; consult "Recurrence Pattern," on page 343, for details about how to set them.

The one difference between setting recurrence patterns for a task and for a calendar item is the Regenerate New Task option in the Task Recurrence dialog box. This option is valuable when a task must recur a specified number of days (or weeks, months, or years) after the previous completion of the task (rather than at a specific interval). For example, you could set up the recurring task of changing your security password every 60 days. Then, for one reason or another, you might change your password in fewer than 60 days. If you have turned on the Regenerate New Task option, Outlook will create a new occurrence of the task, resetting the due date to 60 days after the date you mark the previous occurrence of the task completed.

The second area of the Task Recurrence dialog box, Range Of Recurrence, is identical to the area of the same name in the Appointment Recurrence dialog box. It's easy to see how to set a start date; for details about setting end dates, see "Range of Recurrence," on page 345.

When you click OK in the Task Recurrence dialog box, you return to the task window. If you have set up a recurrence pattern, the colored band at the top of the Task tab now displays information about the intervals at which the task will recur. Notice also that if you have changed the recurring task's start date in the Task Recurrence dialog box, Outlook changes the due date in the task window (and in the task list) accordingly.

If you open a recurring task and change the due date or start date for the task in the task window, Outlook displays a message telling you that you have changed the date for only one occurrence of the task and that to change all future occurrences you need to open the Task Recurrence dialog box. If you click OK in the message box to accept the changes you've made to the single occurrence of the task, Outlook lists that occurrence of the task in the task list separately. The start date and due date for the recurring task are updated according to the existing recurrence pattern.

Skipping a Task in a Series

When a recurring task comes due, you might find that you don't need to perform the task this time, although you will need to do so for future due dates. When you want to skip one occurrence of a recurring task, open the task and choose Skip Occurrence from the Actions menu. Outlook resets the due date to the next occurrence of the recurring task.

You cannot undo skipping an occurrence, so if you skip an occurrence in error, you need to reset the start date on the Task tab. If you've made other changes that should be saved, but you also want to undo skipping an occurrence, be sure to reset the start date on the Task tab.

The Skip Occurrence command is not available for recurring tasks you've set up with the Regenerate New Task option in the Task Recurrence dialog box.

Creating a Task from a Calendar Item (and Vice Versa)

If you have set up an appointment, meeting, or event on your Outlook calendar that also involves a task, you can easily use the calendar item to create the task. You can either drag the item from the Calendar window to the Tasks folder, or copy the item and paste it in the Tasks folder.

To drag the item, follow these steps:

1   Open the Calendar folder.

2   Locate the the item you want to make a task for.

3   Drag the item from the Appointments pane and drop it on the Tasks folder in the Outlook Bar. The task window then appears with the calendar information inserted.

4   If appropriate, change the task information.

5   Click Save And Close.

To copy and paste the calendar item instead, select the calendar item in the Calendar, and then choose Copy To Folder from the Edit menu. In the Copy Items dialog box that appears, select the Tasks folder, and then click OK to display the task in the task window.

You can also create a calendar item from a task. This is useful when you want to schedule time to work on or complete the task. The process is similar to the one just described: either drag the task from the task window to the Calendar folder on the Outlook Bar, or use the copy and paste method. (For help with setting up calendar items, see Chapter 11, "Scheduling Appointments, Meetings, and Events.")

Setting Task Dates

Outlook sets up new tasks without a due date. If your task needs a due date, you can specify this date, and you can also specify the date on which you should start the task in order to complete it.

As mentioned earlier, you can add a due date in the task list itself by entering it in the Due Date box. (See "Quickly Setting Up a Task," on page 375.) Alternatively, you can open the task and specify the due date by clicking the Due Date box and then setting a date in it. Outlook also lets you set a start date for the task in the Start Date box.

To enter any of these dates, you can either type a date in the appropriate box or click the small arrow next to each box and select a date from the calendar that appears.

Prioritizing Tasks

Most tasks that you perform are routine, at least within the context of your daily chores. From time to time, however, you'll have very important tasks that require your immediate attention, or at least a large portion of your fund of attention. You may have other tasks that are less important than your routine tasks and can be deferred or delayed without serious consequences.

When you create a new task in the task list, Outlook assigns an importance level (or priority) of Normal to the new task. If you create a new task using the task window, you can enter the importance level directly in the Priority box. Your choices are Normal, High, and Low. You can change the importance level of a task at any time, by using one of these methods:

- Open the task and select the level of importance in the Priority box on the Task tab.

- Open the task and choose Properties from the File menu. Select the level of importance in the Importance box.

- If the Priority column is visible in the task list (the column with an exclamation mark as its label), click the Priority column for the task you want to change. Then select Low, Normal, or High from the list that appears. (The Priority column appears in all views of the Tasks folder window except Simple List view and Task Timeline view. To change the view, see "Viewing Your Tasks," on page 398. You can also customize any view to show the columns you are interested in.)

In the Tasks folder window, a red exclamation mark in the Priority column indicates a task with a High importance level. A task with Low importance is marked by a blue downward-pointing arrow. The Priority column is blank for a task with a Normal level of importance.

Setting a Task Reminder

 SEE ALSO

For information about changing the default reminder time (8:00 AM) for all tasks with due dates, see "Reminder Options," on page 93.

When you create a new task with a due date, Outlook sets up a reminder for 8:00 AM on the due date. If this doesn't suit your work habits—perhaps you'd prefer to be reminded at 3:00 PM the day before the due date for a particular task—you can change the reminder date and time. If your task does not have a due date, Outlook does not automatically set up a reminder; you must set it up yourself if you want one.

It's an easy matter to set up or change a reminder:

1 Open the task, select the Task tab, and then turn on the Reminder option.

2 In the Reminder date box, set the date on which Outlook should display the reminder. If your task has a due date, you'll see that date in the box initially. To change the date, you can type a new date or click the small arrow beside the box and select a date from the calendar that appears.

3 If your task has a due date, you'll see 8:00 AM as the default reminder time in the Reminder time box. To change the time at which the reminder should appear, type a new time, or select a time from the list.

4 Click Save And Close.

> **NOTE**

If you inadvertently set the task reminder for a time that has already passed, Outlook displays a message telling you that the time has passed and that a reminder won't be set. If that's all right with you, click OK to dispense with the reminder. To reset the reminder time, click No. Outlook returns you to the task window, where you can set a new reminder time.

Adding Task Notes

SEE ALSO

For information about attachments, see "Adding Attachments to an Item," on page 336.

The box at the bottom of a task window provides a space in which you can type any text that should accompany the task. This box is like the message area in an e-mail message, which means that you can attach files, messages, and any other Microsoft Windows or Microsoft Office objects to a task. For example, if you're sending a task request to

III

Scheduling Your Time and Tasks

Changing the Task Reminder Sound

When the reminder is triggered, you'll hear a pleasant tone from your computer speaker. You can change the sound that is played with a reminder by designating another sound file with the WAV extension (called a *wave* file). You can find all sorts of interesting wave files on the Internet, or you can record your own using the Sound Recorder application that comes with Windows. Each task can even use its own unique reminder sound.

To change the sound file for a particular task, or to turn off the sound entirely, click the speaker icon in the task window.

When the Reminder Sound dialog box appears, turn off the Play This Sound option if you don't want to hear a reminder sound. If you do want to hear a sound, type in the name of the sound file to be played or use the Browse button to find a file. Click OK to close the dialog box.

---

someone else, you can type directions, goals, concerns, restrictions, and guidance for the task. You can also include attachments with any background or preparatory material related to the task.

Keeping a Task Private

You might want to designate a task as private when it's personal or otherwise sensitive or confidential in nature. When you give others permission to view your Tasks folder, or when you assign a delegate who can perform actions such as responding to task requests on your behalf (see "Using the Delegates Tab," on page 80), these people can normally see the subject of a task. If you have set up a task that should not be seen by authorized users of your Tasks folder, turn on the Private option on the Task tab of the task window to keep the task private.

Setting Up a Task Estimate

? SEE ALSO

For more information about the Details tab, see "Recording Other Task Information," on page 397.

On the Details tab in the task window, shown in Figure 12-3, you can record your estimate of the number of hours that a task is likely to take. You might want to use this number as you estimate the cost and billing for a task. You could also use it to test your estimating skills or tools, by later comparing it to the actual hours worked. (See "Actual Work," on page 394.)

FIGURE 12-3.

The Details Tab of a task window.

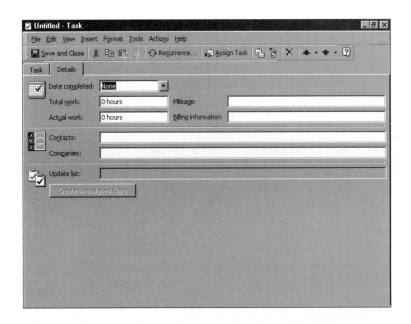

To set a time estimate for a task, simply click the Details tab in the task window and type the estimated number of hours in the Total Work box. Outlook converts the number of hours you type to days or weeks. The conversion is based on the number of hours per day and hours per week that you set in Outlook's Options dialog box (choose Options from the Tools menu, select the Other tab, and then click the Advanced Options button).

 NOTE

> The number of hours you enter in the Total Work box is *not* connected to the due date you set on the Task tab. You must adjust the due date yourself if you want it to correspond to the start date plus the estimated work time.

Adjusting Other Task Properties

SEE ALSO

For more about using AutoArchive, see Chapter 18, "Archiving Folder Items." For more about assigning a level of importance to tasks, see "Prioritizing Tasks," on page 380.

In each task window, you can set additional properties for the task by opening the Properties dialog box. Figure 12-4, on the next page, shows the options and information for a new task. When setting up a new task, you can adjust such items as the priority and sensitivity of the task and whether it is included in AutoArchiving. Other options pertain to task requests you send to someone else, including options to have a receipt sent to you when your request is delivered to the

III

Scheduling Your Time and Tasks

FIGURE 12-4.
The Properties dialog box for a new task.

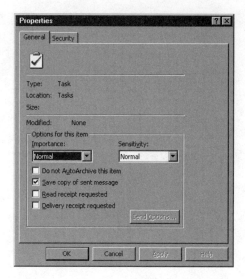

recipient or when the recipient reads (or at least opens) the request. Certain properties are not available after a task is first created, and the Properties dialog box changes accordingly. For instance, the sensitivity level cannot be changed after your task is entered on your task list or sent as a task request, and you can't request a receipt after the task has been set up.

Categorizing Your Tasks

As with other Outlook items, you can assign tasks to categories. This enables you to sort tasks by category so that organizing your tasks is easier. To assign a task to a category, open the task and click the Categories button. (You can also enter a category name in the text box to the right of the Categories button.) In the Categories dialog box, select the category or categories to which you want to assign the task and then click OK. For more information about working with categories in Outlook, see "Working with Categories," on page 560, and also "By Category View," on page 400.

> ### Using Organize to Assign a Category
>
> The Organize button on the Standard toolbar provides another way to create and assign tasks to categories. You'll learn how to create, delete, and manage categories in Chapter 20, "Organizing Folder Items," to quickly assign a task to a category, follow these steps.
>
> **1** Open the Tasks folder.
>
> **2** Select the task you want to assign to a category.
>
> **3** Click the Organize button on the Standard toolbar.
>
> **4** Click Using Categories, if it's not already selected.
>
> **5** Select a category from the first list, or create a new category by typing in the second box. You can place a task in more than one category.
>
> **6** Click Add for each category you select, or click Create for each new category you type.
>
> **7** When you're done, click the Organize button again to close the Organize window.

Sending a Task Request

You might have a task that you need to pass along to someone else to perform. (If you're a manager or a project team leader, that's part of your job.) You can set up a task and send a task request to someone else in order to enlist their aid.

> To send a task request over the Internet, the recipient's e-mail address must be set to use Microsoft Exchange Rich Text Format. See "Adding Someone," on page 171, for more information.

When you send a task request and receive an acceptance, the ownership of the task passes to the person who accepts your request. At that point, you can receive updates to track the progress of the task, but you can no longer make any changes to the task record.

Once a task is assigned, Outlook keeps track of who owns the task and when it is updated. When the task owner updates the task, Outlook updates all copies of that task in the task lists of others who kept a copy of the task. (A task can appear on the task lists of several people because the person you assign a task to might assign that task to someone else. For more information, see "Forwarding a Task Request," on page 390.) When the task has been completed, Outlook sends a status report to those who were assigned the task and who requested a status report. You can see the names of people who will receive updates and status reports about the task by viewing the Update List box on the Details tab in the task window.

 TIP

If you assign the same task to two or more people, you will not receive automatic updates as the task progresses. To keep your finger on the pulse of an assigned task, divide the task into smaller parts and send each part to an individual assignee. That way, you'll receive updates on each segment of the task.

The steps for assigning a task to another person are as follows:

1 Open the Tasks folder, and create a task request in one of the following ways:

- Click the small arrow on the New Task button on the Standard toolbar, and choose Task Request from the menu.

- Choose New Task Request from the Actions menu.

- Point to New on the File menu, and then choose Task Request from the submenu.

- Press Ctrl+Shift+U.

- Create a new task and then, in the task window, click Assign Task on the Standard toolbar or choose Assign Task from the Action menu.

2 Outlook displays a task request window, shown on the next page. Fill out as much of the information on the tabs as you need to—you can set a due date and a start date, prioritize the task, add notes, and so on. The Keep An Updated Copy Of This Task On My Task List option retains a copy of this task on your task list so that you receive periodic status reports. The Send Me A Status Report When This Task Is Complete option provides you with a status report when the assignee marks the task completed.

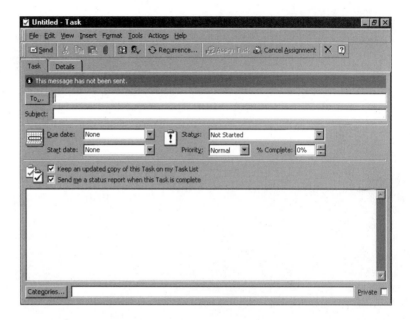

3 In the To box, type the name of the person or persons to whom you're assigning the task. If you'd prefer to select the name (or names), click the To button to open the Select Task Recipient dialog box (a variation of the Address Book dialog box you use for e-mail messages). You can select as many names as necessary. Then click OK.

4 Click the Send button in the task request window to send the task request to the person or persons you've assigned to the task.

> **NOTE**

After you send a task request, you can't change the names of the assignees unless one of them declines the task.

> **Reassigning a Task**
>
> Perhaps you've assigned a task to someone and that someone has accepted the task, but now you change your mind about who should complete the assignment. In such a case, you can create an unassigned copy of the task and assign the copy to someone else. To do this, you must have turned on the Keep An Updated Copy Of This Task On My Task List option on the Task tab of the original task request.
>
> When you create an unassigned copy of a task, everyone who formerly received task updates or status reports will not receive them for the re-assigned task. The original task you assigned stays on the task list of the person you assigned it to, but an updated copy of the original task will not appear on your task list. If you or anyone else who was assigned the original task requested a status report for that task, you and the people who requested it will receive the status report when the owner of the original task marks the task complete.
>
> To create an unassigned copy of a task and reassign the task, you take the following steps. Remember, you must have selected the Keep An Updated Copy Of This Task On My Task List option in the original task request you sent.
>
> 1   In your task list, open your copy of the task you want to reassign.
>
> 2   Click the Details tab.
>
> 3   On the Details tab, click the Create Unassigned Copy button and then click OK. Outlook makes a copy of the task and displays it in the task window.
>
> 4   In the task window, choose Assign Task from the Actions menu.
>
> 5   In the To box, enter the name of the person you now want to assign the task to, and then click Send.

Receiving and Responding to a Task Request

When you receive a task request, you can accept it, in which case it becomes your task and appears on your task list. You can decline the request, in which case the task is returned to the sender and reappears on the sender's task list. You can forward the task to someone else who has more time or expertise. Or you can simply delete the task request message.

In order to process the task request, you must receive it using Outlook. The task request format is not compatible with Outlook Express.

When you receive a task request, you see a message like the one shown on the Task tab in the illustration below:

Click here to accept the task request.

Click here to decline the task request.

Click here to assign the task to someone else.

Click here to delete the task request.

After you've clicked the Accept or Decline button, Outlook displays a message asking whether you want to edit your response or send your reply without a response. If you choose not to edit your response, Outlook sends the message without displaying any further windows. If you choose to edit the response, Outlook provides a typical message window with a colored band showing your response. Your response also appears in the Subject box when the task request is returned. Type any message you want to include, and, when your response is ready, click the Send button.

III

Scheduling Your
Time and Tasks

If you decide to assign the task request to someone else and click the Assign Task button, Outlook displays a task request window that you can use to forward the task request along. See "Forwarding a Task Request," below.

Accepting a Task

When you accept a task request, you take over ownership of the task. You can then make any changes to the task setup that suit the circumstances. You'll probably want (or be required) to send status reports to the person who assigned the task to you. In some cases, Outlook sends a status report automatically; in other cases, you must prepare and send the report yourself. For more information, see "Sending a Status Report," on page 395.

Declining a Task

When you click the Decline button for a task request, you can send your response with or without comment. Outlook returns the ownership of the task to the sender.

If you are the person who assigned the task, you receive a message telling you that the person to whom you assigned the task has declined to accept it. You then have three choices:

- Return the task to your own task list. You can then try to assign it again, or you can perform the task yourself. To return the task to your task list, open the message that declines the task and choose Return To Task List from the Task menu.

- If you simply close the window, the task stays on your task list as a declined task. You can open the task response window in your Tasks folder later and choose the Return To Task List command to make the task active on your own task list.

- Delete the task. Outlook does not ask you to confirm the deletion.

Forwarding a Task Request

If you receive a task request but don't have time to perform the task, you can forward the request to another person who might be able to carry out the task. To forward a task request to someone else, you simply assign the task to that person. The recipient is then in the same

CAUTION

Do *not* forward a task request as a message unless you're only keeping someone else informed about your workload. Forwarding a task request as a message (rather than assigning the task to another person) does not carry with it an assignment mechanism.

boat you were in when you received the task request. If the recipient accepts the task, you're off the hook; the task ownership passes to the recipient. You and the person who originally sent the task request will receive status reports about the task.

You have two ways to forward a task:

- When you open the task request message, click the Assign Task button on the Standard toolbar, or choose Assign Task from the Actions menu. Follow the steps listed in "Sending a Task Request," on page 385, to assign the task. With this method, you don't actually accept the task. You're likely to use this method when you know right away that you need to assign the task to someone else.

- You can accept the task and then assign it to someone else later. Use this method after you've accepted a task but later realize you cannot complete it.

Deleting a Task Request

SEE ALSO

For more about deleting tasks, see "Canceling a Task," on page 398.

If you delete a task request instead of answering it, Outlook asks whether you want to send a message to the sender declining the task request. (It's the polite thing to do.)

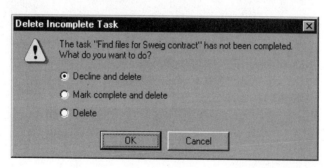

- Click Decline And Delete to send a reply declining the request and then delete the task request.

- Click Mark Complete And Delete to mark the task completed and then delete the task request.

- Delete simply deletes the request without a response and should be avoided.

- Cancel closes the dialog box but doesn't act on the request.

III

Scheduling Your
Time and Tasks

Working with Your Tasks

Outlook's task feature can help you develop efficiency and account-ability in your work and your projects. As due dates approach, you can receive timely reminders. You can track the progress of a task during the course of a project. You can record certain additional information about a task—mileage, billing information, contacts, and names of companies—to help with wrapping up a task. You can send or receive periodic status reports. And, you can keep a list of completed tasks.

Receiving a Reminder

As the due date for a task approaches, Outlook displays a reminder on the date and at the time you set for the reminder. Your reminder will look something like this:

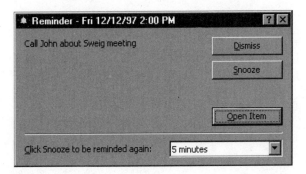

In the Reminder message box, click the Dismiss button to cancel any further reminders. If you need to change the due date for the task, or if the circumstances have changed and should be reflected in the task setup, click the Open Item button to open the task window, where you can make any necessary adjustments.

If you want Outlook to remind you of the task again, you can post-pone the reminder by selecting one of the delay times in the list at the bottom of the message box. The list contains choices ranging from 5 minutes to a week. After you select a delay time, click the Snooze button. Remember that this merely sets when the reminder will re-appear, but it doesn't change the due date for the task.

If you postpone the reminder until after the task's due date and time (not a very useful thing to do), Outlook will display the Reminder message box at the time you set, with the word *Overdue* in the title bar.

> The Reminder message box is the only place where you can assign a Snooze time to a reminder, but you can change the reminder time itself in the task window.

Tracking the Progress of a Task

The task window provides three indicators to help you track the progress of a task: Status, Percent Complete (% Complete), and Actual Work.

Status

The status of each task is displayed on the Task tab. Here you can record the current status of a task by selecting one of these choices from the list:

Not Started.   Outlook assigns this description to all new tasks.

In Progress.   Select this description after you've started a task. If you set the Percent Complete box to a number other than 0, Outlook sets the Status box to In Progress (except when the current status is set to Waiting On Someone Else or Deferred—see below).

Completed.   Select this description when you finish the task. When you mark a task completed in one of the other ways available to you (see "Marking Tasks Completed," on page 396), Outlook sets the Status box to Completed.

Waiting On Someone Else.   If your task requires that someone else complete a prerequisite task before you can continue work on yours, select this description.

Deferred.   Select this description when you defer a task until a later time.

Percent Complete

SEE ALSO

For ways to mark a task completed, see "Marking Tasks Completed," on page 396.

In the Percent Complete box on the Task tab, you can type any percentage from 0 to 100 to indicate how much of the task you've completed, or you can click the arrows to select a preset value of 0%, 25%, 50%, 75%, or 100%.

III

Scheduling Your
Time and Tasks

Note the following points about the Percent Complete box:

- When you set the percentage to any number other than 0 or 100, Outlook changes the Status box setting from Not Started to In Progress. (If the Status box is set to Waiting On Someone Else or Deferred, changing the Percent Complete box doesn't change the Status box setting.)

- If you set the percentage to 100%, Outlook changes the Status box setting to Completed. Likewise, if you set the Status box to Completed, Outlook sets the Percent Complete box to 100%.

- If you reduce the percentage in the Percent Complete box to 0%, Outlook changes the Status box setting from In Progress to Not Started. (If the Status box is set to Waiting On Someone Else or Deferred, changing the Percent Complete box doesn't change the Status box setting.)

- If you reduce the percentage in the Percent Complete box below 100%, Outlook changes the Status box setting from Completed to In Progress, Waiting On Someone Else, or Deferred, depending on what the Status box setting was before the task was set to 100% completed.

Actual Work

In the Actual Work box on the Details tab of the task window (the Details tab is shown in Figure 12-3 on page 383), you can record the number of hours that a task has taken so far. You can use this number to estimate the percentage of a task that has been completed. You can also use it to check the accuracy of your early estimates, by comparing it to the figure you entered in the Total Work box when you set up the task. (See "Setting Up a Task Estimate," on page 382.)

When you type the number of hours worked so far in the Actual Work box, Outlook converts that number to days or weeks. The conversion is based on the number of work hours per day and per week that you set as your standard in Outlook's Options dialog box (choose Options from the Tools menu, select the Other tab, and then click the Advanced Options button.

The number in the Actual Work box is not connected to the settings in the Status box or the Percent Complete box on the Task tab. You have to set the values in those boxes manually if you want them to reflect the Actual Work values.

Sending a Status Report

Whether you're working on a task that you set up yourself or a task that someone assigned to you, you might need to send periodic status reports. Sending a status report is a pretty simple matter.

To send a status report, take these steps:

1 Open the task whose status you're going to report.

2 Update the status of the task, ensuring that the information in the Subject, Priority, Due Date, Status, Percent Complete, Total Work, and Actual Work boxes of the task window is accurate. Outlook will add this information to the text of the status report message.

3 Choose Send Status Report from the Actions menu.

4 You'll see a message window like the one shown here. Outlook has already supplied the status information and has filled in the information in the message header boxes.

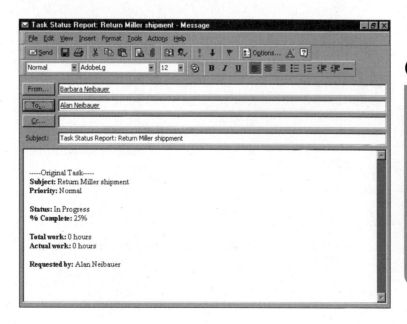

5 Add any message you want to the status report.

6 Click Send.

Sending an Automatic Status Report

If you have been assigned and have accepted a one-time (nonrecur-ring) task, Outlook automatically creates and sends a status report to the person who assigned the task when you mark the task completed.

For recurring tasks that have been assigned to you, Outlook sends an automatic status report only at the end of the series. For a series without an end date, Outlook does not send a status report.

 TIP

To prevent Outlook from automatically sending a status report at the completion of an assigned task, turn off the Send Status Reports When Assigned Tasks Are Completed option. To reach this option, choose Options from the Tools menu, click Advanced Options on the Other tab, and then click Advanced Tasks.

Marking Tasks Completed

When you've finished a task, you'll want to cross it off your task list by marking it completed. Marking a task completed draws a line through the task in the task list, removes the task from your list of active tasks, sets up the next task in a series, shuts off reminders for the task, and (for assigned tasks) sends a status report to the person who assigned the task to you.

To mark a task completed, use any of the following methods:

- In the task window, choose Mark Complete from the Actions menu.

- Select Completed in the Status box on the Task tab of the task window.

- Set the Percent Complete box on the Task tab of the task window to 100%.

- Set the Date Completed box on the Details tab of the task window to today or a date before today. Type the date, or click the down arrow beside the box to select a date from the calendar. (This method is especially useful if you actually finished the task earlier than the date you marked it completed. If you used another method to mark it completed on the later day, Outlook inserts that date in the Date Completed box. In this case, you'll want to reset the completion date to the actual date you finished the task.)

- Click the Complete box in the TaskPad of the Calendar folder when it's in Day/Week/Month view. (See "TaskPad," on page 302.)

- Click the Completed box for the task in the Outlook Today window.

As you'll learn later in this chapter (see "Viewing Your Tasks," on the next page), Outlook gives you numerous ways to set up and view the task list in the Tasks folder window. In certain views, you can use these additional methods of marking a task completed:

- If you have selected Simple List view, click the Complete column in the Tasks folder window (the one that shows a check mark in the column heading).

- If you have selected a view that displays the Status column in the tasks folder, click the task's entry in that column and select Completed from the list that appears.

- If you have selected a view that displays the Percent Complete column in the tasks folder, set the task's entry in that column to 100%.

- If you have selected a view that displays the Date Completed column in the tasks folder, set the task's entry in that column to today's date or to an earlier date.

Recording Other Task Information

? SEE ALSO

For information about the Total Work and Actual Work boxes on the Details tab, see "Setting Up a Task Estimate," on page 382, and "Actual Work," on page 394.

In addition to task status and particulars, you might want to record other information about a task, such as mileage, billing information, contact names, or client and company names. You can record this information on the Details tab of the task window, shown in Figure 12-3.

On the Details tab, you can record valuable information that can help you perform your ongoing work, evaluate your efforts on this task, and plan for future tasks. For instance, you can type the number of miles you've logged for this task in the Mileage box. In the Billing Information box, enter any particulars about billing for this project. In

III

Scheduling Your
Time and Tasks

the Contacts box, type the names of people you've contacted while carrying out the work, either as clients or as resources. Type the names of the companies for whom you are performing the task in the Companies box.

Canceling a Task

When you want to cancel a task, locate it in the Tasks folder window and select the task. Then use one of the following methods to delete it:

- Click the Delete button on the Standard toolbar.

- Press the Ctrl+D shortcut key.

- Choose Delete from the Edit menu.

- Right-click the task item, and then choose Delete from the short-cut menu.

- Open the task, and then click the Delete button on the Standard toolbar.

Outlook moves deleted tasks to the Deleted Items folder.

If you delete a recurring task, you'll see a dialog box asking whether you want to delete just the current task or the entire series. If you're not sure or if you want to postpone the deletion, click the Cancel button.

Viewing Your Tasks

 SEE ALSO

You can also change the task view using the Organize button on the Standard toolbar. For information on viewing tasks on the TaskPad in the Calendar folder, see "Selecting a TaskPad View," on page 314.

Outlook provides several ways to view your tasks. Initially, Outlook displays the Tasks folder window in Simple List view. To select a different view, point to Current View on the View menu, and then choose a view from the submenu.

All of Outlook's built-in views for the Tasks folder (except the Task Timeline view) are table views. A table view displays task information in columns and rows: each task is displayed on its own row and the type and number of columns varies with the particular view you select. In two of the table views (By Category and By Person Responsible), the rows of tasks are also grouped. The Task Timeline view shows tasks graphically along a calendar, similar to the Gantt-chart style popular in project management software. (You can find instructions for changing the format of both a table view and a timeline view in "Formatting Views," on page 593.)

In addition to Outlook's built-in views for tasks, you can set up your own views to look at folder contents in various ways. For information about views, see Chapter 21, "Setting Up Views." For details about grouping, sorting, and filtering items in a folder, see Chapter 20, "Organizing Folder Items."

Simple List View

Simple List view, shown in the second graphic in this chapter, on page 373, shows all the tasks in your Tasks folder in a table that has four columns: the Icon column (in which different icons indicate the type of task—one-time, recurring, or assigned), the Complete column (in which a check mark indicates a completed task), the Subject column, and the Due Date column.

Detailed List View

Detailed List view is similar to Simple List view in design, but it displays eight columns: Icon, Priority, Attachment, Subject, Status, Due Date, Percent Complete, and Categories.

Active Tasks View

Active Tasks view displays the same eight columns as Detailed List view but filters the tasks to show you only those that are active. Completed tasks are not displayed.

Next Seven Days View

Next Seven Days view also displays the same eight columns as Detailed List view but filters your tasks to show only those with due dates occurring within the next seven days.

Overdue Tasks View

Overdue Tasks view also displays the same eight columns as Detailed List view but filters your tasks to show only those that are overdue. All completed tasks as well as tasks that are not overdue as of today are hidden from view.

By Category View

If you assign your tasks to categories, you can view the tasks grouped by category. By Category view lists the tasks in a table with the same eight columns as Detailed List view. The tasks are then grouped by category, with headers showing each category you've used. If you assign a task to more than one category, Outlook lists that task in each of the assigned category groups.

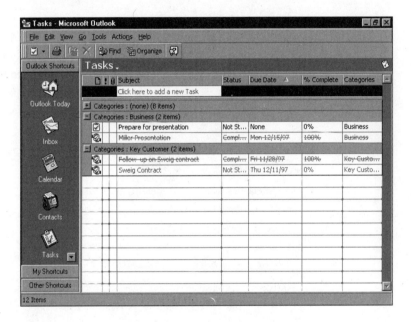

Assignment View

Assignment view shows only those tasks that you have assigned to someone else (tasks for which you sent a task request). The assigned tasks appear in a table with seven columns: Icon, Priority, Attachment, Subject, Owner (the person to whom you sent the task request), Due Date, and Status. Tasks are listed if the recipient of your task request has accepted the task or has not yet replied to your request.

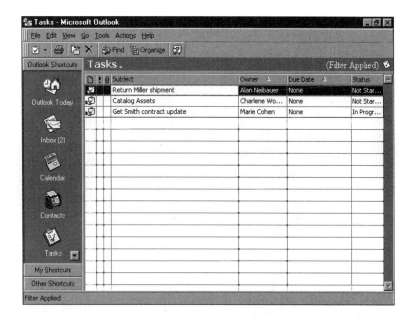

By Person Responsible View

By Person Responsible view displays all the tasks in your Tasks folder grouped according to who owns the tasks (you and those to whom you've assigned tasks). If you assigned a task to more than one person, the task appears in the group for each owner. This view shows tasks in a table with eight columns: Icon, Priority, Attachment, Subject, Requested By (for tasks that were assigned to you), Owner, Due Date, and Status. The groups are separated by headers indicating the name of each owner.

Completed Tasks View

Completed Tasks view displays only those tasks that you have completed. This view's table contains seven columns: Icon, Priority, Attachment, Subject, Due Date, Date Completed, and Categories.

Task Timeline View

Task Timeline view arranges all the tasks in your Tasks folder on a timeline that shows the dates in a band across the top of the window. Tasks are listed below the dates. A task bar delineates the date range for each task.

Scheduling Your
Time and Tasks

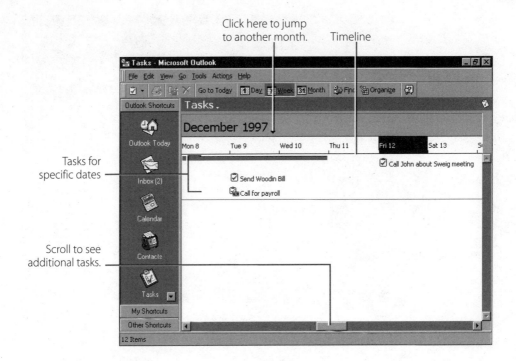

Click here to jump
to another month. Timeline

Tasks for
specific dates

Scroll to see
additional tasks.

The three time scale buttons on the Standard toolbar work as follows:

Day. Click the Day button to see tasks for a single date, listed by
the hour.

Week. Click the Week button to see tasks for a single week, listed by
the day.

Month. Click the Month button to see tasks for a month, listed by the
day of the year. When you're viewing tasks for a month, you see only
task icons, not the subjects of the tasks. Place the mouse pointer on a
task icon or on the bar marking the duration of the task to quickly display the task's subject.

After you use Outlook for a while, you'll have task entries so far away
from today's date that you can't easily or quickly scroll to them in Task
Timeline view. When you want to jump to a date far away from today's
date, you have two choices: clicking the small arrow beside the month
name or choosing the Go To Date command from the Go menu.

To jump to a date within the current year, click the small arrow beside the month name in the Tasks folder window, and use the calendar that appears. You can select any date in the currently displayed month or click the Today button. To select a different month, use the left and right arrows on either side of the month name or click the month name in the calendar and select the month from the list that appears.

To jump to any date, you can use the Go To Date command on the Go menu in the Tasks folder window. For detailed information about how to do this, see "Using the Go To Date Command," on page 309.

PART IV

Keeping Track of People and Things

Managing Your Contacts

For some people, their Filofax is their most valuable possession. Most people who deal with other people keep some kind of list of names, addresses, phone numbers, and fax numbers—a rotary file, a pouch of business cards, an address book (the infamous "little black book"), or an electronic personal information device.

Microsoft Outlook 98 provides the Contacts folder, in which you can keep a list of your contacts, along with all the information you want to record about each one. To see your contact list, click the Contacts folder on the Outlook Bar. Once you've set it up, your list might look something like the one shown in Figure 13-1, on the next page.

FIGURE 13-1.

A contact list in the Contacts folder window.

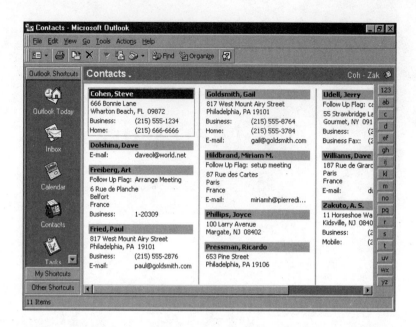

You can set up your address books—which you use for sending messages in Outlook and for addressing letters and envelopes in Microsoft Word—to include your Contacts folder as an address book. For details, see the sidebar "Oh, No! The Show This Folder As An E-Mail Address Book Option Is Not Available!," on page 547.

Setting Up Your Contact List

The first task in compiling a useful list of contacts is to set up entries for the people with whom you work and socialize regularly. You can (and probably will want to) add information for all your friends and family members, too.

Using the Contact Window

To add a new entry to your contact list, use one of the following methods:

- Click the New Contact button on the Standard toolbar.

- Choose New Contact from the Actions menu.

- Point to New on the File menu, and then choose Contact from the submenu.

- Press Ctrl+N.

Outlook opens the contact window, in which you supply the information for the new contact. Each of the five tabs in this window has a specific function, as explained in the following sections.

When you've entered all the information, click the Save And Close button to close the contact window and add the new contact entry to your contact list. Notice, however, that the contact window also contains the Save And New button.

Save and Close   Save and New

When you want to add several new contacts, click the Save And New button, which appears to the right of Save And Close. Clicking Save And New saves the information you've just entered, adds the new entry to your contact list, and displays an empty contact window, ready for you to enter information for another new contact.

To review or change the information for a contact, double-click the contact's listing in the Contacts folder to reopen the window. If you add or change information, however, you must click Save And Close or Save And New again.

Adding a New Contact from a Different Folder

If you are working in an Outlook folder other than the Contacts folder, you can add a new contact using one of the following methods:

- Click the down arrow beside the New button on the Standard toolbar, and then choose Contact from the menu.

- Point to New on the File menu, and then choose Contact from the submenu.

- Press Ctrl+Shift+C.

General Tab

On the General tab of the contact window, you can enter the name, address, phone numbers, and other basic information for a contact.

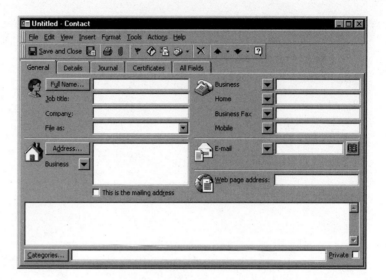

> If you have a low-resolution display, be sure to maximize the contact window when you use the General tab. Because this tab doesn't have scroll bars, you might not be able to see the full contents of some of the boxes at a low resolution unless you maximize the window.

Full Name. Type the contact's name in this box. You can enter a contact's complete name—first, middle, and last—in the Full Name box (and include a title, such as Ms., or a suffix, such as Jr.). Outlook recognizes the distinct parts of the name (the name fields) and saves the information appropriately. Notice that the name you enter in the Full Name box appears by default in the File As box as well.

> A field is a container for a specific type of information. In Outlook, for example, there are separate fields for a person's last name and first name. On a form, a field appears as a blank box that you fill in or select a choice in. In a table, a field is a column.

If you enter only part of a name—for example, only a contact's first name—and then press the Tab key, Outlook displays the Check Full Name dialog box. Use this dialog box to check whether Outlook has correctly recognized the name you entered or to enter the other parts of the contact's name. You can display this dialog box at any time to help you enter a name by clicking the Full Name button on the General tab.

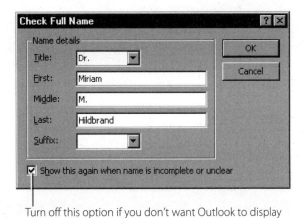

Turn off this option if you don't want Outlook to display
this dialog box when you enter an incomplete name.

File As.   In the File As box, you can select or type the name that should appear as the title of the contact card. Outlook uses the entry in this box to sort the cards in Address Cards, Detailed Address Cards, and Phone List views. (See "Sorting Contacts," on page 434.)

Assuming that you have entered both an individual's name and a company name, the File As list box includes these selections:

- Last name, First name

- First name Last name

- Company name

- Last name, First name (Company name)

- Company name (Last name, First name)

If you don't fill in a company name, the list provides only the first two selections. You can also type in a different title for the contact card if none of these selections is quite right.

Address.   You can enter three different addresses for each contact—business, home, and other. Click the down arrow below the Address button, and select the type of address you want to enter from the list. Then type the address in the Address box, pressing the Enter key at the end of each line. To enter another address for this contact, select a different description from the list, and type the address in the now-blank Address box.

To designate one of several addresses as a contact's mailing address, select the address from the list to display it, then turn on the This Is The Mailing Address option. (If you've entered only one address for a contact, Outlook considers it the mailing address.)

As with the parts of a name, Outlook stores contact addresses in separate fields—street, city, and so on. When you enter a complete address (street, city, state or province, zip or postal code, and country—if that's necessary), Outlook recognizes the pattern of the address and stores the information appropriately. If you enter only part of an address and press the Tab key or click elsewhere in the window, Outlook displays the Check Address dialog box, which you can use to complete and correct the address entry. You can also open this dialog box by clicking the Address button. Do this to check that Outlook has recognized the address correctly, to enter the contact's address field by field, or to add one or two elements to the address, such as just the country.

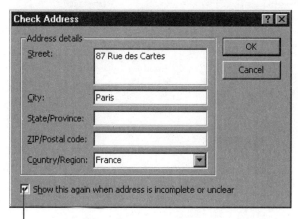

Turn off this option if you don't want Outlook to display
this dialog box when you enter an incomplete address.

Phone.   You can record up to four phone numbers for any one contact. Click the arrow next to each phone number to assign a description to it from the list that appears. This is handy if the four preset labels (Business, Home, Business Fax, and Mobile) aren't appropriate for one or more of the numbers you wish to enter. The phone description list provides nineteen possibilities, such as Car, Callback, ISDN, Home Fax, and Radio. Once you select a description, it becomes the label displayed next to that phone number entry.

When entering phone numbers for a contact, use the following format for international phone numbers and for automatic phone dialing: + *country code (area code) local number*—for example, + 01 (201) 555-1212.

> **NOTE**

Outlook does not recognize letters in a phone number. You can, however, include notes after the phone number—for example, an extension for the contact.

E-Mail.   You can enter up to three e-mail addresses for your contact. If you want to enter only one e-mail address, simply type it in the empty box. To enter additional e-mail addresses, click the down arrow to select a designation for the address (E-Mail 2, E-Mail 3), and then type the address.

If you want to retrieve an e-mail address from one of your address books, click the Address Book button to the right of the box. Select the contact's name in the Select Name dialog box, and click OK.

When you click another field in the window, Outlook underlines the e-mail address, indicating that it is a clickable object.

Web Page Address.   In this box, you can type the URL for a contact's site on the World Wide Web. Outlook uses this information when you want to visit the Web page; see "Connecting to a Contact's Web Page," on page 426.

Notes.   In the large unlabeled box near the bottom of the contact window, you can type any text, comments, or notes about the contact. Also, if you have entered dates for the contact's birthday and anniversary on the Details tab of the contact window (see "Details Tab," on page 416), you'll see small calendar icons in the notes section of the General tab, representing the dates. When you double-click one of these icons, Outlook opens a calendar item window, setting up a recurring event for the birthday or anniversary on that date. Click the Save And Close button in that window to add the event to your Outlook calendar. (Later, when you set up a birthday party or an anniversary dinner, you can change the calendar item to a specific appointment; see "Changing a Calendar Item," on page 332.)

Categories. You can assign a contact to any number of categories. Make up your own categories by typing them in the box, or click the Categories button to select from Outlook's list of categories—for example, Holiday Cards, Key Customer, Personal, Suppliers, or VIP. You can have Outlook display your contact list grouped according to the categories you've specified; for details, see "By Category View," on page 433.

TIP

You can also assign a contact to a category with the Using Categories option in the Organize pane. Click the Organize button on the Standard toolbar, and then choose Using Categories if it isn't already selected. Select the contact in the bottom pane, choose a category from the top list and click Add or type a new category in the Create A New Category box and click Create.

Private. When you give others permission to view your Contacts folder, or when you assign a delegate who can perform actions on your behalf that involve using your Contacts folder (see "Using the Delegates Tab," on page 80), you might prefer that these people not have access to all your contact information. If you want to designate a contact as private because the information is personal or otherwise sensitive or confidential in nature, turn on the Private option.

Mapping a Contact's Address

While Outlook makes it easy to communicate with contacts over your server and the Internet, you may actually have to get out of the office and visit a contact from time to time. When you do have to make a site visit to a new contact, it would certainly help if you had a map of his or her location. That's easy with Outlook.

Sending Meeting and Task Requests over the Internet

You don't have to do anything special to send meeting and task requests to contacts over your Exchange Server. When you click Send in the item window, the request is transmitted and can be picked up by the recipient to be accepted or declined.

To send meeting requests, task requests, and voting buttons to a contact over the Internet, you must send the mail in Rich Text Format. To set up this capability for one or more of the contacts in your Contacts folder, follow these steps:

1   Open or create the contact entry.

2   Type the recipient's e-mail address in the E-mail box on the General tab, or retrieve it by clicking the Address Book button to the right of the box.

3   Press Tab or click elsewhere in the window to have Outlook read and underline the e-mail address you've entered.

4   Right-click the e-mail address, and choose Properties from the shortcut menu.

5   In the Properties dialog box, turn on the option labeled Always Send To This Recipient In Microsoft Outlook Rich-Text Format.

6   Click OK.

The recipient must receive the mail in Outlook in order for meeting requests, task requests, and voting buttons to work.

Notice that when you right-click the e-mail address, you can also choose to add a listing for the contact to the Personal Address Book.

To display and print a map of an address, open the contact item, and then choose the Display Map Of Address command from the Actions menu. You can also click the Display Map Of Address button (the yellow road sign) on the Standard toolbar.

Outlook will then launch your Web browser and connect to the Microsoft Expedia service and map the address. Expedia Maps are part of a more comprehensive travel service that can even provide point-to-point driving instructions and travel agency services. For more information on using Expedia, refer to the Expedia home page. Figure 13-2, on the next page, shows how to use an Expedia map.

FIGURE 13-2.
Mapping a contact
address location.

Click here to get
driving directions
between two locations.

Click here
to choose
a zoom level.

Choose the correct
address, if more than
one is shown.

Click here to look
up another address.

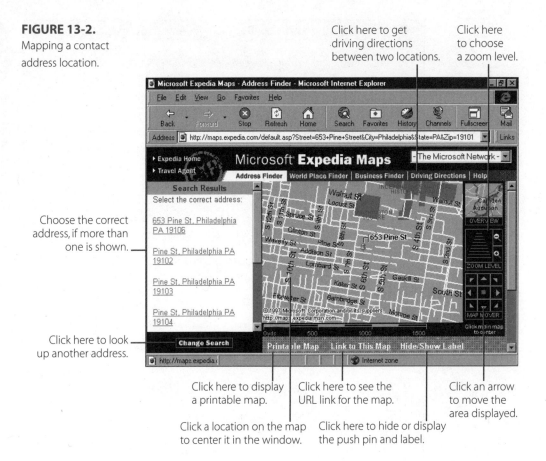

Click here to display
a printable map.

Click here to see the
URL link for the map.

Click an arrow
to move the
area displayed.

Click a location on the map
to center it in the window.

Click here to hide or display
the push pin and label.

Details Tab

To add details to a contact entry, fill out the Details tab of the contact
window, shown on the facing page.

For birthday and anniversary information, you can either type a date
in the appropriate box or click the down arrow to display a calendar
from which you can select a date. Birthdays and anniversaries are then
inserted as annual recurring items in your calendar and shortcuts to
the calendar automatically appear as icons in the notes section of the
General tab of the contact window.

In the Online NetMeeting section of the tab, enter the directory server
where you will log on to conduct the meeting and the e-mail alias for
the contact. Click Call Now to place an Internet call to the contact
using NetMeeting.

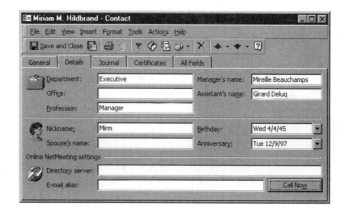

Journal Tab

? SEE ALSO

For information about recording activities for contacts, see "Setting Journal Options," on page 71. For information about Outlook's journal feature, see Chapter 14, "Keeping a Journal."

On the Journal tab of the contact window (shown below), you can view the journal entries for the activities you perform with or for the contact—a log of your interactions with this contact, in other words. You might have journal entries for activities such as e-mail messages, faxes, meeting requests, phone calls, and letters.

You can create a journal entry manually by clicking the New Journal Entry button, which opens a journal entry window. (See "Adding a New Journal Entry Manually," on page 438.) You can click a column heading—Type, Start, or Subject—to quickly sort the list of journal entries. Click a column heading a second time to change the sort order—from ascending to descending (alphabetically) or vice versa.

Turn on this option to record journal entries for activities for this contact.

Select the types of activities you want to see.

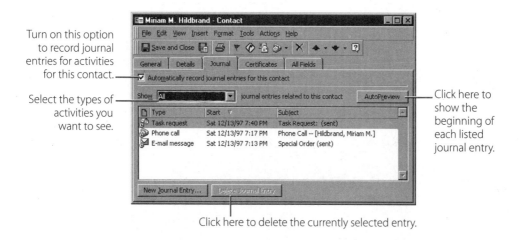

Click here to show the beginning of each listed journal entry.

Click here to delete the currently selected entry.

Certificates Tab

On the Certificates tab of the contact window, you can view the digital IDs that you have on record for a contact in order to send encrypted mail. You can display properties for the ID and choose a default certificate to use.

All Fields Tab

The General tab and the Details tab provide a number of fields that you can use to record information about a contact. However, Outlook includes many other fields related to contacts that you might find useful. You'll find these fields on the All Fields tab in the contact window. You can use these fields to set up each contact entry to fit the circumstances and traits of the individual contact.

Select All Contact Fields to see every field of information you can add for a contact, or select another type of information.

Add or change information for fields not shown on other tabs.

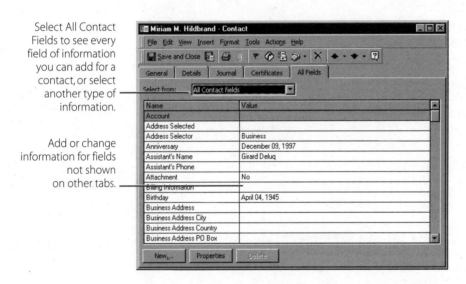

If you find that among all the contact fields provided by Outlook, you still can't find the field you need, you can use the New button on the All Fields tab to create your own field. For information about using custom fields in Outlook, see "Working with Custom Fields," on page 575.

Removing a Contact

To remove a contact from your list, select the contact and click the Delete button on the Standard toolbar or choose the Delete command from the Edit menu. Outlook moves the deleted contact entry to the Deleted Items folder.

Adding Another Contact for a Listed Company

It's not uncommon to know more than one person who works for the same company. Often, all of the people from one company share some of the same contact information—address, business phone, fax. When you already have one contact on your list from a particular organization, you can set up an entry for another person in that organization as follows:

1 Select or open the card of the existing contact.

2 Choose New Contact From Same Company on the Actions menu.

3 When the contact window appears, type the contact's name in the Full Name box.

4 Add or change other information for the contact on the tabs of the contact window, as necessary.

5 Click the Save And Close button.

Working with Your Contacts Folder

The Contacts folder is more than a convenient place to keep a record of names and addresses. Outlook uses the information in the contact entries to help you carry out activities with your contacts, such as the following:

- Dialing a contact's telephone number

- Sending an e-mail message to a contact

- Sending a letter to a contact

- Connecting to a contact's World Wide Web page

- Setting up a meeting with a contact

- Setting up a task that you need to perform for a contact

Phoning a Contact

If you have a modem set up, you can use your computer to dial any of the telephone numbers listed on any folder item in Outlook. The Contacts folder offers an especially rich variety of ways to dial phone numbers from Outlook.

To start an Internet call to a contact, select or open his or her item in the Contacts folder, and then choose the Call Using NetMeeting command from the Actions menu. See Chapter 11, "Scheduling Appointments, Meetings, and Events," for more information on NetMeeting.

When you use Outlook to make a phone call, you must do so from the New Call dialog box, whether or not the contact already has a phone number in his or her listing. To open this dialog box, take one of the following actions:

- Click the AutoDialer button on the Standard toolbar.

- Right-click the contact's name in the Contacts folder, and choose AutoDialer from the shortcut menu.

- In the Contacts folder, or from the open contact window, point to the Call Contact command on the Actions menu, and choose New Call from the submenu.

- If the currently selected contact contains the phone number you want to call, point to the Call Contact command on the Actions menu, and then click the phone number, which appears on the submenu.

- In any Outlook folder, press Ctrl+Shift+D.

After you take any of these actions, Outlook opens the New Call dialog box, shown in Figure 13-3. If the action you took involved a specific phone number—for example, if you right-clicked a contact's card containing a phone number before you chose AutoDialer or you selected a number from the Call Contact submenu of the Actions menu—the New Call dialog box will display the phone number and the contact's name. Otherwise, the dialog box will be empty, allowing you to type in the contact's name and the telephone number that you want Outlook to dial. This is handy if you don't yet have an entry recorded in your address books or Contacts folder for the person you want to call.

FIGURE 13-3.
The New Call
dialog box.

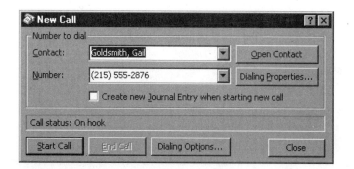

To place a telephone call from the New Call dialog box, follow these steps:

1 If the name of the person you want to call doesn't already appear in the Contact box, you can type it there. (Note, however, that including the name is optional.)

2 If the Number box is empty, type the phone number. If the box already contains a phone number but the contact has several numbers recorded in your address books or Contacts folder, click the down arrow next to the Number box and select the appropriate phone number from the list.

3 To record a journal entry for the call, turn on the option labeled Create New Journal Entry When Starting New Call.

4 Click the Start Call button to have Outlook dial the number.

Outlook displays the Call Status dialog box:

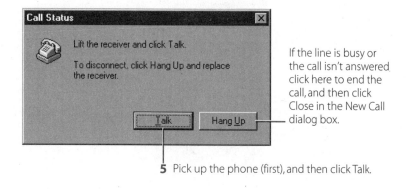

If the line is busy or the call isn't answered, click here to end the call, and then click Close in the New Call dialog box.

5 Pick up the phone (first), and then click Talk.

6 When you've finished your conversation, click the End Call button in the New Call dialog box, and then click the Close button.

> If the name (or part of a name) that you type in the Contact box of the New Call dialog box is already recorded in one of your address books or in your Contacts folder, Outlook completes the name and fills in the phone number for you when you move the insertion point to the Number box.

SEE ALSO

For information about setting up dialing properties, see "Setting Dialing Options," on page 154, and "Setting Up Calling Card Dialing," on page 284.

Notice the Open Contact button in the New Call dialog box. When this button is active, you can click it to review or change contact information in the contact window. You can also use the New Call dialog box to review or change information about the location you're dialing from, about how you dial from this location, or about your calling card. Click the Dialing Properties button to display the My Locations tab of the Dialing Properties dialog box.

Speed Dialing

Many modern telephones provide a memory system that allows you to store several telephone numbers that you call frequently. You can assign each number to a specific button and then call the number simply by pressing the button. In Outlook, you can store a great many frequently called numbers by using the Speed Dial feature.

To set up or change speed dial entries, you need to open the Dialing Options dialog box. The most common way to find this dialog box is to open the New Call dialog box, as explained in the preceding section, and click the Dialing Options button.

To set up or change a speed dial entry, take these steps in the Dialing Options dialog box:

1 Type the contact's name or another designation for the phone number.

2 Type or select the phone number.

3 Click Add.

4 Click OK.

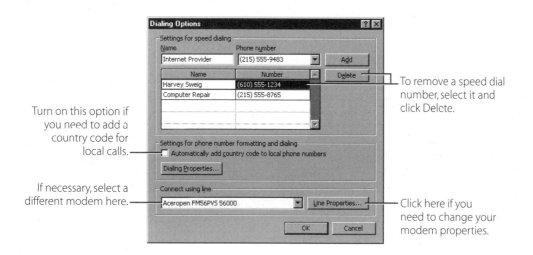

Turn on this option if you need to add a country code for local calls.

If necessary, select a different modem here.

To remove a speed dial number, select it and click Delete.

Click here if you need to change your modem properties.

If you type a name or part of a name that appears in one of your address books or your Contacts folder, Outlook automatically completes the entry for you. You can, of course, modify the results of the automatic completion. If the name you type has more than one telephone number (for example, a voice number or two and a fax number), you can select from the Phone Number list the number you want to set up for speed dialing.

At any time, you can return to the Dialing Options dialog box to change a speed dial name or number. To change the name or number, simply click it, edit the entry, and click OK.

To dial a Speed Dialing number, use either of these techniques:

- Click the small arrow next to the AutoDialer button on the Standard toolbar, point to Speed Dial, and click the number.

- Choose the Call Contact command from the Actions menu, point to Speed Dial, and click the number to call.

Redialing

Outlook keeps a list of recent phone numbers you've dialed from Outlook. When you want to redial a number you've called recently, take these steps:

1 Choose Call Contact from the Actions menu, or click on the small arrow next to the AutoDialer button on the Standard toolbar.

2 Point to Redial and then click the number you want to redial on the submenu.

3 In the New Call dialog box, click the Start Call button.

Recording a Call in a Journal Entry

Although Outlook's Journal folder can keep an automatic record of some of your activities with your contacts (see Chapter 14, "Keeping a Journal," and "Setting Journal Options," on page 71, for more information), it does not include an option for automatically keeping track of phone calls. The New Call dialog box, however, does give you an option for recording telephone calls and for keeping notes of your conversation during the call.

In the New Call dialog box (see Figure 13-3, on page 421), turn on the option labeled Create New Journal Entry When Starting New Call. Then, when you click the Start Call button, a journal entry window appears, as shown here:

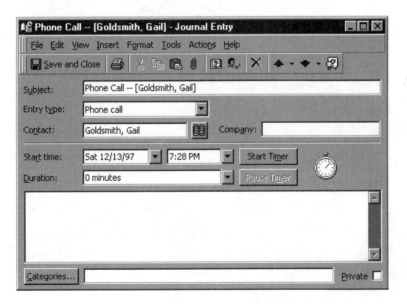

As Outlook dials the number, the window remains on your screen, and the timer immediately begins to time the call. If you don't want to time the call, click the Pause Timer button to stop the timing. (To resume timing, click Start Timer.) During the call, you can type notes, reminders, comments, and so on in the text area at the bottom of the dialog box. At the end of the call, click the Save And Close button to save the record of the call in your Journal folder.

Sending an E-Mail Message to a Contact

Here's an easy way to quickly set up and send a message to a contact. Start by using one of these techniques:

- Right-click the contact's name in the Contacts folder, and choose New Message To Contact from the shortcut menu.

- Click the contact's entry in your Contacts folder, and choose New Message To Contact from the Actions menu.

- If the contact's window is open, you can also choose New Message To Contact from the Actions menu.

The contact item must contain a valid e-mail address.

Each of these techniques opens a new message window and addresses the message to your contact. Complete the message and send it as you learned in Chapter 4, "Exchanging Messages and Faxes."

Here's an even easier way to send a message to a contact. Drag the contact's listing in the Contacts folder to the Inbox icon on the Outlook Bar, compose the message in the window that appears, and then click Send.

Sending a Letter to a Contact

From time to time you may need to print out a letter to send to a contact by snail mail (through the U.S. Postal Service), overnight mail, or fax. You can easily set up and print a letter from an entry in your Contacts folder.

To create a letter from your Contacts folder, you must have Microsoft Word 97 or later installed on your computer.

When you select the contact's entry in your Contacts folder and choose the New Letter To Contact command from the Actions menu, Outlook calls on Microsoft Word 97. Word starts up, and Word's Letter Wizard opens. You can then work through the Letter Wizard to create the letter, and you can print both the letter and an envelope in Word. When you've finished, exit Word if you don't need it for other purposes.

Connecting to a Contact's Web Page

If you entered a contact's World Wide Web page address (URL) in the contact window, you can use that URL to quickly connect to the contact's Web page. To do so, switch to your Contacts folder, and then use one of the following methods:

- Right-click the contact's entry in the Contacts folder, and choose Explore Web Page from the shortcut menu.

- Open the Contact item and choose Explore Web Page from the Actions menu.

- Click or open the contact's entry and press Ctrl+Shift+X.

Setting Up a Meeting with a Contact

When you need to set up a meeting with a contact, you can do so from the contact's entry in your Contacts folder. Simply open your Contacts folder, select the contact's entry, and take one of the following actions:

- Drag the contact's listing to the Calendar folder in the Outlook Bar.

- Choose the New Meeting With Contact command from the Actions menu.

- Choose the Plan A Meeting command from the Actions menu.

With the first two methods, Outlook displays a meeting request window. With the last method, Outlook displays the Plan A Meeting dialog box. For more information, see "Planning a Meeting," on page 327.

Assigning a Task to a Contact

When you have a task you want one of your contacts to perform, you can use the contact's entry in your Contacts folder as the starting point for setting up the task.

Open your Contacts folder, then drag the contact's listing to the Tasks folder in the Outlook Bar. Outlook opens a task window, like the one shown here.

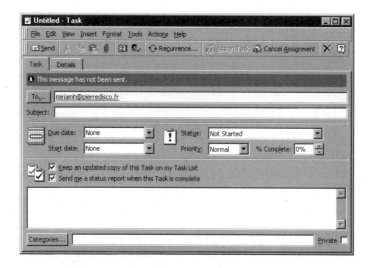

? SEE ALSO

For complete information about setting up tasks and working on them, see Chapter 12, "Controlling Your Tasks."

Outlook fills in the To box on the Task tab with the contact's e-mail address and fills in the Contacts box on the Details tab with the contact's name. You can fill in the subject of the task and as much other information as you need, on both the Task and Details tabs. When you've finished, click the Send button to send the task request to the contact.

Sending Contact Information to Others

People change positions—as a result of promotions, retirements, resignations, or lateral moves. When you change your position within your organization, you might need to turn over at least some of your contacts to your replacement. It's easy to do this in Outlook: you simply forward the contacts to your replacement.

To send contact information to someone else, take these steps:

1 Open the Contacts folder, and select the contact entry you want to send to someone else. To select more than one contact entry, hold down the Ctrl key as you click each entry. To select several consecutive entries, click the first entry, and then hold down the Shift key while you click the last one. To select all the contacts, choose the Select All command from the Edit menu or press Ctrl+A.

2 Choose the Forward command from the Actions menu, or right-click and choose Forward from the shortcut menu. (If you selected more than one item, the command is labeled Forward Items on the shortcut menu.) Outlook opens a message window. The message area contains an icon representing each contact, as shown below.

3 Fill in the To box.

4 Type any message you want to send with the contact information.

5 Click the Send button.

When the recipient receives the message containing the contact icons, he or she can select the contact icon in the message area and drag it to the Contacts folder icon on the Outlook Bar to add the contact information to the contact list.

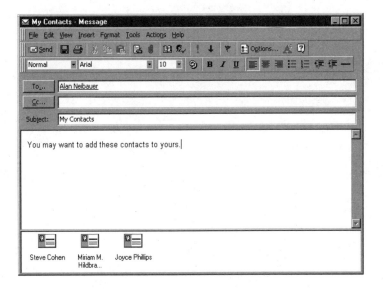

To create a vCard for a contact, right-click his or her listing in the Contacts folder and choose Export To vCard from the shortcut menu, and then click Save in the dialog box that appears.

IV

Flagging Contacts for Follow Up

Sometimes you need to remember to perform some action regarding a contact. You may want to remind yourself to make a call, set up a meeting, send a letter, send an e-mail, or perform some other follow-up. Rather than write the reminder down on a scrap of paper, you can add a follow-up flag directly to the contact's item.

Use these steps to set a follow-up flag:

1 Open the contact's item in the Contacts folder.

2 Choose Flag For Follow Up from the Actions menu, click the red Flag For Follow Up button on the Standard toolbar, or press Ctrl+Shift+G.

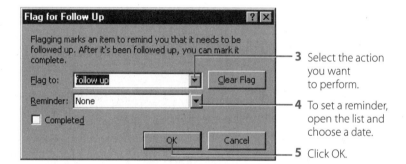

3 Select the action you want to perform.

4 To set a reminder, open the list and choose a date.

5 Click OK.

A note about the follow-up flag appears with the contact's listing in the Contacts folder view, as shown here, and a reminder will appear if you set one.

If you open the contact, you'll also see a colored banner that runs across the top of the General tab and lists the flag information. To remove the flag, redisplay the Flag For Follow Up dialog box and click Clear Flag. To mark the follow-up as completed but leave the flag on the contact item, redisplay the Flag For Follow Up dialog box and turn on the Completed option.

Viewing Your Contacts

Outlook gives you seven standard views of your contacts. The following sections explain each view. To switch from one view to another, point to Current View on the View menu, and then choose the view you want from the submenu.

 TIP

You can also select a view with the Using Views option in the Organize pane. Click the Organize button on the Standard toolbar, choose Using Views, and select the view from the list that appears.

Using Card Views

 SEE ALSO

You can set up custom views for looking at folder contents; see Chapter 21, "Setting Up Views."

In two views of the Contacts folder—Address Cards view and Detailed Address Cards view—Outlook displays the contact information in a "card" format, almost as if you were looking at rotary file cards laid out on a desk.

The cards are arranged alphabetically by the first word in the card title. You can move to a specific alphabetical section of your contact list by clicking the corresponding alphabetical tab along the right side of the folder window, just as you might use tabs to thumb to various sections of a paper address book.

 TIP

If some items on a contact card are incomplete and end with an ellipsis (...), you can widen the card to see the complete information. When you place the mouse pointer on the vertical dividing line in the folder window, the pointer becomes a double vertical line with a two-headed arrow. Drag the line to widen the card until you can see all the information you need.

If you left a box blank on the General tab of the contact window when you entered information about the contact—that is, you entered no data in that field—Address Cards view and Detailed Address Cards view do not initially include that field in the display. (If you want to see all the fields that a contact card can display in these two views, turn on the Show Empty Fields option in the Format Card View dialog box. For details, see "Card Views," on page 600.)

Address Cards View

Address Cards view displays your contacts as small cards that contain some of the basic information from the General tab of the contact window, such as the contact's name, address, phone numbers, and e-mail address. Because the cards are small, Outlook can display a number of them on your screen at one time. This view helps you scroll quickly through a section of your contact list when you are looking for an entry. Figure 13-1, on page 408, shows the Address Card view. Click an alphabetical tab to jump quickly to the contacts whose last name starts with that letter.

Detailed Address Cards View

When you need to see more of the information from the General tab of the contact window, use Detailed Address Cards view. Because the cards are larger and contain more data in this view, you'll see fewer of them on the screen than you would see in Address Cards view, as shown here:

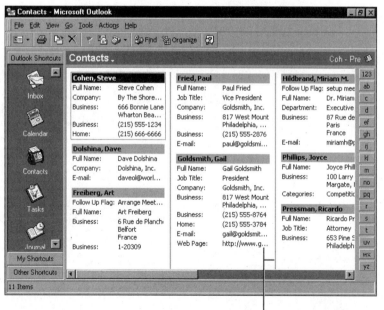

If some entries aren't visible, drag the vertical line to widen the card.

Using Table Views

The card views of the Contacts folder display your contact list succinctly and attractively, but the cards take up a lot of space in the

You can change the format of a view. For details about formatting table views, see "Formatting Views," on page 593.

window. To see more contacts at one time, and to sort the list in different ways, switch to one of these table views: Phone List, By Category, By Company, By Location, or By Follow Up Flag.

These views display your contact information in a table arrangement with rows and columns. The names are listed down the left side of the screen, and various pieces of information (depending on the view) appear in columns to the right. You'll usually need to scroll horizontally to see all the columns. The table views also enable you to enter a new contact directly in the Contacts folder without opening a new contact item.

Phone List View

In Phone List view, you see a simple tabular list of your contacts, with columns for Full Name, Company, File As (the title of a contact card), and numerous telephone and fax numbers. You'll also find a Categories column listing the categories to which you've assigned the contact and a

---

Icons in Contact Lists

In the various table views of your contact list, you'll see several icons that act as column headings or indicate information about the contact entry. The following table explains the meaning of each icon.

Icon	Meaning
	This icon appears at the top of the column that shows the item type.
	This icon appears at the top of the column that indicates whether the item has an attachment.
	This icon appears at the top of the column that indicates whether each item has been flagged for follow-up action.
	This icon indicates that the item is a contact.
	This icon indicates that Outlook will automatically record interactions with this contact in the Journal folder.
	This icon indicates that this contact entry has an attachment.
	This red flag indicates an item flagged for follow-up action.
	This gray flag indicates a follow-up action has been completed.

Journal column, where a check mark indicates that you've chosen to record interactions with this contact in your Journal folder. Like the card views, Phone List view alphabetizes your contact list by the title you entered in the File As box on the General tab of the contact window.

By Category View

If you assign contacts to categories, you can see your contact list grouped by category. If you assign a contact to more than one category, Outlook lists that contact in each category. An example of By Category view is shown here:

This (none) category lists contacts that have not been assigned a category.

Click the minus sign to hide the contents for a category.

Click the plus sign to show the contents for a category.

By Company View

Because you might have several contacts at a single company, you might find it handy to view your contacts grouped by company name. This way, you can quickly find the contact you need for a particular company.

By Location View

Many organizations now conduct business internationally. If your Contacts folder lists contacts in a variety of countries, you might find that using By Location view is a quick way to locate a contact in a specific country. (In this view, the term "location" refers to a country rather than to a city, state, province, or region.)

By Follow Up Flag View

Follow-up flags are terrific for reminding you that some action has to be performed. While you can easily see the flag in the contact's listing, in any of the other views you'll have to scroll the contact list to see the flags that are set.

In By Follow Up Flag view, your contacts are organized by flags, so items that are flagged are easy to identify. In By Follow Up Flag view, your contact list might look something like this:

This heading shows red-flagged contacts, those whose activity is not completed.

This heading shows gray-flagged contacts, those whose activity has been completed.

This heading shows the contacts that are not flagged.

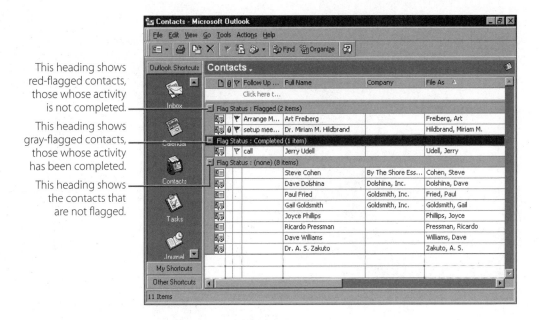

Sorting Contacts

 SEE ALSO

For details about sorting in table views, see "Sorting," on page 566.

By default, Outlook sorts contacts alphabetically by the File As entry. In table views, you can sort the list by clicking a column heading. In card views, to change the order in which the contacts appear, you must actually change the File As information for each contact—not something you want to do frequently. However, for those contacts that don't appear in the order you'd like, open each one and select or type a new entry in the File As text box.

Keeping a Journal

Remembering everything you've done during a day can be difficult. You probably remember the big events pretty easily, but can you honestly remember every e-mail message you sent, every appointment you made, every document you worked on, every note you took, and every person you contacted?

Microsoft Outlook 98 can keep a journal of Outlook activities such as e-mail messages, task and meeting requests, and task and meeting responses as well as your work with any Microsoft Office 97 (or later) document. You can direct Outlook to automatically insert entries in the Journal folder for your interactions with selected contacts. The journal entry identifies the action and records the date and time you performed it.

By assigning each journal entry to a category, you can then group the entries by category so that you can review the actions you've taken for an individual project or task. You can then review the work you've done and more readily compile a list of activities and accomplishments.

In addition to having Outlook record activities, you can manually add journal entries for activities that you've already performed and for activities that Outlook cannot record automatically. You can even add entries that act as shortcuts to files on your hard disk or to files on another computer on your network so that you can open those files from your Journal folder.

Setting Up Your Journal

You can set Outlook to record a journal entry each time you create, open, close, or save a file in an Office 97 or later application. Outlook creates a shortcut to the Office file in the journal entry, even if Outlook isn't running. You can also record Outlook activities in your Journal folder.

The Journal folder displays a timeline showing each document you worked on and each call, meeting, or other Outlook activity for which you created a journal entry, as shown in Figure 14-1.

FIGURE 14-1.

The Journal folder.

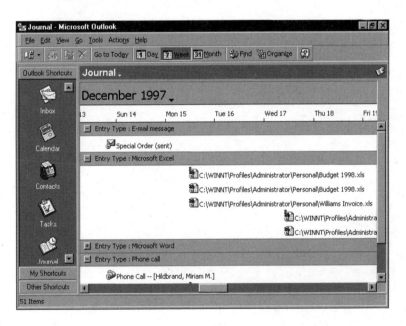

Before using the Journal folder, you should do the following:

■ Choose which Outlook activities are recorded in the journal.

■ Choose the contacts for whom Outlook activities are recorded.

■ Choose the Microsoft Office programs for which activities are recorded.

You can set up the folder using the Options command on the Tools menu, or you can wait until you open the folder for the first time. If you have not yet set up the folder, you'll see this dialog box the first time you open it.

Turn on this option if you do not want to see this message again.

Click Yes to record actions in the Journal.

Click No to skip recording actions.

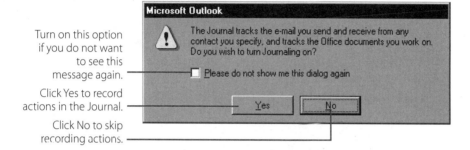

Microsoft Outlook

The Journal tracks the e-mail you send and receive from any contact you specify, and tracks the Office documents you work on. Do you wish to turn Journaling on?

☐ Please do not show me this dialog again

Yes   No

? SEE ALSO

You can have Outlook record journal entries for selected activities for any contact in your Contacts folder. See "Journal Tab," on page 417.

If you click Yes, you'll see the Journal Options dialog box, shown in Figure 14-2, on the following page. You can also display this dialog box, to turn on or change journal settings, by choosing Options from the Tools menu, clicking on the Preferences tab, and then clicking Journal Options.

The For These Contacts box on the Journal tab includes only the names listed in your Contacts folder. If you haven't set up any contact entries, this box is empty. If a name you want to select is not listed, click OK to close the Options dialog box, add the new contact to the Contacts folder, and then reopen the Journal tab of the Options dialog box, where the name now appears in the list.

For details about double-clicking a journal entry and the specific settings on the Journal tab, see "Choosing What to Open," on page 443. On the Journal tab, you'll also see a button called AutoArchive Journal Entries; for information about the AutoArchive feature, see Chapter 18, "Archiving Folder Items."

FIGURE 14-2.
The Journal tab of the
Options dialog box.

1 Select the contacts for whom Outlook will record activities.

2 Turn on the
activities you
want to record.

3 Turn off
applications
whose file
activities you
don't want
Outlook
to record.

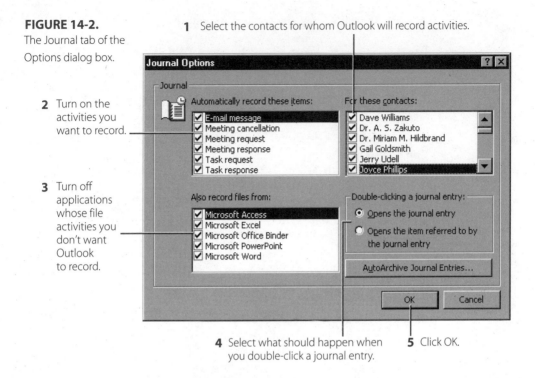

4 Select what should happen when
you double-click a journal entry.

5 Click OK.

Adding Entries to Your Journal

In addition to journal entries for Office 97 (and later) application activities, e-mail messages, task and meeting requests, and task and meeting
responses, you might also want to record journal entries for appointments and notes, for phone calls, for Office files and documents that
you haven't opened, or for files and documents you create with applications that aren't part of Office. In these cases, you can add journal
entries manually.

Adding a New Journal Entry Manually

You can add any type of journal entry manually. Doing so does not create
a related Outlook item, but you can copy the journal entry to the proper
Outlook folder to create an item. For example, if you manually add a
journal entry concerning a task, Outlook doesn't automatically create a
new task item in your Tasks folder. But if you copy the journal entry to
the Tasks folder, Outlook opens a new task window for the item, where
you can set up the task and add it to your task list. (For more information, see "Moving and Copying Folder Items," on page 462).

To add a new journal entry manually, you need to open the Journal folder and then open a new journal entry window. After you've opened the Journal folder, you can use any of the following methods to open the journal entry window:

- Choose the New Journal Entry command from the Actions menu.

- Point to New on the File menu, and then choose Journal Entry from the submenu.

- Click the New Journal button on the Standard toolbar.

- Press Ctrl+N.

When the journal entry window appears, follow these steps:

1 If you want to include the time you are about to spend creating this entry as part of the time spent on the activity, click Start Timer.

2 Type a subject line.

5 Type a company name, if needed.

3 Select the entry type from the list.

4 Type the contact's name, or click the Address Book button to select a name.

6 Add comments, notes, or additional information here.

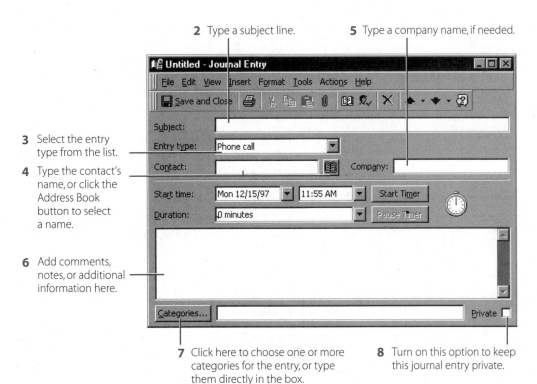

7 Click here to choose one or more categories for the entry, or type them directly in the box.

8 Turn on this option to keep this journal entry private.

9 If you started the timer, click Pause Timer to stop it.

10 When you are finished, click Save And Close.

⭐ **TIP**

> You can also assign a journal entry to a category by selecting the Using Categories option in the Organize pane. Click the Organize button on the Standard toolbar, and then choose Using Categories, if it's not already selected. Select the entry in the Journal folder, and choose an existing category in the Add Entries list and click the Add button, or type in a new category in the Create A New Category box and click the Create button.

Using the Timer

A journal entry's timer can give you a record of how much time you spend on activities such as completing a task, making a phone call, or meeting with a contact. To use the timer, simply open the journal entry window and click the Start Timer button. As you work, leave the journal entry window open. (Minimize the window if you need to see more of the screen.) You can pause the timer if you are interrupted by a phone call or a visit that isn't related to the matter at hand.

When you finish the activity, click the Save And Close button in the journal entry window. Outlook stops the timer for you.

Adding Existing Outlook Items to Your Journal

When you've worked on a task, held a meeting, or e-mailed a contact, for example, and have not recorded a journal entry for the activity, you might want to add an entry afterward. Here's how to add a journal entry for an existing Outlook item:

1 Open the Outlook folder containing the item for which you want to add a journal entry.

2 Select the item.

3 Drag the selected item to the Journal folder icon on the Outlook Bar.

4 Outlook opens a journal entry window for the item, such as the one just shown on page 439. You can add or change information for the entry as needed. Outlook sets the entry type on the basis of the type of item you added. For example, if you add a contact to your journal, Outlook sets the entry type to Phone Call. If necessary, you can select a more accurate description from the Entry Type list.

5 When you've made your adjustments to the journal entry, click Save And Close.

 TIP

When you add an existing Outlook item to your journal, Outlook adds a shortcut to the original item in the lower-left corner of the journal entry window, in the text and attachments area. The icon used for the shortcut (a contact card, a small calendar, a task checklist, or an envelope, for example) represents the type of the original Outlook activity or document. If you double-click the shortcut, Outlook opens the window in which you set up the item—the contact window, the calendar item window, the task window, or the message window, for instance— allowing you to review details about the item or make any necessary changes.

Adding Existing Documents to Your Journal

You've probably already created documents and files in other applications that you might want to add to your Journal folder. Adding existing

---

Adding a New Journal Entry from a Different Folder

If you're working in an Outlook folder other than the Journal folder when you need to set up a new journal entry, use one of these methods to open the journal entry window:

- Click the down arrow beside the New button on the Standard toolbar, and then choose Journal Entry from the menu.

- Point to New on the File menu, and then choose Journal Entry from the submenu.

- Press Ctrl+Shift+J.

files and documents to your journal allows you to organize a list of entries that all relate to a single project or task. Also, a journal entry makes it possible for you to open the file or document from Outlook rather than searching with other tools—such as the Windows Explorer or My Computer.

To add a journal entry for an existing file or document created in another application, take these steps:

1 Open My Computer or Windows Explorer.

2 Open the folder containing the file or document you want to add as a journal entry, and select the file or document.

3 Arrange the My Computer or Explorer window and the Outlook window so that you can see both windows on screen at the same time.

4 Drag the selected item to the Journal folder icon on the Outlook Bar.

5 Outlook now opens a journal entry window for the file or document. A shortcut icon for the file or document appears in the message area of the window, and the name of the file or document appears in the Subject box. You can change the entry name or the entry type and add other information that you want to record with the journal entry.

6 Click the Save And Close button.

 TIP

You can also open disk file folders from the Outlook Bar. For details, see "Other Shortcuts Group," on page 28.

Opening and Changing Journal Entries

To open a journal entry to view or edit its details, perform one of the following actions in the Journal folder:

- Right-click the entry, and then select Open from the shortcut menu.

- Double-click the entry.

- Select the entry, and then choose the Open command from the File menu.

- Select the entry, and then press Ctrl+O.

In the journal entry window that opens, you can review, add, or change information. If you make additions or changes, be sure to click the Save And Close button when you want to close the window.

Choosing What to Open

By default, Outlook opens the journal entry window when you double-click an entry in the Journal folder or use any of the other methods described previously to open a journal item. But, if you prefer, you can change this behavior and instead have Outlook open the item referred to by the journal entry, such as a calendar item for a meeting or a task window for a task.

As you saw in Figure 14-2, on page 438, the Journal Options dialog box contains a section labeled Double-Clicking A Journal Entry. If you want to open the Journal Entry window when you double-click an entry in the Journal folder, keep the Opens The Journal Entry option turned on. If you'd rather open the item associated with the journal entry when you double-click the entry, turn on the option labeled Opens The Item Referred To By The Journal Entry.

This setting affects not only the double-click action but also the following actions:

- Choosing the Open command from the File menu

- Right-clicking the journal entry and choosing Open from the shortcut menu

- Pressing Ctrl+O

In other words, if you set a double-click action to open the related item rather than the journal entry, these three actions will also result in opening the related item rather than the journal entry. If the journal entry relates to an Office file, Outlook will open the associated application and the file. For example, if the entry relates to an Excel worksheet, double-clicking the entry will both start Excel and open the worksheet from that entry.

Bypassing the Double-Click Setting

Regardless of how you set the Double-Clicking A Journal Entry option, you can always choose which item to open—the journal entry or the related item.

If you set the double-click action to open the related item rather than the journal entry, you can open the journal entry by right-clicking it and choosing Open Journal Entry from the shortcut menu. If there is no related item for a particular entry (it's a simple journal entry), double-clicking opens the journal entry, regardless of the setting on the Journal tab.

If you set the double-click action to open the journal entry, you can open the related item using either of these techniques:

- Right-click the journal entry and choose Open Item Referred To from the shortcut menu.

- Open the journal entry and double-click the shortcut for the associated item, which appears in the lower portion of the journal entry window.

Removing a Journal Entry

? SEE ALSO

You can archive journal entries before deleting them. For details, see Chapter 18, "Archiving Folder Items."

When you no longer want or need a journal entry, you can remove it from your Journal folder. To remove a journal entry, simply open the Journal folder, select the entry you want to remove, and click the Delete button on the Standard toolbar. Deleting a journal entry does not affect any associated file, document, or Outlook item.

When you delete a journal entry, Outlook moves the entry to the Deleted Items folder. To permanently delete the journal entry from Outlook, you have to empty the Deleted Items folder by choosing Empty "Deleted Items" Folder from the Tools menu.

Viewing Journal Entries

Outlook provides several ways to view a listing of your journal entries. The next several sections explain each view.

SEE ALSO

For details about
formatting views or
setting up custom
views, See Chapter 21,
"Setting Up Views." For
details about grouping
journal entries as well
as specifying sorting
procedures, setting up
special filters, and add-
ing custom fields, see
Chapter 20, "Organizing
Folder Items."

To switch to a different view, use one of the following methods:

- Point to Current View on the View menu, and then choose the view you want from the submenu.

- Click the Organize button on the Standard toolbar, choose Using Views in the Organize pane, and select the view from the list that appears.

By Type View

The first time you look into your Journal folder, you'll see journal entries listed in By Type view, as shown previously in Figure 14-1, on page 436.

When you've used Outlook for a while, your journal entries might range over a long period of time, and you won't be able to scroll to them easily or quickly. You can use one of the following techniques to quickly jump to another date:

SEE ALSO

For information about
timeline views, see
"Timeline Views," on
page 597.

- To jump to a date within a few months of the current date, click the down arrow beside the month name in the Journal folder window and select the date from the calendar that appears.

- To jump to any date, use the Go To Date command on the Go menu in the Journal folder window (or press Ctrl+G). For more information about using the Go To Date dialog box, see "Using the Go To Date Command," on page 309.

 TIP

In By Type view, By Contact view, and By Category view, you can click the Day, Week, or Month buttons on the Standard toolbar to determine the number of days displayed on the screen. Click Day, for example, to display a single day on the screen with the timeline divided into hours.

By Contact View

If you include contacts in your journal entries, you can see the entries listed by contact. If you assign more than one contact to a journal entry, Outlook lists that journal entry under each contact name. An example of a Journal folder window in By Contact view is shown on the next page.

Click here to display a calendar for jumping to another date.

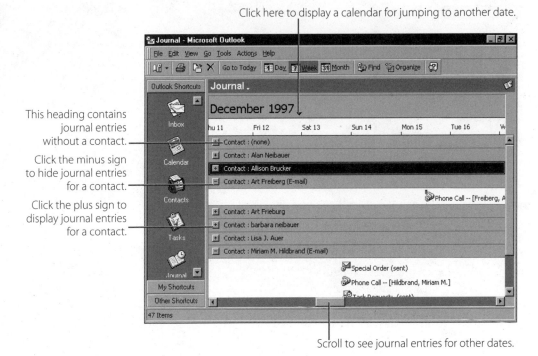

This heading contains journal entries without a contact.

Click the minus sign to hide journal entries for a contact.

Click the plus sign to display journal entries for a contact.

Scroll to see journal entries for other dates.

By Category View

When you assign your journal entries to categories, you can see the entries listed by category. If you assign a journal entry to more than one category, Outlook lists that entry in each category. There will also be a group for entries that have no category assigned to them.

Entry List View

SEE ALSO

For details about changing the columns you see in Entry List view, see "Setting Up Columns," on page 554. You can group your journal entries by some of the columns you set up in Entry List view; for details, see "Grouping," on page 563.

The views that display entries on a time scale are useful in their own way, but when you are using one of these views, you can't see all the information Outlook can display for a journal entry unless you open the entry window. To display more information about all your journal entries at one time, switch to Entry List view. In this view, your entries are listed in a table arrangement, with columns for the following items: icons for entry types, attachments, descriptions of the entry types, subjects, start dates and times, times spent so far on the journal entries (duration), contact names for each entry, and categories to which each entry has been assigned. On the next page, you'll see a typical Journal folder displayed in Entry List view.

■ Journal entries are initially sorted with the most recent start date and time at the top of the list and the oldest start date and time at the bottom of the list. To sort the journal entries a different way in Entry List view, click the column heading for the column you want to use to sort the journal entries. The first click sorts either alphabetically (A–Z) or newest to oldest. A second click sorts either reverse alphabetically (Z–A) or oldest to newest. You can sort the list of journal entries by attachment (with or without), type, subject, start date and time, or duration.

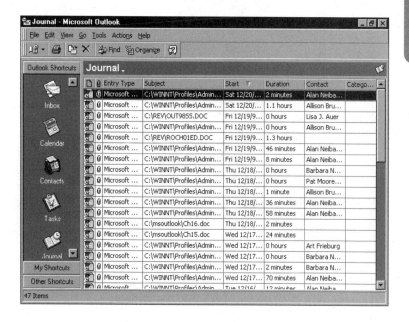

> **NOTE**

You cannot sort journal entries by category or by contact in Entry List view. To sort your journal entries by category or contact, choose By Category view or By Contact view.

Last Seven Days View

Over time you'll collect a lot of journal entries. Even though you might be conscientious about deleting old journal entries that you no longer need, you'll undoubtedly keep some entries around for a very long time. In your daily work, however, you might find that you are interested only in the recent past. That's where Last Seven Days view can help out. In this view, Outlook displays your journal entries for the past seven days only, in a table arrangement similar to Entry List view. You can sort these entries in all the same ways you can sort in Entry List view; see "Entry List View," on page 446.

Phone Calls View

When you select Phone Calls view, Outlook displays only those journal entries for phone calls you made from the Contacts folder and journal entries you've created yourself by adding a contact to your journal. Phone Calls view displays journal entries as shown here:

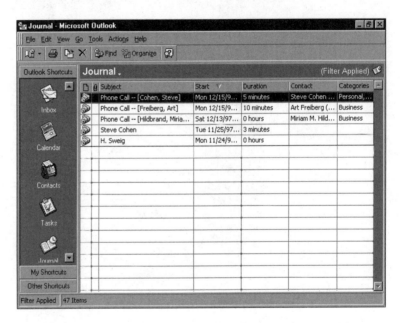

You can sort these entries in all the same ways you can sort in Entry List view; see "Entry List View," on page 446.

Making Notes

J otting down points that we want to remember or commu-nicate to others seems to be one of the major jobs we do just about every day. Microsoft Outlook 98 comes with a folder for notes—a place where you can type notes and keep track of them. You can even print your notes (as explained in Chapter 17, "Printing Folder Items"), and you can forward a note to anyone with an e-mail address.

Adding a Note

To create a new note, open the Notes folder, and use one of the following methods:

New Note

- Click the New Note button on the Standard toolbar.

- Point to New on the File menu, and then choose Note from the submenu.

- Press Ctrl+N.

- Double-click an empty space in the Notes folder window.

When you use any one of these methods, Outlook opens a note window, as shown here:

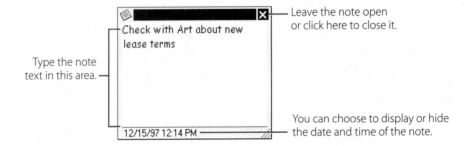

Type the note text in this area.

Check with Art about new lease terms

Leave the note open or click here to close it.

You can choose to display or hide the date and time of the note.

12/15/97 12:14 PM

Once you have a note open, you can also create a new note by clicking the icon in the upper-left corner of the note window and choosing New Note from the menu, shown here:

If you're working in an Outlook folder other than the Notes folder when you need to create a note, use one of the following methods:

- Click the down arrow beside the New button on the Standard toolbar, and then choose Note from the menu.

- Point to New on the File menu, and then choose Note from the submenu.

- Press Ctrl+Shift+N.

After you finish a note and click the Close button, Outlook displays the note text and a note icon in your Notes folder window.

Working with Notes

? SEE ALSO

For details about printing options, see Chapter 17, "Printing Folder Items."

You can edit the text of a note, change the note's color, assign the note to various categories, forward the note to someone else, and copy or move the note to another folder. You can also adjust the default settings for all your notes, changing the default color, size, font, and time and date display.

Editing Note Text

When you want to change the text of a note, simply open the Notes folder and double-click the note you want to edit. Then type your text changes and click the Close button.

You can also open a note for editing in the following ways:

- Right-click the note and choose Open from the shortcut menu.

- Select the note and choose the Open command from the File menu.

- Select the note and press Ctrl+O.

Giving a Note Some (Other) Color

By default, Outlook's notes have a yellow background and a yellow icon. But you can easily change a note's color to one of four other colors: blue, green, pink, or white. (You can also change the default note color, as explained in "Changing Default Note Settings," on page 453.) Keeping notes of different colors is a handy way to organize your notes. You might make personal notes one color and notes related to your job another color.

Here's how to change the color of a note:

1 Open the Notes folder and select the note you want to color differently.

2 Right-click the note, point to Color on the shortcut menu, and then choose the new color from the submenu.

 TIP

If you have a note open, you can click the icon in the upper-left corner of the note window, point to Color on the menu, and then choose the new color from the submenu.

Assigning a Note to a Category

As with other Outlook items, such as e-mail messages, meetings, or tasks, you can organize notes by assigning a note to one or more categories. To assign a note to a category, open the note and click the icon in the upper left corner of the note window. Then choose Categories from the menu. (You can also right-click the note in the Notes folder window and choose Categories from the shortcut menu.) You can use one or more of Outlook's built-in categories or enter a category of your own. For more information about using categories with Outlook items, see "Working with Categories," on page 560.

Sending a Note to Someone Else

If you want someone else to benefit from your careful note taking, you can send the note to another user in one of two ways. You can send the text of the note as the message, or you can include the note as an attachment.

- To send the text of the note as the text of the message, drag the note from the Notes folder to the Inbox folder on the Outlook Bar.

- To send a note to someone else as an attachment, open the note, click the icon in the upper-left corner of the note window, and then choose Forward from the menu.

IV

In the message window that Outlook displays, type the name of the recipient to whom you want to forward the note, or click the To button to select a name. If you dragged only one note, or selected only one note to forward, the Subject line will show the note text. If you selected more than one note to forward, the Subject line will be blank. Add any text you want to send with the notes and message. When you're ready to send the message with the note(s) attached, click the Send button on the Standard toolbar.

Copying or Moving a Note to Another Folder

You can move a note to another folder the same way you move any Outlook item. You can drag a note and drop it on a folder icon on the Outlook Bar to move the note to another folder. For example, if you want to use a note to create a task, open the Notes folder window, select the note you want to use to set up the task, and drag it to the Tasks icon on the Outlook Bar. Outlook opens a task window, which you can use to enter more details about the task. For more details about moving items from one folder to another, see "Moving a Folder Item," on page 463.

Changing Default Note Settings

Outlook's default note settings display a note in a medium-sized yellow window, in a default font and font size. (The note icons are also yellow.) If you want to change the default color, size, and font settings for all your notes, choose Options from the Tools menu, click the Preferences tab of the Options dialog box, and then click Note Options to display the Notes Options dialog box:

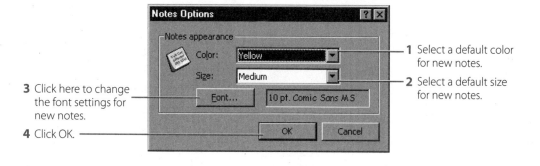

3 Click here to change the font settings for new notes.

4 Click OK.

1 Select a default color for new notes.

2 Select a default size for new notes.

> Changes you make to the default note settings affect only new notes. Existing notes will retain their original appearance.

Date and Time Stamping Notes

If you want, you can have Outlook display the date and time that the note was created at the bottom of a note. To turn this setting off or on, choose the Options command from the Tools menu, click the Other tab, and click Advanced Options. In the Advanced Options dialog box, turn on or off the option labeled When Viewing Notes, Show Time And Date.

> Turning off the Show Date And Time option merely omits the date and time from the note window; Outlook still records the date and time you created the note (or last updated it) and displays this information in a column in certain views.

Viewing Your Notes

The views available for the Notes folder include views based on displaying icons as well as views that use a list format. When you first begin to work in your Notes folder, you'll see the window in Icons view, which is the default setting.

To switch to a different view of your Notes folder, use one of the following methods:

- Point to Current View on the View menu and then choose the view you want from the submenu.

- Click the Organize button on the Standard toolbar to display the Organize pane, click Using Views, and choose the view from the list.

> **NOTE**

You can also resize a note. To do so, point to a corner or border of the note so that the mouse pointer appears as a two-headed arrow and then drag. Drag outward to make the note larger; drag inward to make it smaller. The direction of the arrow indicates how the note will be changed. The lower-right corner has a larger area to grab if you want to change both the height and width of the note at the same time.

Icons View

SEE ALSO

You can set up custom views for looking at your notes. For information, see Chapter 21, "Setting Up Views." You can also set up special filters and sorting procedures for your notes; for details, see "Filtering," on page 568, and "Sorting," on page 566.

Icons view displays your notes with an icon and the note text. In Icons view, you can choose how to display the icons: as large icons, as small icons, or as an icon list.

To select one of these icon displays, click one of the three icon buttons on the Standard toolbar, as shown here:

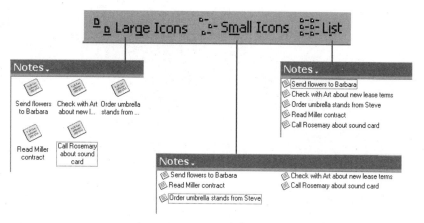

If you click the Large Icons button or the Small Icons button, Outlook gives you several ways to arrange the icons in the Notes folder window. The easiest way to arrange a few notes is to simply drag the icons where you want them to appear in the window. (If you display the icons as a list, however, you can't arrange the icons in the window.)

If you want to align notes automatically in relation to each other, however, use the Format Icon View dialog box:

1   Open the Notes folder, point to Current View on the View menu, and then choose Icons view.

2 Point again to Current View on the View menu and then choose Customize Current View. Outlook opens the View Summary dialog box.

3 Click the Other Settings button in the dialog box to display the Format Icon View dialog box.

4 Select the view type. These buttons have the same effect as the similarly named buttons on the Standard toolbar.

5 Select the icon placement option.

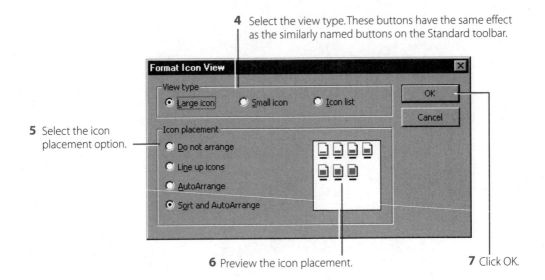

6 Preview the icon placement.

7 Click OK.

The Format Icon View dialog box provides four choices for arranging the icons in the Notes folder window:

- The Do Not Arrange option lets you drag the icons to any spot in the Notes folder window, giving you the freedom to arrange the icons yourself.

- The Line Up Icons option arranges the icons according to a preset grid in the Notes folder window but leaves them close to their original positions. It does not close up gaps between icons.

- The AutoArrange option lines up the icons in rows and columns, closing any gaps.

- The Sort And AutoArrange option sorts the icons alphabetically by the first word of the note and then lines up the icons in rows and columns, closing any gaps.

Notes List View

SEE ALSO

To learn other ways to sort notes, see "Sorting," on page 566. For details about changing the columns in Notes List view, see "Setting Up Columns," on page 554. You can group your notes by some of the columns you set up in Notes List view; for details, see "Grouping," on page 563.

To see more information about your notes than Icons view can display, switch to Notes List view. In this view, Outlook lists your notes with columns for icons, subjects, creation dates and times, and categories, as in the following illustration:

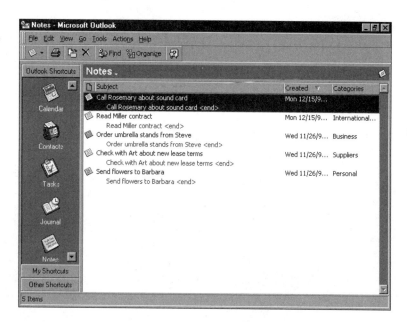

Notes List view initially sorts notes alphabetically by subject. To sort the notes differently in this view, click the column heading for the column you want to use to sort the notes. The first click sorts alphabetically or newest to oldest. A second click sorts reverse alphabetically or oldest to newest.

Last Seven Days View

If, for some reason, you need to focus your attention only on notes from the current time period, Last Seven Days view can be useful. The view looks just like the Notes List view but only displays notes created in the past seven days.

By Category View

If you have assigned at least some of your notes to categories, you can switch to By Category view to see the notes listed by category. A single note can appear in as many categories as you have assigned it to.

> To assign a note to an additional category in By Category view, drag that note's icon to the new category. The note then appears in both categories.

By Color View

If you use different colors for different types of notes, you can see your notes listed by color when you choose By Color view:

Click the plus sign to display the notes for that color.

Click the minus sign to hide the notes for that color.

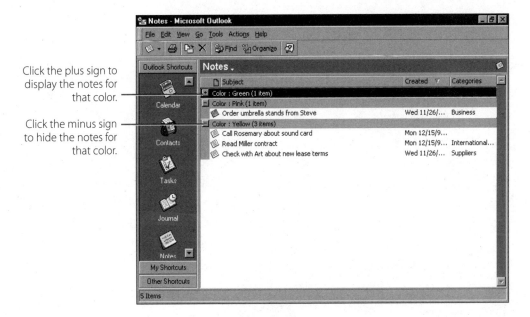

> To change a note's color, drag that note's icon to the section that lists the new color. The note then appears with the new color.

PART V

Bending Folders to Your Will

Managing Folder Contents

To get the most from Microsoft Outlook 98, you need to manage folder contents, to clean up the loose ends that inevitably arise from managing your mail, appointments, contacts, tasks, notes—in short, your life. Can't you just hear your parents telling you, "Straighten up your room—it's a pigsty"? Well, this chapter describes the tools you need to straighten up the messes in your Outlook folders. (Your room is your own business.)

Moving and Copying Folder Items

You can move or copy folder items to any other Outlook folder or to any folder on your system. Outlook generously provides several ways to move and copy folder items. Use whichever method you find convenient.

When you move or copy an item to a folder of another type (such as moving a task to the Inbox or a message to any non–e-mail folder), Outlook opens a new item window for that folder. Except in the Journal, the moved item appears as text in the new item window. Figure 16-1, for example, shows how an appointment appears when moved to the Inbox. The details of the appointment become the text of the message. You can change any of the information in the new item window and fill in the rest before clicking the Save And Close button.

> Drag a contact to the Inbox to send a message, to the Calendar to set up an appointment, or to the Tasks folder to assign a task. The name of the contact will automatically appear in the To text box as the recipient of the message, appointment notice, or task assignment.

When you move or copy an item to the Journal folder, the item appears as an attachment in the journal entry window.

FIGURE 16-1.

An appointment moved to the Inbox.

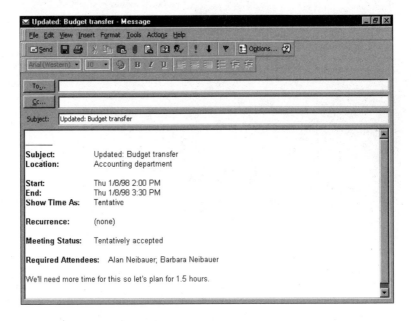

Moving a Folder Item

You can move a folder item either while it's open or while it's closed. The easiest way to move a folder item, however, is when it is closed. Just drag the item to the folder where you want to place it, using the following steps:

> **NOTE**
>
> When you drag an item to a folder of a different type, Outlook actually copies rather than moves the item.

1 Open the folder containing the item you want to move.

2 Click the item you want to move. Hold down the Ctrl key if you want to select multiple items, or use the Shift key to select a series of consecutive items.

3 If necessary, scroll the Outlook Bar, or choose another group on the Outlook Bar, to see the icon for the folder where you want to place the item.

4 Drag the item from the open folder to the folder on the Outlook Bar.

> **NOTE**
>
> If the folder list is displayed, you can also drag the item to the destination folder on the list.

You can also move an item by selecting a destination folder from a dialog box. To move the item without opening it first, follow these steps:

1 Open the folder containing the item you want to move.

2 Click the item you want to move. You can select and move more than one item at the same time.

3 Click the Move To Folder button on the Standard toolbar to see the list of folders shown at the top of the next page.

V

Bending Folders to Your Will

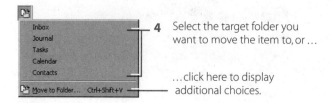

4   Select the target folder you want to move the item to, or ...

...click here to display additional choices.

The Move To Folder command displays a dialog box from which you choose the target folder. You can open this dialog box using any of the following techniques:

- Click the Move To Folder button on the Standard toolbar and choose Move To Folder from the menu.

- Press Ctrl+Shift+V.

- Right-click the item in the folder window and choose Move To Folder from the shortcut menu.

- In the folder window, choose the Move To Folder command from the Edit menu.

- If the item is open, choose the Move To Folder command from the File menu.

If you want to use a new folder, select an existing folder where you want to add the new subfolder, click New, type a name for the new folder, and then click OK.

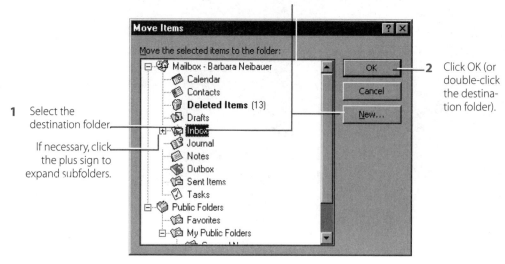

1   Select the destination folder.

If necessary, click the plus sign to expand subfolders.

2   Click OK (or double-click the destination folder).

Moving Folder Items with Organize

Another way to move items to other folders is to use the Organize command. You can use this command from all folders except the Calendar folder, Journal folder, and Public Folders folder in the Other Shortcuts group.

If the Organize pane is not displayed, click the Organize button on the Standard toolbar, or choose Organize from the Tools menu. Choose one or more items that you want to move, and then follow these steps:

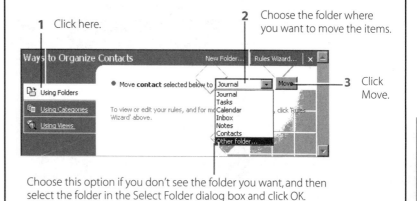

1 Click here.

2 Choose the folder where you want to move the items.

3 Click Move.

Choose this option if you don't see the folder you want, and then select the folder in the Select Folder dialog box and click OK.

Copying a Folder Item

You can copy a folder item either while it's open or while it's closed. If the item is closed and displayed in the folder window, hold down the Ctrl key while you drag the item to the destination folder on the Outlook Bar or in the Folder List. You do not have to hold down the Ctrl key to copy an item to a folder of a different type.

 TIP

You actually do not have to hold down the Ctrl key the entire time you are dragging an item. Just make sure the Ctrl key is pressed down when you release the mouse button. When you press the Ctrl key, a small plus sign will appear next to the mouse pointer indicating that you are making a copy of the item rather than moving it.

V

Bending Folders to Your Will

To copy the item using a dialog box instead of dragging, follow these steps:

1 Open the folder containing the item, and select the item or open it. You can select more then one item in a folder window.

2 Choose Copy To Folder to see the following dialog box. Copy To Folder appears on the Edit menu when you're viewing a folder and on the File menu when you have opened an item.

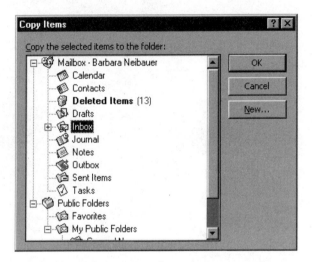

3 Select the destination folder.

4 Click OK (or double-click the destination folder).

Copying a Folder Item to an Office Application

You can copy messages, contact information, or notes to other Office 97 (or later) applications in one of two ways: you can copy the folder item as an embedded object, or you can add the text of the item to a document in the application.

In this chapter, references to Microsoft Office always refer to Office 97 and later versions.

To copy a folder item to an Office application as an object, take these steps:

1 Select the folder item you want to copy.

2 Start the Office application to which you want to copy the folder item, and then create or open the document to which you'll copy the item.

3 Arrange the Outlook window and the Office document window on your screen so that you can see both at the same time.

4 Drag the folder item into the document window.

The folder item is displayed as an icon in the document. You can double-click the icon to see the folder item.

If you want to copy the text of the folder item into the Office document, take these steps:

1 Select the folder item you want to copy.

2 Choose the Save As command from the File menu in Outlook to open the Save As dialog box.

3 Open the Save As Type list, and select Rich Text Format (RTF).

4 Type or edit the filename in the File Name box.

5 Click Save.

6 Switch to or open the Office application, and then choose the Open command from the File menu in that application to open the Rich Text Format (RTF) file for the folder item. You see the text in the appropriate format for the Office application. An example of a Rich Text Format journal entry opened in Microsoft Word is shown on the next page.

7 Save the Office document.

V

Bending Folders to Your Will

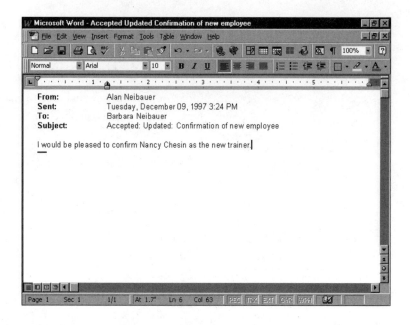

Posting Your Ideas in a Folder

As another way to add new information to a folder—especially to a public folder that is shared by members of a group—you can post a notice, or you can post a response to a previous posting. Many public folders are designed for posting information that is of interest to specific groups of people. These folders are different from e-mail folders because they're designed for public rather than private use. Although you can compose new postings both in e-mail folders and in public folders, posting in an e-mail folder is less common. You cannot compose new postings or post replies in file system folders.

To post a new notice in an e-mail or public folder, follow these steps:

1   Open the e-mail or public folder where you want to add a new posting.

New Post
In This Folder

2   If you open a public folder, click the New Post In This Folder button on the Standard toolbar. For public folders as well as all e-mail folders (Inbox, Outbox, Drafts, and Sent Items), you can also press Ctrl+Shift+S, or click the down arrow beside the New button on the Standard toolbar, and then select Post In This Folder from the menu.

3 Type the topic of your posting.

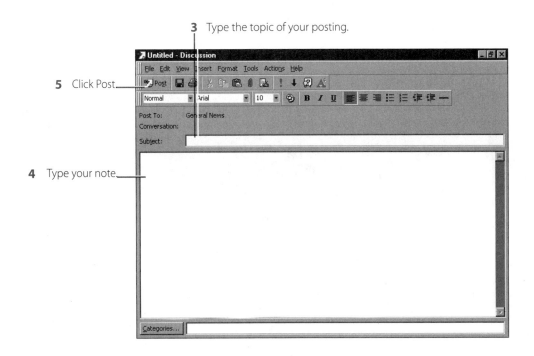

5 Click Post

4 Type your note

After you click the Post button, Outlook adds the notice to the folder, marking it with the icon shown at the left.

To reply to a posted notice, first double-click it to open a discussion window containing the notice. Click the Post Reply button to open a window in which you can type your reply. Enter the subject, type your reply, and then click the Post button. Then close the first discussion window by clicking the Close button in the upper-right corner of the window.

If you read the message in the Preview Pane and want to post a reply without opening the item, do this:

1 Open the folder containing the item to which you want to post a reply, and select the item.

2 Right-click the item and choose Post Reply To This Folder from the shortcut menu in e-mail folders and public folders.

3 Type your reply in the message window.

4 Edit the original item text, if you like.

5 Click Post.

Adding Files to a Folder

In addition to moving an Outlook item to another folder, you can copy files from your disk to an Outlook item. For example, you might want to attach a Word document or an Excel worksheet to a journal entry or task.

To put a file from your file system into an Outlook folder, take the following steps:

1 Open the Other Shortcuts group on the Outlook Bar, and then choose My Computer.

2 Locate the disk, folder, and then the file using the Folder List (if open) or the item list.

3 Select the file.

4 Return to the Outlook Bar and open the group that contains your destination folder. If necessary, scroll so that the folder is visible. (Don't click the folder.)

5 Drag the selected file to the Outlook folder on the Outlook Bar. Outlook creates an item that is appropriate for the folder. In the example shown below, a shortcut to the file has been placed in a journal entry window, opened for your review.

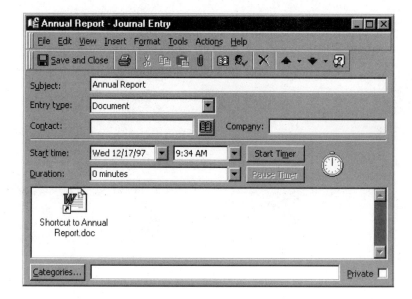

6 Make any changes you want to the information in the item window. You can add text in the message area where the file shortcut appears, if you wish.

7 Click Save And Close.

The new folder item contains a shortcut to the file. For details about using the shortcut, see "Viewing File Attachments and Shortcuts Stored in Outlook Folder Items," on the next page.

The button you click in step 7 depends on the type of folder item Outlook creates and on what you want to do with it. For example, if you want to send the shortcut in a new message, click the Send button. If you don't want to send a message but do want to keep the item in an e-mail folder, click the Save button and then close the message. For other folder item types, click the Save And Close button.

As an alternative to dragging a file to the Outlook folder, you can use the File command on the Insert menu as follows:

1 Open the Outlook folder in which you want to place the file.

2 Create a new item in the Outlook folder.

3 In the folder item window, choose the File command from the Insert menu (or click the Insert File button on the Standard toolbar).

4 Switch to the disk and folder that contain the file.   **7** Click OK.

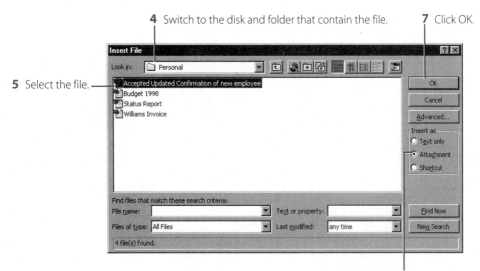

5 Select the file.

6 Select one of these options

8 Fill in the folder item window with the information you want. You might, for example, want to enter a description of the file on the Subject line.

9 If you are working in an e-mail folder, click the Save button, and then click the Close button in the folder item window. For other folder item types, click the Save And Close button.

Notice the Insert As section of the Insert File dialog box (step 6). Which option you choose here depends on what you plan to do with the folder item and on the type of file you're inserting.

■ The Text Only option inserts the file as standard text. Typically, you'll select this option when you want to insert plain (unformatted) text files in order to send the file in a message across the Internet. This option makes sense only for simple text files. Art files and files containing formatted text appear as gibberish.

■ The Attachment option inserts a complete copy of the data from the file, represented as an icon. Select this option if you will need to readily access the file from the folder item. Because the entire file is stored as part of the folder item, you should select the Shortcut option instead if the file is extremely large.

■ The Shortcut option inserts a pointer to the original file, represented as a shortcut icon. Select this option to include a large file. Note, however, that anyone else whom you want to view the file must have direct or network access to the disk, folder, and file, including permission to access it. For the Shortcut option, it's a good idea to store the file on a network server or in a public folder to which others who must view the file have access.

Viewing File Attachments and Shortcuts Stored in Outlook Folder Items

Whether you copied a file to an Outlook folder as an attachment or as a shortcut, you can easily view the contents of the file. In the folder window, right-click the folder item, and choose View Attachments from the shortcut menu. Then select the attachment name from the submenu.

NOTE

What's the difference between a file attachment and a shortcut? A file attachment sends the entire file within the message. If you have a large file that you'd like to share, you might want to attach a shortcut instead. A shortcut sends the location of the file within the message and is much faster to send and open than a file attachment. Of course the recipient must have access to the location of the file itself, or else the shortcut will be useless. This method works well for those connected via an Exchange Server network.

If you open the item, you can use any of these methods in the folder item window to view the file:

- Double-click an attachment or shortcut icon.

- Right-click an attachment or shortcut icon, and choose Open from the shortcut menu.

- Right-click an attachment or shortcut icon, and choose Quick View from the shortcut menu. (Microsoft Windows 95 Quick View must be installed on your computer for this method to work.)

Adding Items to the Favorites Folder

The Favorites folder contains shortcuts to items, documents, and other folders that you use frequently. You can add items to the Favorites folder in several ways:

- You can drag folder items to the Outlook Favorites folder. (This operation takes place within Outlook.)

- You can add icons to the Favorites toolbar on the Office shortcut bar.

- You can add the address of a World Wide Web page (a URL) to the Favorites list in Microsoft Internet Explorer.

 TIP

If you add a favorite to your Favorites folder (either in Outlook or in the Favorites folder inside the Windows folder), to the Favorites list in Microsoft Internet Explorer, or to the Favorites toolbar of the Office shortcut bar, the new favorite automatically appears in all of these places.

V

Bending Folders to Your Will

Dragging a Folder
Item to the Favorites Folder

You can drag any Outlook folder item (or any file) to the Outlook Favorites folder. Depending on how you drag the item, and the type of item you drag, you either move it to the Favorites folder or copy it.

To copy an item to your Outlook Favorites folder, take these steps:

1 Open the Outlook folder (or disk folder) that contains the item you want to move.

2 Click the Other Shortcuts label on the Outlook Bar to display the Favorites folder icon. Do *not* click the Favorites folder icon.

3 Drag the folder item to the Favorites folder icon. If you want to copy a file from My Computer or My Documents, you must hold down the Ctrl key while you drag the item. You don't need to hold down the Ctrl key to copy an item from an Outlook folder.
   Use the same technique to move an item to your Outlook Favorites folder, but with these exceptions:

   • To move a file from My Computer or My Documents, just drag the file to the Favorites folder icon without holding down any key.

   • To move an item from an Outlook folder, hold down the Shift key while you drag it to the Favorites folder icon. When you release the mouse, you'll see a shortcut menu with the options Move Here and Cancel. Choose Move Here.

Adding to Favorites in
Microsoft Internet Explorer

In Microsoft Internet Explorer, you can add World Wide Web sites to your Favorites folder. With Internet Explorer version 4.0 and later, you can also *subscribe* to a Web site. This means that Internet Explorer will periodically check the site to determine if it has changed since you last viewed it. Here's how to add a Web site to your Favorites folder and how to subscribe to it.

1 Start Microsoft Internet Explorer.

2 Locate the web page (URL) you want to add to your Favorites folder.

3 Choose the Add To Favorites command from the Favorites menu.

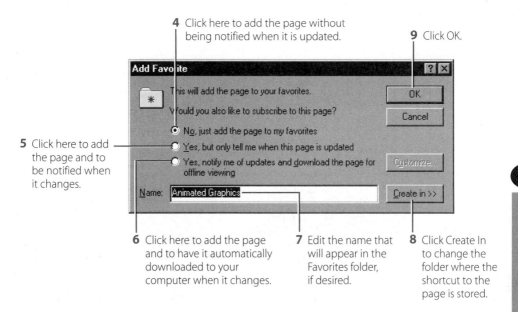

4 Click here to add the page without being notified when it is updated.

9 Click OK.

5 Click here to add the page and to be notified when it changes.

6 Click here to add the page and to have it automatically downloaded to your computer when it changes.

7 Edit the name that will appear in the Favorites folder, if desired.

8 Click Create In to change the folder where the shortcut to the page is stored.

These Web pages are now available in Outlook through your Favorites folder in the Other group on the Outlook Bar.

Searching Folder Contents

Outlook provides two ways to help locate items in a folder. You can use the Find command to search just for words or phrases in folder items, or you can use Advanced Find to specify what folders are searched and to look for specific values within the items searched.

Performing a Simple Search

When you want to locate all folder items that contain a certain word or phrase, follow these steps:

1 Click the Find button on the Standard toolbar, or choose Find from the Tools menu.

2 Type a word or phrase to search for.

3 Turn off this option to search just the message subject lines.

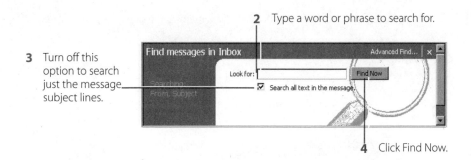

4 Click Find Now.

Outlook displays, in list form, all of the folder items containing the text that you entered.

To look for something else, enter a new search phrase and click Find Now.

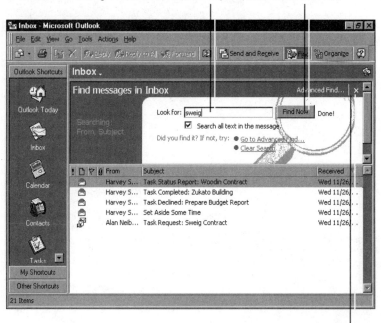

To return to the previous folder view, click here to close the Find pane.

Conducting an Advanced Search

To conduct a more sophisticated search for items in a folder, you need to use the Advanced Find dialog box, shown in Figure 16-2. Open this dialog box in any one of these ways:

■ Choose the Advanced Find command from the Tools menu.

■ Right-click the folder you want to search, and then choose Advanced Find from the shortcut menu.

■ Click Find on the Standard toolbar, and then click Advanced Find.

■ Press Ctrl+Shift+F.

FIGURE 16-2.

Using the Advanced Find dialog box.

Specify the type of folder item here ...

...and the tab name, and its contents, change accordingly.

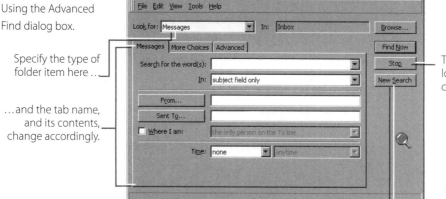

To stop a long search, click Stop.

To clear all search criteria, click New Search.

 **SEE ALSO**

To see a list of the folders Outlook searches by default and to find out how to expand a search beyond them, see "More on the Find Dialog Box," on page 479.

The entry in the Look For box of the Advanced Find dialog box shows the type of item for the open folder, such as messages for the Inbox folder or journal entries for the Journal folder. To search for a different type of item, select another type from the list. The In box beside the Look For box shows the default folder in which Outlook searches for the items.

The first of the three tabs in the Advanced Find dialog box corresponds to the type of folder item you're looking for. As you change the setting in the Look For box, this tab changes, becoming, for instance, the Messages tab or the Journal Entries tab. Although the tabs for different types of folder items vary somewhat, you set them up in similar ways. For instance, on the Messages tab, shown in Figure 16-2, you specify search criteria as follows:

■ In the Search For The Word(s) box, type a word or phrase that appears in all the messages you're searching for. (If you want to choose words you used in past searches, you can select them from the list, where Outlook stores them.)

- In the tab's In box, tell Outlook whether to look for the specified word or phrase only in the Subject line of messages (the subject field), in both the Subject line and the body of messages, or in other text fields.

The term "field" simply refers to a location that shows data or to an empty box that you can fill in with details about an item.

To narrow the search even further, you can also set up the following optional criteria:

- Specify messages that were received from or sent to certain people. Type the names of these people in the appropriate boxes, or click the From button or the Sent To button to display the Select Names dialog box, where you can choose names from your address books.

- Tell Outlook to search for messages in which you are the only addressee, messages in which you are the addressee along with others, or messages for which you received copies. To do this, turn on the Where I Am option and select from the adjoining list.

- Specify a time. By selecting options in both the Time boxes, you can narrow the search to messages that were, for instance, received or sent within a certain timeframe.

When you've set as many search criteria as you need, click the Find Now button to begin the search.

When Outlook completes the search, the Advanced Find dialog box expands to display the items that match your criteria. If the list includes folder items you don't want, you can add additional criteria to search the list only and then click the Find Now button again. This way, you can pare the list down to the items you really want to find. If none of the folder items shown fits your needs, click the New Search button and set up different criteria.

When you change your selection in the Look For box after a search, Outlook notifies you that the previous search will be cleared. If you want to start a fresh search, click OK. If you want to keep the previous search, click Cancel.

TIP

You can open any found item directly from the Advanced Find dialog box by double-clicking the item.

More on the Find Dialog Box

The next several sections take a closer look at some of the features of the Advanced Find dialog box.

Look For box.   As mentioned earlier, the setting in the Look For box of the Advanced Find dialog box determines which tab you see in the dialog box. This setting also affects where Outlook will search for the items you're seeking. The In box next to the Look For box indicates the folder that Outlook will automatically search for the folder items you've specified. Table 16-1 summarizes how the setting in the Look For box determines which folder is searched by default and which tab you see in the Find dialog box.

TABLE 16-1.   Effects of Settings in the Look For Box

Choosing This Setting in the Look For Box	Shows This Default Folder in the In Box to Be Searched	And Displays This Tab for Setting up the Search
Any Type Of Outlook Item	Personal folders or server mailbox	Any Items
Appointments And Meetings	Calendar	Appointments And Meetings
Contacts	Contacts	Contacts
Files	My Documents	Files
Files (Outlook/ Exchange)	Inbox	Files
Journal Entries	Journal	Journal Entries
Messages	Inbox	Messages
Notes	Notes	Notes
Tasks	Tasks	Tasks

Bending Folders to Your Will

Browse button.   If you need to expand Outlook's search beyond the folder indicated in the In box, you can specify additional folders that Outlook should search. You can't type directly in the In box, but you can click the Browse button to open the Select Folder(s) dialog box, shown below.

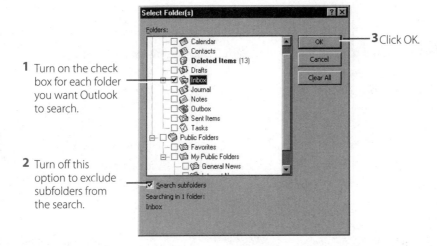

1 Turn on the check box for each folder you want Outlook to search.

3 Click OK.

2 Turn off this option to exclude subfolders from the search.

After you click OK in the Select Folder(s) dialog box, Outlook adds the folder names you selected to the In box and includes those folders in the search.

 NOTE

If you select Files in the Look For box and then click the Browse button, you'll see a Select Folder(s) dialog box that contains a list of all the folders in your file system rather than a list of Outlook's folders.

Files tab.   If you're searching for a file with the Advanced Find dialog box, you'll notice that the tab Outlook displays when you select Files in the Look For box is a little different from the tabs displayed for other items. In particular, the Named box on the Files tab lets you enter either a filename or a file specification.

To enter a filename, type the complete filename and filename extension. For a file specification, use one of these methods:

- Type an asterisk (*) to include all filenames or extensions—for example, type *.pst to include all files that have the .PST filename extension.

- Type word*.* to find all files of any type (any extension) whose filenames start with word.

- Type one or more question marks (?) to include files regardless of the character(s) at those locations. For example, type fig??-01.?if to include all filenames that start with fig, end with –01, and whose extensions end with if.

If you've looked for files before by typing a filename or a file specification in the Named box, you can find these entries listed by clicking the down arrow in the Named box.

If you want to search for all the files of a certain type—for example, all Microsoft Excel workbooks—choose the file type from the Of Type box.

> **NOTE**

When you type a filename or a file specification in the Named box on the Files tab, Outlook's search ignores the selection in the Of Type box.

More Choices tab and Advanced tab.   The other two tabs in the Advanced Find dialog box, More Choices and Advanced, offer still more options for structuring your search. These two tabs are the same as the More Choices tab and the Advanced tab in the Filter dialog box, discussed in Chapter 20, "Organizing Folder Items." For information about setting up these tabs, see "Setting Up the More Choices Tab," on page 571, and "Setting Up Advanced Criteria," on page 573. The next section also provides an example of using the Advanced tab.

Searching for Items by Fields on a Form

When you're looking for specific folder items, you might consider searching for the individual fields that appear on the various types of forms. A form is a window that you use or create to display, enter, or edit information. To use a field as a search criterion, you have to first select the form that contains the field. Here's how.

1 Choose the Advanced Find command from the Tools menu to display the Advanced Find dialog box.

2 In the Look For box, select the type of folder item you want to find, or select Any Type Of Outlook Item to include all item types in the search.

3 If the folder you want to search does not appear in the In box to the right, or if you want to search more than one folder, click Browse to select from a list. In the Select Folder(s) dialog box, turn on the check boxes next to the folders you want to search, and turn off the boxes next to the folders you don't want to search. Click OK.

4 Click the Advanced tab in the Advanced Find dialog box.

5 Click the Field button to display the list of fields.

6 Click Forms on the list.

9 Click Add to place the form in the Selected Forms box.

7 Select the forms library you want to use.

8 Click the form containing the field that you want to use in the search criteria.

10 Click Close.

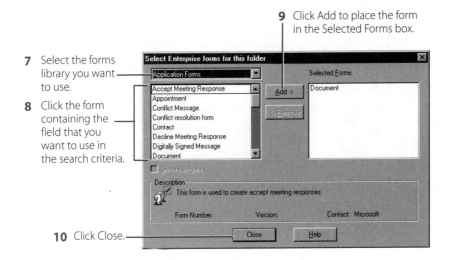

11 In the Advanced Find dialog box, click the Field button again to display the list, and point to the name of the form you selected. On the submenu, click the specific field you want to use in the search criteria. Outlook displays the name of the field in the box under the Field button.

> **◯ NOTE**
>
> The key to this search is targeting forms—either standard or custom—that have been created for use with a folder. For example, if you select Document as the form type in the Select Enterprise Forms For This Folder dialog box, many fields will be available in step 11. If you select Contact in that dialog box, no fields will be available in step 11 unless someone has created a custom form for the Contacts folder. This is because Outlook doesn't provide forms for the Contacts folder.

12 In the Condition box, you can select a condition to use with the field to set up a specific search criterion.

13 If the condition you select requires a value in order to make sense, Outlook activates the Value box, in which you can enter a value to complete the criterion.

14 Click the Add To List button.

15 To use additional fields from the selected form as search criteria, repeat steps 11 through 14.

16 Click the Find Now button to conduct the search with the new criteria.

What's a Forms Library?

A forms library is where Outlook stores published forms and where Outlook searches for the forms you select, as shown in the illustration opposite. If you have a custom form that you've designed and you want to share it with others, you publish it in one of the three types of forms libraries: a Personal Forms library, a Folder Forms library, or an Organizational Forms library.

Bending Folders to Your Will

> **NOTE**

When setting search criteria, if you select more than one search criterion, Outlook finds only the items that meet all the search criteria. However, if you use the same field to set multiple criteria, Outlook finds items that meet any one of the multiple criteria within that field.

Opening Documents or Starting Programs from Outlook

Because you can show any disk folder on the Outlook Bar and, more importantly, because you can display the Folder List, which can show all the folders on all the disks connected to your computer, it's relatively easy to open any document or start any program from within Outlook.

All you need to do is switch to the Other Shortcuts group on the Outlook Bar and open the folder that contains the document you want to open or the program you want to start. (If the folder does not have an icon on the Outlook Bar, display the Folder List, and click the icon for the folder there.) Then simply double-click the icon for the document or program file.

Forwarding Folder Items

> **SEE ALSO**
>
> You can also set up Outlook to automatically send new messages to another person or to any other folder, which is especially useful when you're out of the office. For details, see "Getting Help from Outlook Assistants," on page 44.

You can send any folder item in Outlook to someone else—you simply forward the item. Here's how to send a folder item to someone else:

1 Open the folder, and then select the folder item you want to send to someone else. (To select more than one item, hold down the Ctrl key as you click each item. To select several consecutive folder items, click the first item, and then hold down the Shift key while you click the last item. To select all the folder items, choose the Select All command from the Edit menu or press Ctrl+A.)

2 Choose the Forward command from the Actions menu. In e-mail folders you can also click the Forward button on the toolbar.

5 Click Send.

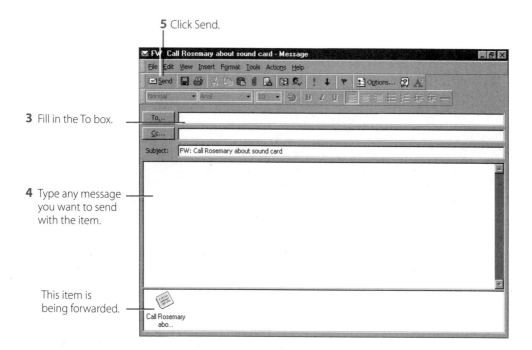

3 Fill in the To box.

4 Type any message you want to send with the item.

This item is being forwarded.

Removing Items from a Folder

Clutter, clutter, clutter! What a mess! You'll find that you receive many messages that you don't need and don't want to keep. Just as you can quickly dump unwanted postal deliveries in the recycling bin, you can dump folder items in the Deleted Items folder.

To delete a folder item, simply select the item in the folder window or open the item, and then click the Delete button on the Standard toolbar. As an alternative, you can move the folder item to the Deleted Items folder. (See "Moving a Folder Item," on page 463.)

Retrieving Deleted Items

How many times have you thrown something away by accident? If you delete an item from Outlook and then change your mind, you can easily recover it. Just move the item from the Deleted Items folder back to its original, or some other, location. (See "Moving a Folder Item," on page 463.) However, you must retrieve the folder item *before* you empty the Deleted Items folder. After you empty that folder, the folder item is gone for good. Your only recourse then is to have someone send you a copy of the folder item, restore it from a backup copy, or, as the final resort, recreate it.

Purging Deleted Items

When you are certain you no longer need the items you deleted, you can empty the Deleted Items folder. Just remember: deleting items from the Deleted Items folder wipes them out forever. Here are ways to remove items from the Deleted Items folder.

■ To completely empty the Deleted Items folder, choose the Empty "Deleted Items" Folder command from the Tools menu. When Outlook asks whether you want to permanently delete all the items and subfolders in this folder, click the Yes button.

■ When you want to purge only certain folder items and folders from the Deleted Items folder, open the Deleted Items folder, and select the items and folders you want to delete. Click the Delete button on the Standard toolbar, choose the Delete command from the File menu, or press Ctrl+D. When Outlook asks whether you want to permanently delete the selected items, click the Yes button.

 TIP

You can set up Outlook to automatically purge your Deleted Items folder when you quit an Outlook session. To do this, choose the Options command from the Tools menu, click the Other tab, turn on the Empty The Deleted Items Folder Upon Exiting option, and then click OK. From now on, when you quit Outlook, you'll see a message asking whether you want to empty the Deleted Items folder.

Viewing Files in the Other Group Folders

? SEE ALSO

For more information about folders in the Outlook Bar's Other Shortcuts group, see "Other Shortcuts Group," on page 28.

You can use the miscellaneous group of folders, labeled Other Short-cuts, on the Outlook Bar to view files and folders throughout your file system. The My Computer folder, for instance, displays the same icons you see in the My Computer window on your desktop. By clicking one of these icons, you can see a list of all the folders on a disk drive. The My Documents or Personal folders, which may also be part of the Other Shortcuts group, contains documents that you've saved with Microsoft Office applications. Outlook provides a number of options for viewing the files in these folders. Switch to a different view of the folder by pointing to Current View on the View menu, and then choosing the view you want from the submenu.

> NOTE

> If your installation of Outlook doesn't contain file system support, you will need to add it as an additional component.

? SEE ALSO

You can set up custom views for looking at your files; for information, see Chapter 21, "Setting Up Views." You can also group your files, specify sorting procedures, set up special filters, and add custom fields to file properties; for details, see Chapter 20, "Organizing Folder Items."

Icons view.   In this view, disk drives, folders, and files are displayed with an icon and their name. When you select Icons view, Outlook adds three buttons to the Standard toolbar: Large Icons, Small Icons, and List. Clicking one of these buttons varies Icons view, displaying either large or small icons or an icon list. You can also decide how to arrange the file icons in the window.

Details view.   This view provides more information about your files, similar to Details view in a My Computer or a Windows Explorer window. You see your files listed with columns for icons, filename, author, type, size, date and time of the last modification, and keywords.

By Author view.   In this view, your files are grouped by their author, making it easier to find files created by a specific person.

By File Type view.   In this view, files are grouped by their file type, making it easier to find files created by a specific program.

For details about changing the columns in Details view, see "Setting Up Columns," on page 554. You can group your files by some of the columns you set up in Details view; for specifics, see "Grouping," on page 563. For more information on arranging icons, see "Icons View" on page 455.

Document Timeline view.   In this view, your files are arranged on a timeline that shows the dates in a band across the top of the window. Document Timeline view resembles the Journal window.

Programs view.   This is the standard view you see the first time you look at the files in one of the folders in the Other group. Programs view is a filter that permits only program files (a file that starts an application, for example) and folders to appear in a files folder window.

Files shown in Details view are initially sorted alphabetically by filename. To arrange the files a different way in Details view, click the column heading for the column you want to use to rearrange the files. The first click sorts alphabetically, smallest to largest, or newest to oldest. A second click sorts reverse alphabetically, largest to smallest, or oldest to newest.

You can also change Document Timeline view in the following ways:

- Click the Day button on the Standard toolbar to see documents for a single date, listed by the time.

- Click the Week button on the Standard toolbar to see documents for a single week, listed by the day of the week.

- Click the Month button on the Standard toolbar to see documents for a month, listed by the date.

When you have files so far away from today's date that you can't scroll to them quickly in Document Timeline view, you can jump to a date in one of three ways:

- Click the down arrow beside the month name in the files folder window, and use the calendar that appears.

- Choose the Go To Date command from the Go menu. For details about how to use this command, see "Using the Go To Date Command," on page 309.

- Click the Go To Today button on the Standard toolbar, or choose the Go To Today command from the Go menu, to display the current date in the timeline.

CHAPTER 17

Printing Folder Items

Printing a copy of an item from a Microsoft Outlook 98 folder is a simple matter. If you want to use Outlook's standard print style, it's merely a question of selecting an item and clicking a toolbar button. But if the standard print style doesn't meet your needs, you can select a different print style—Outlook offers several built-in styles for various folders. You can also print a view of an entire folder rather than an individual item, and you can adjust the printing options for either items or views. And if you can't find a built-in print style that suits your purposes, you can modify one of the built-in styles or even create your own print style.

Printing with Outlook's Standard Style

For each Outlook folder—and for each view of that folder—Outlook has a default print style set up. To print folder items using that standard print style, follow these steps:

1 Select the folder item or items that you want to print. (To select more than one item, hold down the Ctrl key as you click each item. To select several consecutive items, click the first item and then hold down the Shift key while you click the last item you want to select. To select all the items in a folder, choose Select All from the Edit menu or press Ctrl+A.)

Print

2 Click the Print button on the Standard toolbar.

You can preview the printed copy before you actually print it. Select the folder item, and choose Print Preview from the File menu. See "Previewing Printing," on page 496.

Changing Printing Settings

If you're not pleased with the default print settings used when you click the Print button on the toolbar, you can change the settings before you print. To set print options, open the Print dialog box in one of the following ways:

- Choose the Print command from the File menu.

- Point to Page Setup on the File menu, and then choose a style (or define a new style and then choose it). Then click the Print button in the Page Setup dialog box.

- Choose the Print Preview command from the File menu, and then click the Print button on the Print Preview toolbar. (See "Previewing Printing," on page 496.)

Figure 17-1 shows the Print dialog box. Use this dialog box to set the following print options:

Printer Name.   If necessary, select a different printer.

Properties.   If necessary, click this button to adjust the printer setup.

Print To File.   Turn on this option to send the job to a file instead of the printer.

Print Style.   Select one of the available print styles, or click Define Styles to make your own.

Number Of Pages.   Select which pages to print (All, Even, or Odd).

Preview.   Click this button to see a preview of the printed page on your screen.

Number Of Copies.   Set the number of copies you want to print.

Collate Copies.   If you are printing multiple copies of more than one page, you can turn on this option to print complete sets of the job. If you turn this option off, printing may be faster, but all your page 1s will print first, then your page 2s, and so forth. You will have to manually collate them into sets.

Print Options.   Choose print options, or select a print range, if available.

FIGURE 17-1.

The Print dialog box.

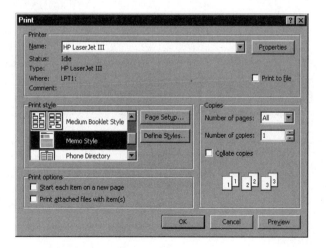

V

Bending Folders to Your Will

Choosing an Alternate Built-In Print Style

Outlook comes to you with certain print styles that are set up for each view in each folder, as listed in Table 17-1. The print styles available for the current folder and view appear in the Print dialog box and on the Page Setup submenu on the File menu.

TABLE 17-1. Outlook's Built-In Print Styles, by Folder and View

Folder	View	Print Style
Inbox	Message Timeline	Memo
	All other views	Table, Memo
Calendar	Day/Week/Month, Day/Week/Month with AutoPreview	Daily, Weekly, Monthly, Tri-Fold, Calendar Details, Memo
	All other views	Table, Memo
Contacts	Address Cards, Detailed Address Cards	Card, Small Booklet, Medium Booklet, Memo, Phone Directory
	Phone List, By Category, By Company, By Location, By Follow Up Flag	Table, Memo
Tasks	Task Timeline	Memo
	All other views	Table, Memo
Journal	By Type, By Contact, By Category	Memo
	Entry List, Last Seven Days, Phone Calls	Table, Memo
Notes	Icons	Memo
	All other views	Table, Memo

If you want to use another print style, follow these steps:

1 Open the folder that contains the folder items you want to print.

2 Use the Current View command on the View menu to change the view setting if necessary. If you want to print one or more individual folder items, select the item or items.

3 Choose the Print command from the File menu to open the Print dialog box.

4 Select the print style you want to use.

5 Click OK to print.

As an alternative, you can also point to Page Setup on the File menu, choose the style from the submenu that appears, and then click Print in the Page Setup dialog box. You'll learn more about using the Page Setup dialog box later in this chapter.

> **NOTE**

For views that you have created, you can use the built-in print styles that are available for other views of the same type. For example, if you create a new card view in the Contacts folder, the print styles are the same as those for Address Cards view.

As you can see in Table 17-1, Memo style, which lets you print one or more individual folder items, is available in all views. When you print an open Outlook item, Memo style is the only print style available. With other built-in print styles, you can print an entire view (as well as individual items, in some cases).

> **NOTE**

When a view is based on displaying a timeline or icons, you cannot print the entire view. In this case, Outlook offers only the Memo print style, and you can print only individual items.

Here's a brief description of what Outlook's built-in print styles do by default:

Memo. Prints one or more selected folder items in a standard memo format. For instance, a printout of an appointment on your calendar might look like this:

Subject:	Lunch with Mark
Start:	Tuesday 3/18/98 12:30 PM
End:	Tuesday 3/18/98 2:00 PM
Recurrence:	(none)

V

Bending Folders to Your Will

Table. Prints either selected folder items or an entire view. The information appears in a table arrangement with the items in rows with the same column headings that are shown in the current view.

Daily. Prints your calendar for the selected day, 7 AM to 7 PM, and includes the TaskPad and a Notes section.

Weekly. Prints your weekly calendar on one page. This style does not include the TaskPad or a Notes section.

Monthly. Prints your monthly calendar on one page. Like Weekly style, this style does not include the TaskPad or a Notes section.

Tri-Fold. Prints your daily calendar, weekly calendar, and TaskPad in three equal sections, using landscape orientation.

Calendar Details. Prints the currently displayed items in a list format.

Card. Prints either selected contact cards or an entire view of your Contacts folder. Contact cards appear in alphabetical order, marked by letter tabs, from top to bottom on the page in two columns. Outlook prints two blank cards at the end.

Small Booklet. Prints either selected contact cards or an entire view of your Contacts folder. This style is designed for printing on both sides of a sheet of paper, with eight pages per sheet. You can cut, fold, and assemble the pages to form a booklet.

Medium Booklet. Prints either selected contact cards or an entire view of your Contacts folder. This style is designed for printing on both sides of a sheet of paper, with four pages per sheet. You can cut, fold, and assemble the pages to form a booklet.

Phone Directory. Prints names and telephone numbers for all your contacts or for selected contacts. The list is in alphabetical order, marked by letter tabs. Other contact information is omitted.

Setting the Print Range or Options

The settings below the Print Style section of the Print dialog box may be labeled either Print Options or Print Range, based on the selected style. Table 17-2 lists the print styles and the options available for each style.

TABLE 17-2.   Print Range Options Available for Each Print Style

Print Style	Print Range Options	Description
Table	All Rows	Turn on this option to print all items in a folder view.
	Only Selected Rows	Turn on this option to print only the folder items you selected before opening the Print dialog box.
Phone Directory, Card, Small Booklet, Medium Booklet	All Items	Turn on this option to print all items in a folder view.
	Only Selected Items	Turn on this option to print only the folder items you selected before opening the Print dialog box.
Memo	Start Each Item On A New Page	Turn this option on to print each folder item on a separate page.
	Print Attached Files With Item(s)	Turn on this option to print the contents of attachments with the text of each folder item.
Daily, Weekly, Monthly, Tri-Fold, Calendar Details	Start	Select or type the earliest date of the items you want to print.
	End	Select or type the latest date of the items you want to print.

V

Bending Folders to Your Will

 TIP

Most of the time, you'll want to select All in the Number Of Pages box in the Print dialog box to print all the pages of folder items. But when you need to collate the pages in a special way, you can select Odd or Even to print only the odd-numbered or even-numbered pages. For information about printing odd-numbered and even-numbered pages to form a booklet, see the sidebar, "Printing and Assembling a Booklet," on the following page.

Printing and Assembling a Booklet

The booklet print styles are designed so that you can print pages on both sides of a sheet of paper and then cut and staple the pages to create a booklet. (In Outlook, *paper* refers to a physical sheet of paper. *Page* refers to the area of the paper that is actually printed.) The layout and page numbering for the booklet are arranged automatically by Outlook.

You can print a booklet on either a duplex printer (a printer that can print on both sides of the paper) or a printer that prints on only one side of the paper at a time. When using a duplex printer, be sure it is set up for duplex printing. Click the Properties button in the Print dialog box to open the Properties dialog box for your duplex printer. Select the Flip option you prefer. (Note that None is the default and is for one-sided printing only.) If you are using a printer that prints on only one side of the paper at a time, print odd-numbered pages first (by selecting Odd in the Number Of Pages box in the Print dialog box), load the paper in the printer again so that the blank side will be printed on, and then print the even-numbered pages. (Select Even in the Number Of Pages box.)

Before you start printing, click the Page Setup button, and then click the Paper tab. In the Page Size box, select 1/2 Sheet Booklet, 1/4 Sheet Booklet, or 1/8 Sheet Booklet. Click Print Preview to see how the pages will appear when printed. Click OK to start printing.

After the booklet's pages are printed, cut the paper into the number of sections you specified. For example, if you specified a 1/8 Sheet Booklet, cut the paper into four sections. Each section will show two pages (the odd numbered page on the left or right side and the even numbered page on the opposite side). Stack the sheets of paper in the order of the page numbering, and fold along a ruler or straight edge. You can then staple the sheets of paper together into a booklet.

Previewing Printing

Before you print an item or a view, you can preview it to see what it will look like on paper. Print Preview uses the settings for the currently selected print style in the Print and Page Setup dialog boxes.

To preview a selected item or a view before printing, take one of the following actions:

- Choose the Print Preview command from the File menu.

■ Point to Page Setup on the File menu, choose the print style you want to preview, and then click the Preview button in the Page Setup dialog box.

■ Choose the Print command from the File menu, and then click the Preview button in the Print dialog box.

Figure 17-2 shows a preview of several notes in the Memo print style and points out useful buttons on the Print Preview toolbar.

Print Preview displays the full page layout of the items to be printed, reducing the size of the folder item text in order to display an entire page on screen at one time. It's an extremely useful feature when you want to check how the various print styles look on the page, how columns line up, whether the print style needs adjustment, and so on.

If you don't like what you see in Print Preview, you can click the Page Setup button on the Print Preview toolbar to open the Page Setup dialog box. You can then adjust the current print style as explained in "Modifying a Print Style," on the next page, returning to Print Preview whenever you want to check the results of your changes. Or, if you decide to try a different print style, you can click the Print button either

FIGURE 17-2.

Notes in Print Preview, using the Memo print style.

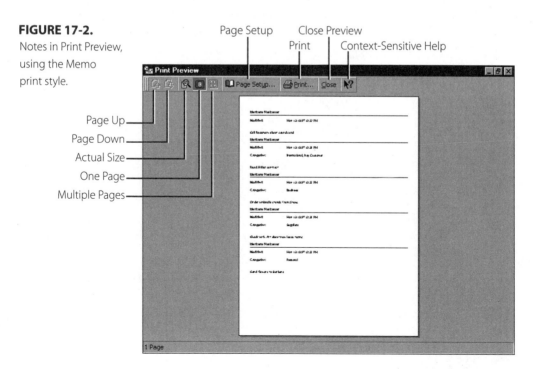

on the Print Preview toolbar or in the Page Setup dialog box to open the Print dialog box and select a new style.

If you need to see the text in actual size while you are in Print Preview, you can either click the Actual Size button on the Print Preview toolbar or click anywhere inside the page area. To switch the view back to full page, click again inside the page area.

When you're ready to print, click the Print button on the Print Preview toolbar, and then click OK in the Print dialog box.

Modifying a Print Style

⊗ CAUTION

If you decide to modify a built-in print style for all print jobs, the changes will affect that print style in all folders and views where you can use it. For example, if you change the Table style to print with a landscape orientation instead of portrait, all printing you do using this style will be in landscape. If you change a built-in print style, you can return it to its original settings—see "Resetting a Print Style," on page 506.

You can make a number of changes to a print style, including changes to its format, to its standard paper settings, and to the information included in headers or footers.

To change the print style, you have to open the Page Setup dialog box. You can do this using any of these techniques:

- Point to the Page Setup command on the File menu, and choose the print style you want to use from the submenu. (The submenu lists the available built-in styles as well as any print styles you have created that apply to the view—see "Creating a Print Style," on page 507.)

- Choose Print from the File menu, choose the print style you want to change, and then click the Page Setup button.

- Point to the Page Setup command on the File menu, and choose Define Styles. In the dialog box that appears, choose the style you want to change and then click the Edit button.

Now you can review and change any of the settings shown in the Page Setup dialog box (described in more detail in the next three sections) to customize the print style.

You can also use the Print Preview feature in this process. As you make your changes in the Page Setup dialog box, you can click the Print

Preview button at any time to see how your adjustments affect the printed page. If you're dissatisfied with the results, click the Page Setup button on the Print Preview toolbar to return to the Page Setup dialog box so that you can continue refining the print style.

When you're satisfied with what you see in Print Preview (and if you don't want to change another print style), click the Close button on the Print Preview toolbar to return to Outlook, or click the Print button on the same toolbar to open the Print dialog box, where you can begin printing as soon as you click OK.

Changing the Format

The Format tab of the Page Setup dialog box always provides a small preview picture of the print style as well as the three standard options indicated in Figure 17-3. (This figure shows the Format tab for the Table print style; the tab for the Memo style is very similar.) For all print styles, you can change the fonts used in headings and in the body of the folder items, and you have the option of printing with or without gray shading.

FIGURE 17-3.

The Format tab for the Table print style.

You can change the font for column headings (in Table style) or titles (in Memo style).

You can change the font for rows (in Table style) or fields (in Memo style).

Turn on this option to add gray shading; turn it off for faxing or if your printer doesn't print gray.

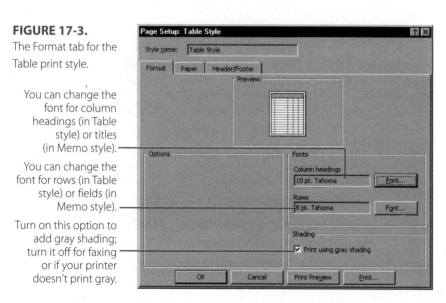

The Format tab for the Calendar Details print style is similar to the tab shown in Figure 17-3, except it also contains these options:

Start A New Page Each.   This option lets you choose to start a new page for each day, week, or month.

Print Attachments.   This option lets you choose whether to print attachments with the calendar item.

You can also change the format of the Daily, Weekly, Monthly, and Tri-Fold print styles, which are used to print calendar items. Again, you can use different fonts for date headings and for appointments, and you can print with or without gray shading. But you also have some additional layout options, as shown here for the Daily print style.

In the Layout box, you can tell Outlook to print the day's calendar on two pages rather than one, giving you more room to write in information about your appointments and meetings. You can specify the range of time to be printed for the day (in the Print From and Print To boxes), and you can choose to include or omit the TaskPad (which is lined) and the Notes section (which is lined or unlined).

The Format tabs for the Weekly and Monthly print styles are similar to that for the Daily print style, with the following variations:

- The Format tab for the Weekly print style offers the same options you find for the Daily print style. (In this case, of course, you choose whether to use one or two pages to print a week rather than a day.) In addition, this tab contains two Arrange options: click Top To Bottom to have Outlook arrange the seven days down two columns on the page (omitting hour markers), or click Left To Right to have Outlook set up seven columns across the page, one for each day, including hour markers. (If you choose Top To Bottom, Outlook turns off the Print From and Print To boxes—there's no need to specify a range of hours when the hour markers are omitted.)

- The Format tab for the Monthly print style provides the Layout option (which prints a month on one page or two) and the Include options (which print the TaskPad and the Notes section) but omits the Arrange options and the Print From and Print To boxes.

The Format tab for the Tri-Fold print style is a little different. It contains only three options: Left Section, Middle Section, and Right Section. For each section (fold) of a tri-fold printing, you can specify one of the following items to print in that section:

- Daily calendar

- Weekly calendar

- Monthly calendar

- TaskPad

- Notes (blank)

- Notes (lined)

The Format tabs for the Card, Small Booklet, and Medium Booklet print styles, used for printing contact items, are identical, and they contain the options shown here:

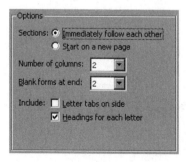

The Sections options on this tab refer to the alphabetical sections of your contact list. You can print alphabetical sections one after another in continuous columns, or you can begin the entries for each letter of the alphabet on a new page. You can also specify the number of columns per page, and you can tell Outlook to include blank contact cards (forms) at the end of the printing—these are useful if you need to hand-write contact information to be entered into your contact list in Outlook later. In addition, you can include or omit headings for each alphabetical section as well as letter tabs on the side of the page. When you include letter tabs, they appear on the right-hand side of the page in a shaded column, as shown in Figure 17-4.

FIGURE 17-4.

A page of contact information, previewed using the Card print style with letter tabs on the side.

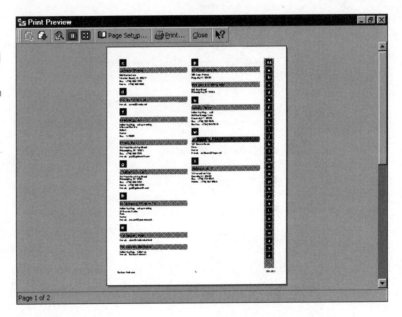

Finally, the Format tab for the Phone Directory print style is fairly simple. You can specify the number of columns to print, and you can include or omit headings for each alphabetical section and letter tabs on the side of the page.

Changing Paper Settings

The various print styles have their own paper settings—paper size (or type), page size, orientation, paper source (the tray(s) in your printer), and margins. You can adjust these settings on the Paper tab of the Page

Setup dialog box, shown in Figure 17-5. The Paper tab displays the same information for all print styles.

When printing Outlook items and views, it's important to understand how Outlook distinguishes between paper and page. In Outlook, paper and paper type refer to the physical sheet of paper you put in the printer. Page refers to the area of that sheet of paper that each formatted Outlook "page" will be printed on. You can print several of these *pages* on a single sheet of *paper*. For example, in the Small Booklet print style, you can select 1/8 sheet booklet and print eight pages of a booklet on a single sheet of paper.

Each print style uses a default paper type and page size. You can modify the paper type and page size for a print style on the Paper tab of the Page Setup dialog box. When you select a paper type, the list of page sizes available for use with that paper type is displayed in the Page Size list. Settings for paper type and page size in the Page Setup dialog box take precedence over any paper settings you select in the Properties dialog box for your printer (which you open by clicking the Properties button in the Print dialog box). Settings you make in the Orientation area of the Paper tab apply to pages, not to paper type.

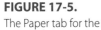

Bending Folders to Your Will

FIGURE 17-5.
The Paper tab for the Memo print style.

Set the area each formatted Outlook page will occupy on each sheet of paper from your printer.

Select the size of paper used in your printer.

If the paper isn't listed above, enter its dimensions here.

Select the appropriate paper feed for your printer.

Set the margins here.

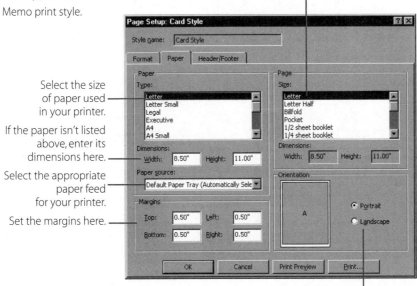

Set the page orientation here.

Let's say you want to use the Daily print style to print four days' worth of calendar items. By default, Outlook prints the items for each day on a separate sheet of 8½ × 11-inch paper. If you want to have all four days appear on one sheet of paper, select ¼ sheet booklet from the Size list on the Paper tab.

Setting a Custom Paper Size

You can set up any custom paper size you want. To specify a custom paper size, simply select Custom in the Paper Type list, and then set the width and height of the paper in the Dimensions boxes in the Paper Type section.

> If you change the width or height of a listed paper type in the Dimensions boxes, Outlook automatically selects Custom in the Paper Type list.

When you set up a custom paper size, the Page Size list includes the appropriate page size choices for that paper size. Outlook also adds Custom and Custom Half as the first two items in the Page Size list.

Setting Margins

When you change the margin settings, you're changing the width and height of the blank space at the borders of the paper. Keep margins small unless you like lots of blank space around the printed information. The larger the margins, the more cramped the information appears because it must fit into a smaller space. You'll often need to print on more sheets of paper if you use large margins.

Outlook's default margins are .50 inch for the top, bottom, left, and right borders of the paper. You can click the Print Preview button in the Page Setup dialog box to see the effect of changes you make to the margins.

Setting Up Headers and Footers

The process of setting up headers and footers is the same for all print styles. The Header/Footer tab of the Page Setup dialog box provides six boxes in which you can insert the text and fields that you want Outlook to print in headers and footers, as shown in Figure 17-6. For some

FIGURE 17-6.

The Header/Footer tab of the Page Setup dialog box.

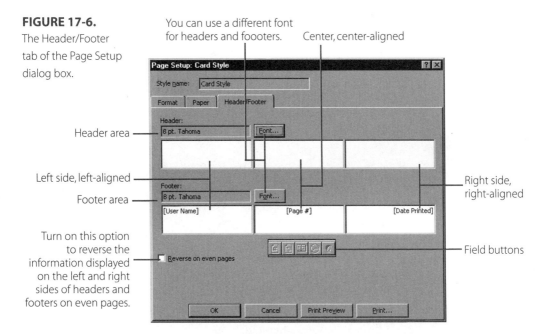

You can use a different font for headers and foooters.

Center, center-aligned

Header area

Left side, left-aligned

Footer area

Right side, right-aligned

Turn on this option to reverse the information displayed on the left and right sides of headers and footers on even pages.

Field buttons

print styles, Outlook presets parts of the header or footer, but you can change any section of the header or footer as you like.

You can use text only, fields only, or a combination of text and fields in your headers and footers. The header and footer boxes (left, center, and right) correspond to the location on the page—if you enter text only in the center header box, for instance, Outlook prints a centered header on each page. For the footer set up in Figure 17-6, Outlook will print the user's name on the left, the page number in the center, and the date of printing on the right.

> **NOTE**

The term "field" refers to a location that shows data or to an empty box that you (or Outlook) can fill in with information.

To insert a field into a header or footer, click in the boxes where you want to insert a field, then click one of the Field buttons on the Header/Footer tab.

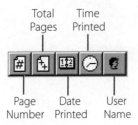

Total Pages
Time Printed

Page Number
Date Printed
User Name

Outlook displays an inserted field as words inside square brackets: *[Page #]*, for example. (You can type the field in the header or footer box instead of clicking a button if you type it in this format.) During printing, Outlook replaces the field with the proper information—the page number, the date of printing, and so on.

You can type any text in any of the header and footer areas. The text might be some special information about the printed items, such as the date range of appointments, meetings, or tasks. You might want to type the word *Page* before the Page Number field. Or you might type the word *of* between a Page Number field and a Total Pages field and then type the word *pages* after the Total Pages field—this way, on each page Outlook prints a header or footer such as *5 of 10 pages*.

If you want the same headers and footers to print on every page, leave the Reverse On Even Pages option turned off. But if you're printing on both sides of the paper or if you're going to photocopy single-sided printed pages back to back to assemble a booklet, you might want to have Outlook always print the text in the left-most area of the header or footer on the outside of all pages. This would, for instance, allow page numbers to appear on the outside edge of each of two facing pages (both odd and even pages). In this case, turn on the Reverse On Even Pages option.

Resetting a Print Style

After you make changes to a built-in print style, you might want to restore the original settings. To reset a built-in print style, take these steps:

1 Point to Page Setup on the File menu, and choose Define Print Styles from the submenu.

2 Select the print style you want to reset.

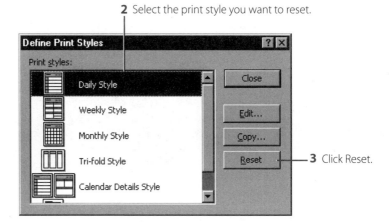

3 Click Reset.

4 When Outlook asks you to confirm resetting the print style, click OK.

5 Repeat steps 2 through 4 for each built-in style you want to reset.

6 When you've finished, click the Close button in the Define Print Styles dialog box.

> **NOTE**
>
> You can't reset a print style that you have created. You can only modify it or delete it.

Creating a Print Style

What if you want to modify a print style but only want it to apply to certain print jobs? Rather than changing a built-in print style, which will affect the printing of all folder items for which you use the style, you can create a print style of your own. You create a print style by first making a copy of a built-in print style (or a copy of a print style you've already created). This method gives you some advantages. First, you start from an existing batch of settings, which means that you need to modify only the specific settings that you want to change rather than having to set all the options yourself. Second, in any instance in which the print style you copied applies, your custom style also appears on the Page Setup submenu (after you exit and restart Outlook) and in the

Print dialog box for easy selection. You don't have to recreate your special print style for every view or folder.

Here's how to create a print style.

1 Point to Page Setup on the File menu, and choose Define Print Styles from the submenu. As an alternative, you can choose the Print command from the File menu, select the print style in the Print Style list, and then click the Define Styles button.

2 In the Define Print Styles dialog box, select the print style you want to copy.

3 Click Copy.

4 Type a name for the new print style.

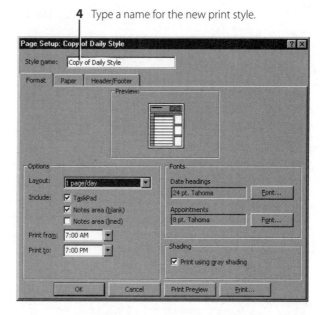

5 Change any settings on any (or all) of the three tabs in the Page Setup dialog box. (For details, see "Changing the Format," on page 499; "Changing Paper Settings," on page 502; and "Setting Up Headers and Footers," on page 504.)

6 Click OK in the Page Setup dialog box.

7 Click the Close button in the Define Print Styles dialog box.

TIP

You can also use the Print Preview feature in this process. As you make your changes (step 5), you can click the Print Preview button at any time to see how your style will appear on the printed page. If you're dissatisfied with the results, click the Page Setup button on the Print Preview toolbar to return to the Page Setup dialog box and continue creating the print style.

Deleting a Print Style You Created

If you no longer want or need a print style that you created, you can delete it. To do so, take these steps:

1   Point to Page Setup on the File menu, and choose Define Print Styles from the submenu. As an alternative, you can choose the Print command from the File menu, select the print style in the Print Style list, and then click the Define Styles button.

2   In the Define Print Styles dialog box, select the print style you want to delete, and then click the Delete button.

3   When Outlook asks you to confirm that you want to delete the print style, click OK. Repeat steps 2 and 3 for each custom style that you want to delete.

4   When you've finished, click the Close button in the Define Print Styles dialog box.

V

Bending Folders to Your Will

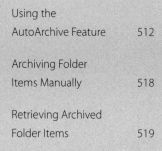

CHAPTER 18

Archiving Folder Items

As you use Microsoft Outlook 98, your folders can eventually become cluttered with items that you no longer need on a day-to-day basis—tasks that were long since completed, e-mail messages about a project that has been canceled, appointments from the past, and so on. You can, of course, simply delete these folder items if you're sure that you'll never need them again. But if the items might be important in the future—perhaps that canceled project comes back to life, for instance—you can put them into storage.

Outlook lets you transfer old items to an archive (storage) file on your hard disk. Outlook removes the items from your current folders, reducing the number of folder items so that the folders are easier to use. If you need the archived items in the future, you can retrieve them from the archive file.

You can archive folder items in two ways:

- Allow Outlook's AutoArchive feature to automatically archive folder items of specified ages on a regular basis.

- Manually archive folder items yourself as the need arises.

 **NOTE**

When you archive Outlook folder items, your existing folder structure is maintained in the archive file. For example, if you choose to archive the items in a subfolder, the main folder is also created in the archive file, but the items in the main folder are not necessarily archived. By doing this, Outlook creates the same folder structure in your archive file as in your mailbox. Even if folder contents are emptied during archiving, Outlook leaves the folders in place. To remove an empty folder, right-click the folder name in the Folder List, and choose Delete from the shortcut menu.

Using the AutoArchive Feature

Outlook is initially set up to automatically archive old items in certain folders every 14 days. Outlook lets you know when it's preparing to run the AutoArchive feature and gives you a chance to cancel it. Every 14 days when you start Outlook, you'll see the following prompt shortly after startup:

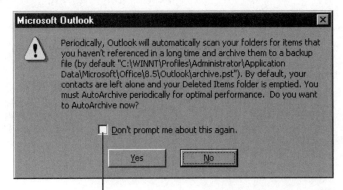

Turn on this option to archive in the future without being prompted.

You can vary the 14-day time span, and you can specify additional folders to be archived. You can also change the definition of an "old" (expired) item, and you can use AutoArchive for both archiving and deleting. To set up automatic archiving the way you like, you first need to review or adjust the AutoArchive settings on the Other tab of the Options dialog box. Then you need to set the AutoArchive properties for each folder that you want Outlook to archive automatically.

> As AutoArchive is running, you'll see an animated icon on the right of the status bar. Right-click the icon if you want to see details of the archiving process or to cancel archiving.

Setting General AutoArchive Options

As you might recall from Chapter 3, "Setting Outlook Options," the Options dialog box contains tabs whose settings govern Outlook's default behavior in various areas. To review or change Outlook's default AutoArchive settings, choose the Options command from the Tools menu, select the Other tab, and then click the AutoArchive button to display the dialog box shown in Figure 18-1.

> AutoArchive runs only when you start up Outlook. If you want to run automatic archiving in the middle of an Outlook session, change the number of days in the AutoArchive Every [ ] Days At Startup option to 1, choose the Exit And Log Off command from the File menu, and then restart Outlook.

FIGURE 18-1.
The AutoArchive dialog box.

Turn off this option if you don't want to see a prompt before automatic archiving begins.

Turn off this option to prevent deletion of expired items from e-mail folders.

Type a different archive filename, if wanted, or click Browse to locate another archive file.

Turn off this option to prevent all automatic archiving.

Enter a number from 1 to 60 to specify how often AutoArchive will run.

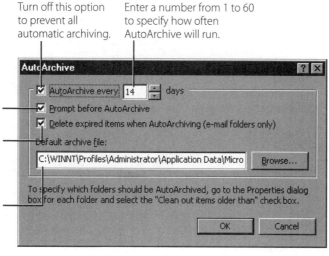

When the option called Delete Expired Items When AutoArchiving is turned on, Outlook moves expired e-mail messages to the Deleted Items folder rather than adding them to the archive file. Turn off this option to prevent deletion of the items. Also, when AutoArchive runs, items in the Deleted Items folder are not moved to the archive file. Instead they are deleted.

Outlook's default archive file is named ARCHIVE.PST. The .PST file-name extension indicates a personal folders file, which Outlook uses for archiving. You can create more than one archive file. For example, you could create a separate archive file for each of your folders, and you can manually select and archive groups of items related to a particular project.

> The location of the ARCHIVE.PST file depends on how your system is set up. Make a note of the location shown in the AutoArchive dialog box for future reference.

> The settings in the AutoArchive dialog box affect both automatic archiving and manual archiving (explained in "Archiving Folder Items Manually," on page 518).

Setting a Folder's AutoArchive Properties

Once AutoArchive is turned on and the settings adjusted (if necessary) on the AutoArchive tab of the Options dialog box, you need to specify which folders Outlook should automatically archive. By default, the AutoArchive feature is turned on for the Calendar, Journal, Tasks, Sent Items, and Deleted Items folders. To turn on automatic archiving for the Inbox folder, the Notes folder, or any folder that you have created (or to turn it off for the default folders), you need to change the folder's properties, as explained below.

1 Right-click the folder icon on the Outlook Bar, and choose Properties from the shortcut menu. (If the folder icon does not appear on the Outlook Bar, choose the Folder List command from the

View menu, right-click the folder in the Folder List, and choose Properties from the shortcut menu.)

2 In the Properties dialog box, click the AutoArchive tab.

3 Turn on this option to archive this folder.

5 Click here to move expired folder items to the archive file, or …

…click here to permanently delete expired folder items.

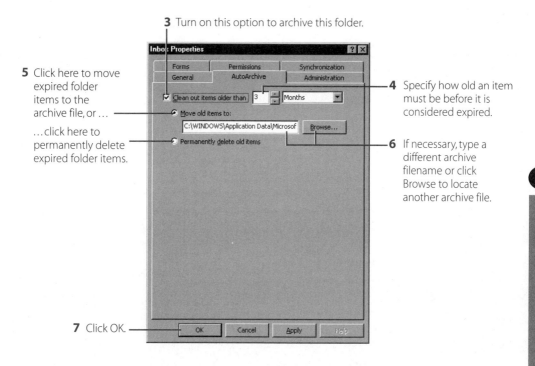

4 Specify how old an item must be before it is considered expired.

6 If necessary, type a different archive filename or click Browse to locate another archive file.

7 Click OK.

Archiving vs. Exporting Outlook Folder Items

When thinking about archiving Outlook folder items, it's helpful to keep in mind some differences between archiving items and exporting items. You can only archive Outlook items by using a personal folder file (a file with a .PST extension), but you can export Outlook items to many file types, such as text. Although Outlook can archive all types of Outlook items, Outlook archives only files (such as an attached Microsoft Excel spreadsheet or Microsoft Word document) that are stored in an e-mail folder. A file that is not stored in an e-mail folder cannot be archived. When you archive, the original items are copied to the archive file and then removed from the folder that is currently open. When you export, the original items are copied to the export file but are not removed from the current folder.

You'll need to repeat this procedure for each folder that you want to set up for automatic archiving. The AutoArchive choices you select for a folder take effect the next time Outlook automatically archives the folder's items or when you manually archive them.

For each folder, you can choose whether the AutoArchive feature should move expired items to the archive file or should permanently delete them. Choosing the Permanently Delete Old Items option means that expired items are permanently removed. They are not moved to the Deleted Items folder, from which you could retrieve them.

Also, for each folder, you can use the Clean Out Items Older Than option to define the number of days, weeks, or months that Outlook should use to consider an item expired. If you enter 60 days, for example, Outlook will consider items expired as follows:

- An e-mail message will expire 60 days after the date it was sent, received, or last modified.

- An appointment or meeting will expire 60 days after the date of the appointment or meeting or 60 days after the date the item was created or last modified.

- A task will expire 60 days after the date it was marked completed or 60 days after the date it was created or last modified.

- A note will expire 60 days after the date it was created or last modified.

- A journal entry will expire 60 days after the date it was created or last modified.

Outlook does not archive items from the Contacts folder. Task items from the Tasks folder (both your own tasks and tasks that you have assigned to someone else) are not archived unless they have been marked completed.

Preventing the Automatic Archiving of a Folder Item

Somewhere, in at least one Outlook folder, you're likely to have an item that you don't want Outlook to archive automatically. Maybe it's an item that you want to keep as a reminder. Or perhaps you've set up AutoArchive to permanently delete expired items from the folder, but you don't want to lose this one particular item. In such cases, you can designate the item as "Do Not AutoArchive."

To prevent a single folder item from being automatically archived (or deleted by AutoArchive), take these steps:

1 Open the item.

2 Choose the Properties command from the File menu, and click the General tab in the Properties dialog box. The dialog box you see will depend on the type of item you opened.

The item title appears in these locations.

3 Turn on this option to exclude the item from AutoArchiving.

4 Click OK.

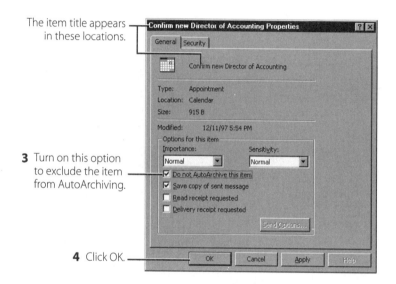

You must repeat this procedure for each folder item that you want to designate as "Do Not AutoArchive." If a folder contains a number of items that you do not want to archive automatically, consider turning off AutoArchive for that *folder* and then archive the other individual items manually.

 NOTE

You can manually archive a folder item that you've designated as "Do Not AutoArchive." This designation simply prevents AutoArchive from taking any automatic action with the folder item.

V

Bending Folders to Your Will

Archiving Folder Items Manually

Even though you set up AutoArchive to archive folder items on a regular basis, you still might want to manually archive items from time to time. Perhaps you've finished a project and want to archive the related items sooner than the next scheduled AutoArchive. Maybe you've turned off AutoArchive for a certain folder but nevertheless want to archive a few items from that folder. Or maybe you're finally ready to archive an item that has previously been designated "Do Not AutoArchive."

To manually archive folder items, follow these steps:

1   Choose the Archive command from the File menu to open the Archive dialog box.

2   If you select the first option in the dialog box, Archive All Folders According To Their AutoArchive Settings, the rest of the options become unavailable and you should move to step 7.

    If you select the second option, Archive This Folder And All Subfolders, proceed to step 3.

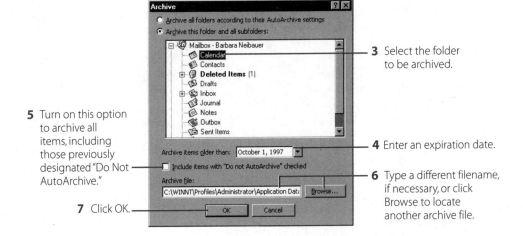

3 Select the folder to be archived.

5 Turn on this option to archive all items, including those previously designated "Do Not AutoArchive."

7 Click OK.

4 Enter an expiration date.

6 Type a different filename, if necessary, or click Browse to locate another archive file.

You must repeat this procedure for each folder that you want to archive manually.

TIP

> To type a date in the Archive Items Older Than box, you can use any standard
> date format: 10-13-97, 10/13/97, Oct-13-97, October 13, 1997, and so on. Alternatively, you can click the down arrow beside the date to display a calendar from
> which you can select the date.

Retrieving Archived Folder Items

The main reason you archive your old items rather than delete them is
so you can retrieve them later if you need to. You can retrieve items
from an archive file either by opening the archive file, by adding the
archive file to your user profile, or by importing the archive file.

To open the archive file (or any file with the .pst extension) point to
Open on the File menu, choose Personal Folders File, and then select
the archive file in the dialog box that appears. You'll probably have to
navigate to the folder containing the file.

To add the archive file to your user profile, you add it as a personal
folders file. In this way, the archive file is attached to your mailbox and
remains a separate file that contains all the archived items.

To add the archive file to your user profile, follow these steps:

1 Choose the Services command from the Tools menu.

2 On the Services tab, click the Add button.

3 In the Add Service To Profile dialog box, select Personal Folders
from the Available Information Services box and click OK.

4 In the Create/Open Personal Folders File dialog box, locate the
archive file you want to add, and then click Open.

5 In the Personal Folders dialog box, name the file. You might want
to give the file a name such as Archived Items or name it after a
particular project.

6 Click OK in the Personal Folders dialog box, and then click OK in
the Services dialog box.

You now have access to the items in the archive file—just display the Folder List and open the folder you need.

To retrieve items from an archive file by importing the file, choose Import And Export from the File menu to start the Import And Export Wizard. In the wizard's first panel, select Import From Another Program or File, and then click the Next button. In the next wizard panel, select Personal Folder File (.pst), and then click the Next button. From there, you can follow the instructions in the Import And Export Wizard. Outlook moves the archived items back into your mailbox.

Managing Folders

Folders are an important and integral part of Microsoft Outlook 98. Outlook stores all items in folders, and it can display the folders and files on any disk that's connected to your computer.

Chapter 16 described how to manage the contents of folders. But to make Outlook work more effectively and efficiently, you also need to be able to manage the folders themselves. That's what this chapter describes.

Opening a Folder

Outlook gives you several ways to open a folder. As you know, icons for most Outlook folders appear in one of the three groups on the Outlook Bar, so opening a folder from the Outlook Bar is usually quick and convenient. You click the group label that contains the folder you want to open, and then you click the folder icon. If necessary, click the small up or down arrow on the Outlook Bar to scroll to the folder you want. In addition to the Outlook Bar, you can use the Folder List and the Go menu to open folders.

Opening a Folder from the Folder List

If you need to use a folder that's not listed on the Outlook Bar, you can open the folder from the Folder List. You can display the Folder List just long enough to select the folder or you can keep the Folder list displayed on the screen.

To temporarily display the Folder List in order to open a folder, follow these steps:

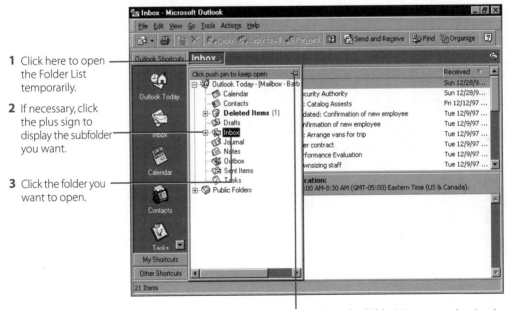

1 Click here to open the Folder List temporarily.

2 If necessary, click the plus sign to display the subfolder you want.

3 Click the folder you want to open.

Click here to keep the Folder List open and resize the right pane so folder items are not partially obscured.

When you select a folder, the Folder List closes. To keep the folder list open, click on the push pin icon when the list appears, or open the Folder List by choosing the Folder List command from the View menu.

> If you open a folder from the Other Shortcut group that is a shortcut to a folder on your computer, the Folder List displays file folders instead of Outlook folders. This list looks just like the lists you see in the My Computer window or the Windows Explorer window.

Opening a Folder from the Go Menu

The Go menu contains a list of the Outlook Today, Inbox, Drafts, Calendar, Contacts, and Tasks folders, as well as four commands for opening folders: Back, Forward, Up One Level, and Go To Folder. To open a folder listed on the Go menu, click the folder name on the menu. To open a folder that is not listed on the Go menu, do the following:

1 Choose the Go To Folder command from the Go menu.

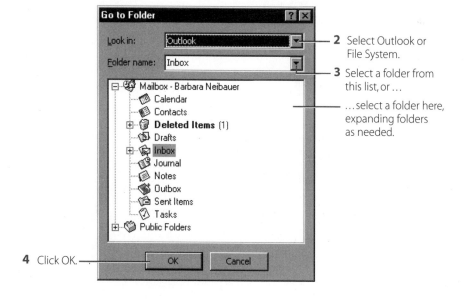

2 Select Outlook or File System.

3 Select a folder from this list, or …

…select a folder here, expanding folders as needed.

4 Click OK.

You can also open folders using three commands on the Go menu. The Back command and the Forward command become available once you've viewed at least two folders in your current Outlook session. These commands let you move backward and forward through folders in the order that you initially selected them. The Up One Level command opens the "parent" folder that contains your currently open folder. If you choose this command from the highest-level folder, Outlook displays a message telling you that there are no folders above the current one.

Opening a Folder in a Separate Window

If you want to see the contents of two folders at the same time, you can open the second folder in a separate window. This arrangement can be convenient for quickly switching from one folder to another.

To open a folder in a separate window, right-click the folder, either on the Outlook Bar or in the Folder List. Then choose Open In New Window from the shortcut menu.

Outlook displays a new Outlook window with the selected folder open. You can set up this Outlook window in all the same ways you set up the first Outlook window. Having separate windows also gives you the opportunity to set up each window differently.

Creating a Folder

Creating a new folder is a pretty simple task. You can add a new folder inside any existing folder or subfolder.

To create a new folder, follow these steps:

1 Point to the Folder command on the File menu, and then choose New Folder from the submenu.

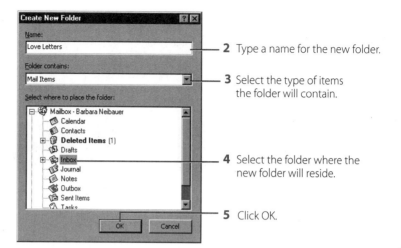

2 Type a name for the new folder.

3 Select the type of items the folder will contain.

4 Select the folder where the new folder will reside.

5 Click OK.

V

Bending Folders to Your Will

 TIP

Most of the folder management commands on the Folder submenu can also be accessed from the Folder List. Right-click the folder, and then choose a command from the shortcut menu that appears.

Copying a Folder

If you have a folder that might prove to be useful in more than one location, you can copy it as a subfolder of another folder (rather than move it). For example, you might copy a server folder to your personal folders. You can even copy a folder to a new folder you create during copying.

Here's the way to copy a folder into another folder:

1 Open the folder you want to copy.

2 Point to the Folder command on the File menu, and then choose Copy from the submenu. Alternatively, you can right-click the folder in the Folder List (not in the Outlook Bar), and then choose Copy from the shortcut menu.

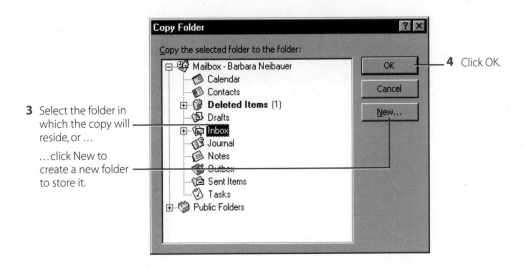

3 Select the folder in which the copy will reside, or...

...click New to create a new folder to store it.

4 Click OK.

For a faster way to copy a folder, display the Folder List, and then hold down the Ctrl key while you drag the folder being copied to the folder in which the copy will reside.

Copying a Folder Design

You can sometimes put a lot of effort into designing a folder—setting up views, grouping items, adding filters, sorting, designing forms, and granting permissions. After you set up the design of a folder, you might realize that another Outlook folder could benefit from having the same, or a very similar, design. Fortunately, rather than going through a laborious setup for each folder, you can simply copy a folder design from one folder to another. Follow these steps:

1 Open the Folder List, and select the folder to which you will be copying the design of another folder.

2 Point to Folder on the File menu, and then choose Copy Folder Design from the submenu.

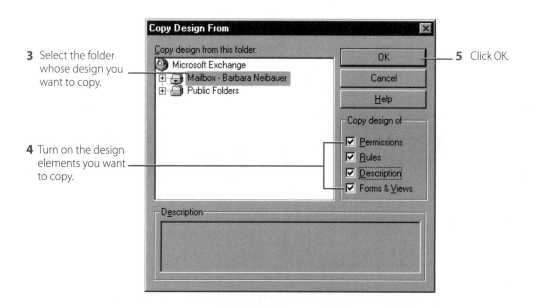

3 Select the folder whose design you want to copy.

4 Turn on the design elements you want to copy.

5 Click OK.

After you copy a folder design, you can adjust it to suit your needs. For information about folder design, see Chapter 20, "Organizing Folder Items."

Moving a Folder

Sometimes you may want to move a folder to another location rather than copy it. You can move a folder into another folder in several ways. The easiest way is by dragging. Simply display the Folder List and expand it as needed so that both folders are visible. Then drag the folder you want to move to the folder where it will be stored (the destination folder).

> You can move only the folders that you have created. You can't move the standard (built-in) Outlook folders, or server folders. Unless you have permission from the system administrator, Microsoft Exchange won't let you move a folder to the Public Folders folder.

Alternatively, instead of dragging the folder, you can point to Folder on the File menu and then choose Move from the submenu. Or you can right-click the folder in the Folder List and then choose Move from the shortcut menu. Either action displays the Move Folder dialog box. This is similar to the Copy Folder dialog box shown on page 526. Select an existing destination folder or click the New button to create a new folder to contain the one you're moving. Click OK to finish the move.

Renaming a Folder

If you didn't get the name right when you created a folder, you can change it. To rename a folder that you created, follow these steps:

1 Open the folder you want to rename.

2 Point to Folder on the File menu, and then choose Rename from the submenu. (The Rename command shows the name of the open folder.) If the Folder List is not displayed, you'll see the Rename dialog box.

3 In the Rename dialog box, type the new folder name.

4 Click OK.

If you choose the Rename command while the Folder List is displayed, Outlook highlights the folder name in the Folder List, allowing you to rename the folder simply by typing the new name and pressing the Enter key.

 NOTE

You can rename only the folders that you have created. You can't rename the standard Outlook folders (although you can rename the shortcuts to these folders—the folder icons—on the Outlook Bar). Renaming a folder does not change the name of the corresponding folder icon on the Outlook Bar. To change the name of a folder icon on the Outlook Bar (whether the icon represents a standard Outlook folder or a folder that you created and renamed), see "Renaming a Folder Icon on the Outlook Bar," on page 32.

Removing a Folder

When you delete a folder, Outlook moves the folder and its contents to the Deleted Items folder. From there, you can retrieve the folder and its contents if you change your mind, or you can permanently delete them. To retrieve (undelete) a folder, move it to some other folder. To completely delete folders and their contents from Outlook, you must delete them from the Deleted Items folder—see "Purging Deleted Items," on page 486.

Outlook gives you a number of ways to delete a folder:

- Select the folder in the Folder List, and then click the Delete button on the Standard toolbar, or press the Delete key.

- Right-click the folder, and then choose Delete from the shortcut menu.

- Select the folder in the Folder List, point to Folder on the File menu, and then choose Delete from the submenu.

- Drag the folder to the Deleted Items folder.

NOTE

You can delete only the folders that you have created. You can't delete the standard Outlook folders. If the folder you delete has an icon on the Outlook Bar, deleting the folder does not remove the corresponding folder icon from the Outlook Bar. To remove the folder icon from the Outlook Bar, see the directions in "Removing a Folder Icon from the Outlook Bar," on page 32.

Working with Public Folders

A public folder is similar to other Outlook folders or disk folders, in that it can contain any type of folder item—a message, an appointment, a contact, a task, a journal entry, a note, a posting, a file, or a form. The purpose of public folders is to allow wide access to folder items that are interesting to everyone in an organization or to a particular group within an organization—for example, a project team or a specific department. Public folders can also be used to organize information by subject matter, which gives people interested in the subject a handy place to browse.

In most public folders, you can read items and add your own items, but you cannot delete items other than those you added. Some public folders are even more restricted—you might be able to see and read the items but be unable to add any items to the folder. In very restricted cases, the public folder is not available to you at all. The difference has to do with permissions. (See the sidebar "Do You Have Permission?" on the next page.) To open a public folder and read its folder items, you must have permission to read items. To add items to a public folder, you must have permission to create items. In most cases, such permission is granted to anyone who has access to the public folder.

Opening Public Folders

Public folders are those contained in the folder labeled Public Folders on your e-mail server, so to view the list of public folders, you must be connected directly to the server. You can't view public folders while you're offline unless you set up public folder favorites and set the shortcuts for working offline. (See "Using Public Folder Favorites," on page 532.)

To open a public folder, take these steps:

1 Click the Other Shortcuts label on the Outlook Bar.

2 Click the Public Folders icon.

3 Choose the Folder List command from the View menu, if the Folder List is not already displayed.

4 In the Folder List, expand the list of subfolders by clicking the plus sign beside Public Folders. The first level of public folders contains only two folders: Favorites and All Public Folders.

5 To see the list of public folders, click the plus sign next to All Public Folders.

Do You Have Permission?

Restrictions can be set on who can access or modify the contents of public folders. Some public folders are open and available to all Outlook users on your system. Other public folders are limited to people who have a special affiliation with the folder, such as a project team. Still other folders might be available by subscription—that is, you sign up with the group whose conversations are kept in the public folder, much like a newsgroup. And you might even be barred from seeing certain other public folders.

In general, if you can open the folder, you'll be able to read its contents. If you are restricted from performing certain functions in a folder, Outlook informs you if you attempt a restricted operation. If you don't have permission to post an item to a folder, you'll see an error message when you try to post the item, or the commands you need to post a message will be unavailable. If you don't have permission to move or delete a folder or its contents, you'll see a message when you try.

You can check your permissions in the public folder's Properties dialog box. To display this dialog box, right-click the folder in the Folder list and choose Properties from the shortcut menu, or click the folder and point to Folder on the File menu and then choose Properties from the submenu. Review your permissions on the Summary tab or Permissions tab, whichever tab the Properties dialog box displays for that folder.

After you review the level of your permissions, you can discuss any changes you want to make with the folder contact listed on the Summary tab in the Properties dialog box. You may be able to change permissions yourself for some public folders, if you have a Permissions tab available. For more information about folder permissions, see "Permissions Tab," on page 543.

V

Bending Folders to Your Will

Each folder can contain folder items and subfolders. You'll know that a folder has subfolders if you see a plus sign next to its name in the Folder List. To see the subfolders, click the plus sign. Click any additional plus signs to expand the subfolders.

You treat items in public folders the same way you treat mail messages, except that you probably won't be able to delete or move the folder items—unless you have administrative privileges, unless you are the owner of the folder, or unless you put the item in the folder yourself. You can, however, copy a folder item to your Outlook folders and disk folders, and you can save any folder item as a file on a disk.

Using Public Folder Favorites

Public folders can contain a wide variety of information about topics that fit within a general category. To help you make some sense of it all, your server administrator is likely to also set up several levels of subfolders.

For example, if your e-mail system includes a public folder for Internet newsgroups, the folder probably contains a subfolder for each newsgroup area. Many newsgroups have a large number of subareas. When you want to check the latest postings to a specific folder, you might have to click (and scroll) many times to get there. Instead, you can set up shortcuts to your favorite public folders.

Outlook provides two ways to help you navigate through public folders—the Other Shortcuts group on the Outlook Bar and the Favorites folder within Public Folders. Each method has its own purpose:

- Setting up a shortcut on the Outlook Bar gives you quick access to a favorite public folder. For details, see "Using the Outlook Bar," on page 20.

- Setting up a shortcut to a public folder favorite lets you open that folder without working through the layers of public folders and also lets you see the folder contents while you're working offline. For details about setting up a favorite folder for offline work, see "Setting Up an Offline Folder File," on page 267. Of course, when working offline, the information in a favorite public folder will be only as current as your last synchronization with the public folder to which it's linked. You can also use a shortcut in the Public Folders Favorites folder to quickly open the related public folder: open the Folder List, open the Favorites folder in Outlook's Public Folders, and then open the shortcut.

NOTE

Do not confuse the Favorites folder in Outlook's Public Folders with the Favorites folder on your hard disk, which may be shown as a separate icon on the Outlook Bar. Outlook's Favorites folder in Public Folders contains shortcuts only to public folders or synchronized copies of their contents. The Favorites folder on your hard disk contains shortcuts to folders, files, and disks connected to your computer, as well as to Web sites that you added using Internet Explorer.

Following a Public Folder Conversation

Some public folders in your organization may be set aside for "conversations" much like newsgroups on a news server. Over time, a large number of different but related threads (conversations) can exist in a public folder. Setting up subfolders for various threads helps to bring some order to the mass of material, but even subfolders can contain diverse conversations. Following a particular thread can be difficult because messages arrive in the folder at different times, with pieces of other threads interspersed.

To solve this problem, Outlook provides By Conversation Topic view, in which you group folder items according to their topics. When you use this view of a public folder, you can readily follow the threads of any conversation from beginning to end.

To follow a thread, do this:

1 Group the folder contents into threads by pointing to Current View on the View menu and then choosing By Conversation Topic from the submenu.

2 Locate the thread (topic) that you want to follow, and then click the plus sign to expand the thread.

3 Double-click the first item in the thread, and read it.

4 Click the Next Item button on the Standard toolbar in the item window to see the next item in the thread.

5 When you've read the entire thread, click the Next Item button. If the next thread is expanded, Outlook opens the first item in that thread. If that thread is not expanded, Outlook closes the item window. If you have read as much as you need before you reach the end of the thread, click the Close box in the upper-right corner of the item window.

Sending Messages to a Public Folder

You can also post a message to a public folder by sending the folder an e-mail. However, to e-mail directly to a folder you need to add the folder to your address book. Sending e-mail to that address posts the message in the folder. Follow these steps:

1 In the Folder List, right-click the public folder, and then choose Properties from the shortcut menu. You can also open the public folder, point to Folder on the File menu, and then choose Properties from the submenu.

2 In the Properties dialog box, click the Summary tab.

3 Click the Personal Address Book button to add the folder address.

4 Click OK.

If the Properties box does not have a Summary tab, look for an Administration tab. Click the Personal Address Book button on that tab instead.

Working with Personal Folders

You can use a personal folder to store related items, hold archived information, or just to organize files for quick reference and retrieval. However, personal folders must first be set up as part of your profile.

Technically, a personal folder is not an actual folder (subdirectory) on your disk but a file with the .PST extension.

Creating Personal Folders

As explained in Chapter 1, "Starting Out," you can change a profile from within Outlook or from the Windows Control Panel. To review, the steps for adding a personal folder from within Outlook are as follows:

1 Choose the Services command from the Outlook Tools menu.

2 On the Services tab of the Services dialog box, click Add to display the Add Service To Profile dialog box.

3 Select Personal Folders.

4 Click OK.

5 Select the location for the new or existing folder.

6 Type the name for the new folder or select an existing .PST file.

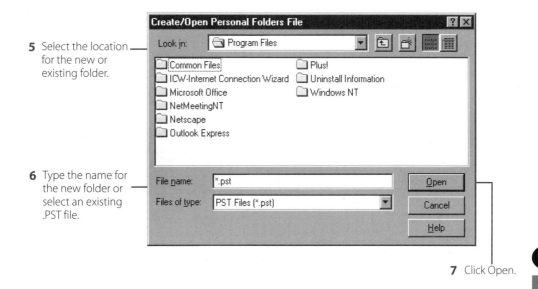

7 Click Open.

8 Type the name you want to appear for this folder in the Folder List.

9 Choose an encryption setting.

12 Turn on this option if you selected a password and don't want to be prompted for it when you use the folder.

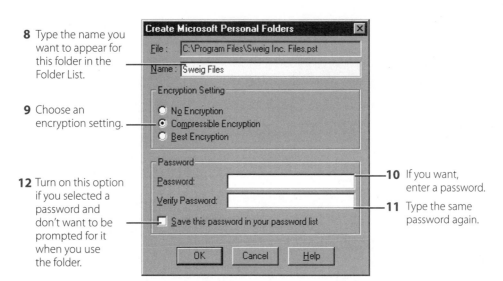

10 If you want, enter a password.

11 Type the same password again.

13 Click OK in both dialog boxes to return to Outlook.

Opening Personal Folders

You open a personal folder and move items in and out of it, as you would any other folder by using the Folder List. To open a personal folder just display the Folder List and click the name of the folder you want to open. If the personal folders file you open has been assigned a password, Outlook displays the Personal Folders Password dialog box. Enter the password for the personal folders file, and then click OK. Each personal folder, by the way, contains a subfolder called Deleted Items, which stores items that you removed from the folder.

You can also open a personal folder even if it is not listed in the Folder List. Removing a personal folder from the profile, for example, does not delete it from your disk. So if you remove a folder from the profile, you can still open it using these steps:

1 Point to Open on the File menu and choose Personal Folders File (.PST) from the submenu.

2 In the Open Personal Folders dialog box, navigate to the location where the folder is stored.

3 Select the folder, and then click OK.

Opening Exchange Folders

If you are connected to Microsoft Exchange Server, you can also open another user's Calendar, Contacts, Inbox, Journal, Notes, or Tasks folder.

1 Point to Open on the File menu, and choose Other User's Folder from the submenu.

2 Click here to select the other user's name, or ... ...type it here.

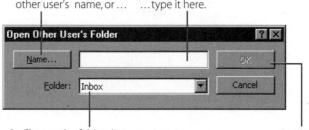

3 Choose the folder that you want to open.   **4** Click OK.

Outlook displays the folder in a separate window. You can then add calendar items, tasks, and other items. Messages you send from the user's Inbox, however, will be sent under your own name. Appointments and tasks that you assign to others will be under your name but listed as "on behalf of" the user whose folder you opened.

Sharing Folders over the Internet

Public folders let you share information over your Microsoft Exchange network. Net Folders, a separate component of Outlook, lets you share folders over the Internet.

To use Net Folders, you must have installed the component using the Add/Remove Components feature of the Outlook installation program. You then designate which folder you want to share and which individuals you want to share it with. The information in the shared folder will be downloaded to the persons sharing it and updated at regular intervals.

 NOTE

> You cannot share public folders or mailbox folders stored on Exchange Server, but you can share personal folders.

Here's how to set up folders for sharing over the Internet, once you've installed the Net Folders component:

1 Click the folder you want to share, in either the Outlook Bar or the Folder List.

2 Point to Share on the File menu, and choose This Folder. The Share command is only available if the Net Folders component has been installed.

3 The introductory screen of the Net Folders wizard appears. Click Next.

Current members with permissions will be listed here.

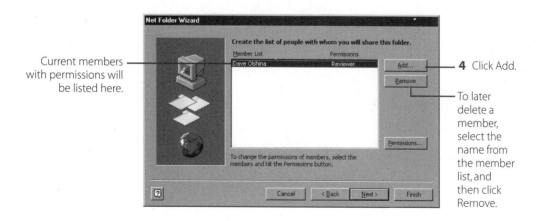

4 Click Add.

To later delete a member, select the name from the member list, and then click Remove.

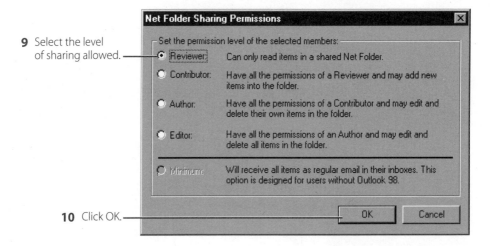

5 Select the person with whom you want to share your folder.

6 Click To.

7 Click OK.

8 In the member list, select the name and click Permissions.

9 Select the level of sharing allowed.

10 Click OK.

11 Click Next.

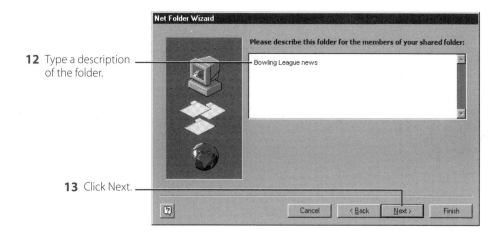

12 Type a description of the folder.

13 Click Next.

14 Click Finish, and then click OK in the next two dialog boxes.

All new members will now be sent e-mail messages inviting them to share your folder. (If necessary, click Send And Receive to send the messages over the Internet.) They will receive an e-mail like the one shown here:

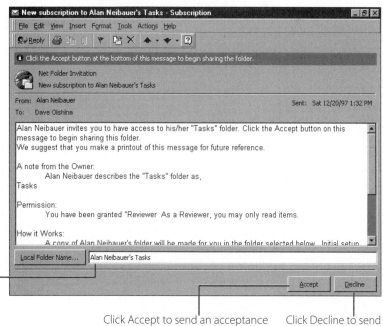

If desired, change the name for the shared folder on your system.

Click Accept to send an acceptance message and to receive the folder.

Click Decline to send a rejection message.

V

Bending Folders to Your Will

Dealing with Folder Properties

You can set the properties for each folder in Outlook and for public folders for which you have appropriate permission. Each folder has its own unique properties as well as certain properties that are common to all folders.

> **NOTE**
>
> To set all the properties of a folder, you must have administrative permissions for the folder. Even so, in some cases, you can't set certain properties because they don't apply to the folder. In almost all cases, it is best to set folder properties while you're working online. You can, however, set folder properties for personal folders while you are working offline.

All Outlook folders (except the Contacts folder) have the same four tabs in the Properties dialog box: General, AutoArchive, Administration, and Forms. Server folders have two additional tabs: Permissions and Synchronization. The Properties dialog box of the Contacts folder has a unique tab, Outlook Address Book, instead of the AutoArchive tab. When you create an Outlook folder or copy an Outlook folder, it has the same properties—and therefore the same tabs—as the folder on which it is based. Disk folders have a different set of tabs: see "Disk Folders," on page 547. Public folders have a tab labeled Internet News that lets you publish the folder for access by newsgroup readers.

The general steps for changing the properties of a folder are as follows:

1 Right-click the folder in the Outlook Bar or Folder List, and then choose Properties from the submenu.

2 Change the property settings on any or all of the tabs.

3 Click OK to close the Properties dialog box.

The following sections illustrate and describe the General, Administration, Permissions, and Outlook Address Book tabs of the Properties dialog box. The AutoArchive tab, see is discussed in "Setting a Folder's AutoArchive Properties," on page 514. The Synchronization tab, is discussed in "Designating Folders for Offline Work," on page 271.

> The Forms tab is used to manage the forms associated with each folder. Forms
> are the templates Outlook uses to present information, such as the message
> form you fill in to send a message. Managing and customizing forms is an
> advanced topic not covered in this book. Consult the Outlook online Help for
> more information about forms.

General Tab

The General Tab of the Properties dialog box, shown in Figure 19-1,
contains information such as the folder name and its description. You
cannot change the names of Outlook's standard folders, nor can you
change the name or description of a public folder without having the
proper permissions. For a custom folder that you created, however, you
can select the folder's name in the box at the top of the tab and type a
new one in its place. In the Description box, you can type or edit the
description of any folder, custom or standard.

The When Posting To This Folder, Use list offers the options Post and
Forms. Select Post to use the default Outlook form for posting items
in this folder—that is, to use a message form for the Inbox folder, an
appointment form for the Calendar folder, and so on. When you select
Forms, you can choose a custom form in this folder.

FIGURE 19-1.

The General tab of the
Properties dialog box.

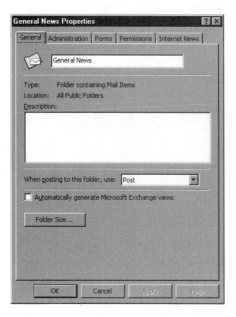

V

Bending Folders to Your Will

If some members of your organization use the Microsoft Exchange client program instead of Outlook, turn on the option labeled Automatically Generate Microsoft Exchange Views so that they can use the views that are set up for this folder.

Administration Tab

The Administration tab is used primarily with public folders. For Outlook folders and for public folders for which you do not have administrative permission, most of the options on this tab are unavailable. If you do have administrative permissions for a folder, you can use this tab to set which view of a folder is used when it is first opened, what happens when you drag and drop an item into the folder, and access permissions as shown in Figure 19-2.

The Initial View On Folder list includes all the built-in views for the folder plus any views you have created for it.

The Personal Address Book button (which can also appear on the Summary tab for public folders, depending on your level of permission) lets you add this folder to your Personal Address Book. For information, see "Sending Messages to a Public Folder," on page 533.

FIGURE 19-2.

The Administration tab of the Properties dialog box.

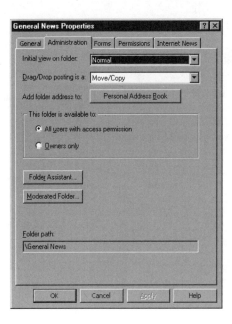

Use the Folder Assistant button to set up rules for dealing with the items sent to this folder. The Folder Assistant is similar to the Rules Wizard. (For information about using the Rules Wizard to set up rules for folder items, see "Getting Help from Outlook Assistants," on page 44. You can easily apply the information in that section to setting up the rules you want to use with the Folder Assistant.) You can use the Folder Assistant to set up rules to take actions on items sent by or to a particular person, items about a certain subject, or items that contain a particular word or group of words in the body of the message. You can return items to the sender, delete items automatically, reply to items automatically, or forward items.

Use the Moderated Folder button to automatically send newly posted messages to an individual for review. The person you assign as the moderator can send a response to the sender and then actually post the message to the folder. This button is active only for public folders for which you have administrative permissions.

Permissions Tab

SEE ALSO

If you have delegates who work in your Outlook folders on your behalf, you can set up delegate permissions on the Delegates tab of the Options dialog box. For details, see "Using the Delegates Tab," on page 80.

The Properties dialog box for server folders and for public folders for which you have appropriate permissions contains a Permission tab, shown in Figure 19-3, on the following page. On this tab, you give others permission to open the folders that you want them to see or use.

A server folder is simply a folder in your Exchange Server mailbox that you access from the server—Outlook automatically sets up the folders in your mailbox on the server. If you are working from a Personal Folder File (PST) on your hard disk, you are not accessing the folders from the server but rather from your own hard disk.

On this tab, you can compile a list of names of the people who have permission to use the folder. Each name is assigned a role, and each role has specific privileges attached to it. Users' names and roles appear in the upper box. You can remove an existing user by selecting the name and clicking the Remove button, and you can add new users by clicking the Add button and selecting them from the Add Users box.

FIGURE 19-3.

The Permissions tab of
the Properties dialog
box for a server folder.

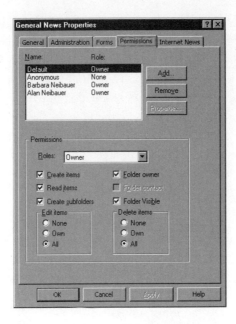

FIGURE 19-3.

The Permissions tab of
the Properties dialog
box for a server folder.

The Permissions area is where you can select, customize, and later modify the permissions for each user. For instance, someone who has an Author role can create folder items, read folder items, and edit or delete his or her own folder items but cannot create a subfolder and cannot edit or delete the items created by other people. Table 19-1 lists the roles and their respective privileges. (The role None is not listed because this role grants no permissions or privileges other than the folder name being visible in the Folder List or Outlook Bar.)

When you create a folder in your mailbox, the default role listed is None (no privileges). When you create a public folder, the default role listed is Author.

To add a name, click the Add button. Outlook displays the Add Users dialog box, in which you can type or select the name or names you want to add. When you click the Add button in this dialog box and then click OK, Outlook adds the names to the list on the Permissions tab, assigning each the default role (None).

TABLE 19-1. Roles and the Permissions They Receive

Permissions	Author	Nonediting Author	Contributor	Editor	Owner	Publishing Author	Publishing Editor	Reviewer
Create items	✔	✔	✔	✔	✔	✔	✔	
Read items	✔	✔		✔	✔	✔	✔	✔
Create subfolders					✔	✔	✔	
Folder owner					✔			
Folder contact								
Folder visible	✔	✔	✔	✔	✔	✔	✔	✔
Edit items	Own	None	None	All	All	Own	All	None
Delete items	Own	None	None	All	All	Own	All	None

To assign or change the role for a person on the list, select the name, and then select a role from the list in the Roles box.

Instead of assigning one of the predefined roles to a name, you can assign privileges one by one to that person by setting individual options in the tab's Permissions area. If the resulting combination of privileges is the same as one of the predefined roles, Outlook displays that role name in the Roles box. If the combination of privileges is unique, Outlook assigns Custom as the role. (You won't see a Custom role listed in the Roles box; it appears only when you change an assigned role in a way that doesn't match any of the predefined roles.)

 TIP

You can change the default role from None to, say, Author or Contributor. But remember that the default role applies to everyone who uses your Exchange Server, even those not listed on the Permissions tab. If you want to limit access to your folder to only those people you specify on the Permissions tab, leave the default role set to None.

V

Bending Folders to Your Will

Outlook Address Book Tab

The Properties dialog box for the Contacts folder contains the Outlook Address Book tab instead of the AutoArchive tab. This tab is shown in Figure 19-4.

FIGURE 19-4.

The Outlook Address Book tab of the Contacts Properties dialog box.

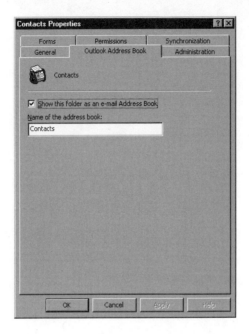

Turning on the option labeled Show This Folder As An E-Mail Address Book adds your Contacts folder items to your Outlook Address Book, giving you access to the names, addresses, fax numbers, e-mail addresses, and URLs of the people you list as contacts. You can use contact entries to send messages and faxes, to place telephone calls, to write letters, and to connect to Web pages while you're working in another Microsoft Office program.

Although you can't change the name of the Contacts folder itself, you can change the name that appears in your Outlook Address Book. For example, if you want your Contacts list to be called "Buddies" in the Outlook Address Book, type *Buddies* in the Name Of The Address Book box in the Contacts Properties dialog box.

> **Oh, No! The Show This Folder As An E-Mail Address Book Option Is Not Available!**
>
> The option on the Outlook Address Book tab of the Contacts Properties dialog box called Show This Folder As An E-Mail Address Book is not available if you have set up Microsoft Schedule+ as your primary calendar. (See "Use Microsoft Schedule+ As My Primary Calendar," on page 68.) To use your Contacts folder as an e-mail address book, you must choose the Options command from the Tools menu, click Calendar Options on the Preferences tab, and then turn off the Use Microsoft Schedule+ As My Primary Calendar option in the Calendar Options dialog box. You must then exit and log off Outlook and restart Outlook for this change to take effect. Once you do this, the Show This Folder As An E-Mail Address Book option will be available, and you can turn it on to use your Contacts folder as an address book.
>
> As an alternative way of setting up your Contacts folder as an address book, open the profile you use for Outlook and add the Outlook Address Book as a service. This replaces Schedule+ as your primary calendar and automatically adds your Contacts folder as an e-mail address book. For information about adding a service to a profile, see "Updating a Profile," on page 10.

Disk Folders

Disk folders that you set up and view in Outlook have the same properties they have in a My Computer window or a Windows Explorer window. The Properties dialog box for a disk folder contains two tabs: General and Sharing. Figure 19-5, on the following page, shows the General tab, which provides a description of the folder and allows you to set the folder's attributes.

On the Sharing tab of a disk folder's Properties dialog box, shown in Figure 19-6, on the next page, you can specify whether or not the folder will be shared with other people. If you designate it as a shared folder, you can also specify how it will be shared.

If you want to make a disk folder available to others, click the Shared As option. Then accept or change the share name for the folder. The share name identifies the folder on the network. To help users make sure that they've found the correct folder, you can add a comment that identifies the folder more fully.

FIGURE 19-5.
The General tab of the Properties dialog box for a disk folder.

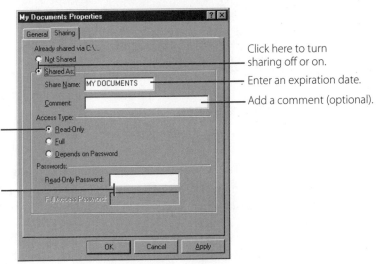

Turn these options on or off to set folder attributes.

FIGURE 19-6.
The Sharing tab of the Properties dialog box for a disk folder.

Click here to turn sharing off or on.

Enter an expiration date.

Add a comment (optional).

Designate how others can use the shared folder.

If you want, enter a password for read-only or full access.

 NOTE

You can share a folder only if you have administrative control over it. You usually have this control over the folders on a disk that's part of your computer.

Depending on the configuration of your system, you may also be able to set sharing levels individually for each user rather than once for everyone who has access to the Exchange Server. If the Sharing tab

FIGURE 19-7.
User-Level Sharing
Settings for a disk
folder.

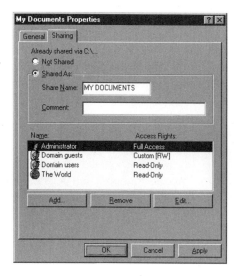

appears as in Figure 19-7, you can choose which users can share the folder and the exact permissions each user or group of users will have.

When your Sharing tab appears as in Figure 19-7, it is set by default to allow full access to everyone on the network, represented by the user name The World. You can limit access to everyone at once by editing The World's access rights, or you can specify individual users or groups of users and their access rights. To change the level of access given to everyone, take these steps:

1 Select The World and click the Edit button.

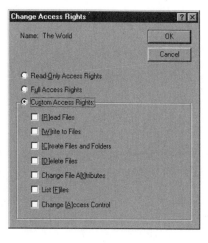

2 In the Change Access Rights dialog box, select from among these three access levels:

- Read-Only Access Rights enables everyone to see and read the files in the folder, but they cannot delete, edit, or add files.

- Full Access Rights is the default and grants everyone complete rights to all file actions.

- Custom Access Rights, when selected, enables the options below it to be individually turned on or off to specify just the level of access you wish to grant.

3 Click OK.

It only makes sense to grant rights to individuals or groups if you have removed full access from The World. Everyone is a member of The World and would therefore automatically have complete access to the folder regardless of what other group or individual status you may give them. To limit access to the folder to specific users or groups of users, first select The World and do one of the following:

- Click the Remove button to remove all access from the network except for those you specifically list.

- Assign a low level of access (such as Read Files) to The World, suitable for everyone who accesses your network, and then selectively assign greater access levels to specific individuals or groups.

When you're ready to grant access rights to specific individuals and groups, follow these steps:

1 Click the Add button on the Sharing tab of the Properties dialog box.

2 Select a user or group from the list.

3 Click Read Only, Full Access, or Custom to move the user to the appropriate access rights box.

4 Repeat steps 2 and 3 for each user whose permissions you want to configure.

5 Click OK.

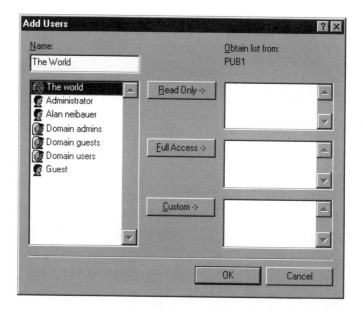

If you assigned Custom access to anyone, you will see the Change Access Rights dialog box with the user's name shown in the upper portion so that you can pick the specific types of access you want to grant. This is the same dialog box you see when you select a user on the Sharing tab of the Properties dialog box and click the Edit button.

Click OK when you've completed assigning custom rights. The names of the people to whom you granted access rights will appear on the Sharing tab of the Properties dialog box for the folder you're configuring. You can select a name in that box and change their access rights or remove the name from the list entirely. Click OK to close the Properties dialog box.

Now that you've learned how to manage the folders that Outlook accesses, the next chapter will show you how to organize the contents of these folders.

Organizing Folder Items

O rganizing information so that it makes sense is an essential part of managing projects and tasks. As you've seen in previous chapters, Microsoft Outlook 98 offers you numerous ways to view your folders and the information they contain. You can choose the view that best meets your needs, one that lets you focus on the most important information in the folder and makes that information clear, readily accessible, and easy to work with. Outlook provides a set of built-in views for each folder, drawn from the five general types of views: table, timeline, card, icon, and day/month/week.

Chapter 21, "Setting Up Views," explains how to modify Outlook's built-in views or even design your own views. To do so, however, you first need to understand the methods and techniques described in this chapter for setting up folders and displaying their contents. What you see in a folder depends on the combination of settings you select for columns, categories, grouping, sorting, filtering, and fields. It's almost impossible to describe, at least in fewer than several dozen pages, how all the variations look. In effect, you'll have to experiment with the combinations to come up with the ones that suit your purpose in any given situation.

Setting Up Columns

Outlook's table views show items in rows and columns. Each item is in a row, with the fields for the items in columns. You can add or remove columns, and you can rearrange the order of the columns to suit your needs. You can also adjust the width of the columns to show more or less information or to fit more columns within the folder window.

Adding Columns from the Field Chooser

The Field Chooser is a window listing the fields that you can add as columns to a table view, and it gives you a visual means to see and add columns. Outlook's fields are arranged into groups, called field sets. When you use Field Chooser, you first select the set that contains the field you want to add, and then you drag the field into the table to the position where you want the column to appear. You can add fields from more than one set. After adding fields from one set, for example, just choose another field set and drag any fields from it to the table.

 NOTE

The term *field* simply refers to a location that stores data of the same type. By organizing similar kinds of data in fields, you can find, sort, and process information quickly.

⊘ SEE ALSO

You can also add a column during the sorting process; see "Sorting with the Sort Dialog Box," on page 567.

To add columns to a folder view using the Field Chooser, follow these steps:

1   Open a folder, and select a view that has columns (any table view).

2   Right-click the column headings, and choose Field Chooser from the shortcut menu.

3   Click the down arrow at the top of the Field Chooser window (shown on the next page), and select a field set from the list that contains the field you want to add. When you select a field set, Outlook displays the fields contained in the set in the lower portion of the window.

4   Drag the field name into the folder window, positioning it in the column headings at the location where you want the column to

appear. (Outlook displays two red arrows to show you where the column will be inserted.) When you release the mouse button, Outlook adds the column to the folder view, with the field name as the new column heading. Outlook also removes the field name from the Field Chooser.

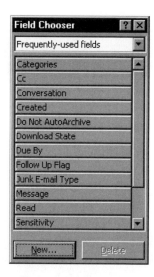

5 When you've added as many columns as you want, click the Close box in the upper-right corner of the Field Chooser window.

TIP

If you can't find an appropriate predefined column, you can click the New button in the Field Chooser to create a new field, which you can then add as a column in the folder view. For details, see "Creating a Simple Custom Field," on page 577.

Removing Columns

If you no longer want a column to appear in a folder view, you can easily remove it from the screen, without actually deleting the information contained in the column. Any fields you remove from a folder view return to the Field Chooser. You can later reinsert the column to display the information again.

V

Bending Folders to Your Will

To delete a column, use either of these techniques:

- Drag the field name away from the column heading until you see a large black X appear over the field, and then release the mouse button.

- Right-click the heading of the column you want to remove, and then choose Remove This Column from the shortcut menu.

Rearranging Columns with the Mouse

When you want to quickly move a column to a new position in a folder window, just drag its column heading to the new location. As you move the column heading between existing columns, you'll see two red arrows pointing to where the column will be inserted when you release the mouse button. When you do so, the column moves to its new location, and the columns to the right of the new position move to the right to make room.

Using the Show Fields Dialog Box

The most general way to add, remove, and rearrange columns in a folder view is by using the Show Fields dialog box. Begin by opening a folder and selecting a view that has columns, and then follow these steps.

1 Point to Current View on the View menu, and then choose Customize Current View from the submenu. You can also right-click the column headings and choose Customize Current View from the shortcut menu.

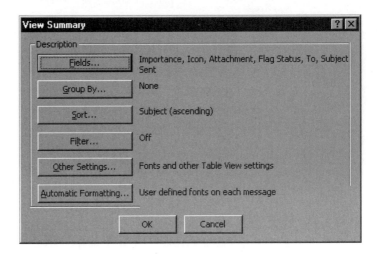

2 You'll learn more about the View Summary dialog box in Chapter 21, "Setting Up Views." For now, click the Fields button to display the Show Fields dialog box.

3 Select and arrange the fields as shown in Figure 20-1.

FIGURE 20-1.
The Show Fields dialog box.

Select a field here, and click here to add it.

Select a field here, and click here to remove it.

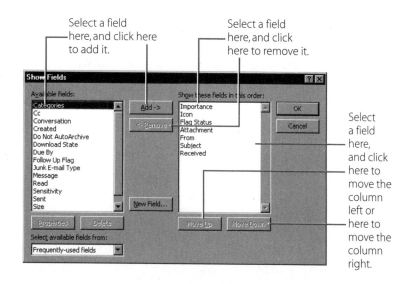

Select a field here, and click here to move the column left or here to move the column right.

Changing Column Format

With either the mouse or a menu command, you can adjust the width of a column, alter the alignment of information within a column, and generally modify the format of a new column in a folder view.

Changing Column Width

To change the width of a column using the mouse, drag the right edge of the column heading to the right or left.

To have Outlook automatically size the column to best suit its contents, right-click the column heading and choose Best Fit from the shortcut menu. You can also double-click the right-hand border of a column to set the column width to best fit.

Setting column width with the Best Fit command is usually a temporary arrangement so that you can fully see a particular column's contents.

V

Bending Folders to Your Will

The Date/Time Fields Dialog Box

If you want to customize a timeline view of a folder, first display a timeline view, then point to Current View on the View menu and choose Customize Current View. When the View Summary dialog box appears, choose Fields. Outlook then displays the Date/Time Fields dialog box rather than the Show Fields dialog box. In a timeline view, Outlook positions folder items on the timeline according to the date in their start and end fields. For a message, Outlook by default uses the time the message was sent and the time it was received as the time interval. If you want to change the fields used to display folder items on a timeline, you can do so in the Date/Time Fields dialog box:

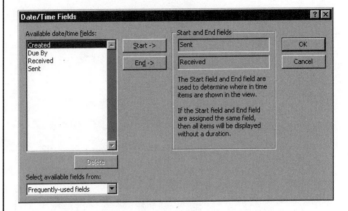

Use the Select Available Fields From box at the bottom of the dialog box to select the field set, and then from the Available Date/Time Fields list, select the field that you want to use as the item start date, and click the Start button. To change the field that Outlook uses to display each item's end date, select a field from this list and click the End button.

When Outlook sets a column width to best fit, it has to adjust the width of other columns in the folder window. Some columns might even be reduced to a single character's width, which makes them pretty useless. In that case, you might want to remove a column or two or adjust the width of other columns, using the techniques described in the preceding sections.

Changing Column Alignment

By default, the contents of columns are left-aligned. To change column alignment, follow these steps:

1 Right-click the column heading.

2 Choose Alignment from the shortcut menu.

3 Choose the alignment you want (Align Left, Align Right, or Center) from the submenu.

Using the Format Columns Command

The Format Columns command lets you change the width, the alignment, the heading, and the information format for a single column from one dialog box.

To change the format of a column using this command, follow these directions:

1 Open the folder, and select a view that has columns.

2 Right-click the column headings, and choose Format Columns from the shortcut menu.

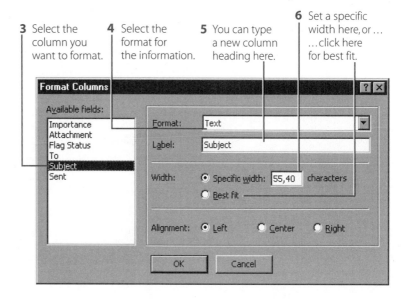

3 Select the column you want to format.

4 Select the format for the information.

5 You can type a new column heading here.

6 Set a specific width here, or ... ...click here for best fit.

7 Select an alignment.

8 Click OK.

 NOTE

> For some columns, you have only one choice in the Format box of the Format Columns dialog box: text. For other columns Outlook provides several format choices. For more information about these formats, see "Creating a Simple Custom Field," on page 577.

Working with Categories

Whether you think of it this way or not, you probably use categories for organizing various activities and records—shopping lists, reminders, house repairs, friends, pets, and so on. In business, you might have categories of folder items for various projects, personal business, daily tasks, customers, suppliers, orders, billing, and so on. Outlook provides a list of 20 built-in categories for folder items, and you can add your own categories as well.

To assign a folder item to a category (or to several categories), follow these steps:

1 Open the folder, and select one or more items that you want to assign to a category.

2 Open the Categories dialog box in one of the following ways:

- Choose the Categories command from the Edit menu.

- Right-click the folder item, and choose Categories from the shortcut menu.

- For calendar items and tasks, open the item and click the Categories button in the folder item window.

- For notes, click the icon in the upper-left corner of the note window, and choose Categories from the menu.

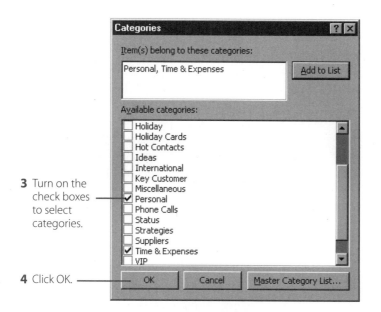

3 Turn on the check boxes to select categories.

4 Click OK.

To remove a folder item from a category, turn off the check box for that category in step 3.

Adding Your Own Categories

Because you are a unique person, you probably have categories of your own that you'd like to add to Outlook's list. This is easy to do:

1 Open a folder, and select an item that you'd like to assign to a new category.

2 Open the Categories dialog box in any of the ways described in the preceding section.

3 Type the new category name in the Item(s) Belong To These Categories box. If you are adding more than one category, separate the names with a comma.

4 Click Add To List. Outlook adds the new category to the list so that you can easily assign other folder items to this new category later. Outlook also adds the new category to the master category list.

5 Click OK.

V

Bending Folders to Your Will

Managing the Master Category List

The master category list contains Outlook's built-in list of categories as well as any categories that you've added. In the master category list, you can add categories, remove categories, and reset the category list to the original 20 categories built into Outlook.

To manage the master category list, you must first open the Categories dialog box. In the Categories dialog box, click the Master Category List button to display the Master Category List dialog box, as shown here:

 NOTE

Deleting a category from the Master Category List doesn't remove the category name from any items that have already been assigned to it.

> ### Organizing Categories with Organize
>
> You can quickly assign a category to a calendar, contact, task, or journal item without opening it, and you can even create new categories directly from the folder window. Here's how.
>
> **1** Open the Calendar, Contact, Tasks, or Journal folder.
>
> **2** Click the Organize button on the Standard toolbar.
>
> **3** Select the items that you want to assign to a category.
>
> **4** Click Using Categories.
>
> **5** Choose an existing category from the top list and click Add, or type in a new category in the lower box and click Create.
>
> **6** Specify as many categories as you want, and then click the Organize button again to close the Organize pane.

Grouping

You can use grouping as a way to organize folder items to more easily find and examine similar items. Views such as By Category, By Company, or By Location group folder items under headings that correspond to the various entries in the Category, Company, or Location field. For example, By Person Responsible groups task folder items according to the person who is responsible for the task.

Outlook gives you two ways to group items. You can group them visually from within the folder window, or you can use a dialog box to group based on up to four fields. The dialog box method is most useful when you want to group items from a field that is not displayed in the current window.

Grouping in the Folder Window

If the column heading you want to use for grouping is displayed on the screen, the quickest way to group items is directly from the folder window. Just right-click that column heading, and then choose Group By This Field from the shortcut menu. You can also display the Group By box first, and then drag a field to it. To display the box, right-click a column heading and choose Group By Box from the shortcut menu. Outlook groups the items by the selected field, and then displays the field name in the Group By box above the column headings, as shown in Figure 20-2. Notice that the field no longer appears in the column headings.

You can then add one or more subgroups to further organize the items. To add a subgroup, use either of these methods:

- Right-click the field, and then choose Group By This Field from the shortcut menu.

- Drag the field to the Group By box.

When you use multiple levels of grouping, Outlook first groups the folder items by the first field you specified for grouping. Then, within each one of those groups, Outlook creates a subgroup based on the second field, and so on. The fields will be indented in the Group By box to visually illustrate this order, as shown opposite. If a folder item contains no information in the specified field, it is listed first and labeled (None).

To change the order in which the fields are used for grouping, rearrange the fields within the Group By box. For example, to change a subgroup into the primary grouping field, drag it to the left of any other groups in the Group By box and then release the mouse.

FIGURE 20-2.
Grouping items using the Group By box.

Group By box —

Click here to switch between ascending and descending order.

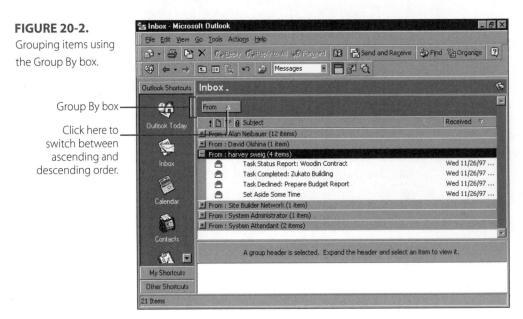

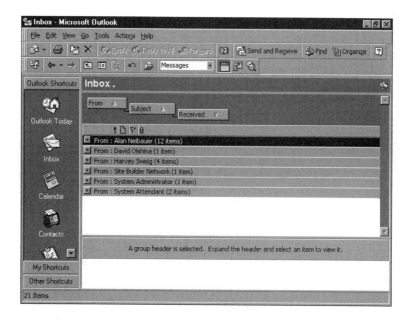

When you no longer want to group by a field, drag it from the Group By box back to the column heading, or right-click the field name in the Group By box and choose Don't Group By This Field from the shortcut menu.

If you no longer want to display the Group By box, right-click the column heading and choose Group By Box from the shortcut menu. You can also turn off the Group By button on the Advanced toolbar. If this toolbar is not visible, point to Toolbars on the View menu and choose Advanced. You can click the Group By button again whenever you want to redisplay the Group By box.

Grouping with the Group By Dialog Box

As an alternative to dragging fields into the Group By box, you can also group items using a dialog box. The Group By dialog box lets you select fields that aren't visible, group using up to four fields, set the order of the fields, and choose how you want the groups expanded or collapsed.

To change the way items are grouped in an open folder, follow these steps:

1 Point to Current View on the View menu, and then choose Customize Current View from the submenu.

2 Click Group By in the View Summary dialog box to display the Group By dialog box.

3 In the Select Available Fields From box at the bottom of the dialog box, select the field set containing the fields that you want to use for grouping.

4 Select a grouping.

5 Turn on this option to display the field in the column heading as well as on a grouping bar.

6 Choose a second, third, and fourth group level, as desired.

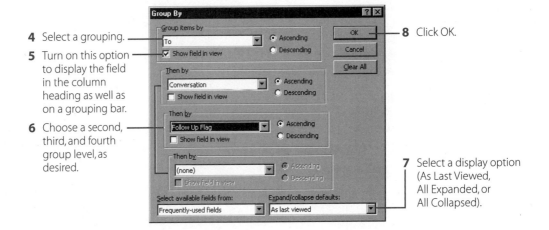

8 Click OK.

7 Select a display option (As Last Viewed, All Expanded, or All Collapsed).

 **TIP**

To remove all the groupings from a folder view, open the Group By dialog box and click the Clear All button.

Sorting

You can sort folder items in any type of view except timeline and day/week/month views. Outlook gives you two ways to sort folder items: with the mouse and with the Sort dialog box. You can sort by as many as four fields. Unlike grouping, sorting does not add headings or labels to the list.

Sorting with the Mouse

Sorting with the mouse is quick and convenient, but you can use this method only in a view with columns. You can sort items in either ascending or descending order. Ascending order is alphabetical, earlier time to later time, or lower number to higher number; descending order is the reverse.

- To sort items in ascending order, click the heading of the column you want to use to sort the items so it contains an up-pointing triangle.

- To sort items in descending order, click the column heading so it contains a down-pointing triangle.

- To sort items by more than one sorting field, click the column headings in reverse order—that is, begin by clicking the heading of the last column you want to sort by, and end by clicking the heading of the first column you want to sort by. For example, if you want to sort tasks first by subject, then by priority, and then by the due date, click the Due Date heading first, then the Priority heading, and then the Subject heading.

Sorting with the Sort Dialog Box

The Sort dialog box gives you more options for sorting than you have using the mouse, such as sorting on a field that is not visible in the current view of the folder. You can also use the dialog box to sort in card and icon views in addition to table views.

To sort folder items using the Sort command, follow these steps:

1 Open a folder, and select a table, card, or icon view.

2 Point to Current View on the View menu, and then choose Customize Current View from the submenu to display the View Summary dialog box.

3 Click the Sort button to display the Sort dialog box.

4 In the Select Available Fields From box at the bottom of the dialog box, select the field set containing the fields that you want to use for sorting. You can select fields from more than one set.

Select the first sorting field, and choose Ascending or Descending order.

Select a second, third, and fourth sort level, as desired, and their sorting orders.

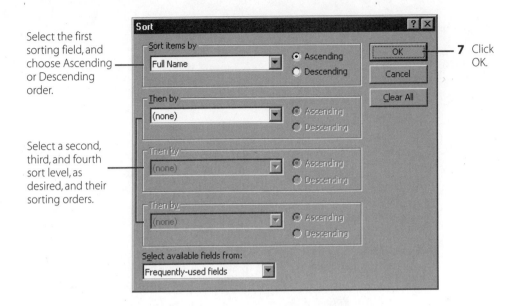

7 Click OK.

If you select a field for sorting that isn't displayed in the current view of the folder, Outlook asks whether you want to display that field. Click Yes to display the field for each item in the view. (If you are using a table view, for instance, this can be a handy way of adding a column to the view.) Click No to keep the current folder view, without displaying the additional field. Whichever choice you make, Outlook can sort items by the fields you choose, whether the fields are visible or not.

 NOTE

If you select (None) as a sorting key in any box in the Sort dialog box, all the boxes below automatically revert to (None).

Filtering

A filter lets you temporarily hide items that you are not interested in seeing. This limited view makes it easier to analyze certain folder items without interference from irrelevant items and the information they contain. When you remove the filter, you can see all the items again.

To set up and apply a filter for the current view, you display the Filter dialog box, shown in Figure 20-3, by following these steps:

1 Open the folder you wish to filter.

2 Point to Current View on the View menu, and then choose Customize Current View from the submenu to display the View Summary dialog box.

3 Click the Filter button.

You can use all three of the tabs in this dialog box to set up criteria for a filter. (As you might notice, the Filter dialog box resembles the Find dialog box, discussed in Chapter 16, "Managing Folder Contents;" see "Searching Folder Contents," on page 475. Setting up a search and setting up a filter are similar in many ways.)

V

Bending Folders to Your Will

FIGURE 20-3.

The Filter dialog box for the Inbox folder showing the Messages tab.

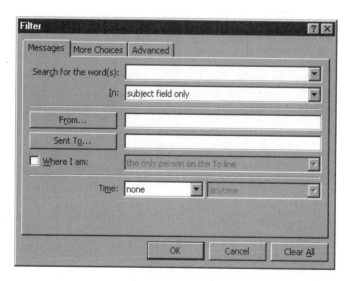

For example, you could use the Filter dialog box to just display all Inbox messages sent by Jane Doe pertaining to a networking project in which your organization is involved using the following steps:

1 Open your Inbox folder.

2 Point to Current View on the View menu, and then choose Customize Current View from the submenu.

3 Click Filter in the View Summary dialog box.

4 On the Messages tab of the Filter dialog box, type the word *networking* in the Search For The Word(s) box.

5 Select Subject Field And Message Body from the In list.

6 In the From box, type *Jane Doe*.

7 Click OK to close the Filter dialog box.

8 Click OK again to close the View Summary dialog box and apply the filter.

Your Inbox folder would now display only messages sent by Jane Doe that contain the word *networking* in either the Subject line or the body of the message. Notice that Outlook adds the words *Filter Applied* to the status bar (in the lower-left corner of the folder window) and to the right of the folder window's title.

If you want to narrow your filter even further, you can set additional filter criteria on the Messages tab—specifying messages sent during a certain time range, for example—or on either of the two other tabs in the Filter dialog box. (See "Setting Up the More Choices Tab," on page 571, and "Setting Up Advanced Criteria," on page 573, for information about the second and third tabs.) A folder item must meet all of the criteria specified on all of the tabs in order to appear in the filtered view of the folder.

The first of the three tabs in the Filter dialog box varies according to the type of folder that is currently open. For instance, you'll see the Messages tab shown in Figure 20-3, on the previous page, if you are setting up a filter for a folder that contains message items. If you open a different type of folder to set up a filter, Outlook changes not only the name of the first tab in the Filter dialog box but also the options it contains. Table 20-1, on the following page, lists the options available on the first tab for each type of folder. If you're not sure how to fill in any of the fields, click the question mark button in the upper-right corner of the Filter dialog box, and then click on top of the field you want help with. Specific information for that field will appear on screen. Click again to close it.

TIP

You don't have to fill out all the tabs of the Filter dialog box. You can set conditions on any tab of the Filter dialog box either in addition to or instead of conditions you set on other tabs.

TABLE 20-1.   Filter Options on the First Tab of the Filter Dialog Box for Each Folder Type

Folder	Tab Name	Available Filters
Inbox	Message	Search for the word(s), In, From, Sent To, Where I am, Time
Calendar	Appointments and Meetings	Search for the word(s), In, Organized By, Attendees, Time
Contacts	Contacts	Search for the word(s), In, E-Mail, Time
Tasks	Tasks	Search for the word(s), In, Status, From, Sent To, Time
Journal	Journal Entries	Search for the word(s), In, Journal Entry Type, Contact, Time
Notes	Notes	Search for the word(s), In, Time
Disk Files	Files	Named, Type Of, Search for the word(s), In, Time

Setting Up the More Choices Tab

The More Choices tab of the Filter dialog box, shown in Figure 20-4, on the next page, is the same for most types of folders, except that some options are unavailable for a few types, as noted in the following summary:

Categories.   When you use categories as filter criteria, Outlook displays folder items that have been assigned to the categories you list. Type the category names, separated by a comma, or click the Categories button to select category names in the Categories dialog box. (If you want to specify categories you used in a previous filter, select them from the list, where Outlook stores them.)

Only Items That Are.   Turn on this option, and then select either Read (for folder items that you have already read) or Unread (for folder items that you haven't yet read).

Only Items With.   After you turn on this option, you can select One Or More Attachments (to filter for folder items that contain attachments) or No Attachments (to filter for items that have no attachments). This option is unavailable for the Notes folder.

Whose Importance Is.   This option filters for folder items that have the specified level of importance: High, Normal, or Low. Turn on the option, and then select a level from the list. This option is not available for folders that contain contact items, note items, or journal entries.

Match Case.   Turn on this option to display only those folder items whose uppercase and lowercase characters exactly match the uppercase and lowercase characters you typed in the Search For The Word(s) box on the first tab.

Size.   You can use this option to restrict the filter to only those folder items whose size, in kilobytes, matches a specified size range. Select Doesn't Matter from the list if you don't want to filter for a particular size. If you select Equals (Approximately), Less Than, or Greater Than (size conditions), Outlook activates the first box to the right, and you must enter a specific size value. If you select Between, Outlook activates both boxes to the right, and you must enter two size values (the upper and lower end of a size range).

FIGURE 20-4.

The More Choices tab of the Filter dialog box.

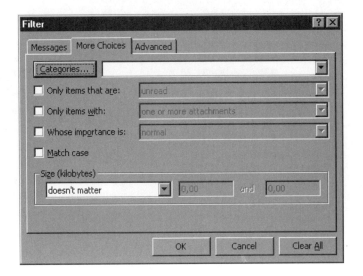

When you set up a filter for a folder that contains disk files, the More Choices tab offers only three options: Match Case, Match All Word Forms, and Size. You can set up the Match Case and Size options exactly as you do for other types of folders. If you choose the Match All Word Forms option, you are in effect widening the scope of your filter criteria to include all files that contain variations of the words you typed in the Search For The Word(s) box on the first tab. For instance, if you've set up the word *write* as a filter criterion in the Search For The Word(s) box, choosing Match All Word Forms means that files containing the text *write, writes, wrote, written,* and so on will be displayed in the filtered view.

Setting Up Advanced Criteria

If you need to refine the filter for your folder view beyond the settings available on the first two tabs of the Filter dialog box, you can click the Advanced tab, shown in Figure 20-5. On this tab, you can select a field, specify a condition and a value for the field, and then have Outlook filter folder items according to this criterion. This tab is the same for all types of folders, including folders that contain disk files. (The More Advanced button is not available for the Disk Files folder type.)

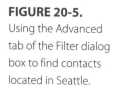

FIGURE 20-5.
Using the Advanced tab of the Filter dialog box to find contacts located in Seattle.

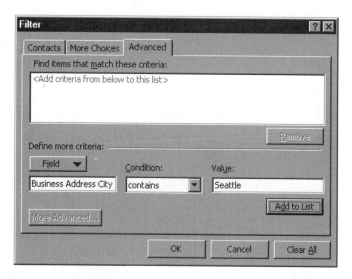

Bending Folders to Your Will

The following steps show you how to set up advanced criteria, using a simple example:

1   In the Filter dialog box, click the Advanced tab.

2   Click the Field button to open a menu of the available lists of fields.

3   Point to a list name to display a submenu containing all the specific fields on that list that are available for the open folder. As an example, let's say that you want to set up a filter for your Contacts folder that will display all contacts whose business address is in Seattle. In that case, you'd point to the Address Fields list.

4   Click the field you want to use—for this example, click Business Address City. Outlook adds the field name to the box under the Field button and activates the Condition box and the Value box.

5   Choose a condition from the list in the Condition box. (The set of conditions available in this box depends on the specific field you selected.) For this example, choose Contains.

6   In the Value box, type a value—in this case, type *Seattle*. Outlook activates the Add To List button.

7   Click the Add To List button. Outlook adds the criterion to the Find Items That Match These Criteria box.

8   If you want to add additional criteria, repeat steps 2 through 7. (Remember that when you set up multiple criteria, a folder item must meet *all* the criteria in order to appear in the filtered view.) If you change your mind about including a criterion, select it in the Find Items That Match These Criteria box and click the Remove button.

9   Click OK to close the Filter dialog box and click OK again to close the View Summary dialog box. The folder now appears with its contents filtered. For the example described here, your Contacts folder displays a filtered view of all contact entries whose Business Address City field contains the word *Seattle*.

Not all fields and conditions require a value (step 6). If a condition requires a value, Outlook activates the Value box and does not activate the Add To List button until you've entered the value.

You can enter multiple values in the Value box. For text fields, use the word *and* or a blank space to filter items whose field contents match both values. For instance, to display messages that you've assigned to *both* the categories Key Customer and International, type *Key Customer and International* in the Value box. To display messages that you've assigned to *either* category, use the word *or*, a comma, or a semicolon instead of the word *and*. For date fields—used most often with the conditions On, On Or After, and On Or Before—you can use AutoDate to describe the value. For example, you can assign Birthday for the field contents, On as the condition, and for the value you can type *today*. The filter will alert you to those contacts whose birthday is today.

Turning Off a Filter

To turn off a filter, take these steps:

1 Open the folder.

2 Point to Current View on the View menu, and then choose Customize Current View from the submenu to display the View Summary box.

3 Click the Filter button.

4 In the Filter dialog box, click the Clear All button.

5 Click OK in the two dialog boxes to return to the unfiltered folder.

Working with Custom Fields

Outlook lets you create your own fields when you cannot find a built-in field that serves your needs. Use the field to display information, to perform calculations, or to group items in the folder.

When you create a custom field, you must do so for a specific folder. You'll need to create the custom field again in each folder where you want to use it. The custom field name appears in the User-Defined Fields In Folder in the Sort, Filter (Advanced Fields), and Group By dialog boxes.

V

Bending Folders to Your Will

You can create three kinds of custom fields: simple, combination, and formula.

- Use a simple field to add a basic piece of information to folder items as a column in a table view or as a row on a card. For example, you might add a field called Summary Report Submitted in your Tasks folder, in which you can record the date you wrote and submitted a summary of a completed project. You could then add this field as a column in Detailed List view or Completed Tasks view.

- In a combination field, you can combine existing fields to appear in a single column or a single row in a folder. For example, you might create an Attendees field for your Calendar folder that combines the Optional Attendees and Required Attendees fields, if the distinction between optional and required attendance isn't important or practical in your organization. You could then display the Attendees column in, for instance, Active Appointments view or Recurring Appointments view.

- With a formula field, you perform a calculation that involves the information contained in other fields. You might create a formula field for messages, for instance, that shows the number of days since each message was received and its importance icon with any due dates that might occur for the task associated with the message.

Each new custom field must be based on a specific data type—that is, the field must be able to contain the appropriate kind of data: text, numbers, dates, or other data. The basic steps for creating all three types of custom fields are the same, as explained in the following section. Combination and formula fields involve a few additional complications; see "Creating a Combination Field," on page 580, and "Creating a Formula Field," on page 582.

 NOTE

You can create custom fields only for table views and card views—not for timeline, day/week/month, note, or icon views.

Creating a Simple Custom Field

To create a simple custom field for a folder, follow these steps:

1 Open the folder for which you want to create a custom field.

2 Select a table view or a card view.

3 Point to Current View on the View menu, and then choose Customize Current View from the submenu to display the View Summary dialog box.

4 Click the Fields button.

5 In the Show Fields dialog box, click the New Field button.

6 Type a new field name. ——
7 Select the data type. ——
8 Select the format. ——

9 Click OK. ——

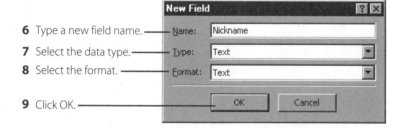

10 In the Show Fields dialog box, you can click the Move Up button to move your new field up the Show These Fields In This Order list if you want to adjust the position in which the field will be displayed in the folder window.

11 Click OK in the Show Fields dialog box, and then click OK in the View Summary dialog box.

 TIP

In the Contacts folder there is another way to create a new field. Double-click the item, click the All Fields tab in the item's window, and then click the New button.

In the following section, you'll find details about how to select a data type and a data type format in the New Field dialog box.

V

Bending Folders to Your Will

Data Types and Standard Formats

When you create a custom field, you select a data type in the Type box of the New Field dialog box. You must base each custom field on a specific data type that is able to contain the kind of information you'll be storing in the field. Table 20-2 lists the data types you can choose.

TABLE 20-2.   Data Types for Custom Fields

Data Type	Use For
Currency	Numbers shown as currency; calculations of money amounts.
Date/Time	Dates and times.
Duration	Numbers. You can enter a duration time as minutes, hours, or days. You can use a standard format to indicate whether duration time is based on a 24-hour day or on the Task Working Hours settings you choose on the Tasks/Notes tab of the Options dialog box (accessed by choosing Options on the Tools menu). For example, if you have set 10 hours as a work day on the Tasks/Notes tab, entering 15 hours shows as 1.5 days. Values are saved as minutes.
Integer	Nondecimal numbers.
Number	Numbers; mathematical calculations except those involving money amounts. (Use the Currency data type for money.)
Percent	Numbers expressed as a percentage.
Text	Text or combinations of text and numbers (as many as 255 characters), such as addresses and phone numbers.
Yes/No	Data that can be only one of two values, such as Yes/No, True/False, or On/Off. (For example, the Do Not AutoArchive field uses a Yes/No data type.) A Yes/No field can also be displayed as an empty box or a box with a check mark.
Keywords	User-defined fields that you can use to group and find related items, in much the same way you use the Categories field. If the text contains multiple values, you must separate them with commas. Each value can be grouped individually in a view.
Combination	Combinations of fields and text in a column (table view) or row (card view). You can show each field of the combination or show the first field containing data.
Formula	Calculations using data contained in any field. Use appropriate functions and operators to set up a formula.

For each data type except combination and formula, Outlook provides
standard formats that you can choose to format your custom field.
Table 20-3 lists these standard formats.

TABLE 20-3.   Some Standard Formats for Data Types

Data Type	Standard Formats
Currency	$12,345.60 or ($12,345.60) $12,346 or ($12,346)
Date/Time	Monday, March 2, 1998 8:15 PM March 2, 1998 8:15 PM (plus 13 other formats)
Duration	12h or 12 hours (assumes a 24-hour day) 12h (Work Time) or 12 hours (Work Time) (based on work time set on the Tasks/Notes tab of the Options dialog box accessed by choosing Options on the Tools menu)
Integer	1,234 Computer: 640 K; 2,300 K; 3,100,000 K Computer: 640 K; 2.3 M; 3.1 G Computer: 640 K; 2.3 MB; 3.1 GB
Keywords	Text
Number	All Digits: 1,234.567 or -1,234.567 Truncated: 1,235 or -1,235 1 Decimal: 1,234.6 or -1,234.6 2 Decimal: 1,234.57 or -1,234.57 Scientific: 1235E+03 or -1235E+03 Computer: 64 K or 128 K or 65,536 K Computer: 64 K or 128 M or 1 G Computer: 64 KB or 256 MB or 2 GB Raw: 12345.67 or -12345.67
Percent	All Digits: 65.4321% Rounded: 65% or -65% 1 Decimal: 64.4% or -64.4% 2 Decimal: 65.43% or -65.43%

(continued)

V

Bending Folders to Your Will

TABLE 20-3. *continued*

Data Type	Standard Formats
Text	Text
Yes/No	Yes or No On or Off True or False Icon—Empty box or Box with a check mark

For a list of standard formats available for a field in a specific view, right-click a column heading and choose Format Columns from the shortcut menu. In the Available Fields box, select the field, and then select a format in the Format box. (If you don't find the format you want, you can create a custom format with a formula data type and the Format function; see "Creating a Formula Field," on page 582.)

Creating a Combination Field

You can combine simple fields (both built-in fields and custom fields) in a single column or row—the result is called a combination field. For example, you can create a column that combines the City and State fields in an address list to save space. (For more examples, see Table 20-4, on page 584.)

To create a combination field, follow these steps:

1 Open the New Field dialog box, as explained in "Creating a Simple Custom Field," on page 577 (steps 1 through 5).

2 Enter the new field name.

3 Select Combination.

4 Click Edit.

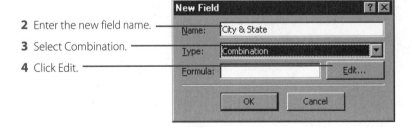

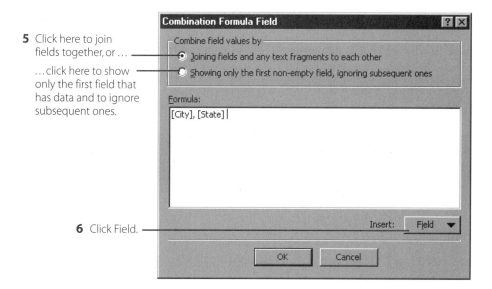

5 Click here to join fields together, or ...

...click here to show only the first field that has data and to ignore subsequent ones.

6 Click Field.

7 Point to the field set containing the first field you want to combine. When Outlook displays the list, click the field.

8 Repeat steps 6 and 7 for each field you want to add to the combination.

9 Click OK in the Combination Formula Field dialog box and in the New Field dialog box.

10 In the Show Fields dialog box, you can click Move Up to move your new field up the list if you want to adjust the position in which the field will be displayed in the folder window.

11 Click OK in the Show Fields dialog box.

To add or change the information in a combination field, you must add or change the information in the simple fields that make up the combination. For example, if you create a combination field consisting of city and state names, you need to add or change the city name in the simple City field and the state name in the simple State field. You can't directly edit the information in a combination field.

Combination fields use the default format of the data type on which they are based. To display a data type with a custom format, you must create a formula field and use the Format function. (See the following section.)

V

Bending Folders to Your Will

NOTE

You cannot sort, group, or filter the contents of a combination field.

Creating a Formula Field

Formula fields combine functions, operators, and fields. To see some examples of formula fields, see Table 20-4, on page 584.

To create a formula field, take these steps:

1 Open the New Field dialog box, as explained in "Creating a Simple Custom Field," on page 577 (steps 1 through 5).

2 Enter the new field name.

3 Select Formula.

4 Click Edit.

5 To insert a function, click Function, point to the category containing the function you want to use, and then choose the function.

6 To insert a field into the function, select the argument in the function where the field name should go.

Formula Field   ? ☒

Formula:

DateValue(Now())-DateValue([Hired]) & " Days"

Insert: Field ▼   Function ▼

OK   Cancel

---

7 Click Field, point to the category containing the field you want to use, and click the field name. The field name will be inserted into the function, replacing the word you highlighted.

8 Repeat step 5 or step 6 until you have completely built the formula.

9 Click OK in the Formula Field dialog box, and then click OK in the New Field dialog box.

10 In the Show Fields dialog box, click the Move Up button if you want to adjust the position of the field in the list.

11 Click OK in the Show Fields dialog box.

You can use a large number of varied functions in formula fields. Describing all the functions and operators that you can incorporate in formula fields is well beyond the scope of this book, but you can find information about functions, operators, and operator precedence in the Outlook Help file. Choose Contents And Index from the Help menu, and then click the Index tab. Type *functions* or *operators* in the top box to see an extensive list of topics and comprehensive lists of functions or operators.

If you need to add or change the information contained in a formula field, you must add or change the information in the simple fields that make up the formula. You can't directly edit the information in a formula field.

Formula fields are updated any time you change a view. For example, if you change the width of a column, the formula fields are updated.

You cannot sort, group, or filter the contents of a formula field.

Examples of Formula and Combination Fields

Formula and combination fields can be a little tricky, but they can also be extremely useful. Table 20-4, on the next page, offers a few examples of such custom fields, showing you what the formulas and combinations look like and providing some sample results for each field.

TABLE 20-4.   Examples of Formula and Combination Fields, with Sample Results

What the Custom Field Shows	Custom Field	Sample Result in Custom Field
Number of days since an item was received (formula field)	DateValue (Now())- DateValue ([Received]) & " Day(s)"	6 Day(s) (if 6 days have elapsed since the date the message was received)
Description of a meeting in your calendar (formula field)	"This meeting occurs" & [Recurrence Pattern] & " in " & [Location]	This meeting occurs every day from 1:00 PM to 1:30 PM in room 10b-3400
Amount charged for a phone call recorded in the Journal at $.75 a minute (formula field)	IIF ([Entry Type] = "Phone call", Format ([Duration] *.75, "Currency"), "None")	$1.50 (if the duration of the call was 2 minutes)
Description of a message flag (formula field)	IIF ([Flag Status] = "2" [Message Flag] & " " & [Due By],"")	Follow up 10/5/97 10:00:00 AM
The first phone number recorded for a contact, in order of appearance in the formula (combination field)	[Business Phone] [Business Phone 2] [Home Phone] [Car Phone]	(555) 555-1234 (555) 555-1234 x564 (555) 555-5000 (555) 555-0000
A description of a field combined with the field itself (combination field)	Task Due: [Due Date]	Task Due: 10/5/97 10:00:00 AM

Changing a Custom Field

You can change a custom field only by changing the format or the formula. You can't change the field name or the data type. If you don't like a field's name or data type, you have to delete the custom field (see "Deleting a Custom Field," on the next page) and then create a new one that suits you.

Here's how to change the format or formula for a custom field:

1 Point to Current View on the View menu, and then choose Customize Current View from the submenu to display the View Summary dialog box.

2 Click the Fields button.

3 If you're using the custom field, remove it from the Show These Fields In This Order list so that it reappears in the Available Fields list. (Either double-click the field name, or select it and then click the Remove button.)

4 Select the field name in the Available Fields list, and then click the Properties button to display the Edit Field dialog box.

5 For a formula field, type a new formula in the Formula box. (You can also click the Edit button, change the formula in the Formula Field dialog box, and then click OK.).

6 Click OK.

7 If you want to use this newly edited custom field in the folder, add it back to the Show These Fields In This Order list. (Either double-click the field name, or select it and then click the Add button.)

8 Click OK in the Show Fields dialog box.

You can't edit Outlook's built-in fields.

Deleting a Custom Field

If you no longer have a use for a field you created, you might as well get rid of it. To delete a field you created, take these steps:

1 Point to Current View on the View menu, and then choose Customize Current View from the submenu to display the View Summary dialog box.

2 Click the Fields button.

3 If you're using the custom field, remove it from the Show These Fields In This Order list so that it reappears in the Available Fields list. (Either double-click the field name, or select it and then click the Remove button.)

V

Bending Folders to Your Will

4 Select the field name in the Available Fields list, and then click the Delete button.

5 When Outlook asks you to confirm the deletion, click OK.

6 Click OK in the Show Fields dialog box.

 NOTE

You can't delete any of Outlook's built-in fields.

CHAPTER 21

Setting Up Views

When you set up a view for Microsoft Outlook 98, you can choose the fields to be included, group and sort the information, and filter the view all in one operation. You can also modify the view, rename it, change its format, and even decide who can use the view and in which folders they can use it. Obviously, you'll need familiarity with the topics covered in Chapter 20, "Organizing Folder Items," so you might want to review that chapter briefly before beginning this one.

Defining a View

While Outlook provides a number of views for each type of folder, you may want to organize a folder in an entirely different way. Rather then make drastic changes to one of the built-in views, you can define a new view just for you.

When you define a view for a folder, you give the view a name, and you also set up the fields, the sorting, the grouping, and the filtering you want to use. Defining a view involves a series of dialog boxes, as outlined here:

1 Open the folder in which you want to define a new view.

2 Point to Current View on the View menu, and then choose Define Views from the submenu to open the Define Views For dialog box.

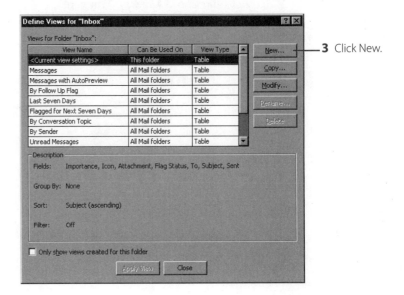

3 Click New.

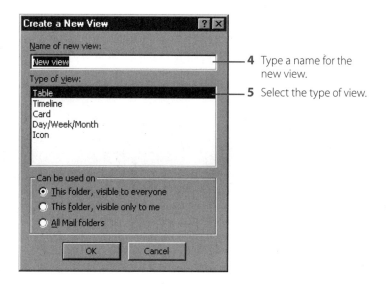

4 Type a name for the new view.

5 Select the type of view.

6 In the Can Be Used On area, select one of the three options to specify where the view can be used and who can use it:

- This Folder, Visible To Everyone makes the view available only in the folder in which you created it. Anyone who has permission to open the folder can choose to display the view from the Current View submenu.

- This Folder, Visible Only To Me makes the view available only in the folder in which you created it and does not allow other people to use the view.

- All [Folder Type] Folders makes the view available to all folders that are the same type as the folder in which you created the view. Anyone who has permission to open a folder of this type can use this view to organize items in a similar folder.

V

Bending Folders to Your Will

7 Click OK in the Create A New View dialog box. Outlook displays the View Summary dialog box, which provides a complete description of the view as it currently exists:

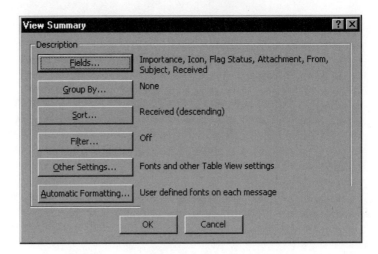

8 Use the buttons in this dialog box to set up the elements of the new view. Clicking one of the first four of these buttons takes you to a dialog box that should be familiar from Chapter 20, "Organizing Folder Items"; for details about how to use these dialog boxes, see "Using the Show Fields Dialog Box," on page 556, "Working with Custom Fields," on page 575, "Grouping," on page 563, "Sorting," on page 566, or "Filtering," on page 568. Clicking the Other Settings button opens the Format View dialog box, discussed in "Formatting Views," on page 593, later in this chapter. Clicking the Automatic Formatting button opens the Automatic Formatting dialog box, discussed in "Adjusting Automatic Formatting," on page 604.

9 When you've finished setting up the elements of the view and closed the relevant dialog boxes, click OK in the View Summary dialog box to close it and return to the Define Views For dialog box.

10 If you want to apply the new view to the currently open folder, select the view from the list, and then click the Apply View button.

11 Click the Close button in the Define Views For dialog box.

Copying a View

Outlook also provides a shorter method for creating a new view. Instead of starting from scratch and defining every part of a new view, you can base a new view on the current arrangement of fields, sorting, grouping, and filtering. Just follow these steps:

1 Open the folder in which you want to define a new view.

2 Point to Current View on the View menu, and then choose Define Views from the submenu to open the Define Views For dialog box.

3 Select the view that you want to use as the basis for the new one, and then click Copy to display the Copy View dialog box.

4 Type a name for the new view.

5 Select a Can Be Used On option.

6 Click OK.

7 In the View Summary dialog box that appears, use the available buttons to change any of the view settings as desired, and then click OK.

Modifying a View

If a view isn't quite right, you can modify it so that it better suits your needs. To modify either a view you created or one of Outlook's built-in views, follow these steps:

1 Open the folder that contains the view you want to change.

2 Point to Current View on the View menu, and then choose Define Views from the submenu to open the Define Views For dialog box.

3 Select the name of the view you want to change.

4 Click the Modify button to open the View Summary dialog box.

V

Bending Folders to Your Will

5 In the View Summary dialog box, use the available buttons to modify the view as needed.

6 When you've finished modifying the view and you've closed the relevant dialog boxes, click OK in the View Summary dialog box to close it and return to the Define Views For dialog box.

7 If you want to apply the modified view to the currently open folder, click the Apply View button in the Define Views For dialog box.

8 Click the Close button in the Define Views dialog box.

 TIP

To open the View Summary dialog box quickly, right-click a column heading in a table view or right-click anywhere in a timeline view, and then choose the Customize Current View command from the shortcut menu that appears.

Resetting a Standard View

As just described, you can modify custom views as well as Outlook's built-in views. If you modify a built-in view but later decide that you'd prefer to use Outlook's original version, you can restore the standard settings for that view. Here's how to do it.

1 Open the folder containing the built-in view you want to reset.

2 Point to Current View on the View menu, and then choose Define Views from the submenu to open the Define Views For dialog box.

3 In the Define Views For dialog box, select the name of the view.

4 Click the Reset button. This button is available only when you select a built-in view; you can't reset a custom view.

5 If you want to apply the restored original view to the currently open folder, click the Apply View button in the Define Views For dialog box.

6 Click the Close button in the Define Views For dialog box.

Renaming a User-Defined View

You can easily change the name of a view you created. (Although you can modify Outlook's built-in views, as you saw in the preceding section, you cannot rename them.)

To change the name of a view you created, take these steps:

1 Open the folder that contains the view you want to rename.

2 Point to Current View on the View menu, and then choose Define Views from the submenu to open the Define Views For dialog box.

3 In the Define Views For dialog box, select the view you want to rename, and then click the Rename button.

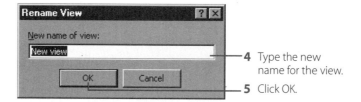

   4 Type the new name for the view.

   5 Click OK.

6 If you want to apply the renamed view to the currently open folder, click the Apply View button in the Define Views For dialog box.

7 Click the Close button in the Define Views For dialog box.

Formatting Views

Each Outlook view is one of these five types:

- Table

- Timeline

- Day/Week/Month (built into the Calendar folder only)

- Card (built into the Contacts folder only)

- Icon (built into the Notes folder only)

V

Bending Folders to Your Will

As this list implies, some views are designed specifically for certain folders (and for custom folders of the same type). Actually, you can set up any view for any folder—for instance, you could set up a day/week/month view for your Notes folder—but you'll need to judge for yourself how much sense this makes in any given situation.

As you've seen in earlier chapters, you can customize views in Outlook in many ways. In addition to defining what items a view displays and in what order or groupings it displays them, you can also change the font, add previews, and set other formatting options for the various views.

To change the format of a view, you have to display the Format View dialog box. You can change the formatting of the current view or any other view available to the folder you have open. To format a view, follow these steps:

1 Open the folder that contains the view you want to modify.

2 If you are already using the view you want to format, point to Current View on the View menu, and then choose Customize Current View. If you want to format a different view, point to Current View on the View menu, and then choose Define Views instead. From the Define Views dialog box, select the view you want to format, and then click Modify.

3 Click Other Settings in the View Summary dialog box to display the Format View dialog box.

> When you use the Format View dialog box to change the formatting of a view, the modifications you make apply only to that view. For example, if you change the formatting of the Tasks folder's Simple List view, the changes apply only to that view and not to any other table views.

Table Views

A table view displays folder items in rows and columns. Each row contains the information for one folder item; each column contains one piece of information about the item (one field). (For details about working with columns, see "Setting Up Columns," on page 554.)

To format a particular table view, open a folder that contains the view, and then open the Format View dialog box using the technique described above. Outlook opens the Format Table View dialog box, shown in Figure 21-1.

FIGURE 21-1.

The Format Table View dialog box.

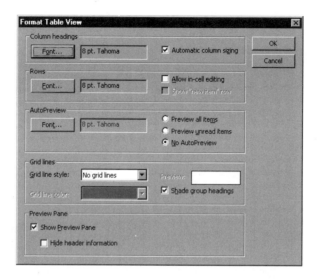

As you can see in the dialog box, Outlook offers numerous options for formatting:

Font buttons.

When you click any one of the three Font buttons, Outlook opens the Font dialog box, where you can change the font, the font style (most fonts offer regular, bold, italic, and bold italic), the font size in points, and the alphabet for the font you've chosen (if your computer is set up to work in such languages as Greek or Russian. You can adjust the font settings for column headings, for rows (the contents of each folder item), or for previews (if you choose to display them).

Automatic Column Sizing. Turn on this option to have Outlook size the columns in the view so that all of them fit on the screen. (Some might be abbreviated in order to fit.) If you turn this option off, you might have to scroll to see all the columns in a view, or you can size the columns yourself to see the ones you want.

Allow In-Cell Editing.   When this option is turned on, you can type or edit directly in the table cells to make changes to folder items. When it's turned off, you cannot edit in the cells and must instead open each folder item to make any changes.

Show "New Item" Row.   This option is available only when Allow In-Cell Editing is turned on. When you select it, Outlook adds a row at the top of the table view that allows you to create a new folder item without opening a new folder item window. (The Tasks folder, for example, displays such a "new item" row by default.)

AutoPreview.   This Outlook feature displays partial contents of a folder item in the table view so that you can quickly determine what each item contains. For messages, Outlook displays the first three lines of the message body; for other folder items, you see the first three lines of the Notes section of the folder item. You can choose whether to show previews for all items or for unread items only, or you can choose No AutoPreview to eliminate previews and see headings only.

Grid Lines.   You can choose to display grid lines between the rows and columns of a table view. If you include the grid lines in the view, you can set both a line style (Small Dots, Large Dots, Dashes, or Solid) and a line color. After you set both these options, Outlook provides a sample grid line in the Preview box. You can also choose whether to shade group headings in those views that group the table rows by a particular field. You'll probably want to leave the Shade Group Headings option turned on in most cases; it's usually easier to distinguish the headings of grouped items when they're shaded.

Preview Pane.   In this section of the dialog box, you can choose to display or hide the Preview Pane and whether to display or hide the header information in the pane.

 NOTE

The default settings in the Format Table View dialog box are not the same for all table views and all folders. For instance, Simple List view in the Tasks folder displays grid lines, allows in-cell editing, and includes a "new item" row by default, whereas Messages view in the Inbox folder (another table view) by default omits grid lines and in-cell editing, and does not contain a "new item" row.

Timeline Views

A timeline view is named for the way dates are displayed along a line running from left to right across the top of the folder window, with the folder items for each date listed below their respective dates, as shown here in a timeline view for a single week:

Timeline ——

Folder items for
a specific date. ———

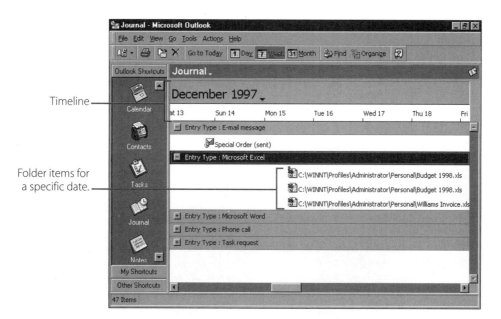

When displaying Journal information, you can click the Day, Week, or Month button on the Standard toolbar to have the timeline band show the folder items in the following ways:

- For a single day, listed by the time

- For a single week, listed by the day

- For a month, listed by the date or by the week of the year—for example, week 14

To format a timeline view, display the view on your screen and open the Format View dialog box as described above. Outlook opens the Format Timeline View dialog box, shown in Figure 21-2, on the following page.

Fonts.   You can click the buttons in this area to set the font, font style (usually regular, bold, italic, or bold italic), font size, and foreign-language alphabet. You can make these font changes for the upper or lower scale of the timeline or for the folder items displayed in the view. You cannot change the color of any of these elements in a timeline view.

Scales.   Turn on the Show Week Numbers option if you want to include week numbers in the view. When you turn on this option, Outlook displays the week numbers in the top band of the timeline when you're looking at a single day or week and in the lower band of the timeline when you're looking at a month.

Labels.   The options in this area affect the labels (names) of the various folder items that appear under the dates in the timeline. You can set a maximum width for these labels (from 0 through 132 characters). When the timeline displays a month rather than a day or a week, you can choose whether to include or omit the item labels by setting the Show Label When Viewing By Month option.

FIGURE 21-2.
The Format Timeline
View dialog box.

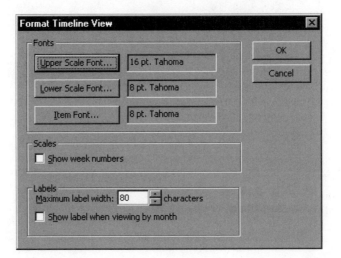

Day/Week/Month Views

A day/week/month view displays folder items in a standard calendar arrangement. By clicking the Day, Work Week, Week, or Month button

? SEE ALSO

For information about Day, Week, and Month views that are built into Outlook's Calendar folder and about elements such as the Date Navigator, see Chapter 10, "Viewing the Calendar."

on the Standard toolbar, you can have the calendar show the items in the following ways:

- For a single date, listed by the time

- For a single work week, listed by the day

- For a single week, listed by the day

- For a month, listed by the day

To format a day/week/month view, display the view on your screen, and then open the Format View dialog box. Outlook opens the Format Day/Week/Month View dialog box, shown in Figure 21-3.

FIGURE 21-3.

The Format Day/ Week/Month View dialog box.

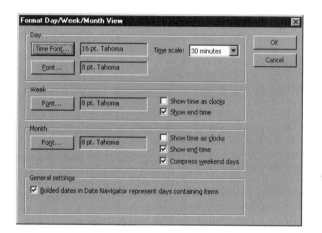

Day. Use the Time Font and Time Scale options to format the times that appear to the left of the appointments (or other folder items) on a one-day calendar. If you want to change the font of the times, click the Time Font button to open the Font dialog box, where you can set the font, font style (usually regular, bold, italic, or bold italic), font size, and foreign-language alphabet. To set the time intervals shown for the calendar items, select a time interval from the Time Scale list (5, 6, 10, 15, 30, or 60 minutes are the choices). Click the Font button if you want to change the font of the folder items that appear in the appointment (or other folder item) slots.

Bending Folders to Your Will

Week.   When you've chosen Week view to display a one-week time span, clicking the Font button in the Week section lets you change the font of both the dates and the folder items. If you'd like to see start times for items shown on small clock faces rather than in digits, turn on the Show Time As Clocks option. To have Outlook display both start and end times for folder items, turn on the Show End Time option; turn it off to omit the end times.

Month.   When you've chosen Month view to display a one-month time span, clicking the Font button in the Month section lets you change the font of both the dates and the folder items. The Show Time As Clocks and Show End Time options are available, as they are in the Week section. You can also choose whether to compress weekend days on the monthly calendar (combining Saturday and Sunday in a smaller space) or to allot equal space to all days of the week.

> **NOTE**

To display the start and end times of appointments in Month view, you must have Show Time As Clocks selected for Month view in the Format View dialog box. Depending on the resolution of your monitor, you might have to hide the Outlook Bar (by clicking Outlook Bar on the View menu) and the Folder List (by clicking Folder List on the View menu) to display both the start and end times of an appointment.

General Settings.   Turn on the option in this area if you want dates containing folder items to appear in boldface in the Date Navigator; turn off the option to remove the boldface.

Card Views

SEE ALSO

For information about the specific card views built into the Contacts folder, see "Using Card Views," on page 430.

A card view displays folder items as small cards containing various fields of information. The card views that are built into Outlook's Contacts folder, for instance, show contact information such as addresses and phone numbers on cards that look like rotary file cards laid out on a desk. You can view a number of cards on the screen at the same time, with the level of detail that you set up.

To format a card view, open an appropriate folder, use the Current View command on the View menu to open the View Summary dialog box for the view you wish to format, and then click Other Settings to open the Format View dialog box. Outlook opens the Format Card View dialog box, shown in Figure 21-4.

Font buttons.   If you want to reformat the card headings (titles) or the body of the card (the contents of the folder item), click the Font button in the appropriate section to open the Font dialog box, where you can change the font, font style, font size, or alphabet.

Allow In-Cell Editing.   Turn on this option if you want to be able to type or edit directly on the card that appears on your screen in the card view. When this option is turned off, you cannot edit the fields of information on the card but must instead open the folder item to make changes.

Show Empty Fields.   Turn on this option if you want each card to display all the fields for the folder item, whether or not the fields contain text. Turn off this option to have Outlook show only those fields that contain information (a more efficient use of screen space in most cases).

Card Dimensions.   You can specify the width of the cards, in characters. If you enter a width that is too large to fit in the window, Outlook resets the card width to the maximum possible for the window. (Note that when you display the Outlook Bar and the Folder List, the maximum width for a card decreases.) In the Multi-Line Field Height box, you can specify the minimum number of lines (1 through 20) that should be allocated to a multiple-line field such as an address field.

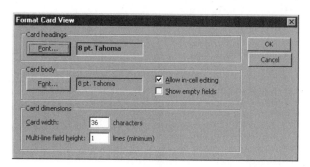

FIGURE 21-4.
The Format Card View dialog box.

V

Bending Folders to Your Will

You can also use the mouse to change card width in the folder window. When you place the mouse pointer on the vertical dividing line between two columns of cards, the pointer becomes a double vertical line with a two-headed arrow. Drag the dividing line to the left to decrease the card width or to the right to increase the card width. If you widen the cards so that some columns move off screen, Outlook activates a horizontal scroll bar so that you can scroll to see all the cards.

Icon Views

An icon view displays folder items as small images (icons) with text labels. You'll see different icons for different types of folders—the specific icon Outlook shows matches the type of item contained in the folder.

To format an icon view, display the view on your screen and open the Format View dialog box. Outlook opens the Format Icon View dialog box, shown in Figure 21-5.

FIGURE 21-5.

The Format Icon View dialog box.

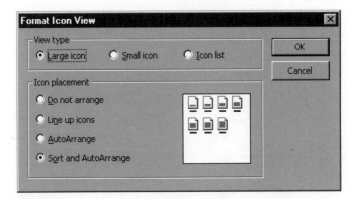

View Type.   You can choose to display the icons in the selected view as large icons, as small icons, or as an icon list. If you select the Icon List option, the options in the Icon Placement section below become unavailable; you can arrange the icons in the window only if you choose the Large Icons option or the Small Icons option.

Icon Placement. You can select any one of the four options in this area. Select Do Not Arrange if you want to arrange the icons yourself, dragging them to any spot in the folder window. The Line Up Icons option lines up the icons according to a preset grid in the folder window, snapping the icon to the nearest grid point. The AutoArrange option also lines up the icons on the invisible grid, but it arranges the icons in continuous rows and columns, so there are no gaps between icons. To have Outlook sort the icons, choose Sort And AutoArrange, which arranges the icons in rows according to the sorting keys you specify in the Sort dialog box. In the box to the right of these options, you can see a small preview of how the icons will be arranged, depending on your choice.

Deleting a View

If you no longer have a use for a custom view, you can delete it from the folder that contains it. (You can delete only those views that you created yourself; you cannot remove Outlook's built-in views.)

1 Open the folder that contains the view you want to delete.

2 Point to Current View on the View menu, and then choose Define Views from the submenu.

3 Select the name of the view in the Define Views For dialog box.

4 Click the Delete button. (This button is available only when you select the name of a custom view.) When Outlook asks whether you're sure you want to delete the view, click the Yes button.

5 Click the Close button in the Define Views For dialog box.

> **NOTE**

If you delete a custom view but then change your mind, you're out of luck—you'll have to recreate the view. Outlook provides no way to retrieve a deleted view.

Adjusting Automatic Formatting

In some folders, not every item is displayed the same way in the item list. In e-mail folders, for example, unread messages are shown in bold, expired messages with a strikeout, and mail that has been submitted but not sent in italic. In the Tasks folder, overdue tasks are displayed in red and completed tasks with a strikeout.

Formatting items based on their condition or status is called "automatic formatting" and it helps you visually distinguish items on the list quickly.

You can modify the formats that Outlook applies to folder items, and you can create your own rules for identifying and formatting items. For example, you may want to display messages from a certain recipient or regarding a specific topic in color to call your attention to them.

To modify the way Outlook formats items, follow these steps:

1 Display the view that contains the type of items you want to automatically format.

2 Point to Current View on the View menu, and then choose Customize Current View from the submenu to open the View Summary dialog box.

3 Click the Automatic Formatting button to display the Automatic Formatting dialog box.

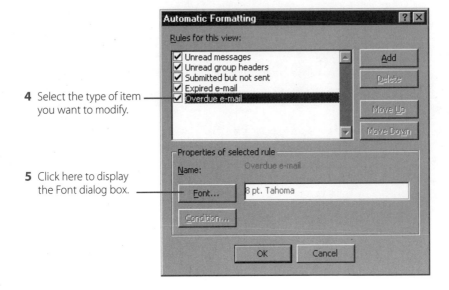

4 Select the type of item you want to modify.

5 Click here to display the Font dialog box.

6 Choose the formats to apply to the item type.

7 Click OK to close the Font dialog box.

8 In the Automatic Formatting dialog box, click OK.

To create your own rules for identifying and formatting an item, you have to establish the conditions that identify the item type. For example, a condition may be the name of the sender for an e-mail item or the subject of a task. You can then apply formats to items that meet those conditions.

Here's how to create a new rule from the Automatic Formatting dialog box:

1 Click Add to create a new rule. Outlook activates the Name text box.

2 In the Name text box, enter an identifying name for the rule.

3 Click Font, choose the formats to apply to the items that meet the rule, and then click OK in the Font dialog box.

4 Click Condition to display the Filter dialog box.

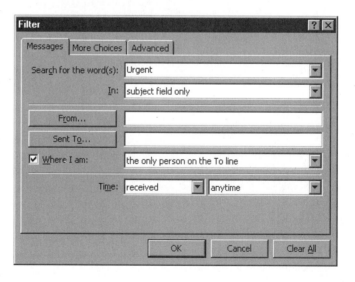

5 Specify the conditions for the item, using the techniques you learned for creating filters in Chapter 20, "Organizing Folder Items."

6 Click OK in the Filter dialog box, in the Automatic Formatting dialog box, and in the View Summary dialog box.

 NOTE

> Formats are applied to items in the order the rules are listed in the Automatic Formatting dialog box. To change the order of a rule, select it in the Automatic Formatting dialog box, and then click the Move Up or Move Down button.

To delete one of your own rules, select it in the Automatic Formatting dialog box and click the Delete button. You cannot delete any of Outlook's built-in rules.

Index

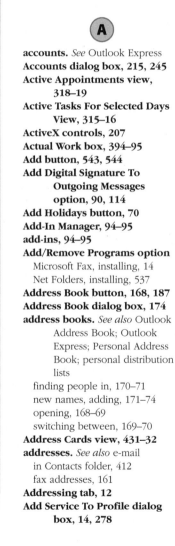

About the Author

Alan Neibauer is a veteran computer book author, with several best-sellers to his credit, including *The Official Guide to the Corel Word-Perfect Suite* and *The ABC's of Windows*. As a computer consultant and trainer, he has helped several companies in the Pennsylvania area implement Outlook as the e-mail client in their organizations. Neibauer has a degree in Journalism from Temple University and a master's from the Wharton School of the University of Pennsylvania. He lives in Huntingdon Valley, PA, with his wife, Barbara, and his yet unpublished mystery novel waiting for any interested offers.

MICROSOFT LICENSE AGREEMENT
(Book Companion CD)

IMPORTANT—READ CAREFULLY: This Microsoft End-User License Agreement ("EULA") is a legal agreement between you (either an individual or an entity) and Microsoft Corporation for the Microsoft product identified above, which includes computer software and may include associated media, printed materials, and "online" or electronic documentation ("SOFTWARE PRODUCT"). Any component included within the SOFTWARE PRODUCT that is accompanied by a separate End-User License Agreement shall be governed by such agreement and not the terms set forth below. By installing, copying or otherwise using the SOFTWARE PRODUCT, you agree to be bound by the terms of this EULA. If you do not agree to the terms of this EULA, you are not authorized to install, copy or otherwise use the SOFTWARE PRODUCT; you may, however, return the SOFTWARE PRODUCT, along with all printed materials and other items that form a part of the Microsoft product that includes the SOFTWARE PRODUCT, to the place you obtained them for a full refund.

The SOFTWARE PRODUCT is protected by United States copyright laws and international copyright treaties, as well as other intellectual property laws and treaties. The SOFTWARE PRODUCT is licensed, not sold.

1. GRANT OF LICENSE. This EULA grants you the following rights:

   a. **Software Product.** You may install and use one copy of the SOFTWARE PRODUCT on a single computer. The primary user of the computer on which the SOFTWARE PRODUCT is installed may make a second copy for his or her exclusive use on a portable computer.

   b. **Storage/Network Use.** You may also store or install a copy of the SOFTWARE PRODUCT on a storage device, such as a network server, used only to install or run the SOFTWARE PRODUCT on your other computers over an internal network; however, you must acquire and dedicate a license for each separate computer on which the SOFTWARE PRODUCT is installed or run from the storage device. A license for the SOFTWARE PRODUCT may not be shared or used concurrently on different computers.

   c. **License Pak.** If you have acquired this EULA in a Microsoft License Pak, you may make the number of additional copies of the computer software portion of the SOFTWARE PRODUCT authorized on the printed copy of this EULA, and you may use each copy in the manner specified above. You are also entitled to make a corresponding number of secondary copies for portable computer use as specified above.

2. DESCRIPTION OF OTHER RIGHTS AND LIMITATIONS.

- **Not For Resale Software.** If the SOFTWARE PRODUCT is labeled "Not For Resale" or "NFR," then, notwithstanding other sections of this EULA, you may not resell, or otherwise transfer for value, the SOFTWARE PRODUCT.

- **Limitations on Reverse Engineering, Decompilation, and Disassembly.** You may not reverse engineer, decompile, or disassemble the SOFTWARE PRODUCT, except and only to the extent that such activity is expressly permitted by applicable law notwithstanding this limitation.

- **Separation of Components.** The SOFTWARE PRODUCT is licensed as a single product. Its component parts may not be separated for use on more than one computer.

- **Rental.** You may not rent, lease or lend the SOFTWARE PRODUCT.

- **Support Services.** Microsoft may, but is not obligated to, provide you with support services related to the SOFTWARE PRODUCT ("Support Services"). Use of Support Services is governed by the Microsoft policies and programs described in the user manual, in "online" documentation and/or other Microsoft-provided materials. Any supplemental software code provided to you as part of the Support Services shall be considered part of the SOFTWARE PRODUCT and subject to the terms and conditions of this EULA. With respect to technical information you provide to Microsoft as part of the Support Services, Microsoft may use such information for its business purposes, including for product support and development. Microsoft will not utilize such technical information in a form that personally identifies you.

- **Software Transfer.** You may permanently transfer all of your rights under this EULA, provided you retain no copies, you transfer all of the SOFTWARE PRODUCT (including all component parts, the media and printed materials, any upgrades, this EULA, and, if applicable, the Certificate of Authenticity), **and** the recipient agrees to the terms of this EULA.

- **Termination.** Without prejudice to any other rights, Microsoft may terminate this EULA if you fail to comply with the terms and conditions of this EULA. In such event, you must destroy all copies of the SOFTWARE PRODUCT and all of its component parts.

3. **COPYRIGHT.** All title and copyrights in and to the SOFTWARE PRODUCT (including but not limited to any images, photographs, animations, video, audio, music, text, SAMPLE CODE, REDISTRIBUTABLES, and "applets" incorporated into the SOFTWARE PRODUCT), the accompanying printed materials, and any copies of the SOFTWARE PRODUCT are owned by Microsoft or its suppliers. The SOFTWARE PRODUCT is protected by copyright laws and international treaty provisions. Therefore, you must treat the SOFTWARE PRODUCT like any other copyrighted material **except** that you may install the SOFTWARE PRODUCT on a single computer provided you keep the original solely for backup or archival purposes. You may not copy the printed materials accompanying the SOFTWARE PRODUCT.

4. **U.S. GOVERNMENT RESTRICTED RIGHTS.** The SOFTWARE PRODUCT and documentation are provided with RESTRICTED RIGHTS. Use, duplication, or disclosure by the Government is subject to restrictions as set forth in subparagraph (c)(1)(ii) of the Rights in Technical Data and Computer Software clause at DFARS 252.227-7013 or subparagraphs (c)(1) and (2) of the Commercial Computer Software—Restricted Rights at 48 CFR 52.227-19, as applicable. Manufacturer is Microsoft Corporation/One Microsoft Way/Redmond, WA 98052-6399.

5. **EXPORT RESTRICTIONS.** You agree that you will not export or re-export the SOFTWARE PRODUCT, any part thereof, or any process or service that is the direct product of the SOFTWARE PRODUCT (the foregoing collectively referred to as the "Restricted Components"), to any country, person, entity or end user subject to U.S. export restrictions. You specifically agree not to export or re-export any of the Restricted Components (i) to any country to which the U.S. has embargoed or restricted the export of goods or services, which currently include, but are not necessarily limited to Cuba, Iran, Iraq, Libya, North Korea, Sudan and Syria, or to any national of any such country, wherever located, who intends to transmit or transport the Restricted Components back to such country; (ii) to any end-user who you know or have reason to know will utilize the Restricted Components in the design, development or production of nuclear, chemical or biological weapons; or (iii) to any end-user who has been prohibited from participating in U.S. export transactions by any federal agency of the U.S. government. You warrant and represent that neither the BXA nor any other U.S. federal agency has suspended, revoked or denied your export privileges.

DISCLAIMER OF WARRANTY

NO WARRANTIES OR CONDITIONS. MICROSOFT EXPRESSLY DISCLAIMS ANY WARRANTY OR CONDITION FOR THE SOFTWARE PRODUCT. THE SOFTWARE PRODUCT AND ANY RELATED DOCUMENTATION IS PROVIDED "AS IS" WITHOUT WARRANTY OR CONDITION OF ANY KIND, EITHER EXPRESS OR IMPLIED, INCLUDING, WITHOUT LIMITATION, THE IMPLIED WARRANTIES OR MERCHANTABILITY, FITNESS FOR A PARTICULAR PURPOSE, OR NONINFRINGEMENT. THE ENTIRE RISK ARISING OUT OF USE OR PERFORMANCE OF THE SOFTWARE PRODUCT REMAINS WITH YOU.

LIMITATION OF LIABILITY. TO THE MAXIMUM EXTENT PERMITTED BY APPLICABLE LAW, IN NO EVENT SHALL MICROSOFT OR ITS SUPPLIERS BE LIABLE FOR ANY SPECIAL, INCIDENTAL, INDIRECT, OR CONSEQUENTIAL DAMAGES WHATSOEVER (INCLUDING, WITHOUT LIMITATION, DAMAGES FOR LOSS OF BUSINESS PROFITS, BUSINESS INTERRUPTION, LOSS OF BUSINESS INFORMATION, OR ANY OTHER PECUNIARY LOSS) ARISING OUT OF THE USE OF OR INABILITY TO USE THE SOFTWARE PRODUCT OR THE PROVISION OF OR FAILURE TO PROVIDE SUPPORT SERVICES, EVEN IF MICROSOFT HAS BEEN ADVISED OF THE POSSIBILITY OF SUCH DAMAGES. IN ANY CASE, MICROSOFT'S ENTIRE LIABILITY UNDER ANY PROVISION OF THIS EULA SHALL BE LIMITED TO THE GREATER OF THE AMOUNT ACTUALLY PAID BY YOU FOR THE SOFTWARE PRODUCT OR US$5.00; PROVIDED HOWEVER, IF YOU HAVE ENTERED INTO A MICROSOFT SUPPORT SERVICES AGREEMENT, MICROSOFT'S ENTIRE LIABILITY REGARDING SUPPORT SERVICES SHALL BE GOVERNED BY THE TERMS OF THAT AGREEMENT. BECAUSE SOME STATES AND JURISDICTIONS DO NOT ALLOW THE EXCLUSION OR LIMITATION OF LIABILITY, THE ABOVE LIMITATION MAY NOT APPLY TO YOU.

MISCELLANEOUS

This EULA is governed by the laws of the State of Washington USA, except and only to the extent that applicable law mandates governing law of a different jurisdiction.

Should you have any questions concerning this EULA, or if you desire to contact Microsoft for any reason, please contact the Microsoft subsidiary serving your country, or write: Microsoft Sales Information Center/One Microsoft Way/Redmond, WA 98052-6399.

Register Today!

Return this
Running Microsoft® Outlook™ 98
registration card for
a Microsoft Press® catalog

U.S. and Canada addresses only. Fill in information below and mail postage-free. Please mail only the bottom half of this page.

1-57231-840-6   *RUNNING MICROSOFT®*   *Owner Registration Card*
OUTLOOK™ 98

_____

NAME

_____

INSTITUTION OR COMPANY NAME

_____

ADDRESS

_____

_____

CITY   STATE   ZIP

Microsoft®*Press*
Quality Computer Books

For a free catalog of
Microsoft Press® products, call
1-800-MSPRESS

BUSINESS REPLY MAIL
FIRST-CLASS MAIL   PERMIT NO. 53   BOTHELL, WA

POSTAGE WILL BE PAID BY ADDRESSEE

NO POSTAGE
NECESSARY
IF MAILED
IN THE
UNITED STATES

MICROSOFT PRESS REGISTRATION
RUNNING MICROSOFT® OUTLOOK™ 98
PO BOX 3019
BOTHELL   WA   98041-9946

II.I..I..I.II...I..I..IIII.I..I.I..I..I.II..II...I